THE NEW STOCK MARKET

HG
4529
.H37
1990
West

☐ Diana R. Harrington
☐ Frank J. Fabozzi
☐ H. Russell Fogler

PROBUS PUBLISHING COMPANY
Chicago, Illinois

Library of Congress Cataloging-in-Publication Data

Harrington, Diana R., 1940–
  The new stock market: a complete guide to the latest research,
analysis, and performance / Diana Harrington, H. Russell Fogler,
Frank J. Fabozzi.
    p. cm.
  Bibliography: p.
  Includes index.
  ISBN 1-55738-056-2
  1. Investment analysis.   2. Stocks.   I. Fogler, H. Russell
II. Fabozzi, Frank J.   III. Title.
HG4529.H37 1989
332.63'22--dc20   89-10257
                                                             CIP

Printed in the United States of America

1   2   3   4   5   6   7   8   9   0

Dedication

For Will, Dessa, and Dierdre

Contents

Preface

Making money in the stock market. That—plain and simple—is the subject of this book. We will not describe our golden theory or secret strategy for making money; instead, we will take a look at the theories, strategies, and tools for selecting stocks used by stock market fundamentalists, technicians, cycle theorists, and academics. We will look at many of the theories and strategies for profiting from equity investing and help you examine their strengths in the hard light of the evidence that supports or refutes them. In short, we will try to help you determine whether these theories, the emperors of equity investing, have on any clothes.

We will look only at profiting from investing in equities, and equity derivatives—options and futures. To include other markets would simply make more complex a subject that is already rich and exciting. We will look at the major theories of investing and profiting from equity investing: cycle theory and technical and fundamental analysis. We will look at familiar theories and strategies and some that are not so widely known. We will follow the evolution of theories and strategies born of the adversity of the 1920s and 1930s and new theories statistically distilled from the market's own history. We will look at the evidence: do the theories and strategies hold potential real profitability (substantiated by the evidence), or is the potential a figment of optimists' imagination? The point throughout this analysis is to find ways to make a profit from investing in common stocks.

We could not have written this book 30 years ago. At that time, finance theory was not really a theory or group of theories but was based on rules of thumb and anecdotes. The job of a financial analyst focused primarily on manipulations of accounting data with the objective of minimizing costs. Over the last 30 years, two things have changed:

1. Finance theory has evolved to the point where anecdotes have given way to testable hypotheses.

2. The excitement and drama of the markets themselves have lured strong, innovative practitioners and academics into the field of investments to search for profitable patterns to exploit.

The search for patterns is a search for the structure (or structures) that underlies the apparently confusing process of common stock pricing. The searching investors and academics over the past 30 years have found theories, and theoretical inconsistencies, unexpected but enduring patterns (anomalies) in the market, and patterns that appeared only because faulty tools were used to measure them. Some of the theories, and the strategies and tools for exploiting them, do seem to provide even the most passive investor with unusual profits. Other theories once held in high esteem have been battered by the strength of the evidence.

For the professional or amateur investor, the critical questions are: How can I make money? What do we know? Are there exploitable theories or persistent anomalies? How do I separate real possibilities from false leads?

Much of what has been written and published has been the work of academics and academically oriented practitioners. Some of them write in ways that are difficult to understand and publish in sources foreign to many people. In addition, many of their tests of the theories are complex and statistical approaches inaccessible to the uninitiated. We will not avoid this evidence; instead, we will help you understand what each theory and test means for the profit-seeking investor, in a language an intelligent nonstatistician can understand. Our aim is for the book to be useful for the sophisticated student of investments (either practitioner or academic) as well as the nascent investor.

Before anyone can make money in the stock market, she or he must have some clear idea how prices are set and later reset. If there is no underlying structure to the way investors set prices, there is no way to outguess them and make money. Whether the theory is one of market efficiency, demand-supply imbalance, fear and panic, or greed, there is some structure to the pricing process—a structure that an intelligent investor can hope to exploit. Thus in the first chapter, we will focus on three critical questions: How do people believe that equity prices are set? What is a profit? How do people know if they have found an exploitable opportunity?

Once we have established the basic groundwork, we will turn to the various ways that people have used to understand and profit from the market's progress and direction. One of the most enduring of these ways is cycle theory: long and short waves, the business cycle, and the impact that the time of the year, month, week, or day has on prices. Thus, Chapter 2 will discuss cycles of various kinds and look at the ways investors have used these data about the market as a whole to make equity investments they believe will be profitable.

Although some investors rely on extrapolating cyclical predictions for the market as a whole into what will happen in various segments or to individual stocks, most investors use a form of technical or fundamental analysis to help them make stock selections. Thus in Chapters 3 through 5, we will look at theories and strategies for stock selection. Chapter 3 discusses some of the more popular forms of technical analysis—analysis of a stock's historical price and volume data; Chapter 4 is devoted to strategies for making profits based on using company earnings reports and earnings forecasts; and Chapter 5 examines other characteristics about a firm or its strategy (e.g., corporate size, market value, or merger activity) that could be used to select valuable stocks. In each of these chapters, we will look at the theories, the strategies used to implement the theories, and when appropriate, the tools available for stock selection, as well as the evidence to support choosing and using them.

In the next three chapters, Chapters 6 through 8, we will examine the theories and evidence about what are called derivative securities: common stock options, stock-index options, and stock-index futures. In the 1980s, the attraction of these instruments has increased to a point where many believe they dominate the underlying action in the market. Thus they are not only interesting, but important to understand. Finally, in Chapter 9 we will look to what the future holds.

As you read through this book, keep in mind that there are only three ways to beat the market:

1. Have different information about a stock or the market from what anyone else has.

2. Have the same information but interpret its meaning differently.

3. Have the same information, interpret it the same way, but act on it differently.

Our aim in this book is to help you sort information from fiction, to help you see more than you did before, understand it better, and exploit it more profitably. With this background, we hope you will be better able to avoid the obvious errors and capitalize on the opportunities. Our reminder: This book is not simple. It is about difficult concepts and sophisticated tests, all of which are needed in today's fast-paced world of computer models and continuously updated data bases. We have, however, taken the complex and made it as accessible as it can be made. We hope that you will find the material in this book enjoyable, provocative, and readable. We believe that, at the least, it will help you avoid avoidable mistakes and thus will allow you to profit from your investments.

In the equity markets, our knowledge of what is real, and what only appears real, changes. This book contains what we know about the stock market and making a profit from it now, at the end of the 9th decade of the 20th century.

What you read is the result of the work of many academics and practitioners whose curiosity and profit seeking led them to search for patterns in behavior and exploitable opportunities for profit. To each of them, whether cited here or not, we say thank you.

Some people in particular made the writing of *The New Stock Market* possible. For Diana Harrington, the Sponsors of the Darden School of Business at the University of Virginia, who provided support for this book; Henry

Wingate, Librarian, and Libby Eshback, Library Assistant, at The Darden School, and the rest of the library staff, who provided the voluminous background needed to write the book; Bette Collins, Darden's superb editor, who was integral to the quality and continuity of this multiple-author book; Ginny Fisher, who typed, but more importantly kept the manuscript and one author organized; Richard Keller, who read the manuscript and suggested important changes; and her husband, Will Harrington, ever steady through the long writing process.

For Frank Fabozzi, the ongoing guidance and insights into the stock market provided by Peter Bernstein (editor of *The Journal of Portfolio Management*) and the works of John Cox, Bob Merton, Bob Whaley, Mark Rubinstein, Rick Bookstaber, and Gary Gastineau on equity derivative products have inspired his own research efforts.

For Russ Fogler, the lifetime motivation and guidance provided by Professor Ira Horowtiz (former Department Chairman at the University of Florida) and the intellectual challenge continuously provided by professional colleagues Roger Murray, George Russell, Peter Dietz, George Keane, and partner Ted Aronson played a major role in the ability and desire to do this book.

Each of us recognizes that without the support and understanding of our families this book would never have been written.

Diana R. Harrington
Crozet, Virginia
Frank J. Fabozzi
Cambridge, Massachusetts
H. Russell Fogler
Gainesville, Florida

CHAPTER 1

Profiting in the Stock Market

"The efficient market hypothesis is the most remarkable error in the history of economic theory"[1] was one person's response to the extraordinary stock market drop of over 500 points in one day on October 19, 1987. On the other hand, "It's conceivable that a change in the well-informed forecast of future economic events moved the market as it did: you can't prove it one way or the other" reflects the sentiments of many efficient-market advocates.[2] Obviously, the dramatic market event of Black Monday encouraged some to question market efficiency, while others looked for, developed, and supported alternative hypotheses.

Regardless of whether Black Monday was its death or not, *market efficiency* is currently still the major theory about how investors price stocks: they engage in a fair game where prices fully reflect available information.[3] Arguments about market efficiency center around exactly what information is fully reflected in the price. There are increasingly rigid definitions of what constitutes a fair game in the different forms of market efficiency. The least demanding form, the *weak form,* of the efficient-market hypothesis concludes that a fair game is one where only historical prices are used by investors as relevant information in pricing equities. The *semi-strong form* of the hypothesis adds publicly available information to historical stock prices as information used in determining a fair price. Finally, the *strong form* adds to past prices and public information, private and insider information as well.

Because a theory gives us a standard against which to test our investment ideas, and market efficiency is the most widely used and tested investment theory, it serves as a necessary and useful benchmark. That is, if any investment strategy can be found consistently to produce a profit from a knowledge of prices, of prices and public information, or of prices and public and private information, then the market is not efficient and we must turn to or develop another theory (or theories) to explain what is happening.

Tests of each version of market efficiency abound. Tests of the profits to be made from technical analysis[4] constitute tests of the weak form of efficiency. Tests of the profitability of strategies based on public reports of corporate earnings and dividends reflect a concern with the accuracy of the semi-strong version of market efficiency. The strong form of market efficiency has been tested using insider (corporate officer) information and the information held by stock exchange specialists. We will report what has been found in some of these tests in the next seven chapters. However, because a violation of any of these forms of market efficiency can be demonstrated by making consistent profits, before we can evaluate the test results, we need to look at what is meant by *profit*. Once we define profit, then if we find a strategy that consistently makes a profit and we know what information was used in the strategy, we can declare inaccurate one or more of the forms of the efficient-market theory, and we can capitalize profitably on the inefficiency.

What Is Profit?

Every investor would like, at the very least, to break even: cover his or her costs and get a return of the principal that was initially invested. To determine whether a profit was made, all we must do is calculate the costs and deduct them from the return earned. If the remainder is positive, a profit was made. To determine, for example, if a profit was made over one year,[5] the following formula would be used:[6]

Annual rate of return =

$$\frac{[(Price_t - Price_{t-1}) + Dividends_t - Transaction\ costs]}{Price_{t-1}}$$

The subscript t indicates either the beginning $(t-1)$ or the end (t) of the holding period. Transaction costs may, of course, be paid both when the stock is purchased and when it is sold. To estimate the return from an investment you are considering, you would use forecasts for the dividends, the price change, transaction costs, and costs of obtaining information.[7] Obviously, one of the real tricks is to determine the costs, which are both direct and indirect.

Costs of Investing

Trading and Information Costs

There are a number of direct costs of investing; such things as brokerage commissions and taxes are measurable and can be easily deducted from the proceeds of the transaction. Often, however, costs are more difficult to esti-mate—for instance, price pressure (the impact on price of buying and selling a large block of stock). Over time, a number of people have attempted to calculate these total trading costs.[8] Loeb [1983] found that the total cost of trading increased as the number of shares traded increased, and that the market-maker's[9] spread was inversely related to both the market capitalization of the stock and the number of shares traded. He calculated the relationship between the spread and the average price per share and estimated the price concessions and brokerage commissions for a large universe of stocks, the Wilshire 5000. The results for a sample of 1,200 trades from March to August 1982 are shown in Exhibit 1-1. As you can see, price impact was the largest on large blocks of small stocks, even though Loeb found the commissions were lower.

Exhibit 1-1

Market Capitalization, Block Size, and Total Spread/Price Cost[a]

Capitalization Sector (millions of dollars)	Block Size (thousands of dollars)								
	5	25	250	500	1,000	2,500	5,000	10,000	20,000
0–10 ($4.58%)[b]	17.3%	27.3%	43.8%						
10–25 ($10.30)	8.9%	12.0%	23.8%	33.4%					
25–50 ($15.16)	5.0%	7.6%	18.8%	25.9%	30.0%				
50–75 ($18.27)	4.3%	5.8%	9.6%	16.9%	25.4%	31.5%			
75–100 ($21.85)	2.8%	3.9%	5.9%	8.1%	11.5%	15.7%	25.7%		
100–500 ($28.31)	1.8%	2.1%	3.2%	4.4%	5.6%	7.9%	11.0%	16.2%	
500–1,000 ($35.43)	1.9%	2.0%	3.1%	4.0%	5.6%	7.7%	10.4%	14.3%	20.0%
1,000–1,500 ($44.34)	1.9%	1.9%	2.7%	3.3%	4.6%	6.2%	8.9%	13.6%	18.1%
Over 1,500 ($57.48)	1.1%	1.2%	1.3%	1.7%	2.1%	2.8%	4.1%	5.9%	8.0%

[a] Round-trip trading cost *including* commission costs.

[b] Average price of issues in capitalization sector.

Source: Loeb [1983], p. 42.

In addition to direct costs, information costs may be higher for some strategies. Many strategies that we will discuss later use computerized data bases, which are or have been expensive. Recently the prices of many good data bases and simple computer programs have declined, which allows individual investors reasonable and cost-effective access to these tools and data.

Risk

As difficult as trading and information costs are to determine, even more daunting is to determine the price for taking risk. The fair price for risk has been one of the most important, controversial, and difficult problems confronting investors and academics. Over the years, several ways to adjust for risk have been devised.[10] One way is to avoid a direct estimation of risk by using a benchmark.

Benchmark Portfolios. Investors have always used benchmarks, whether a personal, internal standard or an explicit, market-derived standard, for evaluating whether a profit has or will be made. The simplest benchmark would be something like the Standard and Poor's (S&P) 500 Index or the Dow Jones Industrial Average (DJIA). A profitable investment would then be one for which the return has been, or is expected to be, above that of the benchmark index or average. Unfortunately, using a general equity index as the benchmark treats the risks of each investment as equal to that of the index.

Specific Benchmark Portfolios. For most investments, and most investors, general indexes are too simplistic to be useful; thus different specific benchmarks are used for investments with different characteristics. The numerous refinements of this approach take relative risk into account more or less explicitly. For instance, a benchmark could be chosen that would have characteristics similar to those of the investment: if the investor were considering a growth stock, the relevant benchmark might be other growth stocks or a portfolio of growth stocks (presumably, growth stocks are different in the level of their risk). In contrast, for investments in small stocks, the results might be compared with returns from indexes that are weighted toward small stocks (e.g., *Value Line,* the Frank Russell Company 2000, or the Wilshire 5000). Indexes reflecting a variety of specific investment characteristics have been developed by performance-evaluation consultants and are widely available.[11]

Benchmark portfolios lie at the root of performance evaluation. The ones mentioned here are widely known and used, but they are not the only benchmarks that can be developed. Some people have attempted to determine with great precision the characteristics (e.g., size, price/earnings ratio, liquidity, etc.) of an investment and then compare the return generated from those charac-teristics with what should have been expected. This kind of benchmarking is often called performance attribution.[12]

Risk-Based Benchmarks. In contrast to a benchmark portfolio of similar types of stocks, sometimes benchmark portfolios are chosen to replicate the risk characteristics of the investment being analyzed. Some who use this approach group investments into portfolios by risk (**variance of return** or **standard deviation**, see box) and then compare the return of this risk-similar benchmark to that of their investment. Using this approach, a stock or portfolio would be considered profitable if it had a rate of return higher than that of its bench-mark risk class.[13] The critical first step in this process is measuring risk.

Relative-Risk Benchmarks. Another method for benchmarking that has been widely used relates the risk and return of any investment or portfolio to a market index. The first measure of performance to include both risk and return was developed by Treynor [1965]. His measure rested, conceptu-ally, on a measure of relative risk em-bodied in the capital asset pricing mod-el (CAPM), described in Appendix A to this chapter.[14]

Treynor's objective was to de-velop a measure of performance that could be used by all investors—that is, did not depend on the characteristics of any investor or group of investors. To do this, he related the excess return of the stock or portfolio to its risk. Excess return is the return from the stock or portfolio less transaction costs, and less the return from a risk-free asset.

> **Variance and Standard Deviation—**_Variance_ is a simple way to measure the risk in a series of data—for instance, a stock's prices over a period of time. It is a measure of the average variation of the data from the mean. To calcu-late the variance, first calculate the simple average, or mean (X), value of the series. This average is then compared with each value(X_i). To prevent positive and negative differences from canceling each other out, the results are squared before summation. The formula to calculate variance is
>
> $$Variance = \sum_{i}^{n} (X_i - X)^2 / n$$
>
> where Σ indicates the sum of the individual prices, and n indicates the number of observa-tions or pieces of data.
>   _Standard deviation,_ another risk mea-sure, is based on variance; in fact, it is the square root of variance. For practical pur-poses, both are measures of variation around a mean. Some theories and portfolio proce-dures have been developed specifying stan-dard deviation rather than variance, however, because standard deviation does have an ad-ditional and often useful feature: when data are distributed according to the normal distribution (described in chapter 2), the data can be stan-dardized and assessed relative to the probabil-ities associated with the normal distribution. From this information, the probability a par-ticular value has of occurring can be deter-mined.

The reason the risk-free rate of return is deducted is that, in theory, no reason-able investors would buy any investment that promised less than this return, since they could have this return without risk by simply investing in the risk-free asset. Of course, no such asset really exists, but the concept certainly does, and it makes sense. Risk for Treynor is a special kind of risk, **systematic risk,** also called **beta:**[15]

> **Systematic Risk—Beta—***Beta* is a measure of the relative volatility of a stock's returns to those of the whole asset market. Based on beta, the concept of risk contained in the CAPM, each investment's returns are compared with what it earned or is expected to earn, given its relative risk. This fair return is called the the market price of risk. Graphically, this relationship is shown in Exhibit 1-2. The upward-sloping line is the security market line (SML), the line detailing the risk-return tradeoff required in the market place.

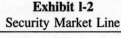

$$\text{Treynor's risk-reward ratio} = \frac{\text{Asset's net return}_t - \text{Risk-free return}_t}{\text{Asset's systematic risk}_t}$$

Obviously, the investor's objective is to obtain the highest reward-for-risk ratio. Treynor's ratio provides a measure of the reward per unit of systematic risk, and thus it depends on systematic risk being what investors use in making their investment decisions.[16]

Because systematic risk presumes that the investor's portfolio is diversified,[17] many people did not like Treynor's ratio. Nevertheless, he did set a precedent for devising a single measure that incorporated both risk and return.

Exhibit 1-2
Security Market Line

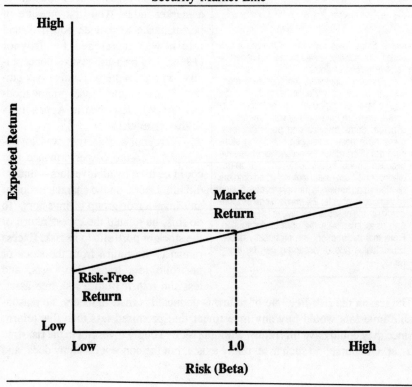

Sharpe [1966] provided another version of the reward-to-risk ratio, one that does not depend on systematic risk alone but uses standard deviation[18] as the denominator:

$$Sharpe's\ measure\ =\ \frac{Asset's\ net\ return_t - Risk\text{-}free\ return_t}{Asset's\ standard\ deviation_t}$$

If the portfolio is perfectly diversified, the Sharpe and Treynor measures will give the same rankings. However, for a single stock or undiversified portfolio, the rankings might differ according to the measure used (the Treynor reward-to-risk ratio will be higher than the Sharpe ratio). The problem with the Sharpe ratio is that it incorporates a measure of total risk, but, at least according to the CAPM, only systematic risk is rewarded; thus this ratio can give an inappropriate ranking.

Another problem exists with both the Treynor and Sharpe measures: they calculate return over a period, however long, without regard to fluctuations in returns over the time. Jensen [1968] took fluctuations into account in developing another reward-to risk ratio. Like Treynor, Jensen based his measure on the CAPM version of risk and calculated the excess, risk-adjusted, returns over time.[19] These excess returns are sometimes called alpha:

$$Asset's\ return - Risk\text{-}free\ return_t =$$

$$Asset's\ alpha + Asset's\ beta\ (Market\ return_t - Risk\text{-}free\ return_t) + Random\ errors$$

or

$$R_i - R_{ft} = \alpha_i + \beta_i\ (R_{mt} - R_{ft}) + e_i$$

Jensen's formula rests on a regression analysis of the excess returns (less the risk-free rate of return) of a stock or portfolio (i) relative to the market's excess returns (R_{mt}). The risk-adjusted return, the return above that expected to compensate for risk, is measured by alpha (α).[20] A positive alpha indicates that the stock or portfolio outperformed what was required by investors.[21] Graphically, alpha is the vertical distance from the risk-return placement for any asset or portfolio to the SML, as shown in Exhibit 1-3. Theoretically, we can conclude that asset A has a positive alpha, which indicates that it outperformed a combination of the market portfolio and a riskless asset—that is, a two-asset portfolio with a similar beta. The drawback to using this measure is that two portfolios could exhibit the same alpha but have different betas, different risks. That is the case with assets A and B in Exhibit 1-3.

Versions of this risk-adjusted approach to performance measurement are in use today. When it is used as a performance-measurement tool, investments

Exhibit 1-3
Jensen's Performance

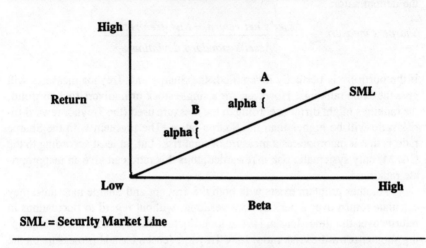

SML = Security Market Line

(portfolios or individual stocks) whose historical risk-return performance is not on the line are determined to have out- or underperformed the average. Used as a forecast tool, the approach implies that, when the returns are above the line (are more than required for a given level of risk), the stock is undervalued and should be bought. The reverse is true if the returns are less than required. This risk-return tradeoff concept can be useful for analyzing past performance as well as anticipating the future.

Are Jensen's, Treynor's, and Sharpe's measures all the same? To see the magnitude of the differences between them, Reilly [1985] calculated the mean, standard deviation, beta, and the three performance measures for one open-end mutual fund. He found that the average return for the fund exceeded that of the S&P 500 from 1968 to 1982, the beta was less than the market average, and the three measures showed a positive risk-reward ratio. Remember, these results depended on the mutual fund being diversified.[22] There was one notable difference among the measures: the Jensen measure showed that the risk-adjusted returns were over 2 percent, but they were not statistically significant. Thus Jensen's measure gave an extra measure of information.[23]

Fama [1972] developed an even more explicit use of the information from the regression analysis of the stock's and market's returns—the so-called market model.[24] He suggested that the various components of the CAPM could be used to analyze a manager's ability to select stocks, diversify, and accept risk. The first step is to estimate the return that would be expected for various levels of risk, which is the security market line.[25] Once this line has been estimated, the return and risk for the stock is estimated for the same period. As shown in Exhibit 1-4, Fama broke down profits into two general sources: (1) the return that comes from managers' abilities to select better than average stocks and (2) that which comes from their willingness to take risk when taking risk is rewarded.[26]

Exhibit 1-4
Performance Measures of Equations

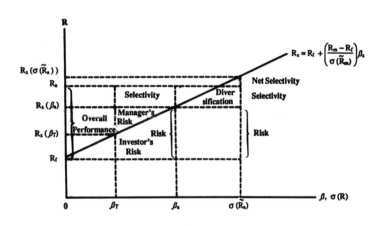

Source: Fama [1972] p. 558.

Moses, Cheyney, and Veit [1987] expanded Fama's ideas to incorporate a benchmark portfolio that has characteristics similar to those of a particular investment. Instead of using the risk-return tradeoffs in the market to develop the security market line, they chose a unique, asset-weighted portfolio. While their benchmark portfolio was used to test a portfolio strategy, and thus included assets other than equities, their concept could be extended for an equity portfolio with concentrations in different kinds of stocks: those from different industries or countries or with different growth characteristics. Exhibit 1-5 shows the differences in relative performance from using three different formulations of the reward-to-risk ratio.

Unfortunately, as interesting as all these performance measures may be, and as rich as they may be, relative to the way we evaluated performance and profit in the past, none tells the whole story. To be accurate measures of the actual profits earned, or the profits expected to be gained, all transaction costs must be included: any profit earned must be attributable only to skill, not to ignored or inaccurate measurement of transaction costs. Thus the right measure of risk must be used. But what is the right measure of risk, and how do we determine what is a fair return for that risk?

Exhibit 1-5

Comparison of Performance-Evaluation Techniques:
Number and Percentage of Funds Outperforming the Market

Fund Classification	n	Jensen [a] Number	Percentage	Sharpe [a] Number	Percentage	Treynor [a] Number	Percentage	PM [b] Number	Percentage
Growth	29	22	75.9	19	65.5	21	72.4	18	62.1
Income	14	12	85.7	12	85.7	12	85.7	7	50.0
Balanced	10	7	70.0	6	60.0	7	70.0	4	40.0
Weighted Totals	53	41	77.4	37	69.8	40	75.5	29	54.7

[a] Performance measure calculated using the S&P 500.
[b] Performance measure calculated using the UABP.

Source: Moses, Cheyney, and Veit [1987], p. 29.

There seems to be some consensus on sources of risk: anything that makes investors' forecasts inaccurate. There are, however, two ways to look at forecast inaccuracy. The first attempts to determine how far from the forecast the actual returns might be at any one time;[27] the second, how much returns may fluctuate over time. In spite of the time, effort, and concern of many, we have not yet found a single, universally applicable measure of risk. For a summary of the evidence about what kind of risk investors look for in potential investments, including whether there is a relationship between risk and return, see Appendix B to this chapter.

Summary

There are four reasons why it is difficult to profit from equity investments: profit is hard to measure; data can mislead an investor; erroneous conclusions can be drawn from the results of studies; and more time than is available is required to evaluate all the original work on potentially profitable equity strategies. In this chapter, we have discussed the first—some of the approaches to measuring a profit and the problems with these methods.

The investor faces many problems in deciding whether an investment has made a profit.[28] Two of the more difficult are measuring price pressure and measuring the market price of risk. Profits are what we all seek, but optimism, rather than reality, can color our perceptions, and profits can be perceived where none really exist. The market is not forgiving, however, and gives up a profit only grudgingly. Since profits are rare, determining as accurately as possible whether an equity investment or strategy has or will make a profit is critical. The three impediments to profit—misleading data, erroneous conclusions and a daunting amount of research to digest—are addressed in the rest of this book. Each of the next eight chapters is designed to help eliminate some of the difficulty and reduce the time needed to find potentially profitable approaches to equity investing, to evaluate those approaches, and to earn profits.

CHAPTER 1

Notes

1. Quote from Robert Shiller, a well-respected academic, reported in Donnelly [1987], p. 7.

2. Quote from William F. Sharpe, Professor at Stanford University, as reported in Donnelly [1987], p. 7.

3. Before the theory of market efficiency, researchers had studied stock-price behavior over time and had generally suggested that the changes in prices had no pattern. The market followed what was called a *random walk:* the next price of a stock is not related to the current price; it can be up, down, or the same; and the investor cannot tell what the next price will be using historical information.

4. Primarily an analysis of historical price and volume data.

5. To determine the annual rate of return for a period longer than one year requires a bit more work and the use of present-value tables or a calculator that gives internal rates of return.

6. As with so many things in finance, there is some disagreement about how the rate of return should be calculated. This formula calculates the return for one period. Returns generated over time may be either arithmetic (to find a simple average of the annual rates of return) or geometric (to compound rates of return).

7. In Chapter 4, we will discuss models that are used to determine the expected return, including the dividend and discounted cash flow models.

8. See, for instance, Cuneo and Wagner [1975], Fouse [1976], Beebower and Priest [1978], and Stoll and Whaley [1983].

9. Those who make a market—that is, hold an inventory, and accept orders to buy and sell a particular stock.

10. All these profit-evaluation tools can be used with historical data to determine whether a profit has been made, or with forecasts for returns to see if one will be made.

11. See, for instance, Capital International's indexes for stock markets outside the United States or First Chicago Investment Advisor's indexes for real estate and U.S. and non-U.S. bonds and stocks.

12. BARRA, a consulting firm, has an evaluation system based on performance attribution. See Rosenberg [1984] for a basic description of the system and Burr, Paustien, and Chernoff [1986] for a discussion of the system.

13. See, for instance, Friend, Blume, and Crockett [1970] for a description of this process.

14. Discussed in detail in Harrington [1987].

15. Systematic risk is risk that cannot be diversified away and is generally driven by changes in macroeconomic factors: factors that affect the returns of all investments to some degree. Theoretically, reasonable investors eliminate any risk that can be eliminated, and unsystematic risk, risk that is peculiar to a given stock (or bond, house, car, or education, for that matter), can be eliminated through diversification. Investors will want to do this because it results in no loss of expected return. These concepts are dealt with in more detail in Appendix A to this chapter and in Harrington [1987].

16. Using this and any other ratio that includes systematic risk also assumes that systematic risk can be measured. There are a variety of problems in forecasting beta, and even more in using history as the basis for the forecast. For instance, Levy [1984] points out that using different horizons (weekly, monthly, or yearly) will result in different betas and thus different results when included in measures of performance. Harrington [1987] provides much more information than is possible here on the differences that can be expected.

17. A perfectly diversified portfolio has eliminated all the unsystematic risk; therefore, beta and standard deviation would provide the same rankings for riskiness.

18. Van Zijl [1987] and Ben-Horim and Levy [1980] discuss the superiority of standard deviation over variance when decomposing risk into systematic and unsystematic sources.

19. The equation is a version of what is called the market model. It is not the CAPM which looks forward to the future. It is a way of looking at history and determining whether the asset earned what was expected for its level of systematic risk. Appendix A explains the differences between the CAPM and the market model.

20. Jensen's model is, in fact, a linear regression of the excess market and asset's returns. The beta is the slope of the regression line; the alpha, the intercept. If the asset returns just enough to compensate for the risk-free return and the returns required for risk, the alpha (the intercept) will be zero.

21. Several investment management companies forecast alphas. Using returns generated by their analysts, and betas from a beta service or calculated from history, they recommend that stocks with positive alphas (returns above those expected for their level of risk) should be considered for purchase, and stocks with negative alphas should be sold.

22. This fund was fairly well diversified; its coefficient of determination was 0.86.

23. Reilly ranked 20 funds on the basis of all three measures. The degree of correlation between the funds' rankings using these measures was over 99 percent.

24. See Note 19.

25. The SML shows the tradeoff between systematic risk (beta) and return. The capital market line uses total risk (standard deviation) as the measure of risk.

26. In prospect, the market line is sloped upward. However, in retrospect, high-risk assets might provide returns lower than what was expected, and lower than the returns gained from investing in lower risk assets. We do not always get what we expect. Thus, in retrospect, the investment's position along the line also says something about the investor's ability to time the market.

27. A number of researchers have speculated on the source of this risk. Lack of skill in forecasting, changes in conditions from the time the forecast was made, and a lack of information have been suggested. Barry and Brown [1986] discuss the latter source.

28. Added problems exist for investments in equities outside the domestic market. Many have written on determining performance in foreign markets; for instance, Errunza and Losq [1987], Mantell [1984], Errunza and Rosenberg [1982], and Stultz [1981].

CHAPTER 1

References

Ang, James, and Chua, J. "Composite Measures for the Evaluating of Investment Performance." *Journal of Financial and Quantitative Analysis*, June 1979, pp. 361-84.

Arditti, Fred. "Another Look at Mutual Fund Performance." *Journal of Financial and Quantitative Analysis*, June 1971, pp. 909-12.

―――. "Risk and the Required Return on Equity." *Journal of Finance*, March 1967, pp. 19-36.

Barry, Christopher, and Brown, Stephen. "Limited Information as a Source of Risk." *Journal of Portfolio Management*, Winter 1986, pp. 66-73.

Beebower, Gilbert, and Priest, William. "An Analysis of Transaction Costs in Equity Trading." Paper presented at the Seminar on the Analysis of Security Prices, Chicago, Illinois, November 3, 1978.

Ben-Horim, M., and Levy, Haim. "Total Risk, Diversifiable Risk and Nondiversifiable Risk: A Pedagogic Note." *Journal of Financial and Quantative Analysis*, June 1980, pp. 289-97.

Burrs, Barry E.; Paustian, Chuck; and Chernoff, Joel. "Few Sponsors Use Performance Attribution." *Pensions and Investment Age*, February 17, 1986, pp. 3, 81.

Cuneo, Larry, and Wagner, Wayne. "Reducing the Cost of Stock Trading." *Financial Analysts Journal*, November-December 1975, pp. 35-44.

Donnelly, Barbara. "Efficient-Market Theorists Are Puzzled by Recent Gyrations in Stock Market." *Wall Street Journal*, October 23, 1987, p. 7.

Errunza, Vihang, and Losq, Etienne. "How Risky Are Emerging Markets?" *Journal of Portfolio Management*, Fall 1987, pp. 62-67.

―――, and Rosenberg, Barr. "Investment Risk in Developed and Less Developed Countries." *Journal of Financial and Quantitative Analysis*, December 1982, pp. 741-62.

Fama, Eugene F. "Components of Investment Performance." *Journal of Finance*, June 1972, pp. 551-67.

Fouse, William. "Risk and Liquidity: The Keys to Stock Price Behavior." *Financial Analysts Journal*, May-June 1976, pp. 35-45.

French, Kenneth R.; Schewart, G. William; and Stambaugh, Robert F. "Expected Stock Returns and Volatility." *Journal of Financial Economics*, September 1987, pp. 3-29.

Friend, Irwin; Blume, Marshall; and Crockett, Jean. "Measurement of Portfolio Performance Under Uncertainty." *American Economic Review*, September 1970, pp. 561-75.

―――. *Mutual Funds and Other Institutional Investors*. New York: McGraw-Hill, 1970.

Fuller, Russell, and Wong, Wenchi. "Traditional versus Theoretical Risk Measures." *Financial Analysts Journal*, March-April 1988, pp. 52-57.

Good, Walter. "Measuring Performance." *Financial Analysts Journal*, May-June 1983, pp. 19-23.

Hagigi, Moshe, and Kluger, Brian. "Safety First: An Alternative Performance Measure." *Journal of Portfolio Management*, Summer 1987, pp. 34-40.

Harrington, Diana R. *Modern Portfolio Theory, The Capital Asset Pricing Model and Arbitrage Pricing Theory: A User's Guide*. Second edition. Englewood Cliffs, N. J.: Prentice Hall, 1987.

Jensen, Michael. "The Performance of Mutual Funds in the Period 1945-1964." *Journal of Finance*, May l968, pp. 389-416.

Joy, D. Maurice, and Jones, Charles. "Should We Believe the Tests of Market Efficiency?" *Journal of Portfolio Management*, Summer 1986, pp. 49-54.

Kon, Stanley. "Models of Stock Returns—A Comparison." *Journal of Finance*, March 1984, pp. 147-65.

Kosmicke, Ralph. "The Limited Relevance of Volatility to Risk." *Journal of Portfolio Management*, Fall 1986, pp. 18-20.

Levy, Haim. "Measuring Risk and Performance Over Alternative Investment Horizons." *Financial Analysts Journal*, March-April, l984, pp. 61-68.

Loeb, Thomas. "Trading Cost: The Critical Line Between Investment Information and Results." *Financial Analysts Journal*, May-June 1983, pp. 39-44.

Mantell, Edmund. "How to Measure Expected Returns on Foreign Investments." *Journal of Portfolio Management*, Winter 1984, pp. 38-43.

Moses, Edward; Cheyney, John; and Veit, Theodore. "A New and More Complete Performance Measure." *Journal of Portfolio Management*, Summer 1987, pp. 24-32.

Reilly, Frank R. *Investment Analysis and Portfolio Management*. Second edition. Hinsdale, Ill.: Dryden Press, 1985.

Rosenberg, Barr. "Prediction of Common Stock Investment Risk." *Journal of Portfolio Management*, Fall l984, pp. 44-53.

Sharpe, William. "Capital Asset Prices: A Theory of Market Equilibrium Under Conditions of Risk." *Journal of Finance*, September 1964, pp. 425-42.

————. "Security Prices, Risk, and Maximal Gains from Diversification: Reply." *Journal of Finance*, December 1966, pp. 743-744.

Shiller, Robert. "Theories of Aggregate Stock Price Movement." *Journal of Portfolio Management*, Winter l984, pp. 28-37.

Stoll, Hans R., and Whaley, Robert E. "Transaction Costs and The Small Firm Effect." *Journal of Financial Economics*, 1983, pp. 57-80.

Stultz, R. "On the Effects of Barriers to International Investment." *Journal of Finance*, September 1981, pp. 923-34.

Treynor, Jack. "How to Rate Management of Investment Funds." *Harvard Business Review*, January-February l965, pp. 63-70.

Van Zijl, Tony. "Risk Decomposition: Variance or Standard Deviation—A Reexamination and Extension." *Journal of Financial and Quantitative Analysis*, June 1987, pp. 237-47.

CHAPTER 1

Appendix A

The Capital Asset Pricing Model and Arbitrage Pricing Theory

The CAPM simplifies risk by viewing each potential investment's risk as relative to the biggest possible portfolio, the market.[1] Thus an investor need only determine the relationship between any investment and the market, not the relationships between that investment and every other possible investment.

Because the relevant risk to investors is that which contributes to their portfolios' risk, that is the only risk for which return is required. This risk that cannot be eliminated is called *market* or *systematic risk,* and it affects all investments to a greater or lesser degree. Prudent investors diversify against all other kinds of risk, called *specific, unique,* or *unsystematic risk* (changes in industry conditions, the competitive environment, or product success), which are related to specific investments. Remember, because unsystematic risk can be diversified away, it has no price.[2] Systematic risk is priced, but not risk from unsystematic sources.

The CAPM specifies that return is related to systematic risk, which is measured by beta (the sensitivity of an asset's returns to changes in the market's returns); because the market's beta is 1.00, if an asset's return moves, for example, 10 percent more than the market's return, its beta would be 1.10. The formula for the CAPM is

Expected return from any investment =
Expected return$_{rf}$ + Beta (Expected return$_m$ − Expected return$_{rf}$)

The risk-free rate of return (*Expected return $_{rf}$*) is the minimum any investor would accept for a riskless investment.

All the factors in the CAPM equation are forecasts and are difficult to make. As an estimate for the risk-free rate of return, analysts often use the

16

return on a U.S. Treasury security.[3] The return on the market and the beta do not have such readily available proxies. To make these estimates, most people resort first to historical data to develop their forecasts. For the market return, the average return for a long period of history is often substituted for an explicit forecast.[4] For beta, many analysts calculate the historical relationship between the market's returns and the returns from the particular investment.

To use history to calculate a beta, one must define what constitutes the market and the nature of the relationship between the market and any investment's returns. The relationship implied by the CAPM is one where more risk requires more return, and the relationship is linear. Seizing on this relationship, many people have used a simple linear regression and historical data to calculate beta. This linear regression is not the CAPM, but the fitting of a straight line to paired data. This linear regression is called the *market model*:

$$Return\ from\ any\ investment = Intercept + Beta \times Return_m + Error$$

The intercept is the return that would be expected if the market return were zero. The error term (also called a *residual*) represents the fact that the returns from the investment and those from the market do not always act in concert; sometimes something special happens to a company, bad or good, that is reflected in the returns. Because the CAPM implies that these special events, which are unrelated to the overall market, are unpredictable, the errors over time or over a large group of companies should average zero. This method of calculating a beta uses historical data (a real problem when things in the world or about the company are changing) and assumes that there has been a close relationship between events that have affected the market returns and those that have affected the returns from the investment.[5]

The CAPM has been put to many uses—forecasting an investment's expected return, identifing over- and undervalued stocks, and determining an equity shareholder's required return.[6] In spite of its widespread use, however, controversy surrounds it. Questions abound about its theoretical strength,[7] appropriate proxies for expectational returns from the market and the risk-free security, and how best to estimate the beta.

The most interesting and obvious question about the CAPM is about beta itself. A legitimate, and provocative, complaint about beta is that it is far too simplistic. Macroeconomic, systematic risk comes not from one factor (the market) but from a variety of factors. Changes in any one of the factors will affect the returns of all investments but will do so differently. Thus lumping all the macroeconomic risks into one index probably is too simple. A multifactor, multibeta, model would really better represent the way things actually work. Such a multifactor model does exist—arbitrage pricing theory.[8]

Like the CAPM, arbitrage pricing theory (APT) relates the returns for an investment to the returns from the risk-free security plus returns relative to a

series of factors. Changes in these factors systematically increase or decrease
the return from all investments. APT still assumes that investors diversify away
unsystematic risk, and the model itself looks much like an expanded version of
the CAPM. As a forecast model (ex ante) it looks like

*Expected return from any investment = Expected return$_{rf}$+ β$_1$ (Expected
return on factor 1 − Expected return$_{rf}$) ... β$_j$ (Expected return
on factor 2 − Expected return$_{rf}$)*

To determine how a security performed relative to the systematic common
factors, we can use an historical, realized (ex post) version:

$$\tilde{R}_j = E[R_j] + \beta_{j1} \, (\tilde{R}F_1 - E[RF_1]) + ... + \beta_{jk} \, (\tilde{R}F_k - E[RF_k]) + e_j$$

where

R_j = the return on an asset,

R_f = the risk-free rate of return,

β_{jk} = the sensitivity of a particular asset (j) to a particular factor (k)—
that is, the covariance of the asset's returns with the changes in the
particular factor,

RF_k = the expected return on a portfolio with an average (1.0) sensitivity
to a factor (k) that systematically affects returns, a factor common
to all asset returns, and

E = to denote an expectation.

e = idiosyncratic risk, assumed to be mutually independent over time
and negligible for large numbers of assets.

˜ = denotes a realized value.

First described by Ross [1976, 1977], APT says nothing about what the
factors are or about the size or signs of each factor's coefficient. What the
theory does say is that, as a result of active trading of investments with different
sensitivities to the common factors, opportunities for profits are arbitraged
away. Over time, and across the market, there are no opportunities to profit
from such arbitrage opportunities. An example of how this works will no doubt
be useful.

Our example market is a simple one: only three investments exist, and
there is only one common factor. One investment, A, is expected to yield 14.0

percent, but if it were properly priced for its common-factor sensitivity, it would yield a return of 12.5 percent. A profit-seeking investor would certainly be attracted to Investment A. The investment is risky, however. With a little creativity, the investor in our three-investment market can get the 1.5 percent profit with no risk at all. Exhibit 1A-1 shows the other two investments available in our simple world and the portfolio that would result in the riskless profit. Obviously, such a riskless profit would be so attractive that investors would leap on it, and it would quickly disappear. Thus APT assumes, and it seems a reasonable assumption, that there are no arbitrage profits for an investor across time or for all investors at any one time.

Exhibit 1A-1
Arbitrage Risk and Return

Action / Amount	Asset	Expected Return[d]	Factor Sensitivity
Buy:			
$1,000	B	14.0%	0.5
Short-sell:			
$667	A	(6.7)[a]	0.0
333	C	(5.8)[b]	(0.5)[c]
Total		(12.5%)	(0.5)
Portfolio:			
$2,000		1.5%	0.0

[a] $.67 \times 10\%$.
[b] $.33 \times 17.5\%$.
[c] $.33 \times 1.5$.
[d] Asset returns

Asset	Factor Sensitivity	Expected Return
A	0.0	10.0%
B	0.5	14.0
C	1.5	17.5

Source: Harrington [1987], p. 193.

There has been no end of discussion about the strength and consistency of the common factors over time. Indeed, many are uncertain about just how many common factors there are,[9] what they are, and how to estimate them. Chen, Roll, and Ross [1986], for example, propose the factors shown in Exhibit 1A-2.

Exhibit 1A-2
Glossary and Definitions of Variables

Symbol	Variable	Definition or Source
	Basic Series	
I	Inflation	Log relative of U.S. Consumer Price Index
TB	Treasury-bill rate	End-of-period return on 1-month bills
LGB	Long-term government bonds	Return on long-term government bonds (1958–78: Ibbotson and Sinquefield [1982]; 1979–83: CRSP)
IP	Industrial production	Industrial production during month (*Survey of Current Business*)
Baa	Low-grade bonds	Return on bonds rated Baa and under (1953–77: Ibbotson [1979], constructed for 1978–83)
EWNY	Equally weighted equities	Return on equally weighted portfolio of NYSE-listed stocks (CRSP)
VWNY	Value-weighted equities	Return on a value-weighted portfolio of NYSE-listed stocks (CRSP)
CG	Consumption	Growth rate in real per capita consumption (Hansen and Singleton [1982]; *Survey of Current Business*)
OG	Oil prices	Log relative of Producer Price Index/Crude Petroleum series (Bureau of Labor Statistics)
	Derived Series	
MP(t)	Monthly growth, industrial production	$\log_e [\text{IP}(t)/\text{IP}(t-1)]$
YP(t)	Annual growth, industrial production	$\log_e [\text{IP}(t)/\text{IP}(t-12)]$
E[I(t)]	Expected inflation	Fama and Gibbons [1984]
UI(t)	Unexpected inflation	$I(t) - E[I(t)\ t-1]$
RHO(t)	Real interest (ex post)	$\text{TB}(t-1) - I(t)$
DEI(t)	Change in expected inflation	$E[I(t+1)\ t] - E[I(t)\ t-1]$
URP(t)	Risk premium	$\text{Baa}(t) - \text{LGB}(t)$
UTS(t)	Term structure	$\text{LGB}(t) - \text{TB}(t-1)$

Source: Chen, Roll, and Ross [1986], p. 387.

Fortunately, we are continually learning more about the way to make estimates about the factors and have found that, among other things, estimates are sensitive to the months of the year and the size of the companies included in the sample tested.[10]

Recent work has found that a simple CAPM is not as effective ex post as APT.[11] APT, even if the model may be hard to use in practice, seems to reflect the reality that many factors are important in pricing investments.[12]

CHAPTER 1   APPENDIX A

Notes

1. Eight assumptions support the CAPM, the first five of which underlie market efficiency:

    1. The investor's objective is to maximize the utility of terminal wealth.

    2. Investors make choices based on risk (portfolio variance) and return (mean portfolio return).

    3. Investors have homogeneous expectations about risk and return.

    4. Investors have identical time horizons.

    5. Information is freely and simultaneously available to investors.

    6. There is a risk-free asset, and investors can borrow and lend unlimited amounts at that rate.

    7. There are no taxes, transaction costs, short-selling restrictions, or other market imperfections.

    8. Total asset quantity is fixed, and all assets can be bought, sold, and/or divided.

For an extensive discussion of modern portfolio theory and the capital asset pricing model, see Harrington [1987].

2. Unsystematic risk is not priced prospectively. However, rewards and losses may come from unsystematic sources, retrospectively. These retrospective rewards are not forecastable, at least in theory, and can best be dealt with through diversification. Thus they are not priced.

3. While most people in the United States who use the CAPM for estimating return on domestic investments use the yield on a U.S. Treasury security as a proxy for the expected risk-free rate of return, there is considerable disagreement over which *maturity* of the security provides the best proxy.

4. Often the estimated return for the Standard and Poor's 500 Stock Index from 1926 onwards, reported in Ibbotson and Sinquefield [1988], is used. Analysts' estimates are used by some analysts. Discussion of proxies for the market is far beyond the scope of this brief introduction. Most people, because the data are available in computer-readable form, have used the S&P 500, but even the most casual observer recognizes that the S&P 500 is not a good representative sample of all possible assets in which an individual could invest.

5. To determine the strength of this relationship, one should examine the R^2 of the regression (the coefficient of determination) and the standard error (a kind of standard deviation) of the beta coefficient. If the R^2 is very low, or the standard error very high, history is not providing data that are very useful for making a forecast.

6. See the appendix to Chapter 3 for a discussion of residual analysis in research.

7. A number of researchers have adapted the CAPM in an effort to reduce problems. For instance, see Breeden [1979], Litzenberger and Ramaswamy [1979], and Merton [1973], among many others.

8. Before APT was developed, many researchers were unsatisfied with the single-factor CAPM. King [1966], Farrell [1974 and 1975], Elton and Gruber [1973], Estep [1979], Sharpe [1982], and others found more than the market factor important in pricing equities.

9. See, for instance, Ross and Roll [1980], Reinganum [1981], and Dhrymes, Friend, and Gultekin [1984].

10. See, for instance Cho and Taylor, [1987].

11. See, for instance, Burmeister and McElroy [1988].

12. For a discussion of the practical differences between APT and the CAPM, see Bower, Bower, and Logue [1984] and Fogler [1982]. For more about APT, see Harrington [1987].

CHAPTER 1   APPENDIX A

References

Bower, Dorothy; Bower, Richard S.; and Logue, Dennis E. "A Primer on Arbitrage Pricing Theory." *Midland Corporate Finance Journal*, Fall 1984, pp. 31-40.

Breeden, Douglas T. "Consumption, Production, Inflation and Interest Rates: A Synthesis." *Journal of Financial Economics*, May 1986, pp. 3-40.

————. "An Intertemporal Asset Pricing Model with Stochastic Consumption and Investment Opportunities." *Journal of Financial Economics*, September 1979, pp. 265-96.

Burmeister, Edwin, and McElroy, Marjorie B. "Joint Estimation of Factor Sensitivities and Risk Premia for the Arbitrage Pricing Theory." *The Journal of Finance*, July 1988, pp. 721-33.

Chen, Nai-Fu. "Some Empirical Tests of the Theory of Arbitrage Pricing." *Journal of Finance*, November 1983, pp. 1393-1414.

————; Roll, Richard; and Ross, Stephen. "Economic Forces and the Stock Market." *Journal of Business*, July 1986, pp. 383-404.'

Cho, D. Chinhyung, and Taylor, William M. "The Seasonal Stability of the Factor Structure of Stock Returns." *Journal of Finance*, December 1987, pp. 1195-1211.

Connor, Gregory, and Korazczyk, Robert A. "Risk and Return in an Equilibrium APT: Application of a New Test Methodology." *Journal of Financial Economics*, September 1988, pp. 255-89.

Dhrymes, Phoebus; Friend, Irwin; and Gultekin, N. B. "A Critical Reexamination of the Empirical Evidence on the Arbitrage Pricing Theory." *Journal of Finance*, July 1984 pp. 323-46.

————; and Gultekin, M. N. "New Tests of the APT and Their Implications." *Journal of Finance*, September 1985, pp. 659-74.

Elton, Edwin, and Gruber, Martin J. "Estimating the Dependence Structure of Share Prices—Implications for Portfolio Selection." *Journal of Finance*, December 1973, pp. 1203-32.

Estep, Tony. "Homogeneous Groupings of Stocks and the Diversification of Portfolios." Kidder Peabody Position Paper, April 11, 1979.

Farrell, James L. "Analyzing Covariation of Returns to Determine Homogeneous Stock Groupings." *Journal of Business*, April 1974, pp. 186-207.

————. "Homogeneous Stock Groupings." *Financial Analysts Journal*, May-June 1975, pp. 50-62.

Ferson, Wayne E.; Kandel, Shimuel; and Stambaugh, Robert F. "Tests of Asset Pricing with Time-Varying Expected Risk Premiums and Market Betas." *The Journal of Finance*, June 1987, pp. 201-220.

————, and Merrick, John J., Jr., "Non-Stationarity and Stage-on-the-Business-Cycle Effects in Consumption-Based Asset Pricing Relations." *Journal of Financial Economics*, September 1987, pp. 127-246.

Fogler, H. Russell. "Common Sense on CAPM, APT, and Correlated Residuals." *Journal of Portfolio Management*, Summer 1982, pp. 20-28.

Harrington, Diana R. *Modern Portfolio Theory, The Capital Asset Pricing Model and Arbitrage Pricing Theory: A User's Guide*. Second edition. Englewood Cliffs, N.J.: Prentice-Hall, 1987.

King, Benjamin. "Market and Industry Factors." *Journal of Business*, January 1966, pp. 139-91.

Lehmann, Bruce N., and Modest, David M. "The Empirical Foundations of the Arbitrage Pricing Theory." *Journal of Financial Economics*, September 1988, pp. 213-54.

Lintner, J. "The Valuation of Risky Assets: The Selection of Risky Investments in Stock Portfolios and Capital Budgets." *Review of Economics and Statistics*, February 1965, pp. 13-37.

Litzenberger, Robert, and Ramaswamy, K. "The Effect of Personal Taxes and Dividends on Capital Asset Prices: Theory and Empirical Evidence." *Journal of Financial Economics*, June 1979, pp. 163-96.

Markowitz, Harry M. "Portfolio Selection." *Journal of Finance*, March 1952, pp. 77-91.

Merton, Robert. "An Intertemporal Capital Asset Pricing Model." *Econometrica*, September 1973, pp. 867-87.

Reinganum, Marc. "The Arbitrage Pricing Theory: Some Empirical Results." *Journal of Finance*, May 1981, pp. 313-21.

Roll, Richard, and Ross, Stephen. "An Empirical Investigation of the Arbitrage Pricing Model." *Journal of Finance*, November 1980, pp. 1073-1103.

Ross, Stephen. "The Arbitrage Theory of Capital Asset Pricing." *Journal of Economic Theory*, 1976, pp. 341-60.

Sharpe, William. "A Simplified Model of Portfolio Analysis." *Management Science*, January 1963, pp. 277-93.

————. "Some Factors in New York Stock Exchange Security Returns." *Journal of Portfolio Management*, Summer 1982, pp. 5-19.

Appendix B

Defining and Measuring Risk

The definitions and measurements of risk are difficult and controversial. Writings about risk range from the philosophical to the empirical. This appendix summarizes the results of some of the research into whether various measures of risk fully capture the inherent riskiness of stock returns.

Return-Risk Relationship

In an early study, Friend and Blume [1970] looked specifically at the relationship between risk-adjusted returns and risk. Obviously, once returns are adjusted for risk (reduced by the market's price for that level of risk), there should be no further relationship between return and risk. That is not what they found: they found that there was a relationship, and the relationship was true regardless of whether the Treynor, Jensen, or Sharpe risk-adjusted performance measures were used.[1] Furthermore, they found that the relationship was inverse: the risk-adjusted performance of the low-risk portfolio was better than that of the higher risk portfolios.[2] Because two of the most widely used measures of risk were used in these ratios, beta by Jensen and Treynor and standard deviation by Sharpe, some believed we might be better off with a different measure of risk.

A number of other researchers have tried to tie returns with risk as measured by volatility. To justify the increased risk premiums of the 1970s, Pindyck [1984], for example, looked to volatility. Shiller [1981] found that price movements were too large to be justified by changes in volatility, and Poterba and Summers [1986] concluded that "volatility shocks (like those in the 1970s) can have only a small impact on stock market prices" (p. 1142). Thus the actual volatility experienced in the stock market was not found to be the culprit behind increases in the required returns for equities.

French, Schwert, and Stambaugh [1987], using a more sophisticated approach to analyzing returns, suggested that part of the problem was that researchers were confusing what had happened (realized volatility) with what was expected to occur, and were confusing what could be forecasted with what could not. Using a two-stage process, they separated the predictable portion of volatility from what was unpredictable and found a "strong negative relation . . . between excess holding period returns and the unpredictable component of volatility" (p. 4). While they did have some difficulty in settling on one model for estimating the relationship between returns and predictable volatility, they found the premiums shown in Exhibit 1B-1.[3] Note that these are monthly premiums. Annualized, a 0.9 percent premium, the highest they found, would be 11.3 percent. The lowest would be an annual risk premium of 6.8 percent.[4]

Exhibit 1B-1
Predicted Percent Monthly Risk Premium to the Standard & Poor's
Composite Portfolio from the Regression on ARIMA Predictions of the
Standard Deviation, 1928–84

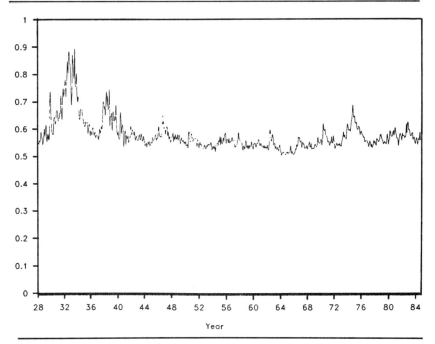

Source: French, Schwert, and Stambaugh [1987], p.22.

On the basis of their research, French et al. concluded that there is a relationship, if indirect, between volatility and expected return. It is important to be aware of the fact that this type of study is relatively new and sophisticated and will no doubt be the subject of further work.

Is volatility the best measure of investors' risk? Kosmicke [1986] puts forth an interesting notion about the usefulness of volatility as a measure of risk. He suggests that volatility is appropriate only if investors are pricing their investments on the basis of long-term forecasts of cash flows. It is not a useful measure if "the market is dominated by investors who act on the basis of short-run forecasts of price changes." Under those circumstances, "prices could change simply because of a change in speculative sentiment." Such changes "will not affect each owner to the same degree; this means that the price of risk of price volatility is different for each owner" (p.19) and would depend on the owner's particular characteristics.

If risk is in the eyes of every beholder, we cannot generalize about how prices are set. As interesting as Kosmicke's notion is, and it certainly is provocative, there does seem to be a relationship between variance and return, but what about relative volatility (beta)? Not wanting to abandon beta (relative volatility) as a measure of risk, Lakonishok and Shapiro [1984] added variance to the simple version of the CAPM to determine whether, in a diversified portfolio, variance is still important. Remember, if the portfolio is diversified, beta should be a complete measure of risk. Using data from the New York Stock Exchange from 1958 to 1980, they found that investors were rewarded for risk, but variance seemed to be a better measure of that risk. They tested four different groupings: based on beta first and then variance (A), and variance first and then beta (B), beta alone (C), and finally on variance alone (D). Their results are shown in Exhibit 1B-2. Variance was important; volatility was not the only priced risk.

Exhibit 1B-2

Summary of Results Over the 1962-80 Period (228 observations)

	γ_0	γ_1	γ_2	$\bar{R}^2$
A	0.0042*	0.0033	-0.0736	0.2995
B	0.0058*	-0.0016	0.3497*	0.3034
C	0.0045*	0.0014		0.2120
D	0.0055*		0.1661*	0.2110

* Statistically significant at the 5 percent level.

where

γ_0 = the regression intercept,
γ_1 = beta,
γ_2 = variance, and
$\bar{R}^2$ = coefficient of determination.

Source: Lakonishok and Shapiro [1984], p. 38.

The results of various researchers are in conflict. Neither beta (systematic risk) nor total risk (standard deviation or variance) seems to tell the whole story about risk.

Cooley, Roenfeldt, and Modani [1977], interested in beta, used a different approach to see whether any measure provided a complete measure of risk. They clustered a variety of risk measures into affinity groups—groups that measured the same or similar things. They found that their first seven measures (listed below) were almost indistinguishable from each other; they measured essentially the same thing. Beta added a bit more information, but **skewness** and **kurtosis** were distinctive measures of risk—that is, unrelated to any of the other measures.

1. Range

2. Semi-interquartile range

3. Mean absolute deviation

4. Standard deviation

5. Variance

6. Semivariance

7. Lower confidence limit

8. Beta

9. Coefficient of quartile variation

10. Skewness

11. Peakedness (kurtosis)

12. Coefficient of variation

Normal Distribution, Skewness, Kurtosis, and Risk—Most economic data have a pattern. Three distinct patterns or distributions are prevalent in investment data: the normal or Gaussian, the Paretian, and the log normal.

Graphically the *normal distribution* is a symmetrical bell-shaped curve that can be explained in terms of its mean (μ) and standard deviation (σ). One especially attractive characteristic of a normal distribution is the fact that a predictable proportion of the data lies within these standard areas, the standard deviations:

Number of Standard Deviations from Mean	Approximate Percentage of the Normal Distribution in the Range from Mean
1	68.00%
2	95.50
3	99.70
4	99.99

Unfortunately, stock returns are not normally distributed. Stock returns tend to exhibit two abnormal tendencies: more outliers (i.e., extremely high or extremely low returns) than predicted by the normal distribution and a more leptokurtic (peaked) shape than the normal, also called *kurtosis*. This can be captured by the Paretian distribution, a distribution that has fat tails:

(continued on next page)

Neither standard deviation nor beta provide complete measures of risk. Skewness and kurtosis both seem to be important to investors, and it makes sense that they should be: if an investor has a choice between a stock with **normally distributed** returns and one where the returns are skewed, the skewed investment would be more attractive.[5]

Two very different conclusions can be reached at this point: (1) the basic models used for estimating profits from common stocks that incorporate standard deviation or beta have ignored some important source or

(continued from previous page)

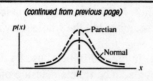

Stock returns also exhibit a tendency to have relatively more extremely high than low values (positive *skewness*). We can use logarithms to solve this problem: when the logarithm of a variable is normally distributed, its underlying distribution will be skewed to the right:

$p(x)$

This tendency can be justified in two ways: a stock's return theoretically is infinite on the upside, but it is limited to a loss of 100 percent on the downside; arithmetic losses do not equal arithmetic gains (that is, a loss of 20 percent requires a gain of 25 percent to break even). Logarithmic returns help solve these problems. By averaging the logarithms of the holding-period returns, we can estimate the return. For instance, by averaging the logarithm of −20 percent and +25 percent, we find the average return is zero.

dimension of risk and we should adapt our models or (2) because market efficiency is critical to the theory behind each of the performance measures we have discussed, the market is not efficient and our theory must be revised.

Skewness

As noted, Roenfeldt, Cooley, and Modani [1977] found that skewness and kurtosis were separate and distinct when they tested them. Furthermore, skewness is much more than just a strangely named measure of risk, it is a fact: an investor, at least an investor long in equities, can only lose 100 percent of an investment, while the upside is theoretically unlimited. Skewness is more upside than downside. It is simply a description of how returns work and, as shown in Exhibit 1B-3, is not a result of a few long shots but of more big winners than losers.[6]

Why then have we rested all our theories on measures of risk that require normal distributions of returns? The short, and correct, answer is that it is easier.[7] Moreover, perhaps in real life, where investors can sell short, buy put and call options, and borrow to buy or sell short, practice may make the distribution returns more normal than not.

Actually, very little effort is needed to make skewness disappear in a portfolio. To diversify away all diversifiable risk, to get the risk of the portfolio down to systematic risk alone, the investor needs to own about 14 relatively unrelated investments (investments where the returns are as uncorrelated as can be found). This fact is shown in Exhibit 1B-4.[8]

Skewness, however, disappears much more quickly than diversifiable risk. Simkowitz and Beedles [1978] found that portfolio skewness (what we might like to call the upside potential) disappears once the investor has about 6 equities. Exhibit 1B-5 shows the results of their study: columns 4 and 6 show that 92 percent of the skewing is exhausted after just 5 stocks are held. It does not take much to offset the benefits of a few winners.

Do investors diversify their portfolios? Blume and Friend [1975] analyzed the major classes of liabilities and assets held by individuals (including home

Exhibit 1B-3
Error Distribution Summary

Standard Deviation Bounds	Frequency of Negative Errors	Frequency of Positive Errors
Between 0 and 1 SDs	57,974	47,255
Between 1 and 2 SDs	14,279	12,395
Between 2 and 3 SDs	1,744	2,955
Between 3 and 4 SDs	247	852
Between 4 and 5 SDs	51	307
Between 5 and 6 SDs	4	128
Between 6 and 7 SDs	1	68
Between 7 and 8 SDs	4	39
Between 8 and 9 SDs	1	9
Between 9 and 10 SDs	2	14
Greater than 10 SDs	1	18

Source: Simkowitz and Beedles [1978], p. 934.

ownership and employment) using the Federal Reserve Board's 1962 *Survey of the Financial Characteristics of Consumers* and a sample of 1971 individual federal income taxes. They found that individuals had remarkably undiversified holdings. This reality is puzzling: if only systematic risk is rewarded, diversified portfolios would be only logical. Conine and Tamarkin [1981] hypothesized that the lack of diversification was not born of a lack of logic, but came about as individual investors sought the positive attractions of skewness.

Skewness appears to be important, and it appears to exist.[9] Even so, there is a question about how skewness should be measured. Some have suggested that it is not skewness but systematic skewness (also called co-skewness) that is relevant to investors.[10] Some of those who have tested systematic skewness disagree.[11] Still, there can be little doubt that all investors, or at least most, would like to find the long-shot winner and would like to do so often.

If skewness is good, and diversification kills skewness, how about incorporating a preference for skewness (upside potential) into a model of investor behavior and into our performance-evaluation ratios? Easier said than done.[12] One of the more widely accepted ways to measure the upside or downside is semivariance. It measures the potential or actual returns from an investor-chosen target. Often used or recommended for use with pension-fund investments,[13] semivariance has the unfortunate problem of resting on a normal distribution, although it can be adapted to focus on returns that are either greater

Exhibit 1B-4
Expected Standard Deviations of Annual Portfolio Returns

Number of Stocks in Portfolio	Expected Standard Deviation of Annual Portfolio Returns	Ratio of Portfolio Standard Deviation to Standard Deviation of a Single Stock
1	49.236	1.00
2	37.358	0.76
4	29.687	0.60
6	26.643	0.54
8	24.983	0.51
10	23.932	0.49
12	23.204	0.47
14	22.670	0.46
16	22.261	0.45
18	21.939	0.45
20	21.677	0.44
25	21.196	0.43
30	20.870	0.42
35	20.634	0.42
40	20.456	0.42
45	20.316	0.41
50	20.203	0.41
75	19.860	0.40
100	19.686	0.40
200	19.423	0.39
300	19.336	0.39
400	19.292	0.39
450	19.277	0.39
500	19.265	0.39
600	19.247	0.39
700	19.233	0.39
800	19.224	0.39
900	19.217	0.39
1000	19.211	0.39
Infinity	19.158	0.39

Source: Statmen [1987], p. 355.

Exhibit 1B-5
Distributional Measures Averaged Over Portfolios of Varying Sizes

Portfolio Size	Number of Portfolios	Holding–Period Return	Variance (×100)	Raw Skewness (×100)	Percentage Return to Standard Deviation	Cube Root of Raw Skew to Standard Deviation
1	549	1.012858	.582320	.046209	.184332	.743956
2	274	1.012864	.373904	.013092	.220674	.608219
3	183	1.012858	.301102	.005399	.241560	.463321
4	137	1.012854	.265995	.002614	.255659	.323158
5	109	1.012888	.247009	.001339	.265002	.165966
6	91	1.012851	.230559	.000571	.272274	.033614
7	78	1.012863	.220846	.000159	.278376	-.036336
8	68	1.012852	.213705	-.000253	.282876	-.112328
9	61	1.012858	.207547	-.000607	.285756	-.262522
10	54	1.012859	.204138	-.000663	.288350	-.291118
11	49	1.012828	.199236	-.000827	.290385	-.328297
12	45	1.012883	.197638	-.000927	.293570	-.366999
13	42	1.012852	.194718	-.001058	.295091	-.428894
14	39	1.012863	.191679	-.001095	.297142	-.438736
15	36	1.012854	.189271	-.001168	.298658	-.472699
16	34	1.012862	.187970	-.001300	.300001	-.493856
17	32	1.012863	.183224	-.001358	.301469	-.504947
18	30	1.012873	.185016	-.001392	.301468	-.535639
19	28	1.012886	.182831	-.001351	.304458	-.526371
20	27	1.012871	.182894	-.001406	.303385	-.536918
21	26	1.012856	.181388	-.001555	.304237	-.559794
22	24	1.012901	.179137	-.001566	.306789	-.569712
23	23	1.012893	.178154	-.001582	.307511	-.570548
24	22	1.012910	.179782	-.001579	.306357	-.563376
25	21	1.012854	.176274	-.001569	.308253	-.593971
26	21	1.012842	.177991	-.001575	.306297	-.582409
27	20	1.012853	.176704	-.001665	.307606	-.598178
28	19	1.012849	.176957	-.001652	.307070	-.569961
29	18	1.012884	.177486	-.001647	.307835	-.597023
30	18	1.012859	.175716	-.001704	.308587	-.606409
31	17	1.012847	.176699	-.001773	.307827	-.613128
32	17	1.012869	.175197	-.001714	.308862	-.613229
33	16	1.012858	.175679	-.001728	.308572	-.611186
34	16	1.012877	.174641	-.001747	.309457	-.617575
35	15	1.012892	.174225	-.001778	.310022	-.620476
36	15	1.012853	.173763	-.001753	.309922	-.620478
37	14	1.012888	.174442	-.001765	.310414	-.619350
38	14	1.012880	.171290	-.001818	.312455	-.629580
39	14	1.012841	.171549	-.001866	.311292	-.636196
40	13	1.012898	.171499	-.001765	.312528	-.626326

Source: Simkowitz and Beedles [1978], p. 936

or less than the investor's chosen target. In general, those who have used some sort of semivariance measure have been those more worried about the downside than the upside.[14]

Other Measures of Risk

We know investors make decisions and are concerned about risk. Our difficulty in generalizing how that is done is that either our measures of risk are not right or we cannot seem to find a way to assure ourselves that any of the measures of risk reflect what is important to investors. Recently, Fuller and Wong [1988] studied the relationship of return to three measures of risk: beta, standard deviation, and safety ranking published by an investment research firm, *Value Line*.[15] Using data from three periods, 1974-77, 1978-81, and 1982-85, they calculated the four-year mean arithmetic return for all stocks on the New York and American Stock Exchanges that also had safety rankings published by *Value Line*. The standard deviation and beta were calculated from data for the four years preceding each of their three periods. They found that the three measures were significantly, but not perfectly, correlated with return, as shown in Exhibit 1B-6.

Exhibit 1B-6
Correlation Coefficients for Risk Measures

Subperiod	Safety Rank and Beta Rank	Safety Rank and Sigma Rank	Beta Rank and Sigma Rank
1974–77	0.705	0.820	0.702
1978–81	0.434	0.703	0.510
1982–85	0.501	0.760	0.616
Averages	0.547	0.761	0.609

Source: Fuller and Wong [1988], p. 54.

Exhibit 1B-7 shows that Fuller and Wong found each of the risk rankings (1 through 5) positively related to the returns for the whole period studied, although the *Value Line* rankings performed best. More than that, for 1982-85, only the *Value Line* rankings were positively related to return.[16]

Because of these results, Fuller and Wong concluded that "intuitive notions of risk utilized by investment professionals in constructing risk measures have been closer to the mark than the theoretically more rigorous risk measures [beta and standard deviation] developed by academics" (p. 57). They suggest

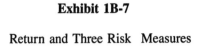

Exhibit 1B-7

Return and Three Risk Measures

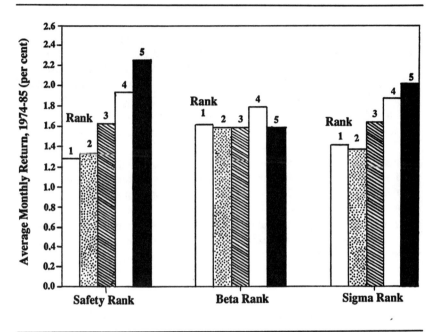

Source: Fuller and Wong [1988], p. 55.

that the analysts at *Value Line* may be taking into account such things as liquidity, firm size, and/or business risk in their rankings, while beta and standard deviation do not adequately account for these sources of risk.[17]

Conclusion

Risk is difficult to measure, and yet it is at the heart of performance measurement, of determining whether a profit was or will be made. The research noted in this appendix is a part of the work that leaves us less than satisfied with the art of risk assessment. The nature of risk, its measurement, and how it is included in evaluating performance has and will continue to be subjects of interest to academic researchers and the basis for creating and marketing products by investment advisors. New work on the nature of risk coming out of such diverse fields as quantum physics, psychology, and sociology makes the problem even more complex, less definite, and immensely more exciting.

CHAPTER 1   APPENDIX B

Notes

1. See text of Chapter 1 for a description of each of these risk-adjustment performance measures.

2. Friend and Blume were concerned that the results could be biased by the nature of the data studied. While Friend and Blume simulated portfolio performance, Klemkosky [1975] studied mutual-fund performance from 1966 to 1971 and found a positive bias (risk-adjusted return and risk were positively related). These researchers all used the Treynor, Jensen, and Sharpe measures.

3. Using other models, they found different premiums.

4. Many others have made estimates of the risk premium. See, for instance, Sorenson [1987].

5. This is true even if the returns are negatively skewed. If the investor expected positively skewed returns, he or she would invest in that stock or buy call options. With negatively skewed returns, the investor could sell short or sell put options. See Chapter 6 for information on options.

6. Reinganum [1981] showed that beta-ranked portfolios also had skewed results, even when extraordinary years were excluded. Singleton and Wingender [1986], however, showed that, while returns for all common stocks (all stocks listed by the Center for Research in Security Prices) have been positively skewed, and consistently so from 1961 to 1980, those for individual stocks and stock portfolios show no such consistency. Thus historical information on skewing does not help in predicting the future direction.

7. Fama [1976] suggested that the relationship is close enough to a normal one that it can be approximated by a normal distribution. Many use log-normal distributions to approximate the positively skewed returns of the equity market.

8. Recent evidence by Statman [1987] suggests that, when borrowing or lending investors' costs are taken into account, 30 stocks are needed for a borrower to diversify and 40 for a lender.

9. Damodaran [1987] theorizes that skewness may come as a result of the way in which a company releases information.

10. See, for instance, Kraus and Litzenberger [1976], who suggest that co-skewness, systematic and undiversifiable, is what is important. They suggest that investors appear to have a preference for increases in beta risk, but that beta is acting as a surrogate for increases in co-skewness.

11. See, for instance, Beedles [1979], Friend and Westerfield [1980], who found that systematic skewness is not important in asset pricing, and Cook and Rozeff [1984] who believe that it is a proxy for dividend yield.

12. Kraus and Litzenberger [1976] developed a version of the CAPM that included a measure of systematic skewness. Ang and Chua [1979] and Prakash and Bear [1986] developed performance measures based on this concept. These models and measures are more difficult to implement, especially when making forecasts of returns.

13. Pension-fund contributions often are predicated on a particular rate of return being

achieved. Consequently, many pension-fund managers are more concerned with avoiding any returns below the targeted rate than with exceeding the rate.

14. See Hagigi and Kluger [1987].

15. More about these rankings is found in Chapter 3.

16. Fuller and Wong also studied the risk-return relationship using regression analysis and found, "Safety rank is the most powerful explanatory risk measure, followed by sigma [standard deviation] rank, with beta rank a distant third" (p. 57).

17. We will discuss liquidity, business risk, and firm size as indicators of potential profits in Chapter 5. We discuss using *Value Line* safety rankings to profit in the stock market in the chapter on technical analysis, Chapter 3.

CHAPTER 1   APPENDIX B

References

Ang, James, and Chua, J. "Composite Measures for the Evaluating of Investment Performance." *Journal of Financial and Quantitative Analysis*, June 1979, pp. 361-84.

Arditti, Fred. "Another Look at Mutual Fund Performance." *Journal of Financial and Quantitative Analysis*, June 1971, pp. 909-12.

————. "Risk and the Required Return on Equity." *Journal of Finance*, March 1967, pp. 19-36.

Barone-Adesi, Giovanni. "Arbitrage Equilibrium with Skewed Asset Returns." *Journal of Financial and Quantitative Analysis*, September 1985, pp. 299-314.

Barry, Christopher, and Brown, Stephen. "Limited Information as a Source of Risk." *Journal of Portfolio Management*, Winter 1986, pp. 66-72.

Beebower, Gilbert, and Priest, William. "An Analysis of Transaction Costs in Equity Trading." Paper presented at the Seminar on the Analysis of Security Prices, Chicago, Ill., November 3, 1978.

Beedles, William. "The Anomalous and Asymmetric Nature of Equity Returns." *Journal of Financial Research*, Summer 1984, pp. 151-60.

————. "Return, Dispersion, and Skewness: Synthesis and Investment Strategy." *Journal of Financial Research*, Spring 1979, pp. 71-80.

Ben-Horim, M., and Levy, Haim. "Total Risk, Diversifiable Risk and Nondiversifiable Risk: A Pedagogic Note." *Journal of Financial and Quantitative Analysis*, June 1980, pp. 289-97.

Blume, Marshall, and Friend, Irwin. "The Asset Structure of Individual Portfolios and Some Implications for Utility Functions." *Journal of Finance*, May 1975, pp. 19-34.

Conine, Thomas, Jr., and Tamarkin, Maurry. "On Diversification Given Asymmetry in Returns." *Journal of Finance*, 1981, pp. 1143-55.

Cook, J., and Rozeff, Michael. "Coskewness, Dividend Yield and Capital Asset Pricing." *Journal of Financial Research*, Fall 1984, pp. 231-41.

Cooley, Philip R.; Roenfeldt, R.; and Modani, N. K. "Interdependence of Market Risk Measures." *Journal of Business*, July 1977, pp. 356-63.

Cuneo, Larry, and Wagner, Wayne. "Reducing the Cost of Stock Trading." *Financial Analysts Journal*, November-December 1975, pp. 35-44.

Damodaran, Aswath. "The Impact of Information Structure on Stock Returns." *Journal of Portfolio Management*, Spring 1987, pp. 53-58.

Donnelly, Barbara. "Efficient-Market Theorists Are Puzzled by Recent Gyrations in Stock Market." *Wall Street Journal*, October 23, 1987, p. 7.

Errunza, Vihang, and Losq, Etienne. "How Risky Are Emerging Markets?" *Journal of Portfolio Management*, Fall 1987, pp. 62-67.

————, and Rosenberg, Barr. "Investment Risk in Developed and Less Developed Countries." *Journal of Financial and Quantitative Analysis*, December 1982, pp. 741-62.

Fama, Eugene. *Foundations of Finance*. New York: Basic Books, 1976.

Fouse, William. "Risk and Liquidity: The Keys to Stock Price Behavior." *Financial Analysts Journal*, May-June 1976, pp. 35-43.

Francis, Jack. "Skewness and Investors' Decisions." *Journal of Financial and Quantitative Analysis*, March 1975, pp. 163-72.

French, Kenneth R.; Schwert, William; and Stambaugh, Robert F. "Expected Stock Returns Volatility." *Journal of Financial Economics*, September 1987, pp. 3-29.

Friend, Irwin, and Blume, Marshall. "Measurement of Portfolio Performance Under Uncertainty." *American Economic Review*, September 1970, pp. 561-75.

————; and Jean Crockett, *Mutual Funds and Other Institutional Investors*. New York: McGraw-Hill, 1970.

————, and Westerfield, Randolph. "Co-Skewness and Capital Asset Pricing." *Journal of Finance*, September 1980, pp. 897-913.

Fuller, Russell, and Wong, Wenchi. "Traditional versus Theoretical Risk Measures." *Financial Analysts Journal*, March-April 1988, pp. 52-57.

Good, Walter. "Measuring Performance." *Financial Analysts Journal*, May-June 1983, pp. 19-23.

Hagigi, Moshe, and Kluger, Brian. "Safety First: An Alternative Performance Measure." *Journal of Portfolio Management*, Summer 1987, pp. 34-40.

Harrington, Diana R. *Modern Portfolio Theory, The Capital Asset Pricing Model and Arbitrage Pricing Theory: A User's Guide*. Second edition. Englewood Cliffs, N.J.: Prentice Hall, 1987.

Jensen, Michael. "The Performance of Mutual Funds in the Period 1945-1964." *Journal of Finance*, May 1968, pp. 389-416.

Klemkosky, R. C., and Martin, J. D. "The Adjustment of Beta Forecasts." *Journal of Finance*, September 1975, pp. 1123-28.

Kon, Stanley. "Models of Stock Returns—A Comparison." *Journal of Finance*, March 1984, pp. 147-65.

Kosmicke, Ralph. "The Limited Relevance of Volatility to Risk." *Journal of Portfolio Management*, Fall 1986, pp. 18-20.

Kraus, A., and Litzenberger, Robert. "Skewness Preference and the Valuation of Risky Assets." *Journal of Finance*, September 1976, pp. 1085-94.

Lakonishok, Josef, and Shapiro, A. C. "Stock Returns, Beta, Variance and Size: An Empirical Analysis." *Financial Analysts Journal*, July-August 1984, pp. 36-41.

Levy, Haim. "Measuring Risk and Performance over Alternative Investment Horizons." *Financial Analysts Journal*, March-April 1984, pp. 61-68.

Loeb, Thomas. "Trading Cost: The Critical Line Between Investment Information and Results." *Financial Analysts Journal*, May-June 1983, pp. 39-44.

Malkiel, Burton. "The Capital Formation Problem in the United States." *Journal of Finance*, May 1979, pp. 291-306.

Mantell, Edmund. "How to Measure Expected Returns on Foreign Investments." *Journal of Portfolio Management*, Winter 1984, pp. 38-43.

Mao, James, and Brewster, J. F. "An E-Sh Model of Capital Budgeting." *Engineering Economist*, January-February 1970, pp. 103-21.

McEnally, Richard. "A Note on the Return Behavior of High Risk Common Stocks." *Journal of Finance*, May 1974, pp. 199-202.

Moses, Edward; Cheyney, John; and Veit, Theodore. "A New and More Complete Performance Measure." *Journal of Portfolio Management*, Summer 1987, pp. 24-32.

Pindyck, Robert. "Risk, Inflation, and the Stock Market." *American Economic Review*, June 1984, pp. 335-51.

Poterba, James, and Summers, Lawrence. "The Persistence of Volatility and Stock Market Fluctuations." *American Economic Review*, December 1986, pp. 1142-51.

Prakash, Arun, and Bear, Robert. "A Simplifying Performance Measure Recognizing Skewness." *Financial Review*, February 1986, pp. 135-44.

Reinganum, Marc. "A New Empirical Perspective on the CAPM." *Journal of Financial and Quantitative Analysis*, November 1981, pp. 439-62.

Sears, R. S., and Wei, K. C. John. "Asset Pricing, Higher Moments, and the Market Risk Premium: A Note." *Journal of Finance*, September 1985, pp. 1251-53.

Shiller, Robert J. "The Use of Volatility Measures in Assessing Market Effects." *Journal of Finance*, May 1981, pp. 291-304.

Simkowitz, M. A., and Beedles, William. "Diversification in a Three-Moment World." *Journal of Financial and Quantitative Analysis*, December 1978, pp. 927-41.

Singleton, Clay, and Wingender, John. "Skewness Persistence in Common Stock Returns." *Journal of Financial and Quantitative Analysis*, September 1986, pp. 335-41.

Sorenson, Eric. *Measuring the Market Risk Premium in ACEs*. New York: Saloman Brothers, February 1987.

Statman, Meir. "How Many Stocks Make a Diversified Portfolio?" *Journal of Financial and Quantitative Analysis*, September 1987, pp. 353-63.

Stultz, R. "On the Effects of Barriers to International Investment." *Journal of Finance*, September 1981, pp. 923-34.

Treynor, Jack. "How to Rate Management of Investment Funds." *Harvard Business Review*, January-February 1965, pp. 63-70.

Van Zijl, Tony. "Risk Decomposition: Variance or Standard Deviation—A Reexamination and Extension." *Journal of Financial and Quantitative Analysis*, June 1987, pp. 237-47.

CHAPTER 2

Market Cycles

The easiest way to make money in the stock market would be to identify cyclical or other repeating patterns. "Long waves," "Blue Mondays," and "the January effect" are all examples of stock market changes that seem to recur. The question we must ask, however, is: Do such patterns really exist? And if they do: How can an investor profit from understanding cyclical behavior?

When we think of cycles in the market, we usually think of general upward or downward movements lasting a few to many years. Various market theorists and practitioners have speculated that such cycles exist and have looked for and found, or thought they found, long cycles lasting a few years and even decades. Recent innovations in computer processing have allowed researchers to see if shorter market cycles exist, and to find new patterns lasting months, weeks, and even days. Such long and short cycles (Elliott waves to the January effect) are the subject of this chapter.

Long and Intermediate Stock-Price Cycles

Technical Market Indicators—Dow Theory and Elliott Wave Principle. Charles Dow, the founder of Dow Theory and much of modern technical analysis, believed a skilled analyst could sort out three simultaneous stock market movements—daily, monthly, and four-year movements or cycles.[1] He likened these three cycles to the movements in water: tides, waves, and ripples. His work was aimed primarily at forecasting business trends, but its most widespread use has been in timing the stock market. While there are many versions of the theory used in practice, in principle, Dow believed that upward movements in the market (tides) were tempered by fallbacks (waves) that lost a portion of the previous gain. A market turn came when the upward movement did not exceed the last gain (a turn in the tide). To determine whether such a turn has occurred, an analyst follows the patterns in three indexes—testing one for movements, then one of the other two for confirmations.

In studying the value of Dow Theory in timing the market, Glickstein and Wubbels [1983] found that, by buying and holding the Dow Jones Industrials from January 2, 1971, to December 31, 1980, an investor would have had a compound return of 1.6 percent. However, if the same investor had "traded on Dow Theory technical indicators . . . one would have experienced an average capital appreciation of 14.6 percent." They further concluded that "successful market timing is by no means impossible" (p. 29). Others also have found moving averages, a technique on which Dow Theory relies, useful in making such forecasts.[2]

Dow Theory is difficult to test objectively. Identifying turning points depends, to a large degree, on the analyst's skill and insight. Therefore, the potential profitability of Dow Theory use is difficult to verify.[3]

R. N. Elliott (a big loser in the markets of 1929), like Dow, believed he could identify major moves. According to Elliott, each major upswing is divided into three parts, or five turning points, as shown in Exhibit 2-1. Downswings are generally believed to have two major parts.

Elliott's patterns are based on Fibonacci number series: each number in a series is the sum of the two preceding numbers (e.g., 1,1,2,3,5,8,13,21,34). The Fibonacci series seems to relate to many phenomena in nature, and Elliott, among others,[4] believed it related to the stock market.[5] However, many have dismissed this material as "numerological nonsense, which, indeed, may be all it is. On the other hand, there may be real and important phenomenon here" (Gehm [1983], p. 53).

Unfortunately, to test such a method, there must be an objective definition of cycles, both up and down, and no such rigor exists with Elliott waves.[6] To test their existence is impossible, and "What evidence there is suggests that Elliott wave theory is not a particularly useful forecasting technique" (Gehm [1983], p. 53). In fact, some authors believe that market technicians, those who follow past market patterns to predict the future, are "members of the lunatic fringe of the investment world. Descriptions of their activities are felt to be a suitable subject for anthropologists, but inappropriate . . . for a serious investor" (Sharpe [1985], p. 613).

Is there a serious economic basis for ripples, waves, and tides, or for stock market cycles in general? Real economic events and factors may lie at the root of Elliott waves or Dow Theory market movements.[7]

Business Cycles, Juglars, Kuznets, and Kondratieff

Even among staid economists, one finds a belief that economic events recur periodically. The shortest of these cycles is the business cycle, a short-term fluctuation of business activity lasting from 3 to 7 years. This cycle is perhaps the most familiar, at least from the wide recognition that it receives in the popular press. A somewhat longer cycle, sometimes called a Juglar, has a length of 9.5 years; less well recognized still is the so-called Kuznets cycle, lasting

Exhibit 2-1
Elliott Wave Stock Market Cycle

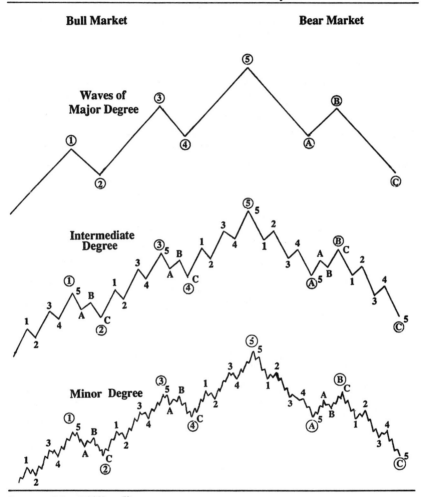

Bull Market

Bear Market

Source: Gehm [1983], p. 52.

from 15 to 25 years. The longest of the cycles that has received recognition and study is the Kondratieff, also called a long wave, lasting from 45 to 60 years. Because almost 60 years have passed since the last bottom of the Kondratieff cycle in 1929, this long cycle has been much discussed recently. The discussion became quite lively following the market decline of October 19, 1987.

If there are periodic patterns in the markets, the critical problem is forecasting where you are in any given cycle. In order to do so, one must determine the source of such cyclical behavior. Kondratieff himself believed that the long cycle was caused by the relationship of various factors in the economic system, but he did not describe the mechanism. The late economist Joseph Schumpeter [1939] believed that the long wave was based on major innovations (railroads in the 1800s, autos in the early 1900s), the intermediate cycles resulted from related or ancillary industries developing in response to the innovations (steel and coal in the 1800s, rubber and glass in the 1900s), and the business cycle was the result of monetary and inventory policy. Schumpeter modeled these three cycles and succeeded in explaining to some degree the U.S. post-World War II economy up to 1962. The 1962 monetary expansion and its accompanying inflation seemed to change the duration of the short cycle.

Forrester [1976] also modeled these cycles, in a somewhat different way. Using a **simulation** of the economy, he showed that the business cycle involved inventories and employment (not money supply, interest rates, and capital spending), that the Kuznets cycle (15 to 25 years in length) related to capital spending (thus interest rates are an important factor in it), and that the long wave resulted primarily from the movement of workers between the consumer- and capital-goods sectors of the economy. Exhibit 2-2 shows representations of each of the three cycles.

Simulation—A *simulation* (computer based by computational necessity) imitates a series of events or a process by programming a set of equations that replicate the process. The equations measure the critical factors, the variables underlying the process. There are two important features of a simulation: (1) the number of time periods and (2) uncertainty of the events. Simulations without uncertainty are characterized as deterministic. One-period simulations with uncertainty are frequently called probabilistic or Monte Carlo simulations: Monte Carlo applies to any simulation that uses random numbers to simulate uncertain outcomes. The outcomes are described by a probability distribution. Stochastic simulations trace uncertain variables over time, and dynamic simulations refer to multiple periods and can be either deterministic or stochastic.

Forrester suggested that the cycle arose from an excess of physical capacity following a cyclical bottom (a depression). This overcapacity comes in several stages over a long period:

1. Slow growth of the capital-goods sector.

2. Gradual decay of the capital plant below what was required.

3. Capital-goods sector rejuvenation, beginning with demand by capital-goods producers.

4. Wage increases and labor shortages in consumer sectors further stimulating capital-goods producers.

5. Capital-goods capacity overexpansion.

6. Over-accumulation of durables by consumers and plant capacity by their producers.

7. Unemployment in capital-goods sectors, reducing wages.

8. Collapse of the capital-goods-producing sectors.

Forrester believed that in 1976 we had reached the top of a long wave. Excess office and hospital space, mothballing of new oil tankers and aircraft, and a nearly complete interstate highway system were symptoms of this peaking. At a peak, monetary largess does not result in increased productive capacity but, rather, provides fuel for speculation and inflation. What has happened since 1976 makes one wonder if Forrester's simulations were prescient.

Exhibit 2-2
Forrester's Three Cycles

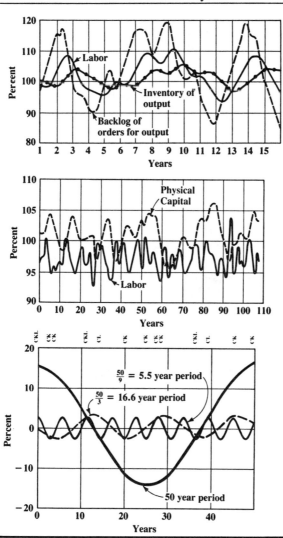

Source: Forrester [1976], pp. 24, 26, and 28.

However interesting long cycles may be in theory, testing for the existence of these longer waves is difficult: extraneous data confound the tests, and overlapping shorter and longer waves confuse the analyst. Analysts have, however, found shorter cycles that are testable.

Election-Year Cycles

Election years, especially U.S. presidential election years, seem to take on a special character. Whether political rhetoric buoys the markets, or policy actions are taken to enhance the economic reality preceding election, many believe that election years are different, and this belief appears to be right. Exhibit 2-3 shows the results up to 1969.

Exhibit 2-3
Victory versus Defeat for the Party in Power
(average market gains and losses)

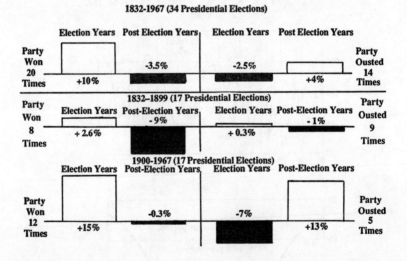

1832-1967 (34 Presidential Elections)

Source: Hirsch [1969], p. 13.

Several researchers have tested whether these election-year cycles really exist. For the 1984 election year, the following two studies, using quite different techniques, reaffirmed their existence.

Hobbs and Riley [1984] used **residual analysis** and found positive excess returns "following a Republican victory and negative following a Democratic victory" (p. 46). Using data from other elections to determine what the optimal buy and sell dates should be during a subsequent election year, they tried to derive an unbiased estimate of the potential profits to be made from buying before election day and selling thereafter. Their results for Democratic and Republican landslides are shown in Exhibit 2-4. As you can see, the optimal buy and sell dates differ markedly depending on the winning party—and so do the profits.

Exhibit 2-4

Results in Landslide and Close Elections

Landslide Election

Year	*Democratic Landslides* Buy	Sell	Profit
1912	E − 6	E + 6	− 0.1
1932	E − 50	E + 4	+ 0.8
1936	E − 6	E + 4	+ 3.9
1940	E − 6	E + 4	+ 2.8
1964	E − 6	E + 4	+ 0.1

Year	*Republican Landslides* Buy	Sell	Profit
1904	E − 35	E + 29	+ 17.1
1920	E − 48	E + 49	− 15.9
1924	E − 33	E + 27	+ 4.5
1928	E − 33	E + 27	+ 11.8
1952	E − 33	E + 27	+ 1.9
1956	E − 50	E + 24	− 5.7
1972	E − 34	E + 27	+ 5.5

Close Elections

Year	Buy	Sell	Profit
1900	E − 48	E + 31	+ 15.4
1908	E − 42	E + 16	+ 12.5
1916	E − 42	E + 41	− 3.3
1944	E − 42	E + 15	+ 0.3
1948	E − 42	E + 16	− 1.4
1960	E − 42	E + 15	+ 4.8
1968	E − 42	E + 15	+ 2.9
1976	E − 42	E + 15	− 7.6

E = Election day.

Source: Hobbs and Riley [1984], p. 50

Residual Analysis—Much of a stock's return can be attributable to whether the market was moving up or down at that time. *Residual analysis* eliminates the portion of return that is due to the coincident market movement, with the remaining return called, appropriately, the residual return. Residual return, therefore, is return that is unique to the stock.

Because this form of analysis has been used extensively by researchers in the late 1970s and 1980s, a further discussion of it is contained in the appendix to this chapter.

Spectral Analysis—*Spectral analysis* is a correlation technique that tests for the existence of cyclical patterns of varying height (amplitudes) and frequency (phase) in a series of data: the greater the frequency, the shorter the cycle. The correlation (actually autocorrelation) of each event with past events is estimated using sine or cosine relationships. The result is a graph of the variation explained using different frequencies of occurrence. To test whether the cycle is genuine, researchers use a Bartels' test: a test result of zero signifies that the outcome could not have resulted from random factors.

Residual analysis, such as that used by Hobbs and Riley, depends on estimates (e.g., beta for removing market effects) that are difficult to calculate with confidence. Thus, others have studied the same phenomena with different methods. They had, however, similar results.

Using **spectral analysis** and data on the Standard and Poor's (S&P) 500 from January 1926 through December 1977, Herbst and Slinkman [1984] confirmed the existence of a four-year,[8] but not a two-year, election cycle.[9] They used this information to test for the existence of cycles that reach their peak during or near November election dates. The four-year cycle reached a peak in mid-December of presidential election years, which was consistent with the Hobbs and Riley results of a peak at about 27 days after election day.

One other piece of evidence is of interest. Huang [1985] found that political control of the economy has become stronger since 1960; Exhibit 2-5 shows the data from which he drew that conclusion. In particular, the returns in the last two years of a presidential election cycle are larger than those in the first two years, and have been becoming larger over time.

Political/economic cycles appear to have existed in the stock market at least up to the 1988 elections, and tests may show that that election also followed form. While many would suggest that an imperfection that has been known to exist at least since the early 1960s should have been arbitraged away, it has not. What could be behind these and other long economic cycles?[10]

Economic Factors and Stock Market Cycles

There are many candidates for the factor most likely to influence the stock market. Among the leaders is monetary policy—more precisely, the supply of money in the U.S. economy—which is one of the factors in the National Bureau of Economic Research's Index of Leading Economic Indicators.

Exhibit 2-5
Mean Annual Rates of Return

Four Years of the Presidential Election Cycle Period

Year of Cycle	1961–1980	1949–1980	1929–1980	1832–1903	1904–1979	1832–1979
1	1.80%	2.00%	3.95%	–4.17%	1.05%	–1.49%
2	–6.94	11.63	8.46	1.06	2.00	1.54
3	23.34	23.04	16.92	4.33	9.68	7.08
4	20.56	16.04	13.04	2.11	9.00	5.65
F-Statistic	7.64[a]	2.92[b]	0.86	1.13	0.99	2.39[b]

Two Halves of the Presidential Election Cycle Period

Year of Cycle	1961–1980	1949–1980	1929–1980	1832–1903	1904–1979	1832–1979
1 and 2	–2.57%	6.81%	6.21%	–1.56%	1.47%	0.03%
3 and 4	21.95	19.54	14.98	3.22	9.34	6.36
t-statistics	4.70[a]	2.11[b]	1.69[b]	1.39[c]	1.73[b]	2.21[b]

[a] Statistically significant at the 1 percent level.
[b] Statistically significant at the 5 percent level.
[c] Statistically significant at the 10 percent level.

Source: Huang [1985], p. 59.

Money Supply

The impact of the money supply on economic activity, including the stock
market, is a persistent source of research and discussion among economists and
market practitioners.[11] Exhibit 2-6 shows the relationship plotted in one article
in *Fortune*.

Exhibit 2-6
Money Moves the Market

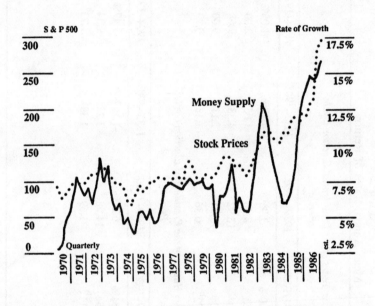

Source: Curran [1987], p. 56.

Theoretically, there should be a relationship: as the quantity of money
increases, investors can be expected to buy more common stock (as well as
other assets). Because such portfolio adjustments occur rather slowly, or at least
did so in the past, one should be able to predict stock-price changes from
changes in the money supply as reported weekly by the Federal Reserve Board.
Does evidence support the hypothesis?

One of the first to relate money-supply changes to changes in the stock
market was Sprinkel [1964 and updated in 1971]. He examined the growth rate
in money (a six-month average) and the S&P 425 from 1918 to 1963 and

concluded that there was, in general, a relationship. Neither the timing of the relationship, however, nor the lag between the two appeared to be consistent over time. Exhibit 2-7 shows data similar to those which Sprinkel analyzed. The relationship does seem to follow the pattern that would be expected. However, it is not as strong as we might have expected—at least not to the naked eye.

Sprinkel tested a trading rule to buy and sell stocks based on the rate of change in the money supply. In contrast to a buy-and-hold strategy, Sprinkel earned an added annual rate of return of 6.7 percent with his strategy from 1918 to 1960.

From today's vantage point, Sprinkel's work was less than complete. His conclusions were largely based on a visual analysis of the data, whereas more recent studies have relied on statistical analysis. Unfortunately, the results of later studies have often been in conflict.

Rozeff [1974] tested Sprinkel's theory using somewhat different, and more realistic, trading rules. His strategy did not outperform a buy-and-hold strategy. Rozeff also used linear regression to examine whether changes in the money supply could be used to predict stock prices. Using current money-supply information to lead stock-price changes, he found a weak relationship. When current changes in money supply were used, the relationship was stronger, and when future money-supply changes were used, the relationship was stronger yet. From this result, one could conclude that money-supply changes do not lead those in the stock market, but stock market changes lead changes in the money supply. These results were in conflict with findings by previous researchers.[12]

Cooper [1974] further investigated the lead-lag relationship between money-supply changes and changes in the stock market. In a spectral analysis of data from 1947 to 1970, he examined the separate cycles in stock prices and the money supply, and found ". . . the relationship between money supply and [stock market] returns significant at the 0.01 confidence level for cycles of six months or more . . . ," and the money series seemed to lag stock-price returns by about one to three months. Thus these results parallel those of Rozeff.[13]

Other research indicates that the relationship is between unexpected, but announced, changes in the money supply and stock prices. While there was work conducted on the long-term relationship between these announcements and interest rates,[14] and stock prices,[15] more recently Pearce and Roley [1983] looked at the short-term effect of unexpected changes in the money supply on share prices. To determine the unexpected portion of the money-supply announcements, they used as the expected money-supply announcement the median money-stock forecasts made by 60 money-market participants surveyed weekly by Money Market Services, Inc., from September 29, 1977, to January 29, 1982. To measure stock prices over the same period, they used the Dow Jones Industrial Average (DJIA) closing prices on the day the money supply was

Exhibit 2-7
Money and Stock Prices

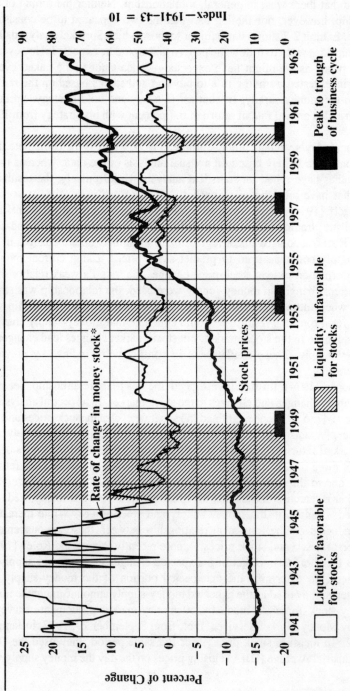

Source: Sprinkel [1964], p. 123.

announced and specialist opening prices the day following a money-supply announcement. They found that "unexpected changes in the money stock have a negative impact on stock prices" (p. 1329). Because there had been considerable change in how the Federal Reserve Board dealt with its monetary policy over this period, they separated the period studied into three subperiods,[16] and found the impact on the stock market unchanged. In addition, they separated the unexpected changes into positive, negative, and other surprises and found that positive surprises (money-supply increases) depressed share prices, while negative surprises had a positive impact on the stock market. Perhaps most important of all to those hoping to make money with this information, they found the "stock price response is essentially complete early in the subsequent trading day" (p. 1332). It appears that a quick profit can be made if the investor can forecast the unexpected changes (the surprises) in the money supply, a difficult task indeed.

One other piece of research worth noting here is work by Klemkosky and Jun [1982] on the relationship between the money supply and the capital asset pricing model. (See Appendix A to Chapter 1 for an introduction to the CAPM.) They discussed the two impacts that money-supply changes have on investors, and thus on any model of investor behavior like the CAPM: (1) the wealth effect and (2) the return-variability effect. Increases in the money supply enhance wealth, and thus increase the level of equity prices. Instability in the growth of the money supply should have a negative impact on stock prices and the market; that is, the market risk premium is positively related to money-supply changes. Using data from the New York Stock Exchange (NYSE) from 1954 to 1980, they found that "past information regarding monetary variation is not important in determining the current market return variability," but that "the market risk premium will be positively related to changes in money supply" (p. 673). Once again, forecasts of money-supply changes were found to affect the stock market.

Money supply, or perhaps more precisely, money-supply surprises, seem to have an impact on the stock market, but the impact appears to be short lived. To capture profits using money-supply information, the investor would have to make better than average forecasts and act quickly.

Inflation

The impact of inflation on the stock market has been of special interest to investors and researchers. For a long period, common stocks were believed to be a hedge[17] against inflation. In part this belief was based on data: over long periods that included times of inflation, deflation, and stability, stocks did return more than enough to offset inflation. When the outburst of inflation in the 1970s drove stock prices down, however, it was recognized that the inflation-beating returns had been an average: in the past, during periods of price stability, stocks' returns had been more than enough to compensate for the losses that had occurred during inflationary periods.[18]

However, in the rush to draw conclusions based on the average, many had ignored the fact that shareholders' required returns should include a premium for both inflation and the basic risk of the equity investment. Returns from common stocks that, on average, just beat inflation are not enough during inflationary times. Thus, when the data about returns from common stocks are reexamined, taking into account different economic environments and the shareholders' nominal required returns, it becomes evident that inflation has a negative impact on common stock returns.

Interpreting Regression Results—Linear regressions relate one variable (e.g., Y_i) to other variables (e.g., X_i, Z_i) and in the following form:

$$Y_i = \alpha_i + \beta_1 X_i + \beta_2 Z_i + e_i$$

The estimates for α, β_1, and β_2 are those that best explain the relationship between the independent (Y_i) and dependent (X_i, Z_i) variables. Specifically they are estimates, signified by a symbol `^` called a hat. The e_i is the residual or error term measuring the variance of the data the regression does not capture or explain.

Basically, the goal in using a regression is to explain the variation in the dependent variable. Interpreting a regression's results requires the answers to three questions:

1. How much of the dependent variable's variation is explained by the regression? The coefficient of determination (R^2) and F-test give the answer. For example, an R^2 of 0.80 would mean that 80 percent of the variation in dependent variable Y_i corresponds to variation in the independent variables. An adjusted R^2 adjusts for extraneous explanatory variables and is somewhat more reliable. While the R^2 is useful, the F-test gives a different view of the quality of the regression: the F-test is the explained variation divided by unexplained variation and thus is a relative measure of the regression's quality taking sample size into account.

2. Which variables are best at explaining variation in the dependent variable and what is the relationship? To answer the questions, look at the t-statistic for each independent variable. A t-statistic over 2.0 generally indicates some statistically significant explanatory power (either positive or negative) to the regression. To

(continued on page 57)

This intuitive look at inflation's impact can be supplemented with evidence. Jaffe and Mandelker [1976] studied several periods from 1875 to 1971 and, using regression analysis, found a negative relationship between inflation and stock returns from 1953 to 1971. Their results for 1875 to 1970 showed no significant relationship between inflation and stock returns (see box on **interpreting regression results**). Using the Consumer Price Index as the measure of inflation and monthly stock returns, Nelson [1976] confirmed that a negative relationship existed between 1953 and 1974.

Both these studies looked at historical, ex post, data. What would happen if expected, not realized, inflation were included in the analysis? The first difficulty in doing this is in obtaining estimates of expected inflation. Most studies use the contemporaneous interest rate, or some adaptation of it, as a proxy for inflation. Gultekin [June 1983], using actual inflation, found a negative relationship, as shown in Exhibit 2-8.[19]

Gultekin went further than current data and used analysts' estimates for inflation.[20] Using expected inflation, he found that "the stock market

Exhibit 2-8
Regressions of Nominal Stock Returns on Concurrent Inflation Rates

$$R_t + \alpha + \beta\pi_t + \hat{e}_t$$

Price Index	α	β	$t(\alpha)$	$t(\beta)$	R^2	F	DW	ρ	Time Period
			Panel A: Semi-annual regressions						
CPI	.0729	-2.4114	3.48	-2.90	.1374	8.44	1.99	-.119	6/1952–12/1979
WPI	.0581	-1.3014	2.86	-2.27	.0889	5.17	2.00	-.101	
CPI	.1039	-8.2093	3.71	-2.51	.2023	6.34	2.03	-.113	6/1952–12/1965
WPI	.0525	-1.0131	2.21	-.42	.0072	.18	1.97	.027	
CPI	.0964	-2.7992	1.99	-2.00	.1384	4.02	1.96	-.187	6/1966–12/1979
WPI	.0525	-1.3274	1.59	-1.71	.1051	2.93	2.00	-1.79	
			Panel B: Annual regressions						
CPI	.1319	-2.0885	3.50	-2.74	.2316	7.53	2.10	-.266	6/1952–12/1979
WPI	.1064	-1.4531	3.37	-2.71	.2276	7.37	2.13	-.236	

R_t is the six- and twelve-month rate of return on the S&P 500 Index;

π_t is the concurrent six- and twelve-month change in the consumer (CPI) or wholesale (WPI) price indexes.

Regressions are adjusted for first-order autocorrelation by the Cochrane–Orcutt method.

DW refers to the transformed series.

ρ is the first-order autocorrelation.

Source: Gultekin [June 1983], p. 666.

Exhibit 2-9
Regressions of Expected Nominal Stock Market Returns on Expected Inflation Rates

$$E(R_t) = \alpha + \beta E(\pi_t) + \hat{e}_t$$

Price Index	α	β	$t(\alpha)$	$t(\beta)$	R^2	F	DW	ρ	Time Period
Panel A									
I. Semi-Annual Forecasts									
CPI	−.0039	1.7896	−.55	4.92	.3137	24.22	1.71	.394	6/1962–12/1979
WPI	.0016	1.5724	.25	4.71	.2951	22.19	1.72	.399	
CPI	−.0058	2.2009	−.73	1.69	.1034	2.88	1.68	.281	6/1952–12/1965
WPI	−.0015	1.8917	−.26	2.29	.1744	5.28	1.73	.235	
CPI	.0038	1.5407	.18	2.01	.1392	4.04	1.66	.480	6/1966–12/1979
WPI	.0210	.9312	1.23	1.49	.0821	2.23	1.61	.475	
II. Annual Forecasts									
CPI	−.0069	2.5657	−1.02	6.76	.6394	28.37	1.81	−.361	6/1952–6/1971
WPI	.0087	2.1573	1.08	4.21	.4569	13.45	1.79	−.158	
Panel B									
I. Semi-Annual Forecasts									
CPI	.0729	1.7224	6.17	3.68	.2031	13.51	1.91	−.3706	6/1952–12/1979
WPI	.0854	1.7520	11.72	5.39	.3539	29.04	1.84	.2349	
II. Annual Forecasts									
CPI	.0686	1.7609	4.98	5.75	.3842	33.06	1.87	.4083	6/1952–12/1979
WPI	.0790	1.9733	9.75	8.96	.6021	80.21	1.79	.1520	
III. Eighteen-Month Forecasts									
CPI	.0638	2.2207	5.87	6.51	.7135	42.33	1.93	−.0974	6/1952–12/1971
WPI	.0734	2.3617	5.42	4.86	.5814	23.61	2.30	.1449	

Panel A uses expectations data. Data in Panel B are computed by the Carlson method. Regressions are adjusted for first-order serial correlation by the Cochrane-Orcutt method. ρ is the first-order autocorrelation.

α = intercept,
β = coefficient for independent variables,
t = t-test (see box),

F = F-test,
DW = Durbin Watson test, and
ρ = correlation.

Source: Gultekin [June 1983], p. 668.

(continued from page 54)
determine the magnitude of the relationship, look at the variable's coefficient itself: it indicates how the independent variable varies with that particular dependent variable.

3. Is there a pattern in the unexplained residual term to the remaining data? Here the Durbin Watson (DW) statistic provides the clue. A DW value near 2.0 indicates no significant auto-correlation. It is especially important with data over time, because we want the independent variables to capture all explainable patterns. Some estimation procedures (e.g., Cochrane-Orcutt) deal with time-dependent relationships (autocorrelation in the errors) and thereby improve the accuracy of the estimated R^2 and t-statistics. The estimated one-period autocorrelation in the errors is often designated by ρ which can vary between -1.0 and $+1.0$.

---

t-Test—A *t-test* asks whether an estimated statistic (e.g., X) is so different from a hypothesized value (e.g., M) that you would conclude that a real difference between the two exists. To decide, you must consider the variance in the data: calculate the sample standard deviation(s) and then adjust it by the number of observations (n). The exact formula is

$$t = \frac{x - m}{s/\sqrt{n}}$$

For a simple rule of thumb, t-values over 2.0 are considered significant.

F-Ratio or Test—At an intuitive level, this is a ratio of the explained divided by unexplained variation. For example, F can be written in terms of the explained variation from a linear regression (R^2) divided by the unexplained variation:

$$F_{k,n-k-1} = \frac{R^2/k}{(1-R^2)/(n-k-1)}$$

where k indicates the number of independent variables and n is the number of observations. Statistical tables for determining the significance of the ratio are indexed by both ($m - 1$) and ($n - 1$). This ratio may be used with any relationship that attempts to explain variations in data. The general formula for the *F*-test is

(continued on next page)

returns and expected inflation are strongly and positively related . . . and in line with the Fisher Effect" (p. 669). The results that led to this conclusion are shown in Exhibit 2-9.[21]

Various researchers have hypothesized different reasons for the curious negative relationship between inflation and stock prices. Fama [1981] concluded that higher unanticipated inflation would cause lower real output. Geske and Roll [1983] believed that the relationship was really a signal for "a chain of events which results in a higher rate of monetary expansion" (p. 1) and that "stock returns signal change in nominal interest rates and changes in expected inflation" (p. 29). In addition to this link, Geske and Roll found that, as the risk of a security increased, the impact of inflation declined. Chang and Pinegar [1987] supported the Geske-Roll notion, concluding that "our findings strongly indicate that risk differences contribute to the negative relationships between stock returns and various measures of inflation" and that "inflation and real activity are not determined independently as Fisher originally assumed" (p. 98).

The negative relationship between contemporaneous stock returns and expected inflation (not based on analysts' estimates) appears to also exist outside U.S. markets. Gultekin [March 1983], in studying the relationship between inflation and stock returns, found "no significant positive relationship between monthly nominal stock returns and expected inflation

(continued from page 57)

$$F_{k,n-k-1} = \frac{(SSR/SST)/k}{(SSE/SST)/(n-k-1)}$$

or

$$F_{k,n-k-1} = \frac{SSR/k}{SSE/(n-k-1)}$$

where

SSR = sum of squares explained by the regression,

SST = sum of the squares of each observation from the sample average, and

SSE = sum of squares of each unexplained residual error.

rates for most of the 26 countries analyzed" (p. 50). However, as shown in Exhibit 2-10, for long-run averages, a positive relationship like that found for the United States exists for almost every country he examined.

These results are similar to those found earlier by Branch [1978]. Solnik [1983], who studied the same phenomena, concluded that "our data provide support for the Geske and Roll [1983] model whose basic hypothesis is that stock price movements signal [negative] revisions in inflationary expectations" and that this relationship "appears to be a structural phenomenon, at least in the recent times of floating exchange rates" (p. 47).

Other Economic Predictors of the Stock Market

A variety of other economic factors have been and could be used to predict the stock market. An indicator that immediately comes to mind is the Index of Leading Economic Indicators, of which both stock market activity and money supply are a part.[22] Because this index signals changes in the economy, some have suggested that it could be used to forecast stock prices.[23] However, results of tests using these data to buy and sell stocks (versus a buy-and-hold strategy over the same period) were mixed.

Interest rates, which are clearly important in the level of equity and debt markets, may also be useful in predicting the stock market. As interest rates rise, the relative value of future cash flows from any investment declines—all else being equal. In a recent paper, Campbell [1987] reported that excess stock market returns can be predicted by using the term structure of interest rates, primarily because stock market risk varies with interest rates and higher returns coincide with periods of high risk.[24]

One of the major components in determining interest rates is inflation, specifically, expected inflation. In fact, until the late 1970s, little controversy existed over the notion that real interest rates (rates net of a premium for expected inflation) were stable. Because Irving Fisher [1930] wrote the major work in this area, the relationship between inflation and stock returns is often called the Fisher effect. After 1980, when interest rates appeared abnormally high, there was discussion about whether real interest rates had risen significantly. Based on the research,[25] they had. Even with changes in the real rate, the major force behind changes in the nominal rate (the rate including a premium for inflation) is changes in expected inflation; thus focusing on inflation effects may subsume real interest rate effects.

Exhibit 2-10
Scatter Diagram of Average Monthly Nominal Stock Returns and Inflation Rates

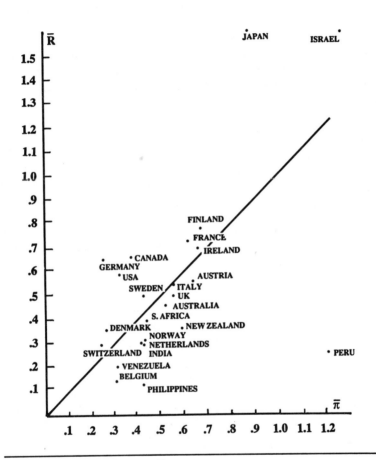

Source: Gultekin [March 1983], p. 62.

Intrayear Cycles

In addition to the preceding effects, recent evidence suggests that a number of cycles occur within the course of a year. These cycles peak as often as once a week. There are economic reasons why some of these intrayear cycles might exist, but there is always the suspicion that the rudimentary nature of some of our tests may be finding patterns where none really exist. In the next sections, we discuss these intrayear trends and the evidence of their existence.

Cycles Peaking Once a Year (January Effect)

The most prominent of the yearly cycles is the January effect. In essence, what researchers have found is that stocks provide an excess return, a return greater than required for the risk, in January. This effect has been found to a minor degree in July also, but in no other month of the year. The earliest work done on this phenomenon was by Rozeff and Kinney [1976]. They used a method that examines the impact on portfolios of risk-level-grouped stocks, which avoids the problems of individual errors. This method is often called the **Fama-MacBeth** approach.

The Fama-MacBeth Approach—Establishing the statistical significance of the coefficients in a regression might appear straightforward, but there are problems: First are errors in measuring the coefficients (betas) when a proxy is used and not the true market index. Second, extreme betas have a tendency to regress toward the mean (e.g., if a beta is estimated as 1.6 in one year, it will probably be lower the next year). Third, portfolio betas are more reliable than stock betas.

To mitigate these problems, Fama and MacBeth [1973] followed four steps. First, after they estimated each stock's beta, they ranked the stocks by their betas, and created a number of portfolios. Second, they reestimated each stock's beta in the subsequent period, and calculated the portfolio beta as the average of the stocks' betas (this step alleviates the regression-toward-the-mean bias). Third, in the subsequent period, a cross-sectional regression (across all stocks instead of for one stock across time) estimated the portfolio coefficients (alphas) using the previous period's beta. And fourth, the preceding steps were repeated for each successive time period until Fama and MacBeth had a time series for each of the coefficients.[26]

Rozeff and Kinney calculated the intercepts and risk premia for 20 portfolios of stocks from 1935 to 1968. They tested the means and standard deviations of their regression estimates for each month of the year, and found a higher mean return for January. In fact, the return for January was an average of 8 times that for the other months of the year.

Later Tinic and West [1984] reevaluated the January effect found by Rozeff and Kinney. Exhibit 2-11 shows their results. As you can see, they found that the returns (γ_1 were much higher in January than the rest of the year and were significant for the years they studied, 1935-68: "The values for γ_1 for the months from February through December are significantly lower than γ_1 for January. Indeed, they are virtually equal to zero! . . . January continues to be the month in which there is a systematic positive relationship between the realized returns and systematic risks of portfolios" (p. 571).

Tinic and West specifically addressed one criticism of Rozeff's work—the index he used. When they tested their results for sensitivity to the index, however, they found that the results did not depend on whether they used a value-weighted or equal-weighted index. In addition to confirming the January findings, they also found an excess return, albeit smaller, in July.

Others have discovered that seasonality exists in more than the U.S. markets. Gultekin and Gultekin [1983] found strong evidence of seasonal patterns in most of the other capital markets. Except for the United Kingdom,

Exhibit 2-11
January Effect

Average values of the Fama and MacBeth estimates of intercept and slope coefficients of the two-parameter model (estimated with monthly data and based on the equally weighted index).[a]

Averaged Over	Intercept Coefficient $(\bar{\gamma}_0)$	Slope Coefficient $(\bar{\gamma}_1)$	Sample Size
January 1935 to June 1968			
January only	-0.000744	0.044509[b]	34
	(-0.1480)	(3.7347)	
Rest of the year	0.006736[b]	0.005136	368
	(3.3674)	(1.5204)	
All months	0.006104[b]	0.008466[b]	402
	(3.2447)	(2.5703)	
January 1935 to September 1951			
January only	-0.002371	0.052459[b]	17
	(-0.2938)	(2.4872)	
Rest of the year	0.005453	0.007852	184
	(1.5878)	(1.2876)	
All months	0.004792	0.011624[b]	201
	(1.4900)	(1.9668)	
October 1951 to June 1968			
January only	0.000882	0.036559[b]	17
	(0.1416)	(3.1689)	
Rest of the year	0.008020[b]	0.002420	184
	(3.8962)	(0.8300)	
All months	0.007416[b]	0.005307[b]	201
	(3.7888)	(1.8232)	

[a] Statistics are presented in parentheses.
[b] Significant at 0.05 level.

Exhibit 2-11 continued

Average values of the updated estimates of intercept and slope coefficients of the two-parameter model (estimated with monthly data and based on the equally weighted index).[a]

Averaged Over	Intercept Coefficient $(\bar{\gamma}_0)$	Slope Coefficient $(\bar{\gamma}_1)$	Sample Size
January 1935 to December 1982			
January only	-0.000645	0.047052[b]	48
	(-0.1443)	(4.6335)	
Rest of the year	0.006689[b]	0.003806	528
	(4.0127)	(1.4145)	
All months	0.006078[b]	0.007410[b]	576
	(3.8635)	(2.7966)	
January 1935 to December 1958			
January only	0.002686	0.041207[b]	24
	(0.4561)	(2.8710)	
Rest of the year	0.008287[b]	0.004445	264
	(3.3063)	(1.0345)	
All months	0.007820[b]	0.007509b	288
	(3.3326)	(1.8111)	
January 1959 to December 1982			
January only	-0.003976	0.052897[b]	28
	(-0.5754)	(3.5543)	
Rest of the year	0.005091[b]	0.003167	264
	(2.3104)	(0.9724)	
All months	0.004335[b]	0.007312[b]	288
	(2.0654)	(2.2053)	
January 1969 to December 1982			
January only	-0.006995	0.060880[b]	14
	(-0.7758)	(2.6394)	
Rest of the year	0.005158[b]	0.001573	154
	(1.6797)	(0.3305)	
All months	0.004145	0.006515[b]	168
	(1.4239)	(1.3340)	

[a] t statistics are presented in parentheses.
[b] Significant at 0.05 level.

Source: Adapted from Tinic and West [1984], pp. 564 and 568.

where the abnormal returns were in April, January was generally the high-return month. Their results for 17 markets are shown in exhibit 2-12.[27] Note that they concluded the seasonal patterns seemed to occur at the "turn of the tax year" (p. 480).

While the Tinic-West and Gultekin-Gultekin results are fascinating, are they enough to suggest that buying and selling should take place using this information? Indeed, these researchers have expressed concern that their results could be caused by statistical errors that result from using the wrong model for risk, the CAPM, or from examining too small a sample.

A recent article by **Rogalski and Tinic [1986]** dealt with these concerns. These authors looked specifically at whether the way others have measured risk predetermined the returns they found. Most previous researchers assumed that systematic risks and required returns are constant during a year. Because the January effect seems primarily a small-capitalization-stock anomaly,[28] they tried to determine whether risk is higher during certain periods of the year for these stocks. If risk is higher during January, then the method used by Tinic and West, which assumes that risk is constant, would find excess returns, or larger excess returns, in January that would not, in truth, be excess.

Rogalski and Tinic formed portfolios based on market capitalization and found that, for all portfolios except the four containing the largest capitalized stocks, the January returns were larger. However, when the variances and betas were estimated, only the five portfolios containing the smallest stocks had higher variances in January. Rogalski and Tinic also tested for bias in the betas that could be caused by **nonsynchronous trading** and found that the small-firm betas might be further underestimated. They concluded that these statistical problems could provide a

Nonsynchronous Trading—Securities like common stocks do not all trade at the same moment. Thus the prices of stocks (for instance, daily closing prices) may actually come from any time during the day and are not fully comparable. Using nonsynchronous data can have a confounding influence on research results.

possible explanation for the January size effect. . . . Assume that the beta of Portfolio 1 [the smallest capitalization stock portfolio] was 1.00 from February to December. Our results demonstrate that this portfolio will have a January beta of approximately 1.30. If the risk-free rate does not increase significantly in January, the returns . . . support a January risk premium for the EW [equally weighted] index that is approximately six times as large as the median of the other months. . . . The combination of the two effects would require . . . a January return about eight to nine times greater than the median for the year (p. 69).

Because, for the smallest capitalization portfolios of stocks they tested, the January returns were more than nine times the returns in other months during

Exhibit 2-12

**Month-to-Month Mean Stock Market Returns and the Tests of Equality of Mean Returns,
January 1959 to December 1979; *Capital International Perspective* Indices**

Country	Jan.	Feb.	Mar.	Apr.	May	Jun.	Jul.	Aug.	Sept.	Oct.	Nov.	Dec.	K-W Tests[b] Stat.	K-W Tests[b] Prob.
Australia	2.649	-0.581	0.506	0.841	0.973	0.428	0.662	-0.365	-2.387	2.130	-0.848	3.993	20.18[f]	0.0430
Austria	0.743	0.890	0.239	-0.414	0.067	0.213	1.237	0.899	0.021	-0.224	0.651	1.233	12.95	0.2965
Belgium	3.215	1.085	0.395	1.482	-1.355	-0.840	1.441	-1.166	-1.866	-0.688	0.415	-0.089	39.40[f]	0.0001
Canada	2.900	0.068	0.789	0.408	-0.963	-0.300	0.689	0.600	-0.061	-0.820	1.435	2.611	18.59[f]	0.0689
Denmark	3.041	-0.407	-1.191	0.584	0.448	0.383	0.506	-0.138	-1.297	0.264	-0.900	2.037	35.53[f]	0.0002
France	3.722	-0.176	1.983	0.936	-0.656	-1.902	1.529	1.028	-1.214	-0.719	0.433	0.152	15.10	0.1779
Germany	3.099	-0.142	1.048	-0.605	-0.016	-0.948	1.559	2.243	-1.681	-0.936	1.356	0.092	24.27[f]	0.0116
Italy	2.229	0.865	0.737	0.723	-1.303	-0.411	-0.573	2.346	-0.724	-1.292	-0.255	-0.171	9.90	0.5398
Japan	3.529	1.128	1.877	0.301	0.975	2.059	-0.321	-0.829	-0.133	-0.976	1.646	1.798	20.30[f]	0.0414
Netherlands	3.762	-0.474	1.298	1.387	-0.982	-1.436	0.492	-0.283	-1.911	-0.246	-0.102	1.308	27.50[f]	0.0039
Norway	4.336	-1.176	-0.627	2.363	0.291	1.953	3.010	0.366	-1.559	-0.508	0.419	-0.320	29.51[f]	0.0019
Singapore[c]	10.591	-0.418	2.093	-2.315	4.015	0.307	-0.487	-0.375	-0.954	2.350	-1.966	5.227	11.51	0.4018
Spain	2.241	1.294	0.321	1.588	-1.873	0.062	0.794	1.290	-1.641	0.189	-0.436	-0.009	26.62[f]	0.0052
Sweden	3.996	0.383	1.006	0.879	-0.795	-0.246	2.409	-1.098	-1.335	-0.673	-0.179	0.823	31.46[f]	0.0009
Switzerland	4.585	-0.747	0.395	0.858	-1.267	-0.020	0.647	1.746	-1.536	-0.194	0.985	1.266	17.60[f]	0.0914
UK	3.406	0.687	1.248	3.129	-1.212	-1.689	-1.112	1.883	-0.239	0.798	-0.608	2.063	17.57[f]	0.0920
US	1.041	-0.410	1.266	0.959	-1.384	-0.560	0.139	0.338	-0.795	0.780	1.027	1.419	12.99	0.2941
US, EW[d]	5.080	0.545	1.545	0.443	-1.418	-1.003	0.734	0.717	-0.416	-0.786	1.792	1.367	17.26	0.1005
US, EW: 47-79[e]	4.449	0.476	1.922	0.523	-0.297	-0.421	1.766	0.759	0.083	-0.156	2.065	2.075	22.52[f]	0.0207

Values under *Month-to-Month Mean Returns*[a].

[a] Means are multiplied by 100. Number of observations is 21 for each month.

[b] The Kruskal-Wallis test statistic is approximately distributed as chi-square with 11 degrees of freedom. It tests the null hypothesis that month-to-month mean returns are equal against the alternative that they are not. Critical value for the chi-square distribution with 11 degrees of freedom at 10% significance level is 17.27. Probability value is the probability that a chi-square statistic is at least as large as the one reported would be realized if the null hypothesis is true, i.e., mean returns are equal.

[c] Data are available for the period 1/1970-12/1979.

[d] Mean returns on the equally weighted (EW) NYSE index for the period 1/1959-12/1979.

[e] For the period 1/1947-12/1979.

[f] Indicates the rejection of the null hypothesis that mean returns are equal at 10% significance level or less.

Source: Gultekin and Gultekin [1983], p. 475.

the year, the entire January effect would not be eliminated by these adjustments for risk. However, what Rogalski and Tinic showed is how important thoughtful analysis can be in sorting out true anomalies from statistical artifacts.

The problems caused by nonsynchronous trading and pricing of less frequently traded equities can cause important distortions in the results. Studies of small-capitalization stock have often found that two patterns exist: lower betas and higher portfolio returns than expected. There are several reasons why this may occur.

First, part of this finding has been shown to be a statistical artifact. An example will demonstrate why. Suppose that the market is up 30 points at 2:00 p.m. when the last trade of the day occurs in a stock, but the market is down 20 at the market close. Obviously, the stock's returns will show a low correlation with the market's closing price because its trade is not priced at the same time: it is nonsynchronous. Calculating betas for stocks that trade like this produces lower betas when ordinary least squares (OLS) regression is used.[29] Nonsynchronous trading can also lead to positive autocorrelation in index and portfolio returns: positive or negative macroeconomic information will affect frequently traded stocks first and less frequently traded stocks later.

A closely related phenomenon, the bid/ask-spread effect, may also produce a downward bias in less active stocks. Suppose that information about a thinly traded stock would support an equilibrium price of $10.00 with a bid/ask spread of ½ (i.e., a spread of $9.75 to $10.25). If a buyer appeared near the market close, the closing price might be pushed close to the top of the spread, $10.25. At the opening the next day, there is a tendency for trades to revert toward the mean, in our example $10.00. Statisticians call such a tendency "negative autocorrelation with a lag of one." Such a lag tends to lower the stock's correlation with the market and thus its beta (Roll [1984]). Furthermore, if you rebalance the portfolio daily to equal weights, the return is greatly increased. Roll [1983] showed that such daily rebalancing doubled the return on small stocks. Similar effects have been theorized to result from using discrete prices such as 1/8, 1/4, etc., prices that do not represent the actual price of trades.[30]

Regardless of which effect we examine, the real question is: How much do these effects matter? Roll [1983] showed they can have an important impact when measuring portfolio returns. However, since autocorrelations are generally positive between daily stock prices of individual stocks,[31] the accepted belief is that the positive autocorrelation in other information is more significant than the negative autocorrelation induced by nonsynchronous trading and dealer pricing.[32] This positive autocorrelation seems to exist for more than a week and represents a large portion of price variance for small stocks, even though the theory of efficient markets suggests that it should be traded away by specialists.[33] Furthermore, these effects have been shown to have other deleterious consequences.[34]

Even taking the problems of measuring small-stock prices into account does not eliminate the January effect. Other research on the January effect has taken quite a different tack. Looking for reasons returns may be higher for all, or small-capitalization, stocks in January, some have suggested that tax-induced selling might be the cause,[35] especially for stocks that had experienced capital losses. In an analysis of taxes and stock returns on the London Stock Exchange, Reinganum and Shapiro [1987] properly pointed out, however, that "tax trading translates into a seasonal pattern in prices only if investors are irrational or ignorant of the stock price seasonality" (p. 281).

What have tests of tax-induced selling in January shown? Tinic, who, along with Barone-Adesi and West [1987], has been active in this area, did not find evidence that tax-induced selling was the sole reason for the seasonality in Canadian returns. Even when adjusted for tax-induced selling, returns were better in January.[36] Still others have looked for different causes.[37]

Another question is: Did stocks paying higher dividends have significantly higher January returns because they would provide investors the returns needed to offset taxes? Keim [1985] found that January returns increased with the dividend yield, but that stocks paying no dividends had higher returns than all those paying dividends—much higher. There does not appear to be a dividend/tax effect.[38]

The January effect is so pervasive that it may provide important clues about stock valuation in general. Chang and Pinegar [1988] showed that Treasury-bill returns have not been statistically lower than stock returns, except in January and July. Recently, Penman [1987] has documented the tendency for good earnings to be reported early in the month, and Chari, Jagannathan, and Ofer [1988] have shown seasonal patterns in stock returns and volatility (especially for small stocks) around these earnings announcements; that is, basic economic data may provide part of the explanation for the January anomaly.

Does a January effect exist? Apparently it does. It has spawned a considerable body of research and at least one practitioner-oriented book, in which Haugen and Lakonishok [1988] conclude that research shows the January effect is greatest for small-capitalization, non-dividend-paying stocks selling well below their past prices.

Cycles Peaking Once a Year (Summer Rallies)

A summer rally is another bit of Wall Street folklore that may be a fact. Market technicians like Joseph Granville find this potential seasonality of interest. Granville [1960] calculated the percentage of years from 1886 to 1960 in which each month showed a rise or fall in the DJIA and found support for summer rallies.

To test whether a significant relationship existed in the Granville data, Osborne [1962] converted Granville's percentages into the number of times such a rise or fall occurred and tested whether a relationship existed between the rises and falls and the month of the year. His findings are shown in Exhibit 2-13. What you see are the number of days there were advances or declines in the index, and the **chi-square** (X^2) analysis of those data. From the data, he concluded that the seasonal pattern existed but was small: the chi-square was significant at the 5 percent level but not at the 1 percent level.

Chance [1986] defined a summer rally as a DJIA high in July-September that exceeded a May-June low. Using these criteria, he found that a rally occurred in 37 of the 38 summers through 1983. By the laws of chance, however, a rally is virtually certain to occur under the definition he used. Thus Chance went on to refine the summer-rally definition as an increase in the rate of return that is statistically significant. He found that, while the average returns for the DJIA were higher in July-September, the standard deviations were not. When the huge summer rally of 1932 was removed, and when broader market indexes were tested, he found neither returns nor standard deviations that were significantly higher. The data did not support the existence of summer rallies.

Chi-Square (X^2)—The *chi-square* statistic tests whether actual results (A_i) are so different from expected results (E_i) that chance could not be the cause. For example, if there were 438 market advances and 450 market declines, then out of 74 times, you would expect (E_1) 36 advancing days (i.e., $438/888 \times 74$) and (E_2) 38 declining days. *Chi-square* would then report how each of the actual results differed from those expected. It also allows you to test whether the difference was statistically significant.

To calculate *chi-square*, the following formula is used.

$$X^2 = \sum_{i}^{n} \frac{(A_i - E_i)}{E_i}$$

where the ratio is summed (Σ) for all outcomes ($i = 1,...,n$). Among other things, independence is assumed.

While summer rallies may not exist, there do appear to be seasonal effects within market groups. For instance, Merrill, Lynch, Pierce, Fenner and Smith published the results of a study of seasonal patterns in industry groups that found, from 1954 to 1964 (updated to 1975 by Hirsch [1986]), investors who traded in and out of these industries would have done about 300 percent better than those buying at the beginning of the period and holding until the end. This study took trading costs and commissions into account. The results of the updated Merrill Lynch study, shown in Exhibit 2-14, provide reasons to wonder whether the seasonal patterns found in the overall stock market might be attributable to industry effects.

Cycles Within a Month

Another approach to making money is to take advantage of the higher returns that accrue the first half of every month.[39] Exhibit 2-15 shows histograms of the mean returns for the nine trading days before and after the end of the month. Clearly, the returns are positive during the first nine days of the month, and

Exhibit 2-13

Osborne's Test for Seasonality

	Jan.	Feb.	Mar.	Apr.	May	Jun.	Jul.	Aug.	Sep.	Oct.	Nov.	Dec.	Total
N (market advance)	38	26	26	38	40	40	44	47	30	36	36	37	438
N (market decline)	36	48	48	36	34	34	30	27	44	38	38	37	450
Total	74	74	74	74	74	74	74	74	74	74	74	74	888

$X^2 = 24.6$; $P(X^2 > 24.6) = 0.011$; $n = 11$ degrees of freedom

Source: Osborne [1962], p. 367.

Exhibit 2-14
10-Year Profits, 1954-64

Industry	Seasonal Strategy		Trading Seasonally	Holding 10 Years
	Buy	Sell		
Air conditioning	Oct.	March	347.2%	63.4%
Meatpacking	Sept.	Feb.	313.8	81.9
Machine tools	Sept.	April	235.8	82.5
Fire/Casualty insurance	Oct.	Feb.	222.5	104.6
Aerospace	Sept.	Jan.	215.7	36.8
Eastern railroads	Oct.	Feb.	165.4	49.3
Agricultural machinery	Oct.	Feb.	145.0	72.5
	Average Profit		235.0	70.1

Source: Hirsch [1986], p. 140.

Ariel [1987] showed that the differences were statistically significant using data from 1963-81 for both the value- and equal-weighted NYSE and American Stock Exchange (ASE) stocks.[40]

He found that, not only were the returns significantly different, but the mean cumulative returns for both equal- and value-weighted indexes were also different. The results, shown in Exhibit 2-16, were not caused by **outliers**, biases in the data, the problem of misallocating dividends, or the January effect.

> **Outliers**—*Outliers* are events that are unusual—often defined by visually examining a graph of data and looking for extremely high or low values. Alternatively, outliers can be defined as data that lie more than three standard deviations from the mean of the distribution.

If one can make money using Ariel's findings (that significantly different and higher returns exist in the first nine trading days of a month), are there patterns of positive or negative returns over even shorter periods that one could exploit? There appear to be.

Weekend Patterns (Blue Mondays)

A number of researchers have found that returns early in the week, particularly on Monday, are consistently negative.[41] Others have found that the negative returns for large firms come between the Friday close and Monday opening, while for small firms the negative returns come during Monday trading.[42] Exhibit 2-17 shows the results of one such study that took the market values of the stocks into account. Mondays are indeed blue.

Exhibit 2-15
Monthly Effect in Stock Returns*

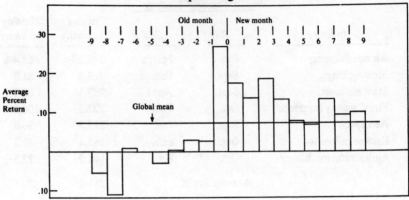

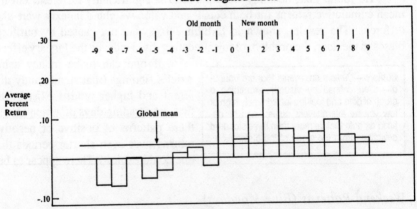

* CRSP indicates Center for Research in Security Prices, University of Chicago Index.

Source: Ariel [1987], p. 163.

Exhibit 2-16
19-Year Cumulative Returns

	Equally-Weighted Index	*Value-Weighted Index*
First half of trading month	2552.40%	565.40%
Last half of trading month	- 0.25	- 33.80
19 years	2545.90	339.90

Source: Ariel [1987], p. 165.

What could be the cause of these abnormal returns? Some have suggested that Friday closing prices might be abnormally inflated or contain a specialist bias, but analysis of these prices suggests that such is not the case.[43] One academic involved in research on such time-related anomalies concluded that "January/firm size/turn-of-the-year effects appear to be interrelated with day of the week returns" (Rogalski [1984], p. 836). Recently, Keim [1987] has untangled many of these interrelationships, showing that ". . . Friday abnormal returns explain 63 percent of the average magnitude of the size effect over the period 1963-1985." In addition, he concluded that small firms showed weekly effects more than large firms and that weekend effects persist even outside of January.

Holidays

Finally, we'll end our discussion of cyclical patterns with a holiday. Scott [1987] reported that Ariel found "over one-third of the return earned by the market accrued over the last 20 years has occurred over the eight trading days which annually fall before holidays" (p. 8). Exhibit 2-18 shows Ariel's results as reported in Scott.

Ariel used data from CRSP (Center for Research in Security Prices) from 1963 to 1982 for returns on the days before and then after holidays that resulted in stock market closings. The average returns he reports are not risk adjusted. When he tested for differences in risk (standard deviation) for holiday periods versus nonholiday periods, he found what is shown in Exhibit 2-19: holding-period volatility was actually lower during the holidays. In addition, he calculated that 35 percent of all the returns from the market over the 23-year period came from holiday periods—just over 3 percent of the trading days.[44]

Intraday Patterns

Although, except in January, Mondays are blue and Fridays hold a greater potential for profit, what about one last rule: buy at the open? Except on Monday, it may hold true.

Exhibit 2-17

Mean Portfolio Close-to-Close, Close-to-Open, and Open-to-Close Returns by Weekday and Market Value Capitalization

Market-Value Decile	Mon. (1)	Tue. (2)	Wed. (3)	Thu. (4)	Fri. (5)	F_5 (6)	F_{Mon} (7)	F_4 (8)
			Means in Percent					
		Panel A: Close-to-close-returns						
All firms	-0.202	0.138	0.146	0.170	0.195	1.86	7.30^b	0.06
(Std. error)	(0.154)	(0.117)	(0.118)	(0.095)	(0.100)			
Smallest	-0.117	0.177	0.096	0.136	0.304	1.95^a	5.74^b	0.82
2	-0.211	0.085	0.211	0.175	0.262	3.23^b	11.33^b	0.62
3	-0.227	0.112	0.174	0.223	0.234	2.79^b	10.41^b	0.29
4	-0.220	0.137	0.197	0.155	0.208	2.30^a	8.91^b	0.10
5	-0.202	0.130	0.203	0.166	0.250	2.19^a	8.19^b	0.21
6	-0.208	0.125	0.166	0.194	0.160	1.96^a	7.62^b	0.07
7	-0.205	0.138	0.167	0.191	0.150	1.51	5.92^b	0.04
8	-0.204	0.131	0.115	0.143	0.144	1.28	5.11^b	0.01
9	-0.229	0.191	0.070	0.166	0.118	1.48	5.46^b	0.18
Largest	-0.196	0.156	0.060	0.149	0.124	0.82	3.05^a	0.09
F_{mv}	0.48	0.53	2.16^b	0.55	2.12^b			
N	53	56	61	60	56			

Panel B: Previous close-to-open returns

All firms	−0.095	0.001	0.052	0.018	0.066	1.63	5.40[a]	0.44
(Std. error)	(0.065)	(0.049)	(0.045)	(0.041)	(0.040)			
Smallest	−0.029	−0.045	−0.054	−0.027	0.042	0.46	0.02	0.66
2	−0.074	−0.032	0.037	0.005	0.056	1.31	3.08[a]	0.82
3	−0.029	0.040	0.061	0.051	0.081	0.83	2.87[a]	0.18
4	−0.096	−0.001	0.051	0.011	0.047	1.61	5.42[b]	0.36
5	−0.108	0.018	0.060	0.026	0.076	2.15[a]	6.47[b]	0.81
6	−0.072	0.015	0.064	0.001	0.045	1.36	4.13[b]	0.50
7	−0.101	0.005	0.073	0.029	0.066	1.70	5.66[b]	0.42
8	−0.139	−0.008	0.048	0.015	0.047	2.22[a]	7.97[b]	0.34
9	−0.121	0.023	0.072	0.027	0.084	2.09[a]	7.41[b]	0.37
Largest	−0.177	0.034	0.105	0.047	0.114	2.87[b]	10.39[b]	0.44
F_{mv}	4.09[b]	2.47[b]	5.85[b]	1.43	1.43			
N	53	56	61	60	56			

Source: Adapted from Harris [1986], p. 103.

Exhibit 2-18
Returns Around Holidays

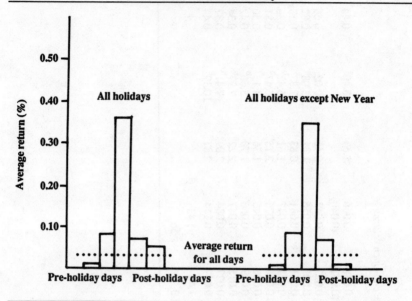

Source: Scott [1987], p. 9.

Exhibit 2-19
Holiday Patterns: Average Percentage Returns
(1963 through 1982)

Trading Days (number in test)	Average Return	Standard Deviation
Pre-holiday (160)	36.5%	60.9%
Non-pre-holiday (4,860)	2.6	78.3
All (5,020)	3.6%	78.0%

Source: Adapted from Scott [1987], p.10.

Harris [1986] studied the 14 months from December 1981 through January 1983 for all transactions on the NYSE. As Exhibit 2-20 indicates, prices changed most during the first and the last hours of trading, and the changes were generally positive. This pattern has been dominant in recent years, but was not so in earlier periods (1950-89).[45]

Exhibit 2-20
Cumulated 15-Minute Intraday Returns, by Weekday
December 1, 1981 - January 31, 1983

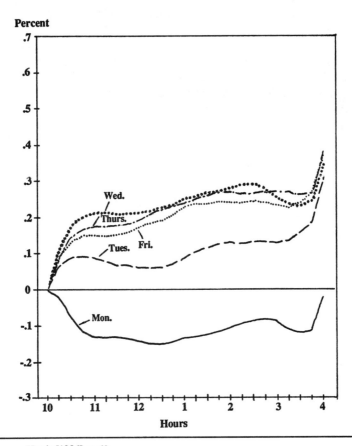

Source: Harris [1986], p. 63.

Conclusion

Cycles do affect stock prices. The cycles may be as long as six decades or as short as a day.[46] As statistical techniques become more refined, we may even find cycles within certain periods of the day, even minutes within the hour. Perhaps there is a mid-morning coffee break effect, or a mid-afternoon glucose slump!

The real questions, however, are not whether cycles exist, but what is behind them, and can the clever investor make profits using them—returns greater than those from a buy-and-hold strategy or from a risk-adjusted portfolio. Many of the cycles seem immune to such systematic profit making (e.g., monetary and inflation cycles appear to be coincident with stock market cycles). Some (e.g., four-year or election cycles and intramonth cycles) may be profitable, although the statistical evidence is not strong enough for high confidence. Seasonal patterns do seem to exist, for some industry groups. And still other patterns, particularly the January effect, are providing a basis for trading strategies being widely sold by investment management organizations.

What you as an investor must be wary of is cycles that seem to rely on unfounded folklore. The key is to capitalize on the enduring patterns, especially ones that have a solid economic rationale.

CHAPTER 2

Notes

1. For a further discussion of Dow Theory, see Bishop [1961].

2. For other tests of moving averages as predictive tools, see James [1968] and Van Horne and Parker [1967].

3. We will discuss Dow Theory more thoroughly in Chapter 3.

4. For instance, see Prechter [1986], p. 50.

5. See, for instance, Vorob'ev [1961], Adams [1972], and Louprette [1972].

6. This lack of definition is, of course, not necessarily a reason not to use a theory. Robert Prechter is an Elliott wave analyst, and his forecasts have been reported in such *Futures* articles as "Stock Market's Hottest Forecasters . . ." [1987].

7. For instance, Schumpeter's [1939] economic cycles and Forrester's [1976] capital goods capacity-based cycles, discussed in the next sections.

8. Granger and Morgenstern [1963], using data from October 1875 to March 1952, found a 40-month cycle, but that cycle was statistically insignificant. Their test covered a very long period, however, during which significant changes in the variance of the data could have occurred. Thus a shift in the data variance (including changes in the data after 1952) or the use of more refined spectral analysis tools could be reasons for the differences between theirs and the Herbst and Slinkman [1984] results.

9. Earlier, Granger and Morgenstern [1963] found the same thing.

10. Prechter [1986], an Elliott wave analyst, discussed the confluence of political and economic cycles.

11. In Friedman and Schwartz [1963], pp. 32-78, the authors documented the historical relationship between changes in the money-supply growth rate and aggregate economic activity. They found that, on average, declines in money-supply growth precede economic contractions by 20 months, and expansions precede economic expansions by 8 months.

12. For instance, Keran [1971] related stock-price changes to money-supply changes, economic growth, price-level changes, and expected corporate earnings. While the model had a very high R^2, it had two flaws. The data were stock prices and earnings with trends, not changes in prices and earnings: data will be positively correlated because of their trends, even if the changes are negatively correlated. In addition, many lagged terms were included for each variable: few degrees of freedom were left, thus essentially forcing high correlations. Others who have found similar results include Homa and Jaffee [1971] and Hamburger and Kochin [1972].

13. Auerbach [1976] found less strong support for the same lead-lag relationship.

14. See, for instance, Urich and Wachtel [1981] and Grossman [1981].

15. See, for instance, Berkman [1978], who found that unanticipated increases in the money supply had a depressive effect on stock prices, and Lynge [1981], who found lowered share prices following positive money-supply announcements. He did not distinguish expected from unexpected announcements.

16. Lynge [1981] studied the impact of weekly money-supply announcements on the stock market index. He found that the market was sensitive to money-supply announcements, but he did not use unexpected changes, nor did he break the data into the three periods studies by Pearce and Roley [1983].

17. Stocks were expected to be a hedge against inflation because the companies that issued the stocks could insulate their earnings from inflation's ravages. Evidence suggests, however, that, on average, profit margins are eroded by inflation, thus reducing the returns that investors might expect.

18. Several researchers have confirmed this finding. For instance, Oudet [1973] found that returns from common stocks were lowest during inflationary periods and highest when the economy had the least inflation.

19. To interpret the coefficients in Exhibit 2-8, refer to the box entitled "Interpreting Regression Coefficients."

20. Gultekin used inflation forecasts gathered by a newspaper columnist Joseph Livingston. Livingston has gathered estimates for 6 and 12 months of inflation from 50 economists twice a year since 1946. There are some problems in using these data, which Gultekin discusses, and they are further discussed in Hasbrouck [1984] and Gibbons [1981].

21. Gultekin also concluded that the results "indicate that the risk premium may vary over time positively with expected inflation, rather than substantially with the relation between the 'real' rate of interest and expected inflation" (p.672). Chang and Pinegar [1987] also discuss the relationship between risk and inflation.

22. In addition to prices for the S&P 500, the index includes manufacturing production hours, unemployment claims, new manufacturing orders, supplier delivery performance, plant and equipment orders, new businesses formed, building permits for private housing, money supply, and changes in inventories, sensitive materials' prices, and business and consumer credit.

23. For instance, see Heathcotte and Apilado [1974].

24. See Chapter 9 for a discussion of how risk premia change over time (nonstationarity).

25. Fisher [1930] concluded that the real interest rate was stable. Examining data from different time periods, Hess and Bicksler [1975] and Schwert and Nelson [1977], among others, found that the real rate changes.

26. Further studies tended to confirm the usefulness of this method. However, recent insights have been added about the impacts of stock size and time-of-the-year effects. In addition, studies by Carroll and Wei [1988] and Litzenberger and Ramaswamy [1979] illustrated how individual stock data (rather than portfolios) might be used in pooled time-series cross-sectional studies.

27. See also Brown et al. [1983], who studied seasonality in the Australian stock market, Van den Bergh and Wessels [1983], who studied Dutch stocks, Berges, McConnell, and Schlarbaum [1984], in a study of Canadian stocks, and Corhay, Hawawini, and Michael [1987], who studied seasonality in the U.K., Belgian, and French stock markets.

28. The small-firm effect will be discussed in detail in Chapter 5.

29. Adaptations to take this problem into account have been made by Scholes and Williams [1977] and Dimson [1979].

30. See, for instance, Ball [1988].

31. See, for instance, Fama [1981] and Hasbrouck and Ho [1987].

32. See, for instance, Atchison, Butler, and Simonds [1987].

33. See, for instance, Grossman and Miller [1988].

34. See, for instance, Chiang and Venkatesh [1988].

35. This cause was earlier suggested in Wachtel [1942] and more recently in Roll [1983].

36. Others have looked at the impact of tax-induced selling on January returns. See, for instance, Reinganum [1983] and Roll [1983]. Schultz [1984] found that the January effect did not seem to exist before 1917, but using a longer, early, period, Jones, Pearce, and Wilson [1987] argue for a pre-tax January effect.

37. For example, DeBondt and Thaler [1987] used quite a different approach.

38. The relationship among dividends, dividend yield, and stock profits will be discussed in Chapter 4.

39. See, for instance, Hirsch [1979].

40. Linn and Lockwood [1988] found these higher returns during the firms' nine days of each month in stocks traded on the NYSE, ASE, and over the counter (OTC). Merrill [1975] traced the same pattern for the DJIA from 1897 to 1974.

41. This effect was first identified by French [1980].

42. In addition to French [1980], see Gibbons and Hess [1981], who found negative returns on Mondays and positive Friday returns. Harris [1986] and Jaffe and Westerfield [1985] found evidence for the weekend effect in the United Kingdom, Japan, and Australia; Lakonishok and Levy [1982 and 1985] attributed the weekend effect to check clearing and settlement procedures. See also Linn and Lockwood [1988], who found the effect existed for NYSE, ASE, and OTC stocks.

43. See, for instance, Kolb and Rodriquez [1987].

44. Ariel also found an impact on the weekend effect when holidays were removed. In fact, the largest returns were earned on Wednesday, not Friday.

45. See Hirsch [1986], p. 40.

46. Keim and Stambaugh [1984] even show that Friday the 13th is less profitable than other Fridays.

CHAPTER 2

References

Adams, John. "A Forecasting Tool: The Fibonacci Indicator." *Financial Analysts Journal,* September-October 1972, pp. 95-96.

Adleman, Irma. "Long Cycles, Fact or Artifact?" *American Economic Review,* June 1965, pp. 444-63.

Ariel, Robert. "A Monthly Effect in Stock Returns." *Journal of Financial Economics,* 1987, pp. 161-74.

Atchison, Michael; Butler, Kirt; and Simonds, Richard. "Nonsynchronous Data and Market Index Correlation." *Journal of Finance,* March 1987, pp. 111-18.

Auerbach, Robert. "Money and Stock Prices." *Federal Reserve Bank of Kansas City Monthly Review,* September-October 1976, pp. 3-11.

Ball, Clifford. "Estimation Bias Induced by Discrete Security Prices." *Journal of Finance,* September 1988, pp. 841-66.

Berges, Angel; McConnell, John; and Schlarbaum, Gary. "The Turn of the Year in Canada." *Journal of Finance,* March 1984, pp. 185-92.

Berkman, Neil. "On the Significance of Weekly Changes in M1." *New England Economic Review,* May-June 1978, pp. 5-22.

Bishop, George W., Jr. "Evolution of the Dow Theory." *Financial Analysis Journal,* September-October 1961, pp. 23-26.

Bonin, Joseph, and Moses, Edward. "Seasonal Variations in Prices of Individual Dow Jones Industrial Stocks." *Journal of Financial and Quantitative Analysis,* December 1974, pp. 963-91.

Branch, Benjamin. "Testing the Unbiased Expected Theory of Interest Rates." *Financial Review,* 1978, pp. 51-66.

Brown, Philip; Keim, Donald; Kleidon, Alan; and Marsh, Terry. "Stock Return Seasonalities and the Tax-Loss Selling Hypothesis: Analysis of the Arguments and Australian Evidence." *Journal of Financial Economics,* 1983, pp. 105-27.

Campbell, John. "Stock Returns and the Term Structure." *Journal of Financial Economics,* 1987, pp. 373-99.

Carroll, Carolyn, and Wei, K. C. John. "Risk, Return, and Equilibrium: An Extension." *Journal of Business,* 1988, pp. 485-99.

Chan, K. C. "Can Tax-Loss Selling Explain the January Season in Stock Returns?" *Journal of Finance,* December 1986, pp. 1115-28.

Chance, Don, and Ferris, Stephen P. "Summer Rallies." *Financial Analysts Journal,* January-February 1986, pp. 6-9.

Chang, Eric, and Pinegar, J. Michael. "Risk and Inflation." *Journal of Financial and Quantitative Analysis,* March 1987, pp. 89-99.

Chari, V. V.; Jagannathan, Ravi R.; and Ofer, Aharon. "Seasonalities in Security Returns." *Journal of Finance,* September 1988, pp. 10-21.

Chiang, Raymond, and Vankatesh, P. C. "Insider Holdings and Perception of Information Asymetry: A Note." *Journal of Finance,* September 1988, pp. 1041-48.

Cho, D. Chenhyung, and Frees, Edward. "Estimating the Volatility of Discrete Stock Prices." *Journal of Finance*, June 1988, pp. 451-66.

Cooper, Richard. "Efficient Capital Markets and the Quantity Theory of Money." *Journal of Finance*, June 1974, pp. 887-908.

Corhay, Albert; Hawawini, Gabriel; and Michael, Pierce. "Seasonality in the Risk and Return Relationship: Some International Evidence." *Journal of Finance*, March 1987, pp. 49-68.

Cross, F. "The Behavior of Stock Prices on Fridays and Mondays." *Financial Analysts Journal*, November-December 1973, pp. 67-69.

Curran, John J. "The Forces Driving Stocks Even Higher." *Fortune*, March 30, 1987, pp. 54-58, pp. 60-61.

DeBondt, Werner, and Thaler, Richard. "Further Evidence on Investor Overreaction and Stock Market Seasonality." *Journal of Finance*, July 1987, pp. 557-81.

Dimson, Elroy. "Risk Measurement When Shares Are Subject to Infrequent Trading." *Journal of Financial Economics*, June 1979, pp. 197-226.

Dyl, Edward, and Martin, Stanley A. "Weekend Effects on Stock Returns: A Comment." *Journal of Finance*, March 1985, pp. 347-50.

Estep, Tony. "Manager Styles and Sources of Equity Returns." *Journal of Portfolio Management*, Winter 1987, pp. 4-10.

Fama, Eugene. "Stock Returns, Real Activity, Inflation and Money." *American Economic Review*, September 1981, pp. 545-65.

————, and Gibbons, Michael. "A Comparison of Inflation Forecasts." *Journal of Monetary Economics*, May 1984, pp. 327-48.

————, and MacBeth, J. "Risk, Return and Equilibrium: Empirical Tests." *Journal of Political Economy*, May-June 1973, pp. 607-36.

————, and Schwert, G. W. "Asset Returns and Inflation." *Journal of Financial Economics*, November 1977, pp. 115-46.

Fisher, Irving. *The Theory of Interest: As Determined by Impatience to Spend Income and Opportunity to Invest It.* New York: Augustus M. Kelly, 1930.

Fisher, Lawrence. "Some New Stock-Market Indexes." *Journal of Business*, 1966, pp. 191-225.

Forrester, Jay W. "A New View of Business Cycle Dynamics." *Journal of Portfolio Management*, Fall 1976, pp. 22-34.

French, Kenneth. "Stock Returns and the Weekend Effect." *Journal of Financial Economics*, March 1980, pp. 55-69.

Friedman, Milton, and Schwartz, Anna. "Money and Business Cycles." *Review of Economics and Statistics*, February 1963, pp. 32-78.

Gehm, Fred. "Who is R.N. Elliott and Why Is He Making Waves?" *Financial Analysts Journal*, January-February 1983, pp. 51-58.

Geske, Robert, and Roll, Richard. "The Fiscal and Monetary Linkage Between Stock Returns and Inflation." *Journal of Finance*, March 1983, pp. 1-33.

Gibbons, Michael, and Hess, Patrick. "Day of the Week Effects and Asset Returns." *Journal of Business*, October 1981, pp. 579-96.

Givoly, Dan, and Ovadia, Arie. "Year-End Tax-Induced Sales and Stock Market Seasonality." *Journal of Finance,* March 1983, pp. 171-85.

Glickstein, David, and Wubbels, Rolf. "Dow Theory Is Alive and Well!" *Journal of Portfolio Management,* Spring 1983, pp. 28-32.

Glosten, Lawrence, and Harris, Lawrence. "Estimating the Components of the Bid/Ask Spread." *Journal of Financial Economics,* May 1988, pp. 123-42.

Granger, C. W. J., and Morgenstern, O. "Spectral Analysis of New York Stock Market Prices." *Kyklos,* 1963, pp. 1-27.

Granville, Joseph. *A Strategy of Daily Stock Market Timing for Maximum Profit.* Englewood Cliffs, N.J.: Prentice Hall, 1960.

Grossman, Jacob. "The Rationality of Money Supply Expectations and the Short-Run Response of Interest Rates to Monetary Surprises." *Journal of Money, Credit and Banking,* November 1981, pp. 409-24.

————, and Miller, Merton. "Liquidity and Market Structure." *Journal of Finance,* July 1988, pp. 617-33.

Gultekin, Mustafa, and Gultekin, Bulent. "Stock Market Seasonality: International Evidence." *Journal of Financial Economics,* December 1983, pp. 469-81.

Gultekin, N. Bulent. "Stock Market Returns and Inflation Forecasts." *Journal of Finance,* June 1983, pp. 663-73.

————. "Stock Market Returns and Inflation: Evidence from Other Countries." *Journal of Finance,* March 1983, pp. 49-65.

Hamburger, Michael, and Kochin, Lewis. "Money and Stock Prices: Channels of Influence." *Journal of Finance,* May 1972, pp. 231-49.

Harris, Lawrence. "How to Profit from Intradaily Stock Returns." *Journal of Portfolio Management,* Winter 1986, pp. 61-65.

————. "A Transaction Data Study of Weekly and Intradaily Patterns in Stock Returns." *Journal of Financial Economics,* May 1986, pp. 99-118.

Hasbrouck, Joel. "Stock Returns, Inflation and Economic Activity: The Survey Evidence." *Journal of Finance,* December 1984, pp. 1293-1310.

————, and Ho, Thomas S. Y. "Order Arrival, Quote Behavior, and the Return-Generating Process." *Journal of Finance,* September 1987, pp. 1035-48.

Haugen, Robert, and Lakonishok, Josef. *The Incredible January Effect.* Homewood, Ill.: Dow-Jones Irwin, 1988.

Heathcotte, Bryan, and Apilado, V. P. "The Predictive Content of Some Leading Economic Indicators for Future Stock Prices." *Journal of Financial and Quantitative Analysis,* March 1974, pp. 247-58.

Herbst, Anthony, and Slinkman, Craig. "Political-Economic Cycles in the U.S. Stock Market." *Financial Analysts Journal,* May-June 1984, pp. 38-44.

Hess, Patrick, and Bicksler, James. "Capital Asset Pricing Versus Time Series Models on Prediction of Inflation." *Journal of Financial Economics,* December 1975, pp. 341-60.

Hirsch, Yale. *Don't Sell Stocks on Monday.* New York: Hirsch Organization, 1986.

————. *The Stock Trader's Almanac and Record.* New York: Hirsch Organization, 1969.

Hobbs, Gerald R., and Riley, William B. "Profiting from a Presidential Election." *Financial Analysts Journal*, March-April 1984, pp. 46-52.

Homa, Kenneth, and Jaffee, Dwight. "The Supply of Money and Common Stock Prices." *Journal of Finance*, December 1971, pp. 1056-66.

Huang, Roger. "Common Stock Returns and Presidential Elections." *Financial Analysts Journal*, March-April 1985, pp. 58-61.

Jacobs, Bruce, and Levy, Kenneth. "Calendar Anomalies: Abnormal Returns at Calendar Turning Points." *Financial Analysts Journal*, November-December 1988, pp. 28-39.

Jaffe, Jeffrey, and Mandelker, Gershon. "The Fisher Effect of Risking Assets: An Empirical Investigation." *Journal of Finance*, May 1976, pp. 447-58.

———, and Westerfield, Randolph. "The Week-End Effect in Common Stock Returns: The International Evidence." *Journal of Finance*, June 1985, pp. 433-54.

James, F. E. "Monthly Moving Averages—An Effective Investment Tool?" *Journal of Financial and Quantitative Analysis*, 1968, pp. 315-26.

Jones, Charles; Pearce, Douglas; and Wilson, Jack. "Can Tax-Loss Selling Explain the January Effect? A Note." *Journal of Finance*, June 1987, pp. 453-61.

Kalay, Atner. "The Information Content of the Timing of Dividend Announcements." *Journal of Financial Economics*, July 1986, pp. 373-87.

Keim, Donald. "Daily Returns and Size-Related Premiums: One More Time." *Journal of Portfolio Management*, Winter 1987, pp. 4-47.

———. "Dividend Yields and Stock Returns: Implications of Abnormal January Returns." *Journal of Financial Economics*, September 1985, pp. 473-89.

———, and Stambaugh, Robert. "A Further Investigation of the Weekend Effect in Stock Returns." *Journal of Finance*, 1984, pp. 819-35.

Keran, Michael. "Expectations, Money and the Stock Market." *Federal Reserve Bank of Saint Louis Review*, January 1971, pp. 16-30.

Klemkosky, Robert, and Jun, Kwang. "The Monetary Impact on Return Variability and Market Risk Premia." *Journal of Financial and Quantitative Analysis*, December 1982, pp. 663-81.

Kolb, Robert, and Rodriguez, Ricardo. "Friday the Thirteenth: Part VII—A Note." *Journal of Finance*, December 1987, pp. 1385-87.

Lakonishok, Josef, and Levi, Maurice. "Weekend Effects on Stock Returns: A Note." *Journal of Finance*, December 1982, pp. 883-89.

———. "Weekend Effects on Stock Returns: A Reply." *Journal of Finance*, March 1985, pp. 351-52.

Linn, Scott, and Lockwood, Larry. "Short-Term Stock Price Patterns: NYSE, ASE, OTC." *Journal of Portfolio Management*, Winter 1988, pp. 30-34.

Litzenberger, Robert, and Ramaswamy, Krishna. "The Effects of Personal Taxes and Dividends on Asset Prices: Theory and Empirical Evidence." *Journal of Financial Economics*, June 1979, pp. 163-96.

Louprette, William. "Fibonacci Sequence in the Stock Market." *Financial Analysts Journal*, November-December 1972, p. 102.

Lynge, Morgan, Jr. "Money Supply Announcements and Stock Prices," *Journal of Portfolio Management*, Fall 1981, pp. 40-43.

Merville, A. *Seasonal Trends in Stock Prices*. New York: Analysis Press, 1975.

Neiderhoffer, Victor. "Clustering of Stock Prices." *Operations Research*, 1965, pp. 258-265.

————, and Osborne, M. F. M. "Market Making and Research in the Stock Exchange." *Journal of American Statistical Association*, December 1966, pp. 897-916.

Nelson, Charles. "Inflation and Rates of Return on Common Stocks." *Journal of Finance*, May 1976, pp. 471-83.

Officer, Dennis. "Seasonality in Australian Capital Markets: Market Efficiency and Empirical Issues." *Journal of Financial Economics*, March 1975, pp. 29-51.

Osborne, M. F. M. "Periodic Structure in the Browninan Motion of Stock Prices." *Operations Research*, May-June 1962, pp. 345-79.

Oudet, Bruno. "The Variation of the Return on Stocks in Periods of Inflation." *Journal of Financial and Quantitative Analysis*, March 1973, pp. 247-58.

Pearce, Douglas, and Roley, Vance. "The Reaction of Stock Prices to Unanticipated Changes in Money: A Note." *Journal of Finance*, September 1983, pp. 1323-33.

Penman, Stephen. "The Distribution of Earnings News over Time and Seasonalities in Aggregate Stock Returns." *Journal of Financial Economics*, 1987, pp. 199-228.

Prechter, Robert R., Jr. "1986 Stock Market Battle: Elliott Wave vs. Four-Year Cycle." *Futures*, January 1986, p. 50.

Reinganum, Marc. "The Anomalous Stock Market Behavior of Small Firms in January: Empirical Tests for Tax-Loss Selling Effects." *Journal of Financial Economics*, June 1983, pp. 89-104.

————, and Shapiro, Alan. "Taxes and Stock Return Seasonality: Evidence from the London Stock Exchange." *Journal of Business*, 1987, pp. 281-95.

Riley, William, and Luksetich, William. "The Market Prefers Republicans: Myth or Reality." *Journal of Financial and Quantitative Analysis*, September 1980, pp. 541-60.

Rogalski, Richard. "Discussion of Keim and Stambaugh." *Journal of Finance*, July 1984, pp. 835-37.

————, and Tinic, Seha. "The January Size Effect: Anomaly or Risk Mismeasurement?" *Financial Analysts Journal*, November-December 1986, pp. 63-70.

Roll, Richard. "A Simple Implicit Measure of the Effective Bid-Ask Spread in an Efficient Market." *Journal of Finance*, September 1984, pp. 127-39.

————. "Vas Ist Das?" *Journal of Portfolio Management*. Winter 1983, pp. 18-28.

Rozeff, Michael. "Money and Stock Prices: Market Efficiency and the Lag in Effect of Monetary Policy." *Journal of Financial Economics*, September 1974, pp. 245-302.

————. "The Money Supply and the Stock Market." *Financial Analysts Journal*, September-October 1975, pp. 18-26.

————, and Kinney, W. R. "Capital Market Seasonality: The Case of Stock Returns." *Journal of Financial Economics Analysis*, 1976, pp. 379-402.

Scholes, Myron, and Williams, Joseph. "Estimating Betas from Nonsynchronous Data." *Journal of Financial Economics,* December 1977, pp. 309-27.

Schultz, Paul. "Personal Income Taxes and The January Effect: Small Firm Stock Returns Before the War Revenue Act of 1917: A Note." *Journal of Finance,* 1985, pp. 333-43.

Schumpeter, Joseph. *Business Cycles.* New York: McGraw Hill, 1939.

Schwert, G., and Nelson, C. R. "Short-Term Interest Rates as Predictors of Inflation: On Testing the Hypothesis that the Real Rate of Interest is Constant." *American Economic Review,* June 1977, pp. 478-86.

Scott, Maria. "Market Patterns: High Returns Before Holidays." *American Association of Individual Investors Journal,* May 1987, pp. 8-12.

Shanken, Jay. "Nonsychronous Data and the Covariance-Factor Structure of Returns." *Journal of Finance,* June 1987, p. 221.

Sharpe, William F. *Investments.* Third edition. Englewood Cliffs, N.J.: Prentice-Hall, 1985.

Solnik, Bruno. "The Relation Between Stock Prices and Inflationary Expectations: The International Evidence." *Journal of Finance,* March 1983, pp. 35-48.

Sorenson, Eric. "Rational Expectations and Impact of Money Upon Stock Prices." *Journal of Finance and Quantitative Analysis,* December 1982, pp. 649-62.

Sprinkel, Beryl. *Money and Stock Prices.* Homewood, Ill.: Richard D. Irwin, 1964.

———. *Money and Markets: A Monetarist View.* Homewood, Ill.: Richard D. Irwin, 1971.

"Stock Market's Hottest Forecasters See Doubling of DJIA Still Ahead." *Futures,* January 1987, pp. 48-51.

Tinic, Seha; Barone-Adesi, Giovanni; and West, Richard. "Seasonality in Canadian Stock Prices: A Test of the 'Tax Loss-Selling' Hypothesis." *Journal of Financial and Quantitative Analysis,* March 1987, pp. 51-73.

———, and West, Richard. "Risk and Return: January vs. the Rest of the Year." *Journal of Financial Economics,* December 1984, pp. 561-74.

Urich, Thomas, and Wachtel, Paul. "Market Response to the Weekly Money Supply Announcements in the 1970s." *Journal of Finance,* December 1981, pp. 1063-72.

Van den Bergh, Willem, and Wessels, Roberto. "Seasonality of Individual Stock Returns: Recent Empirical Evidence from the Amsterdam Stock Exchange." Working Paper, Erasmus University, Rotterdam, Holland, 1983.

Van Horne, J. C., and Parker, George. "The Random Walk Theory: An Empirical Test," *Financial Analysts Journal,* 1967, pp. 87-92.

Vorob'ev, Nikalain. *Fibonacci Numbers.* New York: Blaisdell Publishing, 1961.

Wachtel, S. B. "Certain Observations on Seasonal Movements in Stock Prices." *Journal of Business,* 1942, pp. 183-93.

CHAPTER 2

Appendix

Residual Analysis to Evaluate the Impact of Events on Stock Prices

Suppose a company's stock soars after an earnings increase. Should you design a strategy to buy stocks of companies that announce increases in earnings? Perhaps, but first you must separate two events: the information event (for instance, a positive earnings announcement) from the market event (did most stocks also soar about the same time?).

Many researchers have used a tool called cumulative average residual (CAR) analysis to determine whether an event like an earnings announcement or merger was expected, and whether profits could be made from information about it. Such analysis frequently rests on the capital asset pricing (actually the market) model described in the Appendix A to Chapter 1 to eliminate the effect of a rising and falling market from the stock's total return. A t-test is then used to evaluate whether the remaining after-event returns (the residuals) are significantly different from those before the event (the estimation period).[1]

The first step is to calculate the daily mean excess return (the residual) by one of three methods:

1. estimate the stock's mean return for the estimation period and subtract this mean from each subsequent observation;

2. subtract the market return for each period from the stock's return for the same period; or

3. estimate alpha and beta using the market model:

$$R_{it} = alpha_i + beta_i \, R_{mt} + e_i$$

where R_{it} = the stock return in period t,
              R_{mt} = the market's return in period t,
         $alpha_i$ = the intercept from the regression,
           $beta_i$ = the slope coefficient, and
              e_i = the unexplained error, the residual
               i = to designate a particular stock.

Subtract the estimated return from each subsequent (e.g., daily) return (R_{it}) thusly:

$$A_{it} = R_{it} - (alpha_i + beta_i \, R_{mt})$$

The A_{it} is the excess return or residual. This is called the beta or market-model method.

The second step is to determine whether the information event had an unexpected impact on the returns of the shares of the companies experiencing the event. There are two approaches to determine this. First, an average of the residuals for all companies experiencing the event can be plotted across time. The time-sequenced data look like those shown in Exhibit 3-16. A second approach calculates t-statistics for average excess returns for each day. A sufficiently large t-statistic suggests that the returns are unexpected and significant.[2]

There has been considerable controversy about the effectiveness of this analysis. Discussions center on the stark simplicity of its first two excess-return methods, which ignore risk adjustment, as well as a myriad of problems that are encountered in estimating the market model and its parameters when using the third method.

What has surprised many is how effective and robust the third approach appears to be. Brown and Warner [1980] tested the effectiveness of all three methods on monthly data, and all three performed well, but the last method (the simple market-model or beta method) for calculating excess returns performed the best. Subsequent tests by Brown and Warner [1985] on daily data (the data used by most researchers) indicated that, in spite of daily-data problems,[3] when compared with using more sophisticated methods for calculating beta,[4] the simple beta method held up. In other studies using data from bull and bear markets[5] or more sophisticated approaches designed to deal with systematic patterns in the residuals,[6] the simple market-model approach still worked well.[7]

In spite of the obvious problems with the approach (for instance, the beta before the event may change once the news is announced)[8], this method of analysis has provided one of the best ways to measure the impact of news on a stock's excess returns—its profits. Thus it remains a popular technique.

CHAPTER 2   APPENDIX

Notes

1. The t-test is implemented after making the usual assumptions about residual returns being independent between successive observations and being identically and normally distributed.

2. For those interested in the detailed mathematics behind the residual analysis, a straightforward analysis is provided in Brown and Warner [1985], pp. 6-7.

3. Autocorrelation, kurtosis, and skewness.

4. See, for instance, Dimson [1979] and Scholes and Williams [1977].

5. See, for instance, Klein and Rosenfeld [1987].

6. See, for instance, Malatesta [1986].

7. Some suggest that the simple market-model, beta, approach is robust because the market and stock betas capture about 30 percent of return variation for most stocks. Other systematic factors account for only an additional 5-8 percent, as shown by Sharpe [1982].

8. Others, including Chan [1987], have discussed how beta should be updated if the test period is a long one.

CHAPTER 2   APPENDIX

References

Brown, Stephen, and Warner, J. "Measuring Security Price Performance." *Journal of Financial Economics,* June 1980, pp. 205-58.

————. "Using Daily Stock Returns: The Case of Event Studies." *Journal of Financial Economics,* March 1985, pp. 3-31.

Chen, K. C. "On the Contrarian Investment Strategy" *Journal of Business,* April 1988, pp. 147-163.

Dimson, E. "Risk Measurement When Shares Are Subject to Infrequent Trading." *Journal of Financial Economics,* June 1979, pp. 197-226.

Klein, April, and Rosenfeld, James. "The Influence of Market Conditions on Event-Study Residuals." *Journal of Financial and Quantatitive Analysis,* September 1987, pp. 345-51.

Malatesta, Paul H. "Measuring Abnormal Performance: The Event Parameter Approach Using Joint Generalized Least Squares." *Journal of Financial and Quantative Analysis,* 1986, pp. 27-38.

Scholes, Myron, and Williams, J. "Estimating Betas from Nonsynchronous Data." *Journal of Financial Economics,* December 1977, pp. 309-327.

Sharpe, W. F. "Factors in New York Stock Exchange Security Returns, 1931-1979." *Journal of Portfolio Management,* Summer 1982, pp. 5-19.

CHAPTER 3

Technical Analysis

The previous chapter discussed stock market cycles of various lengths and how knowledge of them might be used to make a profit. These cycles seem to be driven by basic economic factors—the money supply, inflation, taxes, seasonal information, and industrial capacity. Understanding where we are in such cycles can help an analyst to understand the direction the market may take. As a science, however, cycle analysis is quite inexact: cycles overlap each other, and lengths of the cycles vary.

Information about cycles is only one kind of data a profit-seeking investor might use. Another kind of information comes from the market itself. Analysis of market information is called technical analysis: mechanical rules are used to look for recurring patterns in such things as trading volume, price movements, short interest (those investors selling stocks short), and odd-lot trading. From these patterns (the results of opinions and actions of those in the market), technicians hope to determine the beginnings of a change in prices and to profit from it. Technical analysis is used for the market as a whole, for groups of stocks, or for individual common stocks.

The efficient-market theory had a major impact on technical analysis. Before the advent of efficient-market theory, most stock market analysts and investors were divided into two groups—fundamental or technical analysts. Fundamental analysts look to basic economic factors to estimate the intrinsic value (the expected risk and return) of any given security. Technical analysts, on the other hand, believe that all the market's opinion is summed up in the behavior of investors. This behavior is reflected in the prices and the enthusiasm with which the stocks are bought (volume). Technical analysts hope to improve their investment returns by trading on what they believe is investors' lack of historical perspective: they believe investors overbuy, oversell, and repeat their past mistakes.[1]

While efficient-market theory dampened enthusiasm for technical analysis for some time,[2] technicians and technical analysis have recently been rediscovered. In fact, Bernstein [1978] suggested,

Today's technical analyst is as much a social philosopher and observer of world events as his fundamentalist colleague. The distinguishing feature . . . continues to be his belief that the market tells its own story. . . . The Chartist sought to define price trends, which were assumed to be intact until evidence of a change in trend emerged; today's technical analyst is more of a contrary thinker who goes behind the price trends and seeks to define investor sentiment. (p. 2)

Technicians hope to profit from detecting changes in supply-demand relationships in the market,[3] for whatever rational or irrational reasons, long before fundamental analysts can detect that change in fundamental economic or corporate data. Remember, for "profit from," we have a very specific meaning. We do not mean simply that the active strategy should make a positive return; profit is a return in excess of that which would have been obtained by a simple investment process over the same time period. That simpler process might be one where a portfolio of stocks is bought and held, sometimes called a passive portfolio strategy, or it might be another active stock-selection strategy adjusted for risk, brokerage commissions, and/or taxes. Let's see if the use of technical trading rules can result in such a profit.

Technical Indicators

Simple Filter Rules

> **Filter Rules**—A *filter rule* seperates stocks that have behaved in a particular way or have a particular characteristic(s) from other stocks. A frequently used rule depends on stock price movements: suppose you decided to buy stocks when prices rise 5 percent from the previous low and sell when prices decline by the same amount from the previous high. This simple filter rule would be called a "5 percent filter." Other filters could be designed to test for a price deviation from a long-term average price or to choose stocks from companies with particular characteristics.

One of the simplest forms of technical analysis is buying or selling on the basis of pre-set changes in a stock's price. To do this, an investor sets a rule for buy and sell signals called a **filter** and hopes that prices follow particular patterns over time (are serially dependent). Filters dictate that the investor buy a stock if the daily price of the security rises more than a given percentage and hold it until the price moves down a particular percentage from a subsequent high, at which time, the investor should sell the stock and assume a short position, i.e. sell short. This short position is held until the price rises again. Price movements smaller than the target percentages are ignored. For this rule to work, a trend must develop and persist while economic news is slowly assimilated by investors.

Over 20 years ago, Alexander [1961] tested simple filter rules. While Alexander did not include brokers' commissions or test the value of his strategy against a buy-and-hold portfolio, he did find several interesting results. One was that his rule brought about substantial profits. The profits came from making theoretical trades at the time of the signal, however, and critics questioned whether actual trades could take place at his exact triggering points. In later research, Alexander [1964] corrected for the impact of price discontinuities and found that profits persisted. Still, he had not compensated for commissions and dividend payments.

Fama and Blume [1966] studied the Dow Jones Industrial Average (DJIA) stocks from 1957-62 using 24 filters ranging in size from 0.5 percent to 50 percent. Without commissions and dividends, the rate of return for the period was calculated and generalized to the overall rate of return for all transactions.[4] You can see their results with and without commissions in Exhibit 3-1. Long positions, owning the stock, seemed to provide profits; **short positions** did not, which confirmed Alexander's earlier findings. However, and far more importantly, after the data were adjusted for both commissions and dividends, both long- and short-position returns suffered: the adjustment for dividends increased the passive buy-and-hold portfolio returns and lowered the filter-strategy returns.

Although Alexander's failure to adjust for dividends was a serious one, Fama and Blume's work continued to find serial dependence in price changes (persistent trends)—but the dependencies were too small to exploit after the costs of executing the strategy were appropriately assessed.

> **Short Position-Short Sale**—There are two ways to make money, buy low and sell high, or sell high and buy low. A short sale is the latter. Suppose you forecast that a stock's price will drop. If you do not own any of it, you can profit from your forecast by borrowing some shares, selling them, and buying them back later at the lower price. Your broker helps you by borrowing stock from an investor who owns the stock and giving them your IOU. The borrowed stock is sold, and you are given the proceeds. Later, when you sell the stock, the transaction is reversed. In the meantime, you must pay any dividends declared by the company plus a fee for borrrowing the stock. Short sales yield profit only when your market forecast is realized. If the market for the shorted stock rises instead of falling, the cost of replacing the shares is greater than the proceeds from the sale. That results in a loss.

Moving Averages

Simple filter rules are not the only possible ways to find exploitable serial dependencies in prices. Moving averages are widely believed to be useful in sorting out random fluctuations in market prices, thus capturing changes in trends. A 200-day moving average is simply the sum of each of the last 200 prices, weighted equally. Generally, buying (and selling) rules are built on a stock's or the market's price movement exceeding (falling below) the moving

Exhibit 3-1
Nominal Annual Rates of Returns by Filter
Averaged over All Companies

| Filter | Average Return per Security | | Breakdown of Average Return per Security before Commissions | | No. of Profitable Securities per Filter | Total Transactions |
	Before Commissions (1)	After Commissions (2)	Long (3)	Short (4)	(5)	(6)
0.005	.1152	−1.0359	.2089	.0097	27/30	12,514
.010	.0547	−.7494	.1111	−.0518	20/30	8,660
.015	.0277	−.5614	.1143	−.0813	17/30	6,270
.020	.0023	−.4515	.0872	−.1131	16/30	4,784
.025	−.0156	−.3732	.0702	−.1378	13/30	3,750
.030	−.0169	−.3049	.0683	−.1413	14/30	2,994
.035	−.0081	−.2438	.0734	−.1317	13/30	2,438
.040	.0008	−.1950	.0779	−.1330	14/30	2,013
.045	−.0117	−.1813	.0635	−.1484	14/30	1,720
.050	−.0188	−.1662	.0567	−.1600	13/30	1,484
.060	.0128	−.0939	.0800	−.1189	18/30	1,071
.070	.0083	−.0744	.0706	−.1338	16/30	828
.080	.0167	−.0495	.0758	−.1267	15/30	653
.090	.0193	−.0358	.0765	−.1155	17/30	539
.100	.0298	−.0143	.0818	−.1002	19/30	435
.120	.0528	.0231	.0958	−.0881	21/30	289
.140	.0391	.0142	.0853	−.1108	19/30	224
.160	.0421	.0230	.0835	−.1709	17/30	172
.180	.0360	.0196	.0725	−.1620	17/30	139
.200	.0428	.0298	.0718	−.1583	20/30	110
.250	.0269	.0171	.0609	−.1955	15/29	73
.300	−.0054	−.0142	.0182	−.2264	12/26	51
.400	−.0273	−.0347	−.0095	−.0965	7/16	21
0.500	−.2142	−.2295	−.0466	−.1676	0/4	4

Source: Fama and Blume [1966], p. 237.

average by a particular percentage. The percentage is often 5 percent, and the average is often calculated using 200 days of data.

A number of studies have been done on moving average strategies. Cootner [1962] used weekly observations for a sample of 45 stocks for the 5 years from 1956 to 1960 and found that using the moving-average rule produced lower returns for the whole period than a buy-and-hold strategy. His data seem to support the notion, however, that superior returns result from acting on buy signals (upward market movements); off-setting losses occur when the investor sells short to avoid the downward movements. Perhaps if the investor adopted a passive investment strategy, but one that produced a positive return, during the idle periods between signals (for instance, investing in U.S. Treasury securities), the moving-average strategy would show positive weekly returns and positive returns for the whole period.

Procedures more sophisticated than simple moving averages have also been tested. James [1968], using monthly data from 1926 to 1960 for 233 stocks, tried **exponential smoothing** to isolate changes in market direction. He assumed that an investor had $100 to invest in each security and bought or sold as the price rose by target amounts above or fell below the exponentially smoothed average. Even though he used several rules and smoothing coefficients, none of them were more successful than the buy-and-hold alternative when the returns were adjusted for dividend payments.[5]

> **Exponential Smoothing**—This technique gives heavier weight to more recent observations. The more recent observations are weighted according to a smoothing coefficient, usually called an alpha.

These simple averaging techniques are only a small part of the tools at the technician's command. Most other tools use more complex rules, or relationships between two or more historical series.

Advance/Decline Line The advance/decline line measures the number of advancing issues relative to those that decline in price in the market. As can be seen in Exhibit 3-2, the change in the advance/decline line may precede major market moves. To test the effectiveness of using the advance/decline line for **forecasting short-term change,** Zakon and Pennypacker [1968] regressed daily price data from September 1966 to October 1967, and monthly data from April 1962 to October 26, 1967, against the Standard & Poor's (S&P) 500 Index. They allowed the advance/decline line to have leads and lags of 15 time periods, and they found some correlation. In testing to see if the changes in one series forecast the changes in the other, however, they found no significant correlation. Testing peak-and-trough data alone indicated a coincident relationship at best. Zakon and Pennypacker's research points out how careful one must be in forecasting changes.

> **Forecasting Change**—Care must be taken in considering the relationship between two series of data. Consider the following two series:
> $Y = 1,5,10,15,10,5,15,20,25,30,20,40$ and $X = 1,2,3,4,5,6,7,8,9,10,11,12$. Obviously, the second series does not forecast the first series, yet the two series have a correlation of 88 percent. The reason is that both series are generally rising. To test forecasting ability, changes should be used. For the example, the first differences (the differences between each succeeding pair of numbers) for all the Xs are
> *(continued on next page)*

Relative Strength

Relative strength focuses on the ratio of stock price to the price of an index.

(continued from previous page)
one; there is no variation. This is not true with the Y series. First differences do vary. Thus, although the correlation between the two sets of raw data is 88 percent, there is no relationship when their first differences are considered.

The object is to determine whether a stock or group of stocks is outperforming the general average.

Levy [1967] used the following procedures on weekly closing prices for 200 New York Stock Exchange (NYSE) stocks from October 25, 1960, through October 15, 1965:

1. Calculate the ratio of current price to the average price (the relative strength) for the current and previous 26 weeks.

2. Rank all securities based on their relative strength.

3. Invest equal dollar amounts in the securities having the highest relative-strength ratios.

4. Sell all securities with relative-strength ratios below the cast-out rank and reinvest all proceeds in the highest relative-strength securities.

Exhibit 3-3 shows Levy's results for a range of cast-out ranks. What he found was that the returns from using this strategy were higher than those from the passive portfolio, but so were the risks. To reduce the risk, Levy devised his so-called variable-ratio plan. He summed the moving averages of the prices of the stocks for each of 234 weeks. These weekly moving averages were ranked by relative strength (i.e., the strongest to the weakest of the 234 weeks), and rankings were used to determine the proportion of common stock to be held in the portfolio, with a minimum of 50 percent. The remainder of the portfolio was invested in U.S. Treasury bills. Using this approach, Levy guaranteed the selection of the best market periods: his data were based on prior knowledge. Exhibit 3-4 shows that this prior-knowledge approach outperformed the buy-and-hold strategy, with lower risk.

Obviously, efficient-market theorists found flaws in Levy's work. Among others, Jensen [1967] found four faults, three of which are worth noting here:

1. *The use of the geometric average (the arithmetic average of geometric rates of return) to represent the return from the random selection policy.* Jensen showed that this calculation assumed a constant-dollar investment in each of the stocks at each point in time, thus forcing proceeds from better performing stocks to be invested in poorer performing stocks. The result was to bias the results of the passive portfolio downward. However, even after recalculating the buy-and-hold returns, the relative-strength strategy performed better.

2. *The definition of portfolio risk.* Levy's use of the variable-ratio plan was also criticized by Jensen. While admitting that the effect of such a procedure was unclear, Jensen suggested an adjustment: that the risks of the relative-strength and buy-and-hold strategies be equalized. After the results were adjusted, the relative-strength strategy still outperformed the passive alternative.

Exhibit 3-2

DJIA versus Advance/Decline Line, May 12, 1930–July 31, 1987

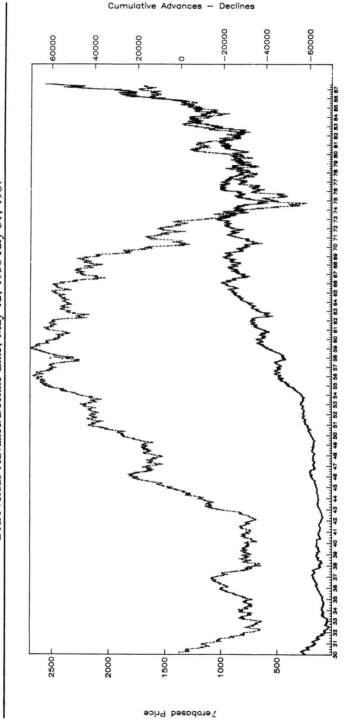

Cumulative Advances − Declines

Zerobased Price

——— DJIA
- - - - Cumulative Advance/Decline Line

Source: **Birinyi and Miller [1987], pp. 8–9.**

Exhibit 3-3

Net Returns Earned by Levy's Relative-Strength Portfolio Policies/Various Cost-Out Ranks

	020	050	100	150	160	180	195	Geometric Average	Buy and Hold
10% Relative Strength —Model A									
Net annual return (%)	-3.2	11.1	16.3	19.1	20.0	17.8	13.2	10.6	13.4
Arithmetic average 4-week returns (%)	-0.19	0.86	1.22	1.41	NA	1.35	1.05	0.83	1.02
Standard deviation of 4-week returns (%)	4.87	4.90	4.39	4.41	4.60	4.55	4.61	3.52	3.5
Number of securities in ending portfolio	NA	NA	NA	NA	72	NA	NA	200	200
Percent of ending portfolio in 5 largest holdings (%)	NA	NA	NA	NA	33	NA	NA	2.5	NA

Other Models	Model B[a]	Model C[b]
Net annual return (%)	26.1	29.1
Standard deviation of 4-week returns (%)	5.40	5.95
Number of securities in ending portfolio	45	3063
Percent of ending portfolio in 5 largest holdings (%)	52	

[a] Model B—"Cast-out rank" = 140, "5 percent relative strength" criteria. That is, the initial portfolio consists of an equal investment in the 5 percent of the securities having the currently highest C/A26 ratios, and all proceeds from sales are reinvested equally in the 5 percent of the securities having the currently highest C/A 26 ratios.

[b] Model C—same as Model B except that to be eligible for selection those securities fulfilling the "5 percent relative strength" criterion must also rank among the 25 securities with the highest coefficient of variation in weekly closing prices over the immediately preceding 6 months.

Source: Jensen [1967], p. 79.

Exhibit 3-4
Results of Selected Portfolio-Upgrading Variable-Ratio Models Compared with the Results of Random Selection

	Model A Results		Model B Results		Model C Results		Geometric Average
	Gross	Net	Gross	Net	Gross	Net	
Annual return (%)	18.3	15.4	23.5	19.9	27.1	23.1	10.6
Standard deviation of 4-week returns (%)	2.79	2.77	3.33	3.33	3.88	3.88	3.52
Modified quadratic mean of 4-week returns (%)	1.4	—	1.6	—	1.7	—	2.4
Extent of 1962 decline (%)	13	—	13	—	13	—	26
No. of weeks of 1962 decline	12	—	12	—	8	—	36
No. of stocks in ending portfolio	38	—	25	—	14	—	200
% of ending stock portfolio value in 5 largest holdings	41	—	40	—	85	—	2

Model A—Cast-out rank 160; 10% relative strength selection.
Model B—Cast-out rank 140; 5% relative strength selection.
Model C—Cast-out rank 140; 5% relative strength selection; 000-024 volatility rank selection.

Source: Levy [1967], p. 76.

Univariate Time-Series Models for Forecasting Stock Prices—In using a univariate (single variable) time-series model, we often assume that future values of a variable are related only to its own past values. For example, suppose today's stock price (P_t) can be forecasted as 90 percent of yesterday's price plus 0.001 percent plus some daily random error (e_i). The formula for the univariate regression representing this relationship would be

$$P_t = .001 + .90P_{t-1} + e_i$$

We might also specify that the error has a memory. For instance, if 40 percent of it relates to the previous day's error, the formula would be

$$P_t = .001 + .90P_{t-1} + .40e_{t-1} + e_i$$

Such time-series processes can be modeled as an ARIMA (Autoregressive Integrated Moving-Average Model) process. ARIMA models provide major benefits over other models. These models deal with such correlated data better than others: although prices in purely efficient markets are not autocorrelated as are actual stock prices.

3. Finally, Jensen noted *several selection biases*. First, because Levy tried 68 variations of 13 major strategies, Jensen suggested that he was bound to find one that fit the data. To correct for this problem, Jensen suggested that half the sample be used to develop the trading rule, the other being used to test the developed rule. Second, Jensen noted that the model's success depended heavily on the 5 largest portfolio holdings (between 33 and 63 percent of the ending portfolio holdings were similar in most of the portfolios).

In spite of the criticisms, Levy's relative-strength rule successfully found nonrandom, exploitable movements in stock prices during the five years he tested. In a later test, Jensen and Bennington [1970] found that the strategy's success was related to the post-World War II period and thus might not prevail during other time periods. Indeed, the more computerized the data and models, the more unlikely that such systems would endure.

Recently Brush [1986] tested the profitability of a number of relative-strength strategies, from simple percentage change to beta-adjusted and an exponentially weighted **generalized least squares** model (called Model E).[6]

Generalized Least Squares (GLS)—A form of time series regression. To test the results of the simple linear (market model), as well as other forms of regression, we assume the errors, or residuals (e_i), are created by a Gaussian (normal) process. Two situations would violate this assumption: first, there are more extremely large or extremely small errors than would be generated from data that conforms to a normal probability distribution; second, successive errors are not independent. If the normally-distributed-errors assumption is violated, GLS can help solve this problem. GLS can be thought of as a weighting process. For exam-

His test was designed to avoid the end-of-the-year reversal effect: that relative-strength models fail in November and December. To adjust for this, he assumed that the annual return would be represented adequately by the returns for a year that excluded January, November, and December. The results for two of his models are shown in Exhibit 3-5. Clearly, ranking by relative strength provided profitable information. Computerization and readily

ple, if some observations have very large errors, these observations can be reweighted to the point where the remaining rescaled errors do not violate the normalcy assumption. Rescaling helps to eliminate extreme effects. Similar adjustments can be made to eliminate the impact of dependencies within error terms.

accessible data did not seem to eliminate potential profits as predicted.

Brush believed that the top and bottom of the relative-strength-ranked stocks showed exploitable momentum that the average stocks did not. He contended that his positive results were different from what others had found and may find because of the way he dealt with the end-of-the-year effect. On the basis of his results, he concluded, regardless of the model used, "Avoid use of price momentum at the end of the year" (p. 24).

Exhibit 3-5
Models E and 6 Rebalanced Every Six Months;
Excess Annualized Compound Returns over Equal-Weighted
Universe

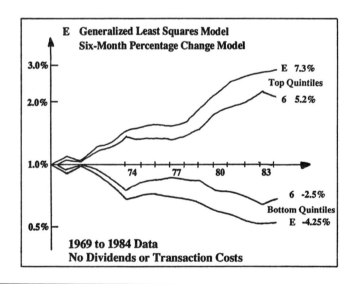

Source: Brush [1986], p. 24.

Two parts of Brush's results are particularly interesting. He found that the less sophisticated the model and the shorter the rebalancing period, the higher the turnover. For instance, the turnover for the simplest model rebalanced monthly was 81 percent, compared with turnover of 23 percent for the most sophisticated model. As the horizon lengthened, both turnover ratios and rates of return converged, as shown in Exhibit 3-6.

Exhibit 3-6
Excess Returns over Equal-Weighted S&P 500 of Shorting Bottom Quintiles
as Identified Using Six Different Models; Four Rebalancing Strategies,
1% Round-Trip Transaction Costs, No Dividends

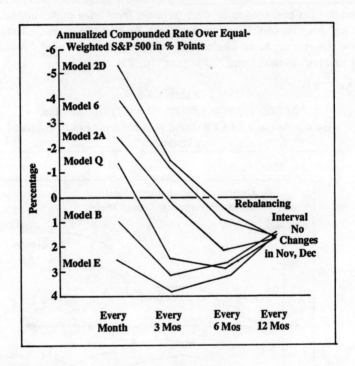

Source: Brush [1986], p. 27.

Thus Brush concluded that, if a relative-strength model is to be used, in addition
to ignoring the end of the year, the investor should use a longer term moving
average (6 months to 200 days) and incorporate the use of the capital asset
pricing model (CAPM). Also, the observations should be weighted in such a
way that more recent prices received higher weights.[7]

Price-Volume Relationships

Another simple technical indicator, and in light of October 19, 1987, perhaps
the most interesting, uses trading volume to look for turning points in the

market as a whole. Together with information about the general movement of prices (for instance, the DJIA), the degree of participation by the whole market can be examined. A price change supported by a change in volume is assumed to signal increased investor interest. A rise in both prices and volume would be expected to continue, but if prices were rising and volume declining, prices might be expected to fall subsequently.

Early studies of volume found interesting patterns, but the results lacked statistical and economic significance. Osborne [1962] noticed that trading volume came in bursts of interest and was not normally, but log-normally, distributed. He suggested that people had herdlike tendencies: once there was some interest in the market, others tended to become interested. He also uncovered a weekly pattern of relatively high volume during the opening and closing hours of trading, a weekly pattern in odd-lot trading, and a seasonal pattern. However, in a study relating volume movements to price changes using spectral analysis, Granger and Morgenstern [1963] found no statistically significant relationship between them.

In a more detailed study of daily price and volume movements for S&P Composite Index stocks, Ying [1966] found evidence confirming the technicians' beliefs. He classified each stock's daily price and volume into one of five categories, based on its mean price and variability, from January 1957 to December 1962 and constructed a **contingency table** showing the number of observations in each class of volume and price changes. From his research, Ying concluded that low volume was usually accompanied by a decline or small change in price, large volume by a rise in price, and large volume increases by a large price change. His results are shown in Exhibit 3-7.

> **Contingency Table**—A *contingency table* displays how often values of two events occur simultaneously. From this table, statistical tests can be performed to determine whether the two events are independent. The most common test is a .chi square (X^2) test, where the actual number in each cell is compared with the expected number based on the marginal probabilities.

Ying also tested the impact of one day's price and volume movements on the next day's price change. He used a three-way classification, **analysis of variance** (instead of the five-class scheme he previously used), to examine the individual effects of each variable on the subsequent price change, and assessed the interaction between the variables and their subsequent movements. He found that one day's change in price (P_t) and volume (V_t) had a significant effect on the next day's price change, but not on volume. Only the interaction of price and volume change was significantly related to subsequent volume at the 1 percent level.

> **Analysis of Variance**—Analysis of variance is used to determine whether, given the magnitude of the residual variation, the variation between parts of a contingency table are so large that a significant relationship should be assumed to be the underlying cause of the variation.

Exhibit 3-7

Contingency Table for Volume (V_t) and Price (P_t) Change

	Class	1	2	3	4	5
				$D \log (P(t))$		
	1	46	80	105	53	25
	2	70	81	90	62	42
$\log V(t)$	3	46	47	76	66	44
	4	36	40	58	65	57
	5	34	46	80	82	69

Source: Ying [1966], p. 679.

How do these positive results fit with the Granger-Morgenstern findings of no significant relationship between volume and price changes? Ying wanted to know too. Because Granger and Morgenstern had used spectral analysis, Ying tested his data using the same technique. He found a strong lead-lag relationship—volume leading price by about four days. However, it was not as strong as he had found before and could not be profitably exploited. From this research, he concluded:

1. A small volume is usually accompanied by a fall in price.

2. A large volume is usually accompanied by a rise in price.

3. A large increase in volume is usually accompanied by either a large rise in price or a large fall in price.

4. If the volume has been decreasing consecutively for a period of five trading days, there will be a tendency for the price to fall over the next four trading days.

5. If the volume has been increasing consecutively for a period of five trading days, there will be a tendency for the price to rise over the next four trading days.

This is not strong evidence on which to build a profit-seeking strategy.

Renewed interest in the relationship between price and volume was spurred by a theoretical paper by Epps [1975]. He examined the Wall Street folklore that volume appears low in bear and high in bull markets. Ying had found large increases in volume related to large price changes and also that price increases (decreases) generally occurred when there were large (small) volumes. Epps developed a theory[8] that "the ratio of volume to price change for upticks exceeds the absolute value of this ratio to downticks" (p. 586). Epps [1977] found support for the hypothesis in the bond market but not in the stock market.

Smirlock and Starks [1985] improved on Epps' test.[9] Epps had assumed that price and volume changes were responses to the arrival of new information, but he did not explicitly designate when information was received. Smirlock and Starks separated the days into those when earnings were announced and those when no earnings announcements were made. They found support for Epps' theory: on upticks, volume was higher when there was new information. However, they found "little support, and some contrary evidence, for the theory when it is applied to trading days for which there is no known information arrival in the market" (p. 224). Thus information affects price and volume, but not quite in the way Epps hypothesized.

One final piece of research provides some interesting insights into the price-volume relationship. Rogalski [1978] found that "security prices and volume are dependent . . . and knowledge of volume may marginally improve conditional price forecasts over price forecasts based on past prices alone" (p. 273). However, he found that the correlations could be the result of volume causing price changes, price changes causing volume, or a feedback relationship between price change and volume.

The studies cited in this section on price and volume are only a few from many that are available.[10] Exhibit 3-8 summarizes the research into the correlation of price changes and trading volume. As you can see, the results are mixed. More important than the actual results may be the various, and sometimes conflicting, conclusions that came about as a result of the research:

1. Trading volume may be abnormally high when there is serial correlation in the returns' absolute values.

2. The size of the price change may be related to the length of the time between transactions.

3. Price variability declines as the number of traders and volume of trades increase.

4. No relationship exists between price and volume.

Dow Theory

In the last chapter, we discussed Dow Theory, a price-volume technique. Because much of modern technical analysis is based on early work by Charles Dow, the theory bears mention here. Recall that Dow believed a skilled analyst could sort out the three simultaneous stock market movements—daily, monthly, and four-year movements or cycles. In principle, Dow believed that upward movements in the market were tempered by fallbacks that lost a portion of the

Exhibit 3-8

Summary of Empirical Studies from Which Inferences Can Be Made About the Correlation of the Absolute Value of a Price Change with Trading Volume[a]

Author(s)	Year of Study	Sample Data	Sample Period	Differencing Interval	Support Positive Price-Volume
Godfrey, Granger, and Morgenstein	1964	Stock market aggregates and 3 common stocks	1959-62, 1951-53,1963	Weekly, daily, transactions	No
Ying	1966	Stock market aggregates	1957-62	Daily	Yes
Crouch	1970	5 common stocks	1963-67	Daily	Yes
Crouch	1970	Stock market aggregates and 3 common stocks	1966-68	Hourly, daily	Yes
Epps and Epps	1976	20 common stocks	Jan. 1971	Transactions	Yes
Morgan	1976	17 common stocks and 44 common stocks	1962-65, 1926-68	4 days monthly	Yes
Westerfield	1977	315 common stocks	1968-69	Daily	Yes
Harris	1983	16 common stocks	1968-69	Daily	Yes
Comiskey, Walking, and Weeks	1984	211 common stocks	1976-79	Yearly	Yes
Harris	1984	50 common stocks	1981-83	Transactions, daily	Yes
Wood, McInish, and Ord	1985	946 common stocks and 1,138 common stocks	1971-72, 1982	Minutes	Yes
Harris	1986	479 common stocks	1976-77	Daily	Yes

Study	Year	Data	Period	Frequency	Correlation
Jain and Joh	1986	Stock market aggregates	1979-83	Hourly	Yes
Richardson, Setcik, and Thompson	1987	106 common stocks	1973-82	Weekly	Yes
Granger and Morgenstern	1963	Stock market aggregates and 2 common stocks	1939-61	Weekly	No
Epps	1977	20 common stocks	Jan. 1971	Transactions	Yes[c]
Rogalski	1978	10 common stocks and 10 associated warrants	1968-73	Monthly	Yes
James and Edmister	1983	500 common stocks	1975, 1977-79	Daily[b]	No
Smirlock and Starks	1985	131 common stocks	1981	Transactions	Yes[d]

[a]This table summarizes the general conclusions of these studies about the correlation of price and volume. Results that indicate no significant correlation are listed as not supporting a positive correlation. These studies use various measures of the price change and trading volume. For more precise descriptions of the data and variable transformations, the reader is referred to the original papers.
[b]Stocks are grouped into deciles ranked by average daily volume. Decile ranking is compared with mean daily return.
[c]Support for a positive correlation between price and volume at the transaction level depends on the treatment of volume over transactions with no price changes.
[d]The data are consistent with a positive correlation between price and volume on days in which there is known information arrival. On other days, the correlation is insignificant or negative.

Source: Adapted from Karpoff [1987], pp. 113 and 118.

previous gain. A market turn came when the upward movement that followed did not exceed the last gain. In other words, the market discounts everything that is known, and it moves in trends over time.

However interesting Dow Theory may be, can money be made with it? One answer came from a study by Glickstein and Wubbels [1983]. They found that using Dow Theory from January 2, 1971, to December 31, 1980, an investor would have earned an average additional return 13 percent over a passive strategy's return. The relationship between their confirmation (a point at which the Dow Industrials and Transportation both exceed a previous high) and a continued trend in the DJIA was positive and significant. Thus although opponents to the theory suggest that its confirmations require subjective judgments, the Dow Theory continues to be used in the search for profits.

Multi-Rule System

Pruitt and White [1988] described a model they call the CRISMA (cumulative volume, relative strength, moving average) Trading System. This model is a multifilter model using, not one, but three of the technical trading rules we have discussed. Using moving averages and filters, it builds on most of the foregoing research on price, volume, and relative strength to create a system to select individual common stocks.[11]

To test the strength of this model, the authors used a variety of ways to estimate the return. Trades were executed at the next available closing price following the buy signal. Testing the CRISMA system over the period from 1976 to 1985, they found that the worst the system performed was 118 profitable trades out of 204 signaled.[12] Exhibit 3-9 shows their results.

Pruitt and White concluded that their CRISMA system can "beat the market" and do so significantly, even when adjusted for transaction costs, trade timing, and risk. Their results are, of course, likely to come under some scrutiny and further testing. However, there appears to be ample evidence to suggest that some or all of the technical trading systems that we have discussed should be considered, and considered carefully, before they are discarded.

Exhibit 3-9

Parametric and Nonparametric Tests of the CRISMA Trading Rule, 1976-85

Panel A: Weighted Mean Daily Excess Returns from Trade Obtained from the CRISMA Trading Rule

Percent Transaction Costs	Market-Adjusted V.W.I.	Market-Adjusted E.W.I.	S-W Market Model V.W.I.	S-W Market Model E.W.I.	Market Model V.W.I.	Market Model E.W.I.	Mean Adjusted
0	0.1344	0.1066	0.1071	0.1084	0.1283	0.1309	0.1426
	(5.79)	(4.35)	(4.42)	(4.41)	(4.98)	(4.89)	(5.39)
0.5	0.1139	0.0861	0.0866	0.0882	0.1078	0.1104	0.1221
	(4.90)	(3.50)	(3.58)	(3.57)	(4.61)	(4.11)	(4.62)
1.0	0.0934	0.0656	0.0661	0.0679	0.0873	0.0899	0.1016
	(4.01)	(2.64)	(2.73)	(2.74)	(3.38)	(3.34)	(3.84)
2.0	0.0523	0.0245	0.0250	0.0273	0.0462	0.0488	0.0605
	(2.23)	(0.94)	(1.03)	(1.07)	(1.77)	(1.78)	(2.28)

Return on V.W.I.: 0.0603   Return on E.W.I.: 0.1032   Total Security-Days: 4970

Panel B: Number of Profitable Trades Obtained from the CRISMA Trading Rule: 1976-85

Percent Transaction Costs	Market-Adjusted V.W.I.	Market-Adjusted E.W.I.	S-W Market Model V.W.I.	S-W Market Model E.W.I.	Market Model V.W.I.	Market Model E.W.I.	Mean Adjusted
0	149	139	141	141	145	142	153
	(6.58)	(5.18)	(5.46)	(5.46)	(6.02)	(5.60)	(7.14)
0.5	145	136	133	132	139	134	150
	(6.02)	(4.76)	(4.34)	(4.20)	(5.18)	(4.48)	(6.72)
1.0	144	134	126	130	130	130	147
	(5.88)	(4.48)	(3.36)	(3.92)	(3.94)	(3.92)	(6.30)
2.0	134	127	121	118	124	125	145
	(4.48)	(3.50)	(2.66)	(2.24)	(3.08)	(3.22)	(6.02)

Total Number of CRISMA Trades: 204

V.W. I. = value-weighted index.
E.W. I. = equal-weighted index.

S–W Market Model = A version of the market model by Scholes-Williams [1977].
All these models are discussed in Brown and Warner [1985].

Source: Pruitt and White [1988], p. 57.

Other Technical Indicators

All the discussion so far in this chapter has related to price, volume, or price and volume trading strategies. Price and volume are not the only factors that technical analysts follow, however. Short interest, odd-lot trading, and insider-trading activities are among others that are used for developing trading strategies.

Short Interest

Short interest, the ratio of the number of shares sold short to average daily volume, is believed to be another signal worth acting on. One problem with the measure is in the interpretation of the signal that is given. Some believe that, when the number of shares sold short relative to volume is high, it is a bullish signal: the short sellers will have to cover their positions, which will result in price-supporting activity. Others, judging more intuitively, believe that it is a bearish signal: many in the market are negative about prospects, and the current price does not yet reflect their opinion. Exhibit 3-10 shows that the relationship between short interest and overall market prices is, at the very least, complex.

The results of early tests of strategies based on short interest were mixed. Biggs [1966], concentrating on long-run relationships, found no consistent relationship between short interest and stock prices. Seneca [1967], using regression analysis, found a negative relationship between short interest and trading volume and stock prices. Kerrigan [1974] found superior returns could be earned based on short-interest information, but the superior returns evaporated after transaction costs were charged.[13]

One early test is interesting because it illustrates the need for extreme care with statistical models. Mayor [1968, p. 85] formulated four possible relationships:

$$P_t = \alpha_1 + \beta_1 S_{t-.5} + e_{1t} \qquad (1)$$

where P_t is the price in time period t, $S_{t-.5}$ is the short interest lagged one-half month, and e_{1t} is a random error termed for time period t of equation (1);

$$P_t = \alpha_2 + \beta_2 S_{t-.5} + \gamma_{2t} + e_{2t} \qquad (2)$$

where γ_2 is a trend factor;

$$P_t d_t = \alpha_3 + \beta_3 (S_{t-.5}/d_{t-.5}) + \gamma_{3t} + e_{3t} \qquad (3)$$

Exhibit 3-10
Short Interest and Stock Prices

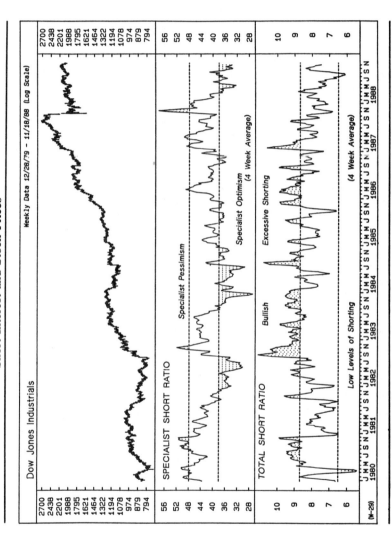

Source: Ned Davis Research, Atlanta, Georgia [1988].

where both price and short interest are adjusted for stock splits and dividends; and

$$P_t d_t = \alpha_4 + p_1 P_{t-1} d_{t-1} + p_2 P_{t-2} d_{t-2}$$

$$+ B_4 (S_{t-.5} d_{t-.5} - p_1 S_{t-1.5} d_{t-1.5} - p_2 S_{t-2.5} d_{t-2.5})$$

$$+ \gamma_4 [t - p_1 (t-1) - p_2 (t-1)] - e_t \tag{4}$$

where the error term in equation (3) is assumed to follow a second-order autoregressive scheme,

$$U_t = p_1 U_{t-1} + p_2 U_{t-2} + e_t$$

Thus equation (4) adjusts for the effect of high serial correlation in equation (3).

Using simple linear regression,[14] Mayor tested the explanatory power of these equations on 14 companies and the aggregate market (the S&P 500 and the NYSE total short interest). Exhibit 3-11 shows his results.

He found positive results when using the aggregate market data, and those results were little affected by the addition of dividends. However, the results disappeared (i.e., t-statistics on the coefficient dropped below significance) when a trend factor (Model 2) was added and when the data were corrected for serial correlation (Model 4).

The strongest evidence for short sales being informative is a study by Hanna [1976]. He used a monthly short-interest ratio (the ratio of monthly number of shares sold short divided by the average daily volume for the month). Hanna's strategy rests on the hypothesis that investors continually run to extremes of under- and overvaluation. To test this hypothesis, he calculated the number of stocks from his sample of 25 stocks from 1962 to 1972 that had rising or declining short-interest ratios, and examined the results for an unexpectedly large number of decliners or risers—unexpected in relation to what would otherwise be expected based on the **binomial probability distribution.** He found that the number was many more times than expected when a large majority of the stocks' short-interest ratios were rising or declining in unison.

From this analysis, Hanna developed a trading rule: If an unexpectedly large number of the 25 stocks' short-interest ratios are moving in either direction, buy or sell the S&P Index. With 25 stocks, and a 50-50 probability based on the binomial distribution, more than 20 ratios moving in a single direction would constitute a buy or sell

Binomial Probability Distribution—A binomial process assigns an event to two outcomes, which have probabilities of p and q. For example, tossing a coin is a binomial process, where the two outcomes are a head or a tail with p = 0.5 and q = 0.5. The binomial distribution function reports the probability that the number of times an event occurs (e.g., the number of heads) is less than a predetermined number, x, in a particular number of trials.

Exhibit 3-11
Regression Results, Models 1, 2, 3, and 4

Firm or Aggregate	Model I					Model II					
	α_1	β_1	T	$\bar{R}^2$	DW	α_2	β_2	T	γ_2	$\bar{R}^2$	DW
Aggregate	48.30	4.401	5.30	.36	.18	65.40	-1.903	-3.30	.89	.88	.50
Addressograph	53.85	-.238	-.30	.00	.28	62.68	-1.136	-1.42	-.29	.13	.88
American Motors	18.69	-.347	-8.31	.59	.47	18.48	-.379	-5.09	1.96	.58	.49
Chrysler	59.98	.006	.03	.00	.52	62.48	.226	.96	-.36	.04	.66
General Electric	93.68	-3.880	-2.32	.09	.13	63.26	-.403	-.52	.93	.82	.48
Litton Industries	108.90	-4.046	-4.12	.25	.22	105.50	-4.024	-4.07	.13	.24	.22
Minnesota Mining	65.38	-2.253	-3.80	.22	.69	65.77	-2.307	-3.38	.01	.21	.70
New York Central	12.83	10.362	12.74	.77	.74	4.02	2.238	1.69	1.03	.89	.43
Pan American Airlines	25.33	2.447	4.07	.25	.41	24.77	2.336	3.02	.04	.23	.40
Pfeizer	54.98	-3.279	-1.90	.05	.26	44.91	-1.763	-1.29	.34	.43	.35
Polaroid	191.12	-4.837	-7.36	.53	.66	199.79	-4.401	-6.40	-.55	.55	.70
Sears Roebuck	104.27	-4.131	-4.35	.28	.35	88.43	-9.446	-12.75	1.51	.78	1.69
Transitron	6.41	.266	1.49	.03	.25	7.88	.267	1.57	-.06	.16	.28
U.S. Steel	61.28	-3.838	-4.50	.29	.63	65.02	-4.258	-4.92	-.11	.32	.75
Zenith	86.94	-4.501	-2.14	.07	.21	47.95	.289	.17	.86	.51	.29

(continued on next page)

Exhibit 3–11 (continued)

Firm or Aggregate	Model III						Model IV					
	α_3	β_3	T	γ_3	$\bar{R}^2$	DW	α_4	β_4	T	γ_4	$\bar{R}^2$	DW
Aggregate	68.20	-1.640	-3.80	.81	.89	.53	11.09	-.264	-.53	.90	.54	1.99
Addressograph	62.68	-1.136	-1.42	-.29	.13	.38	6.32	1.010	1.81	.46	.07	2.08
American Motors	18.48	-.379	-5.09	1.96	.58	.49	3.81	-.094	-.98	-.16	.13	1.91
Chrysler	7.65	.038	.77	1.13	.85	.22	6.52	.042	.71	1.05	.09	1.96
General Electric	63.26	-.403	-.52	.93	.82	.48	10.23	.213	.24	1.24	.39	2.00
Litton Industries	20.71	.133	.81	.58	.63	.24	-.27	.245	1.48	1.25	.27	2.00
Minnesota Mining	65.79	-2.307	-3.38	.01	.21	.70	16.25	-.362	-.48	.20	.02	1.90
New York Central	4.02	2.238	1.69	1.03	.89	.43	-1.98	-1.042	-1.17	1.78	.62	2.02
Pan American Airlines	6.06	.332	2.41	.65	.79	.38	.24	-.044	-.31	.90	.25	2.07
Pfeizer	44.91	-1.763	-1.29	.34	.43	.35	3.35	-.820	-1.29	.80	.17	2.17
Polaroid	30.27	-.170	-1.41	.93	.48	.17	-4.67	.094	.79	3.76	.19	2.00
Sears Roebuck	35.35	-1.026	-3.15	.91	.92	.48	5.79	-.443	-1.49	.92	.53	1.96
Transitron	7.88	.267	1.57	-.06	.16	.28	-4.86	.141	1.21	.19	.09	2.11
U.S. Steel	65.02	-4.258	-4.92	-.11	.32	.75	12.68	-.008	-.01	-.20	.01	2.00
Zenith	23.97	.072	.17	.43	.51	.29	1.02	.194	.64	.87	.13	1.94

Note: DW is the Durbin Watson statistic, and T is the T-ratio for the β coefficients. For convenience the β coefficients are expressed in units of a million for the aggregate and ten thousand for firms.

Source: Mayor [1968], p. 289.

signal. The probability that this signal would occur by chance is 1 percent.

Hanna tested his strategy by investing a hypothetical $10,000 and comparing the results with the actual values for 200 simulated portfolios. The simulated portfolios bought or sold the S&P Index based on random chance. Exhibit 3-12 shows his results.

Exhibit 3-12

Value of Hanna's Simulated Short-Interest-Ratio (SR) Portfolio

Probability of Occurrences	Corresponding # of SRs	Terminal Value of Simulated Portfolio	Terminal Value of Actual Portfolio
.01	≥20	$ 9,899	$ 8,946
.02	≥19	10,134	17,099
.05	≥18	9,885	27,452
.11	≥17	9,127	29,726
.23	≥16	9,769	24,091

Source: Adapted from Hanna [1976], p. 862.

Except for the lowest probability of occurrence, the results were startling. However, Hanna ignored dividends, commissions, taxes, and relative riskiness. Using some rough adjustments for risk, Hanna's trading strategy actually appeared to have lower risk. After adjusting for dividends, taxes, and commissions, the traded portfolio still outperformed the passive alternative. At a probability of occurrence of 5 percent, the value of the passive portfolio would have been $19,652 and the value of the traded alternative $21,519.[15]

Recently, Vu [1987] has looked once again at the value of using short-interest information as a price predictor.[16] Vu tested whether there was a significant increase in a security's price the day following an announcement of a large increase in short interest. He used data from 1975 to 1983 for stocks whose short-interest figures were listed in the *Wall Street Journal* and event-study methodology (see the appendix to Chapter 2 for an explanation of this sort of analysis), with the short-interest announcement date as the event date. The data in Exhibit 3-13 show large changes in short interest have little impact on excess returns, but there is a significant increase in excess returns before the announcement. Vu thus concluded that short-interest signals were neither bullish nor bearish.

Exhibit 3-13
Excess Returns Around the Announcement Date of Large Increases in Short Interest*

Day	Excess Return	Cumulative Excess Return
-40	-0.014%	-0.014%
-30	0.377	1.348
-20	0.326	3.700
-15	0.151	4.646
-10	0.006	5.229
-5	-0.114	5.273
-4	0.117	5.155
-3	0.028	5.183
-2	0.087	5.270
-1	-0.110	5.160
0	-0.121	5.039
1	-0.234	4.803
2	-0.006	4.799
3	0.118	4.917
4	-0.181	4.736
5	-0.055	4.680
10	-0.155	4.701
15	-0.010	4.421
20	0.063	4.408
30	-0.014	4.196
40	-0.174	3.772

*Except for day -30 and day -10, none of the returns is statistically significant at the 5 percent level.

Source: Vu [1987], p. 78.

So, are trading strategies based on short-interest ratios profitable? Maybe. If you find Hanna's results compelling, consider several things before you risk your entire portfolio. First, Hanna used 25 stocks that were continuously listed on the NYSE. Because only the highest short interests were published, Hanna had to use 55 stocks to get his final sample of 25. Thus his sample has what is called a survivor bias: the stocks he could use were known only after the period was over. Second, given the small difference after commissions and taxes, and a high variability of the results when the test is done on different periods (even when extended only one year), the results may really be too close to call. An evaluation of the technique over longer and different periods would be interesting.

If, however, you find Vu's results more compelling than Hanna's, let's consider whether you should ignore short interest in the future. First of all, Vu's results indicate that you could make money if you could estimate large short-interest positions a month before the announcement (the earlier serial correlation and trend effects found by Mayor might help). Also, Vu suggested that short sales by themselves might not be the best way to look at the question. He suggested that the ratio of short interest to trading volume might be more useful. Others have used closely aligned ratios such as the Specialists' Short-Sales Ratio (SSSR).

Specialists' Short-Sales Ratio (SSSR)

The ratio of specialists' short sales to all short sales, published in *Barrons*, has intrigued several researchers. Those who use this ratio believe that specialists have information that others in the market do not. A decline in the proportion of short sales attributable to specialists is believed to precede a rise in stock prices. This ratio was shown graphically in Exhibit 3-10. The major study of the SSSR was by Bowlin and Rozeff [1987] who believed that earlier studies[17] had erred by using overlapping, nonindependent data. To correct for this, Bowlin and Rozeff divided all SSSRs into five groups and calculated the average monthly returns for each group over the following three months. Exhibit 3-14 shows that the higher the SSSR, the lower the actual return for that group in the following three months. The differences between the mean returns for the groups were significant. A strategy based on the SSSR appears to provide clues to potential profits.

Exhibit 3-14

Average Monthly Stock Returns on NYSE in Months Subsequent to Quintiles of the Specialists' Short-Sales Ratio, 1945-84.

	SSSR Quintile					
	Lowest	*2*	*3*	*4*	*Highest*	*All*
12/1945–12/1984						
Average return	0.0215	0.0150	0.0182	0.0021	0.0015	0.0112
Number of months	105	92	70	83	118	468
12/1945–1/1971						
Average return	0.0336	0.0146	0.0204	0.0039	0.0023	0.0106
Number of months	32	44	47	68	110	301
2/1971–12/1984						
Average return	0.0161	0.0154	0.0138	–0.0063	–0.0093	0.0124
Number of months	73	48	23	15	8	167

Source: Bowlin and Rozeff [1987], p. 61.

Using a different approach, Bowlin and Rozeff found that, when the monthly stock returns were regressed against the previous SSSRs, the results were significant, although small. On the basis of all their research, they concluded, "There is little doubt that SSR has predictive power. . . . We make no claim that the specialists' short sale ratio will continue to have predictive power, only that it surely has had such power in the past" (pp. 62, 64).

In addition to making no claims for the future of the SSSR ratio, Bowlin and Rozeff found that the proportion of specialists' short sales to all short sales had declined since 1971. Specialists may have been using other mechanisms to respond to their negative forecasts, such as options: the more sophisticated the investor, the earlier she or he may have recognized and used other markets and other strategies.

The notions of using short interest, the specialists' short interest, and investors' over-enthusiasm and -pessimism to profit are intriguing. Whether there will continue to be evidence supporting the usefulness of these approaches in predicting prices and whether they will be profitable in the future is the question that the investor must now ask.

Odd-Lot Trading

This approach is in the general category of following contrarian technical signals. Contrarian signals are those that go against the prevailing market trends. In general, those that follow odd-lot trading believe that, at market tops and bottoms, small investors are usually wrong. They use odd-lot trading, the purchases and sales of stock in less than round lots (usually 100 shares), as an indicator of small-investor behavior. Exhibit 3-15 graphically shows the relationship between odd-lot trading and major market turning points.

What about tests of the theory? Kewley and Stevenson [1967] calculated the ratio of odd-lot sales to purchases for 75 companies during the 82 weeks from March 1965 through September 1966. The ratios were correlated with prices during the same period, and no significant pattern emerged. Their work was criticized by Drew [1967], who pointed out that odd-lot behavior is a function of changes in odd-lot trends, not in the actual volume of buying and selling.

Incorporating Drew's suggestions, Kewley and Stevenson [1969] studied the odd-lot theory further. In this study, they used the percentage change in the moving average of the sales/purchase ratio to create buy and sell signals. The signals were based on large changes: a buy signal if there was a change of 50 percent over the 3-week average; a sell signal with a 40 percent downward change from the 4-week average; a buy or sell signal with a 20 percent change for the 12-week average. Based on this research, they concluded that the odd-lot theory generated bad buy signals but not bad sell signals. Once again, however,

Exhibit 3-15

Dow Jones Industrials Weekly Data, 12/30/77–11/11/88 (log scale)

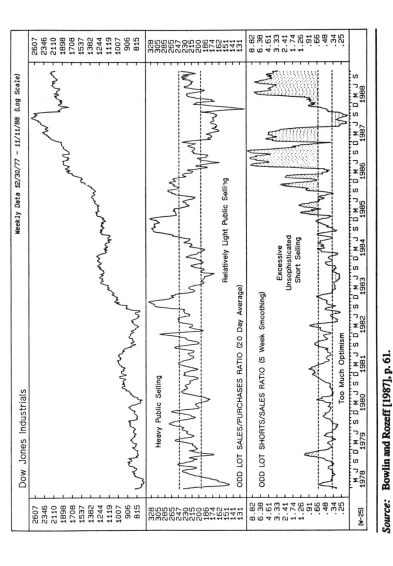

Source: Bowlin and Rozeff [1987], p. 61.

no adjustment was made for risk, and the study covered a short time period. Thus whether excess risk-adjusted returns can be made, and made over long periods of time, is not clear.[18]

Insider Trading

Insiders (corporate officers, directors, and holders of large amounts of a company's common stock) might well have information that predates full public knowledge.[19] Thus many believe that insider trading gives clues to future price behavior. This information has been a featured factor in technical indicators used by many investment analysts, including the one used on *Wall Street Week*, the investment analysis television program. Because the belief is that insiders possess potentially profitable information, and may act on it, the Securities and Exchange Commission (SEC) requires that all trades by insiders be reported, and it publishes the reports.[20] In considering inside information, two questions immediately come to mind: First, do the insiders possess profitable information? Second, if outsiders keep track of, and act on, insider-trading information, can they profit? Let's first consider whether we even want to track insider activity by seeing whether insiders do have special, profitable information.

A number of researchers have concluded that insiders do earn abnormal profits from their transactions.[21] The profits have been estimated at from 3 to 30 percent over periods of from 8 months to 3 years. For instance, Jaffe [1974] examined insider-trading activity and subsequent price changes for 200 companies from 1962 through 1968.[22] He used residual analysis and tested for abnormal returns 15 months before and after any insider trades. He found that insiders' abnormal profits approximated 2 percent for the 2 months after trades and 5 percent for the next 8 months. These were gross returns, however: transaction costs would have reduced or eliminated them. Finnerty's [1976] results, which generally supported those of Jaffe, indicated that insiders did especially well during the first month after a trade. Finnerty also found evidence that insiders tended to buy small companies with larger earnings and dividends than those sold.

Seyhun [1986] attempted to extend previous studies by using different versions of the CAPM, different periods for developing the CAPM parameters (e.g., the beta), and different ways to classify insiders. Exhibit 3-16 shows his results. These data suggest that insiders possess some forecasting ability.

The insider-trading profitability could come from other sources, however: Seyhun also found that small-firm insiders execute more purchases than sales; officers and directors execute most of the trades; officer-directors have the most profitable trades; most of the profits from insider trades go to insiders at small companies; and profits decrease from 7 percent to 1.2 percent over the first 100 days after the trade for companies of $25 million to $1 billion, respectively.[23] Once again we see a small-firm effect, improved on by insiders.

Exhibit 3-16
Excess Returns Around Insider Trading Dates

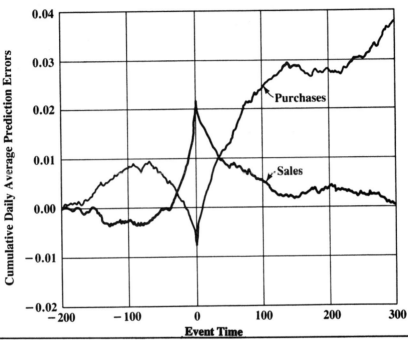

Source: Seyhun [1986], p. 197.

In a later study, Seyhun [1988A] concluded that "net aggregate insider trading in a given month is significantly and positively correlated with the return to the market portfolio during the subsequent 2 months . . . insiders respond to the effects of some economy-wide factors as though they were firm-specific factors by trading in the stock of their own firms" (p. 22).[24] He also reported [1988B] that insiders in small companies tend to buy more in December, apparently capturing the expected profits from the January effect.

Unfortunately, outsiders may not be able to find as much profit. Seyhun found no abnormal profit after transactions costs for outsiders (traders who buy after release of the SEC Insider Transaction Report). Rozeff and Zaman [1988] examined Seyhun's results, and the results of their own research, and concluded that "the anomalous profits to outsiders are a manifestation of the size and earnings/price ratio effects. Controlling for these factors reduces outsider profits by half" (p. 25). Insider trading information is not the source of these profits. Without the returns attributable to price/earnings and small-firm effects, and after taking into account transactions costs, the estimated outsider profits are eliminated.[25] Exhibit 3-17 makes this quite clear.

Exhibit 3-17

Mean Abnormal Returns per Month Earned in October
and Insider Samples, 1973-82

Holding Period in Months	Mean Market Model Excess Returns		Mean Market Model, A Size, and E/P Adjusted Excess Returns	
	No Transactions Costs	25% Transactions Costs*	No Transactions Costs	25% Transactions Costs
A. Outsider samples:				
1	.59	−1.41	−.18	−2.19
	(1.87)	(−4.36)	(1.29)	(−5.03)
3	.55	−.12	.37	−.30
	(2.70)	(−.54)	(2.05)	(−1.29)
6	.44	.10	.23	−.11
	(2.53)	(.50)	(1.94)	(−.23)
12	.47	.31	.19	.02
	(3.60)	(2.38)	(1.56)	(.19)
B. Insider samples:				
1	1.40	−.60	.70	−1.30
	(5.18)	(−1.21)	(3.01)	(−3.81)
3	1.13	.45	.86	.19
	(6.08)	(2.82)	(4.49)	(.98)
6	.81	.48	.47	.14
	(4.94)	(2.90)	(3.50)	(1.23)
12	.72	.55	.43	.26
	(5.39)	(4.15)	(3.50)	(2.09)

Note: Excess returns are expressed in percent. The associated t-statistics based on tests of the standardized abnormal returns are shown in parentheses below the excess returns.

*All transactions costs are assumed and are not data, strictly speaking.

Source: Rozeff and Zaman [1988], p. 37.

Semitechnical Indicators

Another group of methods investors use to make profits is not strictly technical. They rely on information generated by investment advisory services, many of which provide recommendations to their clients. These suggestions may come in the form of a newsletter or lists of buys and sells published periodically by brokerage houses. Investors can examine these suggestions for the reasons behind the suggested moves, or can buy and sell the suggested stocks without any analysis of the stocks themselves. When the investment decisions are made without regard to the nature of the investment—not on the fundamentals of the suggestion, but purely on the buy and sell signals—the method is primarily technical.

One of the most widely read and followed investment advisory services is *Value Line*. It shows periodically the results of using its timeliness rankings to choose stocks.[26] A sample of this report is shown in Exhibit 3-18.

Exhibit 3-18
Record of *Value Line* Timeliness Ranks

Without Allowance for Changes in Rank		Allowing for Changes in Rank	
Average Percentage Change in Price 12/30/86 to 6/30/87		Average Percentage Change in Price 12/30/86 to 6/30/87	
Group 1	+26.9%	Group 1	+30.3%
Group 2	+23.7	Group 2	+23.8
Group 3	+20.2	Group 3	+18.1
Group 4	+21.5	Group 4	+14.9
Group 5	+25.5	Group 5	+13.1
Average	+21.9%		
Dow Jones Industrial Avg.	+27.6%		
NYSE Composite	+23.4%		

Source: "Value Line Ranking System at Midyear" [July 1987], p. 495.

Typical of the controversy surrounding the potential abnormal profits that can be earned by choosing stocks from the most timely of *Value Line's* stocks is an article by Black [1973]. Black's research was undertaken essentially to refute the results of the mid-1960's *Value Line* contest in which investors were allowed to try and beat *Value Line* by choosing 25 stocks from *Value Line's* IV and V (the lowest) timeliness rankings. These portfolios would then compete with a portfolio containing 25 stocks chosen by *Value Line* from its stocks ranked I in timeliness. Performance of these hypothetical portfolios was measured over 6 months, and the *Value Line*-chosen portfolio outperformed all but 20 of the 18,565 contest entries.[27]

Black, a sophisticated contestant, did not succeed in his objective of refuting the potential for profit in using *Value Line* ranking. This efficient-market supporter had to conclude, "It appears that the *Value Line* rankings definitely contain significant information, and are certainly one of the exceptions to my rule that active portfolio management is generally worthless, even before management expenses and transaction costs" (p. 12).

The interest in *Value Line's* timeliness rankings has continued to the present. Holloway [1981] found that an equally-weighted portfolio of *Value Line's* top-ranked securities, bought at the beginning and sold at the end of the year, had abnormal returns, even after transactions costs. His results were large—11.3 percent for 1965 to 1978 before commissions. The size of the results, in addition to some other methodological questions, spurred a flurry of debate.[28] Copeland and Mayers [1982] did not find positive abnormal returns with the top-ranked stocks, but they did find negative abnormal returns with those ranked last—and the negative returns tended to persist.

These studies leave us with the continuing questions of whether the *Value Line* rankings convey profitable information, and, if so, how long the profits persist. Peterson [1987] has made a recent attempt to answer these two questions. Rather than using rankings of all stocks, Peterson relied on initial reviews—assuming that they were likely to contain the newest and most exploitable information. Initial reviews numbered as few as 7 and as many as 120 over the 13 years tested, 1969 to 1982. Using daily returns, Peterson found abnormal (risk-adjusted) returns for the day following the initial review's publication, but no significant abnormal returns after that day.[29]

No doubt, *Value Line* will continue to interest researchers for some time to come, and it is not the only investment advisory service to come under this scrutiny.[30] Even the recommendations provided on *Wall Street Week* have been examined.[31]

Overreaction

Of late, interest has risen in theories based on psychology to understand stock market activity. Evidence from studies done by cognitive psychologists show that people overreact[32] to extreme events; also, they react more strongly to more recent information, and discount older data too strongly. If an investor could define extreme events, both negative and positive, she or he could buy (sell) after the negative (positive) news has affected the share price, and sell (buy) once the temporary overreaction was complete.

Brown and Harlow [1988] tested for the speed at which extreme information affected prices and the relationships between the magnitude of the news and the price changes. They found, as had earlier researchers DeBondt and Thaler [1985 and 1987] and Howe [1986], that extreme price changes were followed by subsequent changes in the opposite direction, and the more extreme the price change, the larger the reaction to it.

Brown and Harlow defined an extreme event by using the residuals from the CAPM: an extreme event was when the residual was positive (negative) after the previous residual had been large and negative (positive). Only extreme events where the direction of the move was different from that of the overall market were tested. Exhibit 3-19 shows the results of their analysis: "extreme movements in equity prices are followed by movements in the opposite direction" (p. 9), but "the tendency to overreact in a systematic manner is much stronger and more predictable when it is induced by a negative stimulus." (p. 11) In addition, the long-term response was a return to the initial price trend, although the return was only significant for those with negative news: only a one-month overreaction was found. While Brown and Harlow did not test whether trading rules could be developed to take advantage of the short-term gains, it is obvious there is a "bad news effect" at work in the market.[33]

Exhibit 3-19
Average Residuals for *First* Month
Following Positive and Negative Events

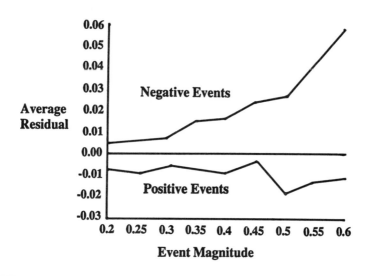

Source: Brown and Harlow [1988], p. 9.

Conclusion

Techhnical analysis is back—after falling out of favor and taking a battering at the hands of efficient-market advocates. Profits do seem possible, albeit small, through using purely historical data. Brokers' recommendations, technical trading rules, and investors' overreaction seem to hold potential for profit, but the profit is vulnerable to transaction costs. We have also seen profits reported from using relative-strength rating and specialists' short sales. Insider trading and the short-sales ratio seem tc be especially affected by transaction costs, however, since profits are eliminated when those costs are considered. Other rules (for instance, volume-based rules) have resulted in conflicting evidence.

Should you rely on technical trading rules? Not without careful thought

and continued vigilance. Every investor must sort out the real from the imag-
ined. Where there is controversy, investors must do their homework (examine
whether adequate commissions were considered, whether the risk adjustment
was adequate, and so on). Where there is profitable information, thoughtful
investors can profit.

CHAPTER 3

Notes

1. Levy [1966] summarized the basic assumptions behind technical analysis: market values are determined by supply and demand; supply and demand are driven by irrational and rational factors; price directions tend to persist; changes in trends depend on changes in supply and demand and can be seen in the action of the market itself.

2. This lack of enthusiasm was reflected in the slacking off of research on the relative profitability of technical analysis in the 1970s. New regard for technical analysis has recently renewed interest in research in this area.

3. For a good summary of the demand and supply theories of stock market movements, see Shiller [1984].

4. Praetz [1976] shows how there may be some bias in this method if the returns are normally distributed and independent.

5. Seelenfreud, Parker, and Van Horne [1968] used a more complex formulation based on a Taylor Series approximation. Several smoothing factors were used. Even so, the passive strategies were superior.

6. Stocks were ranked on alpha, the intercept from a generalized least-squares regression of the stock's returns regressed against the market's returns. Recent returns were weighted more heavily, except for the most recent month. For a full description, see Brush and Boles [1983].

7. He did this except for the very latest month, because he found a one-month reversal tendency.

8. Hanna [1978] extended the work, and Schneller [1978] criticized Epps for errors in model choice and for coming to conclusions inconsistent with the assumptions.

9. Actually, they pointed out that, for the model to hold, the values of the assets must be uncorrelated. Epps [1978] and Schneller [1978] discussed this problem. Smirlock and Starks did not deal with it because they considered it too small to affect the results.

10. A fine summary of the research in this area, and the theoretical reasons for the possible difference in results, is contained in Karpoff [1987].

11. Specifically, they chose those stocks that had a 50-day moving-average price that rose more than 10 percent through the upward-moving 200-day moving-average price, a positively sloped relative-strength graph over the previous 4 weeks, and rising cumulative volume over the previous 4 weeks.

12. The number of profitable trades depended on which of the three versions of the market model and two versions of the index were used to calculate the returns.

13. Goff [1975] and Kerrigan [1984] discussed this problem and the problem of using average number of shares traded, rather than net number of short sales, as the equation's numerator.

14. Hanna [1968], and a response by Seneca [1967], dealt with the problems of using simple linear regression and the specification of the variables in such analysis.

15. To avoid dividend outflows from short sales, we used U.S. Treasury bills as the investment when excessive-optimism signals were given. Trading costs at 1 percent were charged, and taxes were assessed at 30 percent.

16. His work was in response to Figlewski's [1981], which showed a statistically significant negative correlation between short interest and excess portfolio returns.

17. Fosback [1976], who found the SSSR was important, versus Reilly and Whitford [1982], who came to the opposite conclusion.

18. Other research by Wu [1972] and Gup [1973] found mixed results.

19. The weak form of the efficient-market hypothesis implies that insider-trading information would also be incorporated into the current price of a stock.

20. The trades are to be reported to the SEC by the 10th of the month following the trade, although many are not.

21. For major studies other than those mentioned in the text, see Lorie and Niederhoffer [1968], Pratt and DeVere [1970], Finnerty [1976], and Seyhun [1986], among others.

22. Conventional wisdom was that the number of insiders trading, not the amount of money traded, was the key to profits; Wysong's original system, described in Loomis [1967], was to select those stocks with the highest number of insider buyers plus option exercisers minus sellers for the last six months. Jaffe [1974] reconsidered Wysong's intensity of trading.

23. Seyhun also discussed the impact on bid/ask spreads of increases in the possibility of profitable insider trades. He found that the size of the bid/ask spread reflected potential losses to knowledgeable traders.

24. Seyhun used both a value- and an equal-weighted portfolio containing all the NYSE and American Stock Exchange stocks in his test.

25. In Chapter 4, we discuss strategies based on price/earnings ratios, and in Chapter 5, size-based trading strategies.

26. Timeliness rankings are developed by subjecting each stock to three tests: a nonparametric value position; earnings momentum (based on earnings and price rank and price momentum); and earnings surprise. The latter, earnings surprise, is discussed in the next chapter. For more details about the way timeliness rankings are developed, see the *Value Line* for September 19, 1986.

27. Shelton [1967] wrote about this contest.

28. See Hanna [1983], Gregory [1983], and Holloway [1983].

29. *Value Line* is targeted to reach its subscribers on a Friday. If investors act immediately on the highest ranked stocks, Peterson found their excess return could be 3.6 percent. All other *Value Line* ranks were unimportant in developing profitable strategies.

30. Hulbert [1987] looked at the performance ranks for a variety of advisory services; Dimson and Marsh [1984] found profits from acting on brokers' recommendations in the United Kingdom; Bjerring, Lakonishok, and Vermaelen [1983] found that following Canadian brokers' recommendations resulted in post-transaction-cost abnormal returns. Schlarbaum, Llewellen, and Lease [1978] examined individual investors' accounts, and Foster [1979] looked at returns (an 8 percent permanent average decline) for stocks subsequent to critiques of their accounting standards.

31. See Pari [1987] and a study by Salt and Statesman reported in Dorfman [1989]. They looked at the bearish-sentiment index and found that this advisor-optimism/pessimism index did not provide a basis on which to develop a successful trading strategy.

32. See, for instance, Howe [1986].

33. DeBondt and Thaler [1987] found that the effect cannot be attributed to a change in risk that came from the good or bad news, and it is not dependent on the market value of the firm.

CHAPTER 3

References

Akemann, Charles, and Keller, Werner. "Relative Strength Does Persist!" *Journal of Portfolio Management*, Fall 1977, pp. 38-45.

Alexander, Sidney S. "Price Movements in Speculative Market: Trends or Random Walks." *Industrial Management Review*, May 1961, pp. 7-26.

————. "Price Movements in Speculative Markets: Trends or Random Walks, No.2." *Industrial Management Review*, Spring 1964, pp. 25-46.

Amihud, Yakov, and Mendelson, Haim. "Are Trading Rule Profits Feasible?" *Journal of Portfolio Management*, Fall 1987, pp. 77-78.

Arnott, Robert. "Relative Strength Revisited." *Journal of Portfolio Management*, Spring 1979, pp. 19-23.

Bernhard, Arnold. *How to Use the Value Line Investment Survey: A Subscriber's Guide.* New York: Value Line Incorporated, undated material.

Bernstein, Peter. "The Battle of the Century: Technical versus Fundamental Analysis." Peter Bernstein, Inc., April 7, 1978, p. 2.

Biggs, Barton. "The Short Interest—A False Proverb." *Financial Analysts Journal*, July-August 1966, pp. 111-16.

Birinyi, Laszlo, Jr., and Miller, Keith. "Market Breadth: An Analysis." Salomon Brothers Inc., September 1987.

Bjerring, James; Lakonishok, Josef; and Vermaelen, Theo. "Stock Prices and Financial Analysts Recommendations." *Journal of Finance*, March 1983, pp. 187-204.

Black, Fisher. "Yes, Virginia, There Is Hope: Tests of the Value Line Ranking System." *Financial Analysts Journal*, September-October 1973, pp. 10-14.

Blattberg, R., and Gonedes, N. "A Comparison of Stable and Student Distribution as Statistical Models for Stock Price." *Journal of Business*, April 1974, pp. 244-80.

Bohan, James. "Relative Strength: Further Positive Evidence." *Journal of Portfolio Management*, Fall 1981, pp. 36-39.

Boness, A. James; Chen, Andrew; and Jatusipitak, Som. "Investigations in Nonstationarity in Prices." *Journal of Business*, October 1974, pp. 518-37.

Bowlin, Lyle, and Rozeff, Michael. "Do Specialists' Short Sales Predict Returns?" *Journal of Portfolio Management*, Spring 1987, pp. 59-63.

Brown, Keith, and Harlow, W. V. "Market Overreaction: Magnitude and Intensity." *Journal of Portfolio Management*, Winter 1988, pp. 6-13.

Brown, Stephen, and Warner, J. "Using Daily Stock Returns: The Case of Event Studies." *Journal of Financial Economics*, March 1985, pp. 3-31.

Brush, John S. "Eight Relative Strength Models Compared." *Journal of Portfolio Management*, Fall 1986, pp. 21-28.

————, and Boles, Keith E. "The Predictive Power in Relative Strength and CAPM." *Journal of Management,* Summer 1983, pp. 20-23.

Comiskey, E. E.; Walkling, R. A.; and Weeks, M. A. "Dispersion of Expectations and Trading Volume." Working Paper, Georgia Institute of Technology, October 1984.

Conine, Thomas E., Jr., and Tamarkin, Maurry J. "On Diversification Given Asymmetry in Returns." *The Journal of Finance,* December 1981, pp. 1143-55.

Cootner, Paul H. "Stock Prices: Random vs. Systematic Changes." *Industrial Management Review,* Spring 1962, pp. 24-45.

Copeland, Thomas, and Mayers, David. "The Value Line Enigma (1965-1978): A Case Study of Performance Evaluation Issues." *Journal of Financial Economics,* 1982, pp. 289-322.

Crouch, R. L. "A Nonlinear Test of the Random-Walk Hypothesis." *American Economic Review,* March 1970, pp. 199-202.

Damodaran, Aswath. "The Impact of Information Structure on Stock Returns." *The Journal of Portfolio Management,* Spring 1987, pp. 53-58.

DeBondt, Werner, and Thaler, Richard. "Does the Stock Market Overreact?" *Journal of Finance,* July 1985, pp. 793-805.

————. "Further Evidence on Investor Overreaction and Stock Market Seasonality." *Journal of Finance,* July 1987, pp. 557-81.

Dimson, Elroy, and Marsh, Paul. "An Analysis of Brokers' and Analysts' Unpublished Forecasts of U.K. Stock Returns." *Journal of Finance,* December 1984, pp. 1257-92.

Dorfman, John. "Professors Bring Bad News for the Pessimism Theory." *Wall Street Journal,* January 26, 1989, p. e-1.

Drew, Garfield. "A Clarification of the Odd-Lot Theory." *Financial Analysts Journal,* September-October 1967, pp. 107-08.

Epps, Thomas. "Security Price Changes and Transaction Volumes: Theory and Evidence." *American Economic Review,* September 1975, pp. 586-97.

————. "Security Price Changes and Transaction Volumes: Some Additional Evidence." *Journal of Financial and Quantitative Analysis,* March 1977, pp. 141-46.

————. "Security Price Changes and Transaction Volumes: Reply." *American Economic Review,* September 1978, pp. 698-700.

————, and Epps, Mary Lee. "The Stochastic Dependence of Security Price Changes and Transaction Volume: Implications for the Mixture-of-Distributions Hypothesis." *Econometrica,* March 1976, pp. 268-74.

Fama, Eugene, and Blume, Marshall. "Filter Rules and Stock-Market Trading." *Journal of Business,* October 1966, pp. 226-41.

Fielitz, B. D., and Rozelle, J. P. "Stable Distributions and the Mixtures of Distributions Hypothesis for Common Stock Returns." *Journal of American Statistical Association,* March 1983, pp. 28-36.

Figlewski, S. "The Informational Effects of Restrictions on Short Sales: Some Empirical

Evidence." *Journal of Financial and Quantitative Analysis,* November 1981, pp. 463-76.

Finnerty, Joseph. "Insiders and Market Efficiency." *Journal of Finance,* September 1976, pp. 1141-48.

Fosback, Norman. *Stock Market Logic.* Fort Lauderdale, Fla.: Institute for Economic Research, 1976.

Foster, George. "Briloff and the Capital Market." *Journal of Accounting Research,* Spring 1979, pp. 262-74.

Friend, Irwin, and Westerfield, Randolph. "Co-Skewness and Capital Asset Pricing." *Journal of Finance,* September 1980, pp. 897-913.

Glickstein, David, and Wubbels, Rolf. "Dow Theory Is Alive and Well!" *Journal of Portfolio Management,* Spring 1983, pp. 28-32.

Godfrey, M. D.; Granger, W. J.; and Morgenstern, O. "Spectral Analysis of New York Stock Market Prices." *Kyklos,* 1964, pp. 1-30.

Goff, William. "Letter to the Editor." *Financial Analysts Journal,* March-April 1975, pp. 8-10.

Gottschalk, Earl C. "Insider Stock Transactions Are Challenged as a Market Indicator by New Research." *Wall Street Journal,* November 11, 1988, p. 31.

Granger, C. W. J., and Morgenstern, Oscar. "Spectral Analysis of New York Stock Market Prices." *Kyklos,* 1963, pp. 1-27.

Gregory, N. A. "Testing an Aggressive Investment Strategy Using Value Line Ranks: A Comment." *Journal of Finance,* March 1983, pp. 257-58.

Gup, Benton. "A Note on Stock Market Indicators and Stock Prices." *Journal of Financial and Quantitative Analysis,* September 1973, pp. 673-82.

Hanna, Mark. "Price Changes and Transaction Volumes: Additional Evidence." *American Economic Review,* September 1978, pp. 692-95.

————. "Short Interest: Bullish or Bearish?—Comment." *Journal of Finance,* June 1968, pp. 520-23

————. "A Stock Price Predictive Model Based on Changes in the Ratios of Short Interest to Trading Volume." *Journal of Financial and Quantitative Analysis,* December 1976, pp. 857-72.

————. "Testing an Aggressive Investment Strategy Using Value Line Ranks: A Comment." *Journal of Finance,* March 1983, pp. 259-62.

Harris, L. "The Joint Distribution of Speculative Prices and of Daily Trading Volume." Working Paper, University of Southern California, May 1983.

Hausman, Warren H. "A Note on the Value Line Contest: A Test of the Predictability of Stock-Price Changes." *Journal of Business,* July 1969, pp. 317-20.

Holloway, Clark. "A Note on Testing an Aggressive Investment Strategy Using Value Line Ranks." *Journal of Finance,* June 1981, pp. 711-19.

————. "Testing an Aggressive Investment Strategy Using Value Line Rankings: A Reply." *Journal of Finance,* March 1983, pp. 263-70.

Howe, John. "Evidence on Stock Market Overreaction." *Financial Analysts Journal,* July-August 1986, pp. 74-77.

Huberman, Gur, and Kandel, Shmuel. "Value Line Rank and Firm Size." *Journal of Business*, October 1987, pp. 577-90.

Hulbert, Mark. "Investment Newsletters: A 7-year Retrospective." *Journal of the Association of Institutional Investors*, October 1987, pp. 16-17.

Jaffe, Jeffrey. "Special Information and Insider Trading." *Journal of Business*, July 1974, pp. 410-28.

Jain, P. C., and Joh, G. "The Dependence Between Hourly Prices and Trading Volume." Working Paper, The Wharton School, University of Pennsylvania, September 1986.

James, C., and Edmister, R. O. "The Relation Between Common Stock Returns Trading Activity and Market Value." *Journal of Finance*, September 1983, pp. 1075-86.

James, F. E., Jr. "Monthly Moving Averages—An Effective Investment Tool?" *Journal of Financial and Quantitative Analysis*, September 1968, pp. 315-26.

Jensen, Michael. "Random Walks: A Comment." *Financial Analysts Journal*, November-December 1967, pp. 77-85.

———. "Relative Strength as a Criterion for Investment Selection." *Journal of Finance*, December 1967, pp. 595-610.

———, and Bennington, George. "Random Walks and Technical Theories: Some Additional Evidence." *Journal of Finance*, May 1970, pp. 469-82.

———, and Kripotos, Spero L. "Sources of Relative Price Strength." *Financial Analysts Journal*, November-December 1969, pp. 60, 62, 64.

Kaplan, R., and Weil, R. "Rejoinder to Fisher Black." *Financial Analysts Journal*, September-October 1973, p. 14.

———. "Risk and the Value Line Contest." *Financial Analysts Journal*, July-August 1973, pp. 56-61.

Karpoff, Jonathan. "The Relation Between Price Changes and Trading Volume." *Journal of Financial and Quantitative Analysis*, March 1987, pp. 109-26.

Kerrigan, Thomas. "Kerrigan Responds to Critic" (Letter). *Financial Analysts Journal*, May-June 1975, pp. 8-9.

———. "The Short Interest Ratio and Its Component Parts." *Financial Analysts Journal*, November-December 1974, pp. 45-49.

Kewley, Thomas, and Stevenson, Richard. "The Odd-Lot Theory as Revealed by Purchase and Sale Statistics for Individual Stocks." *Financial Analysts Journal*, September-October 1967, pp. 103-06.

———. "The Odd-Lot Theory for Individual Stocks: A Reply." *Financial Analysts Journal*, January-February 1969, pp. 99-104.

Kon, S. J. "Models of Stock Returns—A Comparison." *Journal of Finance*, March 1984, pp. 147-65.

Levy, H. "Equilibrium in an Imperfect Market: A Constraint on the Number of Securities in the Portfolio." *American Economic Review*, September 1978, pp. 643-58.

Levy, Robert. "Conceptual Foundations of Technical Analysis." *Financial Analysts Journal*, July-August 1966, pp. 83-89.

———. "Random Walks: Reality or Myth." *Financial Analysts Journal*, November-December 1967, pp. 69-77.

Lommis, Carol. "A New Inside Track." *Fortune*, December 1967, pp. 216-17.

Lorie, J. H., and Neiderhoffer, V. "Predictive and Statistical Properties of Insider Trading." *Journal of Law and Economics*, April 1968, pp. 35-51.

Mandelbrot, Benoit. "Forecasts of Future Prices, Unbiased Markets, and 'Martingale' Models." *Journal of Business*, January 1966, pp. 242-55.

————. "The Variation of Certain Speculative Prices." *Journal of Business*, October 1963, pp. 394-419.

Mayor, Thomas. "Short Trading Activities and the Price of Equities: Some Simulation and Regression Results." *Journal of Financial and Quantitative Analysis*, September 1968, pp. 283-98.

Morgan, I. G. "Stock Prices and Heteroskedasticity." *Journal of Business*, October 1976, pp. 496-508.

Osborne, M. F. M. "Periodic Structure in the Brownian Motion of Stocks." *Operations Research*, May-June 1962, pp. 345-80.

Pari, Robert. "Wall Street Week Recommendations: Yes or No?" *Journal of Portfolio Management*, Fall 1987, pp. 74-76.

Peterson, David R. "Security Price Reactions to Initial Reviews of Common Stock by the Value Line Investment Survey." *Journal of Financial and Quantitative Analysis*, December 1987, pp. 483-94.

Praetz, Peter. "The Distribution of Share Price Changes." *Journal of Business*, January 1972, pp. 49-55.

————. "Rates of Return on Filter Tests." *Journal of Finance*, March 1976, pp. 71-75.

Pratt, S. P., and DeVere, C. W. "Relationship Between Insider Trading and Rates of Return for NYSE Common Stocks, 1960-1966." In Lorie, J., and Brealey, Richard, eds. *Modern Developments in Investment Management*. New York: Praeger, 1970.

Price, Kelly; Price, Barbara; and Nantell, Timothy J. "Variance and Lower Partial Moment Measures of Systematic Risk: Some Analytical and Empirical Results." *Journal of Finance*, June 1982, pp. 843-55.

Pruitt, Stephen, and White, Richard. "The CRISMA System: Who Says Technical Analysis Can't Beat the Market?" *Journal of Portfolio Management*, Spring 1988, pp. 55-68.

Reilly, Frank, and Whitford, David. "A Test of Specialists' Short Sale Ratio." *Journal of Portfolio Management*, Winter 1982, pp. 12-18.

Renwick, Fred B. "Theory of Investment Behavior and Empirical Analysis of Stock Market Price Relatives." *Management Science*, September 1968, pp. 57-71.

Richardson, G.; Sefcik, S. E.; and Thompson, R. "A Test of Dividend Irrelevance Using Volume Reaction to a Change in Dividend Policy." *Journal of Financial Economics*, December 1986, pp. 313-33.

Rogalski, Richard. "The Dependence of Prices and Volume." *Review of Economics and Statistics*, 1978, pp. 268-74.

Roll, Richard. "R^2." *Journal of Finance*, July 1988, pp. 541-66.

Rozeff, Michael, and Zaman, Mir. "Market Efficiency and Insider Trading: New Evidence," *Journal of Business*, 1988, pp. 25-44.

Schiller, Robert J. "Theories of Aggregate Stock Price Movements." *Journal of Portfolio Management,* Winter 1984, pp. 28-37.

Schlarbaum, Gary; Lewellen, Wilbur; and Lease, Ronald C. "Realized Returns on Common Stock Investments: The Experience of Individual Investors." *Journal of Business,* April 1978, pp. 299-326.

Schneller, M. "Security Price Changes and Transaction Volumes: Comment." *American Economic Review,* September 1978, pp. 696-97.

Scholes, Myron and Williams, Joseph T. "Estimating Betas from Nonsynchronous Data." *Journal of Financial Economics,* 1977, pp. 309-27.

Seelenfreund, Alan; Parker, George; and Van Horne, James. "Stock Price Behavior and Trading." *Journal of Financial and Quantitative Analysis,* September 1968, pp. 263-81.

Seneca, Joseph. "Short Interest: Bearish or Bullish?" *Journal of Finance,* March 1967, pp. 67-70.

Seyhun, H. Nejat. "The Information Content of Aggregate Insider Trading." *Journal of Business,* 1988a, pp. 1-24.

―――. "Insiders' Profits, Costs of Trading, and Market Efficiency." *Journal of Financial Economics,* June 1986, pp. 189-212.

―――. "The January Effect and Aggregate Insider Trading." *Journal of Finance,* 1988b, pp. 129-41.

Shelton, John. "The Value Line Contest: A Test of the Predictability of Stock-Price Changes." *Journal of Business,* July 1967, pp. 251-69.

Shiller, Robert J. "Theories of Aggregate Stock Price Movements." *Journal of Portfolio Management,* Winter 1984, pp. 28-37.

Singleton, C., and Wingender, J. "Skewness Persistence in Common Stock Returns." *Journal of Financial and Quantative Analysis,* September 1986, pp. 335-41.

Smirlock, Michael, and Starks, Laura. "A Further Examination of Stock Price Changes and Transaction Volume." *Journal of Financial Research,* Fall 1985, pp. 217-25.

Smith, Randall. "Short Interest and Stock Market Prices." *Financial Analysts Journal,* November-December 1968, pp. 151-54.

Stickel, Scott E. "The Effects of Value Line Investment Survey Changes on Common Stock Prices." *Journal of Financial Economics,* March 1985, pp. 121-43.

"Value Line Ranking System at Midyear." *Value Line Investment Survey,* July 24, 1987, pp. 495-506.

"Value Line Ranking System in 1986." *Value Line Investment Survey,* January 23, 1987, pp. 717-728.

Vu, Joseph. "Why All the Interest in Short Interest?" *Financial Analysts Journal,* July-August 1987, pp. 76-79.

Westerfield, R. "The Distribution of Common Stock Price Changes: An Application of Transactions Time and Subordinated Stochastic Models." *Journal of Financial and Quantitative Analysis,* December 1977, pp. 13-37.

Wood, R. A.; McInish, T. H.; and Ord, J. K. "An Investigation of Transactions Data for NYSE Stocks." *Journal of Finance,* July 1985, pp. 723-39.

Wu, Hsiu-Kwang. "Odd-Lot Trading in the Stock Market and Its Market Impact." *Journal of Financial and Quantitative Analysis,* January 1972, pp. 1321-41.

Ying, Charles. "Stock Market Prices and Volume of Sales." *Econometrica*, July 1966, pp. 676-85.

Zakon, Alan, and Pennypacker, James. "Advance-Decline as a Stock Market Indicator." *Journal of Financial and Quantitative Analysis*, September 1968, pp. 299-314.

CHAPTER 4

Fundamental Valuation: Corporate Earnings

In the last chapter, we looked at technical strategies for making money in the stock market. Technical analysis attempts to determine the direction of the whole stock market, sectors in the market, or the prices of individual stocks. Price, volume, and insider-trading information constitute the data on which the technical analyst makes predictions. Technical analysts argue that their techniques can be used to forecast the direction of the market before fundamental analysts can do so.

Fundamental analysts, on the other hand, rely on information about a company, or industry, to predict the direction that a company's stock price will take. Information about company management, markets, and competitive and company conditions, now and in the future, concern these analysts.

Among all the data followed or used by fundamental analysts, corporate earnings have received the most attention. Chugh and Meador [1984] found that short-term changes and long-term trends in earnings were two of the most important factors investment analysts used in making their predictions. Therefore, we have separated fundamental analysis into two chapters in order to give the subject of earnings the attention it merits. This chapter deals with earnings, earnings forecasting, earnings surprises, and earnings yields, as they are used by fundamental analysts. Other methods of fundamental analysis will be discussed in the next chapter.

Significance of Earnings

Over time, many researchers have demonstrated the significance of earnings and their relationship to stock prices. The significance they found is not just a statistical relationship, but one that is fundamental to the pricing of a company's common shares. That relationship has a strong base in the theory of investment value.

Investors make investments in the hope that they will earn returns. Returns come from one source alone: the cash sent by the corporation to its shareholders in the form of dividends or liquidating payments (and sometimes in the form of share repurchases). Even companies that do not pay a dividend are expected either to pay one in the future or liquidate. Thus investors find some basis for estimating the value to them of every common share. Of course, the estimated future dividends depend on what the company will be able to pay in the future: on the company's earning capacity and its need to retain funds for future growth. Because these forecasts can change over time, the price of the shares can also change. Changes come from new information about the company, its markets, and the economy in general. Therefore, investors can also make money from their shares in the short term through capital gains if they can predict what the next forecast will be. Exhibit 4-1 shows the sort of forecasts that investors make in valuing shares.

Exhibit 4-1
Conceptual Framework for Calculating
a Company's Present Value

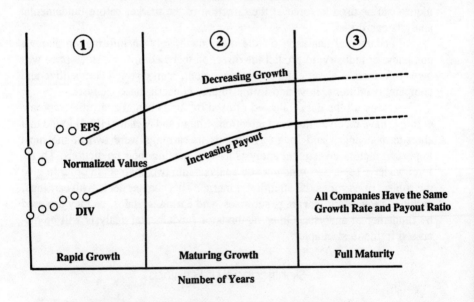

Source: Drexel Burnham Lambert [1987], p. 2.

Because earnings are so fundamental to the value that shareholders will receive, they are the critical factor in determining the fair price for the shares. The unquestioned importance of earnings is obvious when one considers the number of major brokerage firms and other financial institutions that either employ in-house analysts to produce forecasts of earnings, or purchase the forecasts from others. If such analysts neither added potential profits nor were expected to, their jobs would not persist.

Some, perhaps cynical, researchers and investment analysts have insinuated that earnings are concocted "to justify today's lofty stock prices. . . ." (Ozanian [1987]). Treynor [1984], for example, concluded that "the behavior of the accountant [is] essentially drawing on the techniques of accrual accounting to make certain that the earnings number is an appropriate estimate of the [stock's] value" (p. 9). Whether that is true or not, it is important for analysts and investors to know whether all information available from the reported earnings is reflected in the contemporaneous price—regardless of how the earnings figures were derived.

Earnings Announcements

A number of researchers have shown, however, that prices do not fully reflect all information contained in quarterly earnings reports.[1] Morse [1981] looked specifically at the impact of earnings on trading volume and excess, risk-adjusted returns at the time the *Wall Street Journal* reported earnings. The rationale for the study was that trading volume and price changes may occur before any earnings announcement if investors believe there will be unexpected results, and after the announcement if the information is interpreted differently by different investors. While Morse's sample was small (50 stocks), and thus had a bias toward those that survived over the period studied (1968-76), he found significant changes in volume and price the day before earnings were announced, as shown in Exhibit 4-2. Morse attributed those changes to problems in determining the exact day of the announcement. However, there were also significant increases in volume and prices for several days following the announcements. Earnings announcements, therefore, do appear to affect prices and returns and for longer than expected.

Penman [1987] found that the pattern of earnings announcements may explain Blue Mondays: bad news announcements tended to be released on Mondays. There is also a monthly effect. Ariel's [1987] study of earnings announcements from 1971-82 found that announcements made during the first half of a month tended to convey good news, while bad news was conveyed in the latter half of the month. Thus two market anomolies we discussed in Chapter 2 may simply reflect the timing of earnings announcements.

Exhibit 4-2
Mean Absolute Residual Returns Surrounding
the Earnings Announcement

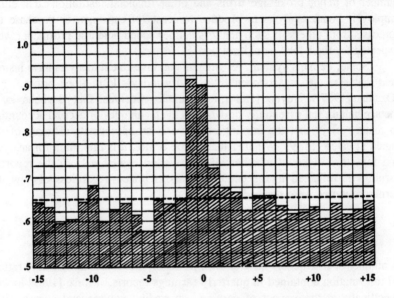

Trading Volume Surrounding Earnings Announcement

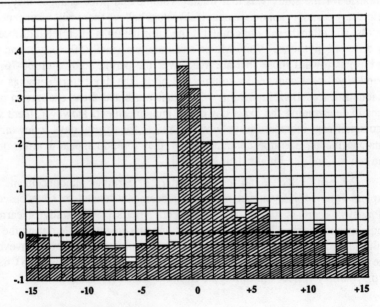

Note: Dotted line = Sample average.

Source: Morse [1981].

Surprise Earnings

To profit from reactions to earnings announcements, it helps to look for the surprises. Joy, Litzenberger, and McEnally [1977] studied the returns of 96 stocks at the time of quarterly earnings announcements from 1963 to 1968. They grouped stocks into portfolios they called unfavorable, favorable, and neutral based on the relationship of the stocks' actual earnings to expected earnings. They used a simple regression estimate and found that those stocks with favorable earnings announcements had large returns after the announcement and continuing upward price trends. Those with unexpectedly low returns relative to what was expected did not show the same results.[2]

A similar study by Rendleman, Jones, and Latane [1982] found that the "surprise" relationship existed for a long time (1971 to 1980) for a large number of stocks (1,496).[3] (Before 1971 a good source of earnings announcement data did not exist.) In their study, the data for earnings came from the COMPUSTAT data base, and the information on stock prices from CRSP. The earnings announcements were gathered by Standard and Poor's Corporation. The stocks were divided into portfolios ranked by their **standardized unexpected earnings (SUEs),** with the lowest SUEs in Portfolio 1. The portfolios were formed in such a way that they were all of the same risk, a beta of 1.0, so that risk would not be a factor in differentiating the returns. Past studies had criticized research that did not explicitly take risk into account, because the differences in excess returns could have been a result of differences in risk rather than true differences in excess returns.[4]

Rendleman et al. used two methods for calculating beta: the Scholes-Williams method, which adjusted for systematic errors induced by differences in measurement lengths, and a more traditional method based on the capital asset pricing model (CAPM) that had also been used by Reinganun [1981]. They tested the impact of using the two different betas on the excess returns and compared the returns with those estimated using no risk adjustment. The results "demonstrate the stability of the excess returns over different types of markets, suggesting the beta effect was not an important part of the explanation of the SUE effect" (p. 280). The results of their analysis are shown in Exhibit 4-3.

Standardized Unexpected Earnings (SUE)—
To classify stocks by the amount of their earnings surprise, Jones, Rendleman, and Latane [1982] compared actual earnings (A) with earnings predicted (P) from a 20-quarter, seasonally adjusted, time-series regression. The standard error of the regression (SEE) was used to normalize the comparison, and the result was called standardized unexpected earnings.

Standardized Unexpected Earnings
$$= (A-P)/SEE$$

The Exhibit 4-3 table shows the cumulative excess returns (not risk adjusted) over the 36 quarters the authors studied. As they noted, "Clearly, SUE works very effectively in predicting subsequent excess returns" (p. 282). They found that the excess returns occured both before and after earnings were announced and that the adjustment continued for some time, at least 70 days. That is, positive portfolio returns could be earned on portfolios purchased even 2 months after earnings were announced,[5] but the major increase in excess returns occurred within 2 days after earnings were announced.[6] They also noted that two other problems should be considered. First, the above-average gain is about 4 percent, but if you have to sell other stocks to buy these stocks, and sell them at the end, the profit may be eliminated by commissions. Second, fully half the excess returns occurred before the announcements were made, which suggests that some investors have ideas about what the earnings announcements will be and act on those ideas.

The foregoing studies, as well as others, provide two inescapable conclusions: the market seems to be inefficient with regard to quarterly earnings, and the adjustment process is not instantaneous. Why? Market inefficiency is only one of the possible explanations for these findings; there are others. For instance, the results could have been specific to the time period or group of stocks studied; or the findings could have been the spurious result of a faulty research technique.

Three such technical problems were dealt with in a study by Brown [1978]: concerns about instability of the CAPM parameters, survivorship bias, and failure to include dividend income. He included dividends, used data that avoided much of the **survivor bias,** and used a different way of calculating the parameters for the CAPM. Because many had been concerned that the risk level of the stock might change after an earnings announcement in the *Wall Street Journal,* Brown estimated the model parameters using data following the quarterly earnings announcement.

Survivor Bias—When companies go bankrupt or are acquired, they are deleted from most current data bases. If the bankrupt companies had low returns before final bankruptcy, ignoring them imparts an upward bias to the results. Since acquired companies may have had high returns, their omission could create a downward bias.

To avoid survivor bias, studies must use all companies in existence at the time a strategy is being tested. Most data-base services can provide histories of the deleted companies.

He still found that significant price trends continued for about 45 days.[7] Thus there seem to be exploitable opportunities, at least in quarterly earnings announcements.

Foster, Olsen, and Shevlin [1984] showed that post-announcement profits seemed to depend on the model used to forecast the expected returns in the first place. Using a regression of historical earnings to forecast future earnings, and placing stocks in ten groups ranked by the amount of earnings surprise, Foster et al. found that risk-adjusted returns exhibited the post-announcement drift reported by the previous studies.[8] As shown in Exhibit 4-4, before and after the announcement, there was the same sort of drift others found.[9]

Foster et al. used several other models to forecast unexpected earnings. One model is especially interesting: it placed stocks in ten portfolios, ranked by the relative size of their abnormal (residual) returns for the day of and day after the announcement. The results of this model are shown in Exhibit 4-5. Notice

Exhibit 4-3
Analysis of Cumulative Excess Returns and Betas over 36 Quarters, September 1971-June 1980[a]

	SUE category								
	1	2	4	5	6	7	8	9	10
Cumulative excess returns[a]									
Days −20 to 90	−8.7	−5.6	−3.6	−1.1	1.2	2.8	3.9	6.9	8.0
Days 1 to 90	−4.0	−3.3	−1.8	−0.8	0.5	1.2	1.6	3.4	4.3
Days −20 to −1	−3.3	−1.7	−1.4	−0.4	0.4	0.9	1.5	2.2	2.4
Day 0	−1.4	−0.7	−0.2	0.1	0.3	0.6	0.8	1.3	1.3
t-statistics									
Days −20 to 90	−3.06	−4.30	−4.35	−3.02	1.51	1.96	2.10	2.55	2.86
Days 1 to 90	−3.69	−5.56	−4.74	−2.63	1.37[c]	2.74	2.44	3.57	4.58
Days −20 to −1	−1.78	−2.12	−3.19	−1.76	0.64[c]	0.83[c]	1.10[c]	1.16[c]	1.17[c]
Day 0	−5.84	−2.72	−1.23[c]	0.21	1.30[c]	2.61	3.29	5.18	5.09
Beta analysis									
Average beta (β)[b]	1.02	0.97	1.00	1.03	1.03	1.01	1.02	1.02	1.02
Maximum beta	1.30	1.25	1.19	1.16	1.16	1.15	1.20	1.49	1.35
Minimum beta	0.67	0.71	0.85	0.89	0.94	0.89	0.76	0.65	0.60
σ_β[d]	0.15	0.12	0.08	0.07	0.05	0.07	0.09	0.16	0.19
$(\beta-1)\sqrt{36}/\sigma_\beta$	0.93	−1.34	0.289	2.47	3.36	0.87	1.33	0.86	0.49

[a] Excess returns are calculated on a daily basis as the difference between an individual stock's return and an equally weighted NYSE-ASE index. Within each SUE category, these excess returns are averaged on a daily basis for each quarter of the analysis. The cumulative averages of the 36 average quarterly excess returns are shown in the table by SUE category. The sample size ranges from a minimum 618 companies (1971) to a maximum of 1,946 in 1980. t-values are calculated via the procedure outlined by Ruback (1982).
[b] The average beta is calculated as follows. For each quarter, average the returns within each of the 10 SUE categories by day and regress this mean daily return against the corresponding market return. This provides a beta for each quarter for each of the 10 SUE categories. These betas are then averaged over the 36 quarters.
[c] Not significant at the 0.05 level.
[d] The standard deviation of 36 betas.

Source: Kendleman, Jones, and Latane [1982], p. 283.

Exhibit 4-4

Behavior of Cumulative Average Risk-Adjusted Returns 60 Days Before and After Earnings Announcement

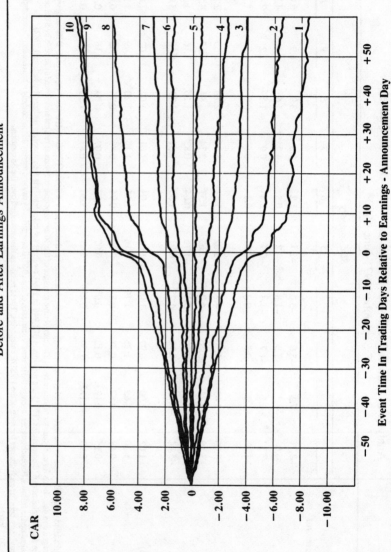

that the drift before the announcement is eliminated by this model, as is the post-event drift: the returns all occur at the event, when earnings are announced.

Exhibit 4-5
Behavior of Portfolio Adjusted Residual Returns
60 Days Before and After Earnings Announcements

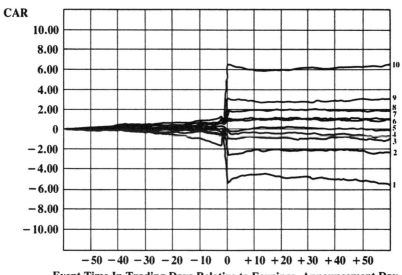

Event Time In Trading Days Relative to Earnings–Announcement Day

Source: Foster, Olsen, and Shevlin [1984], p. 590.

What caused the post-announcement drift to disappear in Foster, Olsen, and Shevlin's later model? Apparently, the market bid the price up or down correctly and immediately, on average. In contrast, when stocks were ranked into groups by their surprise earnings, the average repricing was not completely accurate.[10]

The complexity of analyzing companies with surprise earnings is demonstrated by Jones, Rendleman, and Latane [1984]. Exhibit 4-6 shows their transition matrix of earnings changes over time. The clear message is that winners and losers do not tend to reverse in the next quarter.

If everyone knows this, why aren't the prices of winners bid up immediately? Perhaps surprise earnings indicate that things are changing (are nonstationary). If this is true, because change itself is a risk, earnings must be discounted at a higher rate. As events unfold, the risk declines, as does the rate at which earnings are discounted: prices will rise, at least for the winners. Such subsequent adjustments would not be the result of inefficiencies but of nonstationarities that are difficult to measure and are not captured by a typical beta.

Exhibit 4-6

Percentage of SUEs in any Category One Quarter Later,
Given Their Initial Category over the 36 Quarters
September 1971-June 1980

Initial SUE Category	SUE Category One Quarter Later									
	1	2	3	4	5	6	7	8	9	10
1	13.5	8.9	14.6	16.3	11.3	11.5	9.3	8.6	3.3	2.7
2	11.8	8.6	13.4	20.2	17.7	12.6	7.2	4.7	1.8	2.0
3	7.6	7.1	13.6	21.3	20.5	13.9	7.6	4.5	2.0	2.0
4	5.3	5.1	10.5	20.7	26.0	16.3	8.5	4.0	2.0	1.8
5	3.3	2.8	6.7	15.5	29.2	22.2	10.6	5.1	2.2	2.5
6	2.4	2.3	4.7	11.4	22.6	27.8	16.5	6.5	3.3	2.6
7	2.4	2.2	4.1	8.3	15.8	25.5	23.3	11.2	4.1	3.2
8	2.4	2.5	4.5	7.2	12.2	20.0	24.7	15.9	6.6	4.0
9	2.6	2.6	4.0	7.4	13.3	16.3	20.8	17.8	8.0	7.0
10	2.6	3.2	8.1	10.8	12.8	13.2	13.5	14.5	10.6	10.7
Percentage of all observations in each SUE category*	4.2	3.7	7.3	13.8	21.2	21.0	14.6	7.8	3.5	3.0

*The total number of observations in each column, from 1 to 10, are: 1,766, 1,557, 3,072, 5,855, 8,998, 8,917, 6,180, 3,302, 1,482, and 1,269. The sum of these ten numbers is 42,398.

Source: Jones, Rendleman, and Latane [1984], p. 21.

Finally, more insight into the adjustment process for returns comes from a study by Patell and Wolfson [1984], which focused on companies with large capitalizations. They did not adjust their returns for risk, and they based their test on a simple trading rule: buy (sell) the stock if the announced earnings are larger (smaller) than that forecast by *Value Line*. They looked at the potential return from this strategy for 30-minute periods on the day earnings are announced, the following day, and the evening prior to the announcement. They found "some suggestion of activity beginning 60 to 90 minutes before the release. The 30 minute period beginning at the minute of the announcement exhibits a significant positive return (approximately one quarter of one percent) that is four to five times larger than those in surrounding periods" (p. 234). Within 95 minutes of the announcement, the returns had fallen back to the preannouncement level. Thus the market may be more efficient for large companies than for small companies. This hypothesis seems reasonable, since large firms' stocks are where large institutional traders focus their interests.

Forecasting Earnings

The Value of Accurate Forecasts

Elton and Gruber, with a variety of co-authors over the years [1972, 1981, 1984], have extensively researched the role of earnings. Exhibit 4-7 presents the results of one study. The excess returns are the average CAPM risk-adjusted returns for the months following the forecast, in this case, March (the earliest month in the year for which the prior year's earnings are generally available). The growth-rate forecast used in Exhibit 4-6 was the actual, realized growth for the 7 and 13 months. As you can see, if you had perfect information about the earnings' growth rates, you would profit from using it.

Exhibit 4-7
Excess Returns for 7 and 13 Months Following March

	Earnings Growth Rate				Rank Correlation of Excess Returns vs. Growth
	Upper 30%	*Upper 50%*	*Middle 40%*	*Lower 30%*	
7 Months	0.0591	0.0463	0.0006	–0.0597	0.09*
13 Months	0.0748	0.0411	–0.0191	–0.0493	0.88*

*Significant at the 1 percent level.

Source: Adapted from Elton, Gruber, and Gultekin [1981], p. 982.

Thomas Kerrigan [1984] confirmed these results in tests using data from 1977 to 1982.

Historical Earnings As a Forecast

Over the years, researchers and investment analysts have attempted the difficult task of forecasting earnings using many different methods. Academic researchers have tested a number of ways to use history, particularly the history of the company's earnings, to forecast the future earnings. Most of this research found that simple forecasts from history (for instance, time-series analyses of annual earnings per share for individual companies or groups of companies[11]) were less than helpful in making accurate forecasts. Quarterly earnings-per-share (EPS) data fared a little better. After studying the results of research by analysts who used earnings history as the basis for forecasts, however, Conroy and Harris [1987] concluded that "work using only the past history of annual EPS data has not given rise to predictive ability superior to a random walk. . . . Even in the case of quarterly EPS, Box-Jenkins analysis of each firm's data has not led to significant improvements in forecasting accuracy when compared to simpler models" (p. 727).

> **History-Based Forecasting: Martingale and Submartingale Processes**—A *martingale* process allows successive events to exhibit complex dependence, but it requires the best estimate of the next event to be the most recent event's outcome. Using this approach with stock prices means that the best estimate of tomorrow's price is today's price. With earnings the best estimate of future earnings, is the company's current earnings.
>
> A *submartingale* allows complex dependence in the series but requires that the best estimate of the next event be a continuation of the most recent change. If daily stock prices follow a submartingale process, tomorrow's price would be equal to today's price plus the change in today's price from yesterday's.

Some methods of history-based forecasting appear better than others, but neither the simple nor the more complex methods of forecasting earnings provides good overall results. Because knowledge of future earnings does result in profitable investment opportunities, however, undaunted investors often rely on yet another source of forecasts, investment analysts.

Investment Analysts' Forecasts

Investment analysts' forecasts should be superior to historical forecasts for a number of reasons. First, the analysts can use far more information in developing their forecasts than just the history of the earnings themselves. Second, analysts are paid for their forecasts, and if investors did not believe the forecasts had value, they would not pay for the service, at least not for long, and analysts would not exist.

Although believing that analysts' earnings forecasts are better than time-series extrapolations of history is pleasant, believing something is so, as we have seen in previous chapters, is not enough. We must look at the evidence. Because analysts' forecasts have been around a long time, and have been recorded and collected, researchers have indeed tested their superiority to simple extrapolations of history.

In early studies, Elton and Gruber [1972] concluded that "mechanical techniques have been shown to do about as good a job of forecasting earnings as do security analysts" (p. B-423). In a more recent paper, however, Brown and Rozeff [1978] documented that analysts do add value. They looked at forecasts made by analysts of *Value Line* for 50 stocks, as well as three time-series methods, including a Box–Jenkins formulation. These models were tested over horizons of from one to five quarters, for each of the four years 1972-75. As you can see in Exhibit 4-8, they found that the *Value Line* analysts' forecasts produced smaller errors than any of their history-based models over all the horizons they tested, although the degree of superiority declined as the horizon lengthened.[12] They showed also that Box-Jenkins forecasts were consistently better than more naive martingale process models.

Because Brown and Rozeff tested the *Value Line* forecasts against time-series methods, we should certainly ask: Were the *Value Line* analysts unique in their skill, or can analysts in general outperform history-based forecasts? Fried and Givoly [1982] used forecasts from *Earnings Forecaster*[14] in their research and suggested that the analysts' forecasts, because they are widely read and used by the investment community, provide better surrogates for market expectations than history alone. They found that the analysts' forecast errors were lower than errors of the two time-series methods they analyzed. In addition, they found that forecasts made later in the year, farther from the actual earnings announcement, "rely somewhat less on extrapolation of past earnings data and more on autonomous information and prediction" (p. 102), which confirmed the suspicions of Brown and Rozeff.

Wilcoxon Signed Ranks Test—This test determines whether two paired series are significantly different from each other. Often t-tests are used to determine whether such differences are significant. When individual values are not normally distributed, however (especially if they could be highly skewed with extreme outliers), the Wilcoxon test is used. It ranks the differences, rather than summing individual values; thus it eliminates the impact of extreme values.[13]

Conroy and Harris [1987] went further in testing analysts' forecasts. They used the Institutional Brokers Estimate System data from Lynch, Jones, and Ryan, a service that provides consensus earnings forecasts. The consensus forecasts provided by IBES are analysts' forecasts for EPS for the current and following year.[15] Conroy and Harris tested the consensus mean estimate forecast (MNEST)[16] against five other forecast methods: a simple, no-change-from-the-last-earnings forecast (SF); the best time-series method from the prior period (BEST), and three that combined consensus with either the time-series or simple forecasts. They tested these six forecast methods over five horizons using absolute percentage error as a measure of forecast accuracy. Exhibit 4-9 shows their results.

Absolute Percentage and Mean-Squared Errors—These are two frequently used measures of the size of errors in forecasts. If a negative error is regarded as equally important as a positive error, the common approach is to ignore the sign by taking only the absolute value of the differences. This measure is called the
(continued on page 151)

Note that the consensus forecast was superior for the three shorter forecast horizons, which was also true for Brown and Rozeff's study. When the horizon went beyond seven months, the simple random-walk (martingale) forecast was almost as good, and the

Exhibit 4-8
Summary of Wilcoxon Test Comparisons

A: Value Line vs. Time-Series Models

	Forecast Horizon						Forecast Model			Year			
	Total	1Q	2Q	3Q	4Q	5Q	M	S	BJ	1972	1973	1974	1975
Number of comparisons	52	12	12	12	12	4	16	16	20	13	13	13	13
Comparisons favorable to V[a]	45	12	11	9	10	3	15	15	15	13	12	9	11
Comparisons statistically favorable to V[b]	33	10	8	7	7	1	13	10	10	13	8	4	8
Comparisons statistically unfavorable to V	1	0	0	0	0	1	0	0	1	0	0	1	0
Mean Wilcoxon test statistic ($\bar{t}$)	3.25	4.86	3.75	2.83	2.37	.76	5.27	3.40	1.51	4.84	3.67	1.18	3.29
$\bar{t}/s(\bar{t})$[c]	8.27	5.45	4.51	3.81	3.72	.67	5.65	6.24	3.48	9.98	4.18	1.81	4.24

B: BJ vs. Naive Time-Series Models

	Forecast Horizon					Forecast Model		Year			
	Total	1Q	2Q	3Q	4Q	M	S	1972	1973	1974	1975
Number of comparisons	32	8	8	8	8	16	16	8	8	8	8
Comparisons favorable to BJ[a]	27	7	7	7	6	15	12	8	4	8	7
Comparisons statistically favorable to BJ[b]	24	7	7	6	4	13	11	7	4	6	7
Comparisons statistically unfavorable to BJ	2	0	1	1	0	0	2	0	2	0	0
Mean Wilcoxon test statistic ($\bar{t}$)	3.15	4.87	3.93	2.33	1.48	3.97	2.34	3.98	1.63	3.00	4.00
$t/s(t)$[c]	6.37	4.70	4.16	2.41	2.25	6.23	3.25	6.46	1.05	4.99	4.96

[a] Comparisons are favorable if Wilcoxon statistic is positive.

[b] Comparisons are statistically favorable if Wilcoxon statistic is positive and significant at the 5% level or better.

[c] Both $\bar{t}$ and $s(\bar{t})$ are computed using the number of comparisons in each column of the table.

Source: Brown and Rozeff [1978], p. 10.

(continued from page 149)
absolute percentage errors. If the direction and magnitude of the errors is important, to avoid canceling out the impact of negative and positive errors, the errors are squared before obtaining the arithmetic average—the mean-squared error. This measure is similar to the absolute percentage error when observations are normalized initially.

combinations of the consensus with other forecast methods were superior. Conroy and Harris thus concluded that the hybrid methods performed better than analysts alone, because they dampened the tendency of analysts to over-react.[17] Note that BEST, their best time-series method in the past, did not do any better than the least skilled choice—namely, this year's earnings simply repeated—and these results held true for all three time horizons.

Exhibit 4-9

Forecast Accuracy of Forecast Methods, by Forecast Horizon (1977-83); Entries are MAPE[a] (standard deviation)

Forecast Method	Forecast Horizon				
	3-0	1-3	4-6	7-9	≥9
1. MNEST	24.01 (34.47)	26.70 (37.88)	32.41 (45.97)	38.18 (54.74)	37.18 (55.21)
2. BEST	47.76 (67.05)	42.92 (65.07)	42.05 (63.43)	40.99 (61.64)	38.12 (56.98)
3. SF	42.11 (64.26)	40.00 (61.33)	39.27 (59.68)	38.09 (57.85)	34.92 (54.81)
4. EMNSF	29.47 (40.12)	30.40 (43.00)	33.09 (47.79)	35.48 (52.19)	33.67 (51.68)
5. MNBS	30.01 (49.13)	32.88 (51.83)	35.82 (55.54)	37.89 (58.83)	36.10 (56.81)
6. MNSF	36.28 (53.16)	39.79 (57.02)	44.38 (62.75)	46.79 (67.04)	45.02 (64.18)
Average Value of k[b]					
MNBS	0.470	0.431	0.384	0.350	0.338
MNSF	0.617	0.585	0.543	0.506	0.491

[a] MAPE = Mean absolute percentage error.
[b] k represents weight given to analysts' forecast (MNEST).

Note: Statistical tests are based on a test of differences in means. The calculated t's (essentially distributed normal for these sample sizes) to test for differences between MAPEs for MNEST and SF are as follows: Horizon 1, $t = 25.29$; horizon 2, $t = 20.85$; horizon 3, $t = 10.14$; horizon 4, $t = -0.120$; and horizon 5, $t = -1.46$.

Source: Conroy and Harris [1987], p. 732.

Although analysts' forecasts[18] seem to contain more information than history-based time-series forecasting, the forecasts are far from perfect. *Fortune* regularly gives us information about analysts who have erred; Exhibit 4-10 shows an example review of January 1987 separated by industry.

Exhibit 4-10
Estimated Earnings Growth by Industry—January 1987

Industry	Est. 1986 Earnings Growth as of 1/86	Est. 1986 Earnings Growth as of 12/86	Est. 1987 Earnings Growth as of 12/86
Air carriers	97.3%	−25.3%	181.3%
Auto/truck parts, trucks	28.0	−35.8	108.6
Coal	50.5	13.4	38.9
Electrical equipment	31.9	6.5	44.0
Metal fabricating	72.0	16.2	89.8
Oil producers	12.4	−52.1	45.2
Oil services & machinery	16.0	−128.8	0.0
Railroads	12.0	−13.5	25.1
Toys	17.7	−13.8	42.1
Truckers	41.1	17.6	31.3

Source: Curran [1987], p.123.

What could cause these large errors? Elton, Gruber, and Gultekin [1984] examined analysts' forecasts to see whether they could determine the source of errors. In addition to reaffirming, using an elegant methodology, that analysts' forecasts outperformed time-series methods (especially over shorter horizons and also later in the year), Elton et al. found two sources of error. They first partitioned errors into three segments of misforecasts in EPS: segments for the economy, the industry, or the company (Exhibit 4-11). The major source of errors was not the general forecast for the average level of growth in EPS for the economy, but forecasts for industry and company performance. Note that the errors for industry performance declined over the year, while the errors at the company level remained almost the same regardless of the time of the year.

Elton et al. determined that there were several patterns in analysts' forecasts. First, they found that a poor forecast in one year tended to be followed by a poor forecast in the following year. Second, while analysts' forecasts became more accurate over the year, the differences among their forecasts (measured by the standard deviation between the forecasts) remained fairly stable. Third, differences among their forecasts appeared to be industry related, with certain industries having a wider dispersion of forecasts (at least from 1976 to 1978) than others. Fourth, when forecasts were widely different among analysts,

Exhibit 4-11
Partitioning of Percentage Error in Growth

	Economy	Industry	Company	Bias	Inefficiency	Random Error
January	2.0	37.3	60.7	1.0	27.4	71.6
February	2.2	36.8	61.0	1.1	26.3	72.6
March	2.4	36.2	61.5	1.7	14.2	84.1
April	2.1	33.1	64.8	1.8	8.6	89.6
May	2.5	32.6	64.9	2.2	7.8	90.0
June	2.7	29.4	67.9	2.5	9.5	88.0
July	2.8	30.2	67.0	2.6	6.7	90.7
August	2.7	30.6	66.8	2.4	7.7	89.9
September	2.7	26.5	70.8	2.4	8.5	89.1
October	2.3	26.3	71.5	2.2	6.4	91.4
November	1.3	23.0	75.7	1.6	3.4	95.0
December	0.8	15.5	83.7	0.9	3.0	96.1

Source: Elton, Gruber, and Gultekin [1984], p. 357.

forecast errors (measured as the absolute error in the forecast of growth) had been large previously.[19]

Forecasting Trends in Consensus Forecasts

Because analysts exchange information with other analysts, earnings estimates could move in trends. Kerrigan [1984] tested the possibility of industry trends in earnings estimates. Using 240 companies in 24 industries, he ranked the percentage revisions in earnings and compared the ranks in each month with the subsequent months' ranks. Using the Spearman rank-correlation coefficient, he found that positive correlations existed, but they diminished for each period, as shown in Exhibit 4-12.

Kerrigan then tested the applicability of this information for profitable stock selection. First he tested using analysts' forecasts by themselves and found the results disappointing: stocks with high forecasted growth did not always do well. Thus he concluded that the market had already incorporated these forecasts in prices. He did find that combining analysts' forecasts with the trend in the consensus worked well.[20]

Arnott [1985] substantiated much of Kerrigan's analysis, as well as extending the sample to 700 companies and providing more details. For each of 27 quarters, Arnott ranked the stocks by the expected earnings momentum: the percentage change in 1-year (FY1) and 2-year (FY2) earnings expected based on the consensus IBES analysts' forecast. As shown in Exhibit 4-13, Arnott found that, after 3 months, those stocks in the group showing the largest expected

Exhibit 4-12
Twenty-Four Industry Study:
Industries Ranked by the Net % Plurality of Earnings-
Estimate Revisions for the Month

	Three-Month Rank Correlation Coefficients				Four Quarter Average
Year	Dec./March	March/June	June/Sept.	Sept./Dec.	
1978	.54	.44	.55	.59	.53
1979	.25	.83	.46	.64	.54
1980	.43	.34	.43	.37	.39
1981	.39	.31	.56	.54	.45
1982	.70	.78	.71	.56	.69
5–Yr. avgs.	.46	.54	.54	.54	.52

	Monthly Rank Correlation Coefficients with March								
Year	April	May	June	July	Aug.	Sept.	Oct.	Nov.	Dec.
1978	.83	.49	.44	.39	.22	.08	.19	.30	.27
1979	.91	.84	.83	.45	.44	.43	.49	.16	.23
1980	.70	.72	.34	.25	.43	.35	.34	.48	.49
1981	.63	.49	.31	.50	.63	.60	.55	.61	.50
1982	.80	.76	.78	.76	.52	.55	.50	.46	.46
5–Yr. avgs.	.77	.66	.54	.47	.45	.40	.41	.40	.39

Source: Kerrigan [1984], p. 22.

positive change in earnings (top 5 percent) had a return of 5.2 percent, while the bottom 5 percent earned 3.9 percent. The bottom 5 percent was the group with the largest expected drop in earnings. After 12 months, the return was 24.5 percent versus 16.4 percent, respectively. The **information coefficient** (IC) between the expected earnings changes and the returns for the following 3 months was +0.025 percent, but it was positive only 59 percent of the time. From this result, Arnott concluded that "fully 41 percent of the time this kind of earnings momentum model would have harmed investment performance" (p. 19). For the 2-year forecast horizons, the results were only slightly better.

What is surprising is a joint ef-

> **Information Coefficient**—The IC is merely the statistician's correlation coefficient, representing the degree of relationship between two variables. The square of the correlation coefficient can be thought of as the percentage of variation in one series that relates to the other series (e.g., an IC = 0.50 suggests that 25 percent of the variation in one series is related to the other.) Thus zero would indicate no relationship, 1.0 would indicate a direct, proportional relationship, and −1.0 would indicate that the two series move in opposite proportional directions.

fect: the 12-month returns of the top 5 percent were significantly above the bottom 5 percent (24.5 percent versus 16.4 percent), but the information coefficients were insignificant. This combination tells us that there is a lot of risk to forecasting for individual companies and also that the top performers may come from a few with very high returns; that is, the winners earn any return, while losers are limited to a loss of 100 percent.

So trends in earnings forecasts can provide profitable information. When Arnott created a model for forecasting the trend in consensus forecasts, as well as subsequent stock returns, he was able to raise the ICs from 0 to 89 percent. His basic model, which paralleled work by Kerrigan, revealed that future consensus trends could be forecast from the changes in the past three months. This conclusion seems to be a strong case against market efficiency: profits can be made from widely available information.

Exhibit 4-13
EPS Momentum
(expected percentage change)

	Est. FY1	vs.	Act. FY0		Est. FY2	vs.	Est. FY1
	3-mo.		12-mo.		3-mo.		12-mo.
Total Returns by Decile							
Top 5%	5.2%		24.5%		3.7%		24.2%
1st decile	5.9		23.7		5.2		24.4
2nd decile	4.9		18.3		4.5		20.2
3rd decile	4.0		17.1		4.2		16.5
8th decile	4.4		15.4		3.3		13.7
9th decile	4.5		16.5		3.3		13.6
10th decile	4.1		16.4		3.4		13.6
Bottom 5%	3.9		16.4		3.2		13.8
Correlations							
Mean	+0.025		+0.051		+0.036		+0.090
Best case	+0.229		+0.213		+0.260		+0.294
Worst case	-0.168		-0.181		-0.351		-0.296
% above zero	59%		60%		44%		60%

Note: FY = Fiscal year.

Source: Arnott [1985], p. 19.

Other research indicates that revisions in analysts' forecasts, especially large revisions in consensus forecasts, do appear to affect potential returns. When Hawkins, Chamberlin, and Daniel [1984] constructed portfolios of the 20 stocks with the largest increase in the consensus IBES forecasts, they found positive excess returns, even after adjusting for risk.[21] Benesh and Peterson [1986] also looked at the impact of unexpected earnings declines on share-price changes. From their work, they concluded that stocks should be sold if there is a large downward revision in the forecasts.[22] Givoly and Lakonishok [1984] added more evidence to both of the preceding studies, and Abdel-khalik and Ajinkya [1982], using a sample of data from Merrill Lynch analysts, showed that internal forecast revisions did precede changes in returns and were in the same direction. They did not find, however, that once the forecast was made public, additional return could be earned. Analysts' forecasts, or at least changes in forecasts, can yield information on which profits can be made, especially if you have that information before the general public.

Acting on changes in the analysts' forecasts, particularly private information about these forecasts, appears profitable, but do the announcements of the actual earnings affect these returns? This question is important, because analyst revisions often occur in the same month that earnings are announced by a company. To test whether it is the forecast revision of an earnings announcement that generates excess profits, Givoly and Lakonishok [1979] excluded all stocks for which the revision of earnings and the earnings announcement occurred in the same month and found that, for 49 companies in 3 industries (chemicals, petroleum refining, and transportation equipment), excess profits still existed. In addition, as shown in Exhibit 4-14, they found that excess returns "prevail well after the release of FAF [analyst forecast] revisions—indicating inefficiency of the market with respect to these revisions" (p. 175).

From their analysis, Givoly and Lakonishok devised an investment strategy. They suggested that at the end of each month an investor search for all companies for which the analyst had revised the earnings estimate upward, buy the stocks, and hold them two months before selling. They calculated that the abnormal return for such a strategy would be 2.7 percent for the 2 months (17.3 percent per year), if the upward revision limit was a minimum of 5 percent. This return is in dramatic contrast to a buy-out-hold return of 7.4 percent per year. Even after netting out the transactions costs, the return from the active strategy is attractive.

Revisions in forecasts can have an impact on stock returns, one on which a canny investor may be able to capitalize. Even earnings announcements by themselves seem to yield the possibility of profits.

Price/Earnings Ratios and Earnings Yields

Earnings and earnings forecasts constitute only one kind of information investors use. Price/earnings (P/E) ratios (and their inverse, earnings yields) have long been used to make stock selections. One widely used strategy is simply to purchase low-P/E stocks.[23] Graham and Dodd [1940], the progenitors of fundamental stock valuation, suggested a reasonable P/E ratio as a precondition to buying a stock. They believed a high P/E ratio suggested that investors were

Exhibit 4-14

Average Abnormal Returns per Holding Period by Direction of Financial Analysts' Earnings Forecast Revisions, for Revisions over 5%*

	Direction (upward/ downward)	Monthly Holding Periods								Monthly Return on Buy-and-Hold
		[-1,2]	[0,2]	[1,2]	[-1]	[0]	[1]	[2]	
(1) All revisions	U	4.7	3.1	2.7	1.1	0.9	1.7	1.0	0.6
(standardized)	D	-3.8	-1.9	-1.0	-1.6	-1.2	-0.4	-0.6	
No earnings	U	5.3	4.1	3.4	1.4	0.7	2.5	0.9	0.6
(2) announcements (standardized)	D	-3.2	-2.6	-1.1	-1.1	-0.9	-0.9	-0.5	
(3) All revisions	U	4.9	3.3	2.8	1.1	0.9	1.7	1.0	0.6
(standardized)	D	-3.9	-2.0	-1.0	-1.6	-1.2	-0.4	-0.6	

*All values are different from zero for a two-tailed test at the 5 percent significance level.

Source: Givoly and Lakonishok [1984], p. 176.

enthusiastic about the stock and thus already paying a high price for it (for a share in the company's earnings). Conversely, a low ratio implied that the stock may not have been discovered by investors: if a stock has not been discovered and the price has not been bid up, presumably it has a smaller possibility of a price decline.

There is controversy, however, about the use of P/E ratios, and particularly low-P/E strategies. The ambivalent attitude of some professional money-management organizations toward low-P/E strategies is echoed in a report by Salomon Brothers [1987]:

> Researchers have not agreed over whether the presumed superior results of using the low price/earnings ratio approach are because of errors in risk specification . . . or just a quirk of statistical results. A value-oriented investment discipline is worthwhile. This conclusion is based on historical evidence. Nevertheless, the low price/earnings ratio results are likely because of the law of averages, accompanied by the market's distaste for stocks with little or no growth prospects. In addition, the inferior performance of high price/earnings ratio stocks results from the law of averages and the market's attention to optimistic growth stories. (p. 8)

Some believe that P/E ratios aid in the selection of profitable securities. Others vehemently do not. What does the evidence show?

Some evidence indicates that the price/earnings ratio may be a leading indicator of a change in earnings. For example, Reilly and Drzycimski [1974-75] showed that P/E changes precede earnings changes but are more volatile. A number of early researchers looked at P/E-ratio investment strategies, and their general conclusion was that low-P/E ratio (or high-earnings-yield) stocks provided greater than average returns, and sometimes that differential was very large.[24]

None of these early studies, however, took risk adequately into account, until Basu [1977]. He studied P/E-ratio based investment strategies from an efficient-market standpoint and tested the P/E ratios computed from CRSP and COMPUSTAT data bases for about 500 stocks listed on the New York Stock Exchange from 1956 to 1969. He formed five P/E-ranked portfolios and tested the differential returns using three CAPM-based measures of performance: Jensen's, Treynor's, and Sharpe's.[25] His results are shown in Exhibit 4-15, and a graph of one of the measures is shown in Exhibit 4-16.

Performance Measures and Related Summary Statistics
(April 1957–March 1971)

Performance Measure/ Summary Statistic	CAPM Defined with	P/E Portfolios[a]						Market Portfolios[a]	
		A	A*	B	C	D	E	S	F
Median P/E ratio and inter-quartile range[b]	—	35.8 (41.8)	30.5 (21.0)	19.1 (6.7)	15.0 (3.2)	12.8 (2.6)	9.8 (2.9)	15.1 (9.6)	
Average annual rate of return (r_p)[c]	—	0.0934	0.0955	0.0928	0.1165	0.1355	0.1630	0.1211	0.1174
Average annual rate of return (r'_p)[d]	r_f	0.0565	0.0585	0.0558	0.0796	0.0985	0.1260	0.0841	0.0804
	r_z	0.0194	0.0214	0.0187	0.0425	0.0613	0.0889	0.0470	0.0433
Systematic risk (β_p)	r_f	1.1121	1.0579	1.0387	0.9678	0.9401	0.9866	1.0085	1.0000
	r_z	1.1463	1.0919	1.0224	0.9485	0.9575	1.0413	1.0225	1.0000
Jensen's differential return (β_p) and t-value in parentheses	r_f	−0.0330 (−2.62)	−0.0265 (−2.01)	−0.0277 (−2.85)	0.0017 (0.18)	0.0228 (2.73)	0.0467 (3.98)	0.0030 (0.62)	
	r_z	−0.0303 (−2.59)	−0.0258 (−2.04)	−0.0256 (−2.63)	0.0014 (0.15)	0.0198 (2.34)	0.0438 (3.80)	0.0027 (0.57)	
Treynor's reward-to-volatility measure:[e] r'_p/β_p	r_f	0.0508	0.0553	0.0537	0.0822	0.1047	0.1237	0.0834	0.0804
	r_z	0.0169	0.0196	0.0183	0.0448	0.0640	0.0854	0.0460	0.0433
Sharpe's reward-to-variability measure:[f] $\bar{r}_p/\sigma(\bar{r}_p)$	r_f	0.0903	0.0978	0.0967	0.1475	0.1886	0.2264	0.1526	0.1481
	r_z	0.0287	0.0331	0.0312	0.0762	0.1095	0.1444	0.0797	0.0755

Exhibit 4-15 Continued

Performance Measure/ Summary Statistic	CAPM Defined with	P/E Portfolios[a]						Market Portfolios[a]	
		A	A*	B	C	D	E	S	F
Coefficient of correlation: $\rho(\tilde{r}_p, \tilde{r}_m)$	r_f	0.9662	0.9594	0.9767	0.9742	0.9788	0.9630	0.9936	
	r_z	0.9748	0.9676	0.9780	0.9767	0.9809	0.9705	0.9946	
Coefficient of serial correlation: $\rho(\tilde{\varepsilon}+1, \tilde{\varepsilon}_t)$	r_f	0.0455	0.0845	0.0285	-0.1234	0.0065	0.1623	0.1050	
	r_z	0.0048	0.0681	0.0163	-0.1447	0.0408	0.1485	0.0763	
F-statistics for test on homogeneity of asset pricing relationships (Chow-test)[g]	r_f	2.3988	2.2527	0.4497	1.2249	1.1988	0.2892	0.0496	
	r_z	0.8918	0.2490	0.9767	0.3575	0.6987	0.4761	0.2826	

[a] A = highest P/E quintile, E = lowest P/E quintile, A^* = highest P/E quintile excluding firms with negative earnings, S = sample, and F = Fisher Index.

[b] Based on 1957–1971 pooled data; inter-quartile range is shown in parentheses.

[c] $\tilde{r}_{pp} = \sum_{i=1}^{168} r_{pd}/14$, where r_{pd} is the continuously compounded return of portfolio p in month t (April 1957/March 1971).

[d] $\tilde{r}_p = \sum_{i=1}^{168} r_{pd}/14$, where r_{pt} is the continuously compounded excess return $(r_{pt}$ minus r_{fd} or $r_{zt})$ of portfolio p in month t (April 1957-March 1971).

[e] Mean excess return on portfolio p, $\tilde{r}_p$, divided by its systematic risk, β_p.

[f] Mean excess return on portfolio p, $\tilde{r}_p$, divided by its standard deviation, $\sigma(\tilde{r}_p)$.

[g] None of the computed figures are significant at the 0.05 level: $Pr(F(2,120) \geq 3.07) = 0.01$; $Pr(F(2,120) \geq 3.0) = 0.05$ and degrees of freedom in denominator = 164.

Source: Adapted from Basu [1977], p. 667.

Exhibit 4-16
Basu's Computation of Annual Average Abnormal
Portfolio Returns Based on Jensen's Differential

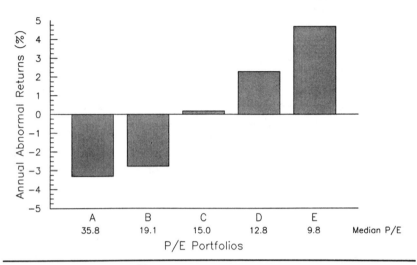

Source: Reinganum [1989], p. 11.

On the basis of his evidence, Basu concluded that "during the period April 1957 to March 1971, the low P/E portfolios seem to have, on average, earned higher absolute and risk-adjusted rates of return than the high P/E securities" and that "securities trading at different multiples of earnings, on average, seem to have been inappropriately priced vis-à-vis one another, and opportunities for earning 'abnormal' returns were afforded to investors" (p. 680). He further concluded that, even after taking transactions costs, taxes, and risk into account, a low-P/E strategy generally provided higher returns and "that disequilibria persisted in capital markets during the period studied" (p. 680). Reinganum [1981], looking at data through the mid-1970s, confirmed Basu's findings.

Because Basu's results obviously challenged efficient-market advocates, they addressed the efficacy of his test: was beta properly measured, or was the source of the abnormal returns a mismeasurement of beta? Banz [1981] said, "Given its [the low-P/E abnormal return's] longevity, it is not likely that it is due to a market inefficiency but it is rather evidence of a pricing model mis-specification" (p. 17).[26]

What is the potential source of the error? There are a number of candidates. One of the first culprits to investigate is problems with the data. Banz suggested that much of the abnormal return could be the result of what he called look-ahead bias. This bias occurs when the research is based on data that would not have been available to the investor at the time. For example, using end-of-year accounting numbers to make decisions in January would bias the results, since most year-end accounting information does not become publicly available until near the end of the first quarter. The COMPUSTAT data base records numbers at the time they occur, not the time they are reported. Thus December 31st data that are reported later, say in March, are shown as of December 31.

Banz and Breen [1986] tested for the importance of this problem to the low-P/E findings. They created a file they called the sequentially collected COMPUSTAT, which adjusted for lags in the announcement of accounting data. Using data from 1974 to 1981, they formed 30 portfolios based on a double sorting by size and earnings yield: portfolios were first sorted into 5 groups by size from largest (1) to smallest (5), then re-sorted into 5 more portfolios based on earnings yield (E/P). A sixth portfolio contained negative-earnings companies. Subtracting the highest E/P portfolio's return from the lowest within each size category removed the impact of size: Any difference in return would be attributable to E/P differences.

Exhibit 4-17 shows the results—for brevity, only the raw, non-risk-adjusted data are presented. Banz and Breen's conclusions:

> With the current COMPUSTAT data file, we conclude that there is a significant relation between earnings-yield and return within size groups. On the basis of the sequentially collected COMPUSTAT file, we come to a different conclusion. There are no significant differences for either the raw or risk-adjusted returns. (p. 789)

To correct for the problem of the time of data availability, most researchers assume that data are not available until the end of the first quarter of the year. Many of them, however, still have found a low-P/E bias in abnormal returns. Why? Are P/Es proxies for something else?

P/E Strategies—Other Issues

Does a P/E provide a signal for growth? Beaver and Morse [1978], using data from 1956 to 1974, placed stocks in 25 P/E-ranked portfolios. Correlating portfolio P/Es over time, they found a high degree of correlation existed between the P/E ratios of portfolios formed in 1956 with their P/Es in following years. While correlations declined over time, the early-year correlations were over 90 percent. In addition, over time the P/Es of the portfolios tended to converge. As for growth, they found a negative correlation between the P/E ratios and earnings growth, but the relationship between the initial P/E and subsequent growth declined rapidly: by the third year, the correlation was 5 percent. From these two findings, Beaver and Morse concluded that "some of

Exhibit 4-17
Test of Strategy: Buy Highest E/P Portfolio, Sell Lowest E/P Portfolio—Current COMPUSTAT Data Base

I. Raw Returns

Size Group	Portfolio	Return (High E/P Portfolio-Low E/P Portfolio)	F-Statistic	t-Statistic
All	Portfolio	$F = 3.61$ [a] $(5,2850\ DF)$		t-Statistic
1	1-5	0.0105	6.54[b]	2.54[b]
2	7-11	0.0066	2.99	1.72
3	13-17	0.0088	7.65[a]	2.75[a]
4	19-23	0.0114	6.90[a]	2.98[a]
5	25-30	0.0082	1.70	2.69[a]

II. Risk–adjusted Returns

Size Group	Portfolio	α (t-Statistic)	β (t-Statistic)	F-Statistic (Total)
All	$F = 2.34$ [a]	$F = 4.5209$ [a]	$F = 2.7226$	
1	1-5	0.0090 (2.16)[b]	0.0882 (1.52)	4.46[b]
2	7-11	0.0069 (1.76)	-0.0183 (-0.34)	1.54
3	13-17	0.0098 (3.00)[a]	-0.0565 (-1.25)	4.62[a]
4	29-23	0.0128 (3.33)[a]	-0.0860 (-1.61)	5.85[a]
5	24-30	0.0077 (2.49)[b]	0.0278 (0.65)	3.85[b]

Sequentially Collected COMPUSTAT Data Base: Sample Period 1974-1981

I. Raw Returns

Size Group	Portfolio	Return (High E/P Portfolio-Low E/P Portfolio)	F-Statistic	t-Statistic
All	Portfolio	$F = 0.94\ (5,2850\ DF)$		t-Statistic
1	1-5	0.0071	2.63	1.61
2	7-11	0.0024	0.41	0.64
3	13-17	0.0022	0.51	0.71
4	19-23	0.0019	1.23	0.51
5	25-30	0.0008	0.14	0.25

Figure 4-17 (Continued)

II. Risk-adjusted Returns: Test of Individual Size Groups

Size Group	Portfolio	α (t-Statistic)	β (t-Statistic)	F-Statistic (Total)
All·	F = 1.2353	F = 0.6927	F = 1.6255	
1	1-5	0.0066 (1.48)	0.0249 (0.40)	1.38
2	7-11	0.0024 (0.61)	0.0037 (0.07)	0.21
3	13-17	0.0022 (0.70)	-0.0016 (-0.04)	0.25
4	29-23	0.0030 (0.81)	-0.0690 (-1.34)	1.01
5	24-30	-0.0004 (-0.13)	0.0757 (1.62)	1.34

Source: Adapted from Banz and Breen [1986], p. 790.

the initial dissipation of the P/E ratio in the first three years after formation can be explained by differential growth in earnings. . . . However, there clearly exists a P/E differential that cannot be explained by differential earnings growth" (p. 70).

Jahnke, Klaffke, and Oppenheimer [1987] also found that P/Es and growth were not directly related. Jahnke et al. focused their analysis on the high-P/E stocks: because investors seem to have a preference for growth, and many investment analysts suggest that high P/E ratios are likely to reflect high-growth companies, the authors believed there should be a difference betweeen the actual growth rates of high- and low-P/E companies.[27] Dividing high-P/E portfolios into high and low sustainable-growth categories did not explain P/E differences. When Jahnke et al. used the P/E ratio divided by historical earnings growth, the portfolios that were rated high did not outperform those rated low. Thus P/E does not appear to be a pure proxy for growth.

Hagin [1985], using forecasts from Kidder Peabody analysts, confirmed that the group with the lowest expected growth rate performed best. He concluded that this group, which also had the lowest P/E, was least prone to unpleasant earnings surprises—torpedo effects.

Other researchers have addressed other potential sources of error. For example, if companies in the same industry had similar P/E ratios in a study, the abnormal returns attributed to the low-P/E ratios could be the result of industry concentrations (e.g., holding utility stocks while ignoring hi-tech stocks). Goodman and Peavy [1983] looked specifically at this problem. In their study, they used a P/E they called a price/earnings relative (PER), which adjusted for average industry P/Es.[28] Each quarter, the resultant PERs were clustered into five portfolios, and the quarterly returns for each portfolio were adjusted for risk (beta). Exhibit 4-18 shows their results.

Exhibit 4-18
Price/Earnings Relative and Portfolio Betas and
Annualized Excess Returns Using Quarterly Rebalancing

PER Portfolio	Mean PER	Portfolio Beta Mean	Portfolio Beta t-Statistic	PER Portfolio	Excess Return	t-Statistic	Significance Level*
1	0.56	1.05	1.42	1	10.89	4.39	0.01
2	0.76	1.01	-1.16	2	3.69	1.49	—
3	0.93	0.97	-3.74*	3	0.69	0.28	—
4	1.13	1.00	-1.81	4	-5.35	-2.16	0.05
5	1.68	1.11	5.29*	5	-9.91	-3.99	0.01
Total	1.01	1.03	—				

*Significant at the 0.01 probability level.

Source: Adapted from Goodman and Peavy [1983], p. 63.

As you can see from the exhibit, excess returns were related to PERs, and the relationship was statistically significant. The relationship held when the portfolios were rebalanced semiannually and annually. Thus, industry concentration does not seem to be the cause of the abnormal returns.

Perhaps a low-P/E strategy worked during only one period in recent history: in some of the research we have discussed, we found that the results reflected some factor or set of factors that were important in one time period but not in another. Jaffe, Keim, and Westerfield [1987] looked at whether an earnings-yield effect existed during 1951 to 1986 and also during two equal subperiods. They found that "much of the controversy over the relative importance of E/P. . . is due to sampling variation in the estimation effects—that is, the results are period specific" (p. 2). They chose their sample so as to minimize errors that might occur because of survivor bias or look-ahead bias—two criticisms of earlier research—and found a relationship between earnings yield and returns during the whole period. They also found, however, that while the relationship was true for all months of the year and for all years in the early part of their test period (1951-69), the relationship was significant "only in January in the latter subperiod [1970-86]" (p. 9).

Reilly, Griggs. and Wong [1983] carried low-P/E strategy one step further: they forecasted a P/E for the overall market. Their explanatory variables were changes in the growth in EPS, the yield on AAA corporate bonds, the risk-free rate, inflation, variability of earnings, dividend-payout, debt levels, corporate failure rate, and the difference in the yields on AAA and BBB bonds. Coincident correlations showed a high and positive relationship between the aggregate market P/E and dividend-payout ratio, and a negative relationship with inflation, earnings variation, and debt levels. In regressions, the payout ratio and the levels of the risk-free rate and inflation were significant and logical. To test the profitability of their findings, they generated predictions for each regression variable using historical data. They used this as a predictor: when a decline in the aggregate P/E was forecast, they invested in U.S. Treasury bills; when an increase was forecast, the Standard & Poor's 400 Index was purchased. On the basis of their simulation, they earned a 9.83 percent return with 1 percent commissions, against a buy-and-hold strategy return of 1.98 percent for stocks and of 7.37 percent for Treasury bills. The risk of their strategy was lower than that for an all-stock portfolio, which suggested that "it is possible to specify macro variables that influence changes in the aggregate stock market earnings multiple" (p. 44). Money can be made, even using aggregate data.

A number of factors could be behind a real or spurious P/E-abnormal return connection: problems with the CAPM and/or the measurment of risk (e.g., infrequent trading could influence the beta calculation), mismeasurement of earnings, or the potential proxying of P/Es for some other fundamentally important variable. One line of research that is of real interest is whether the P/E is a proxy for firm size; that is, do small firms provide abnormal returns relative to large firms? Banz [1981], who questioned Basu's [1977] results, said that "Basu believed he identified a market inefficiency but his P/E effect is just a proxy for the size effect" (p. 17). This research is discussed in detail in the next chapter.[29]

Conclusion

This chapter has shown a number of obvious, and some not so obvious, ways to profit in the stock market. First, it has been widely documented that returns are related to earnings growth, but primarily to unanticipated (surprise) earnings growth. Not surprisingly, simple time-series models are not as effective as analysts in forecasting earnings. This superiority of analysts is especially true for shorter term forecasting (up to six months). And, while the market is relatively efficient in discounting the consensus forecasts by analysts, it appears to be inefficient in using consensus-trends adjusted forecasts. A major remaining question about using earnings data for profitable stock selection is whether simple strategies based on buying stocks with low P/E ratios are profitable.

Research reported in this chapter suggests that some variation of a low-P/E strategy may yield real profits. But how can that be? Low-P/E research has been widely available and acted on by investment professionals for years. Thus the profits should have long ago been arbitraged away. Is it still a real and profitable strategy that can be used today? Is it yet to be revealed as an artifact of improper statistical measurement? Are P/Es proxies for some other factor—for instance, firm size? The next chapter will shed further light on this question of P/Es as proxies for other factors.

CHAPTER 4

Notes

1. Most of the early studies can be criticized for data problems emanating from their use of the COMPUSTAT tapes: there was a survivor bias; a post-announcement earnings revision error; and a large error rate in the data themselves. In addition, most of the studies ignored dividends in calculating returns, used overlapping data, and failed to adjust specifically for risk. Thus while the early studies found that quarterly earnings were not fully incorporated into share prices, one could not be certain that their results were real. Summaries of early research can be found in Joy and Jones [1979] and Ball [1978].

2. This study improved on earlier works that had been faced with the problems inherent in the use of COMPUSTAT data (see note 1).

3. The Rendleman, Jones, and Latane [1982] study was in response to a study by Reinganum [1981], which showed that excess returns could not be earned using the SUE approach.

4. See Mendenhall [unpublished].

5. The authors found that half the excess returns occurred in the 90 days following the earnings announcement.

6. Others—for instance, Bidwell [1979] and Latane and Jones [1977, 1979]—have used SUEs to analyze unexpected returns. They also found that there are excess returns to be made.

7. Brown's [1978] results could have been the result of the time he studied, but Nichols and Brown [1981] replicated the Brown study for two periods, 1963-67 and 1967-71, and concluded that the market did not appear to be becoming any more efficient.

8. For more about this technique, see the Appendix to Chapter 2.

9. See, for instance, Watts [1978].

10. When Foster, Olsen, and Shevlin [1984] tested for the importance of another factor, firm size, they found that 65 percent of the variation in the portfolio cummulative abnormal return in the first 60 days after earnings are announced could be attributed to the size of the company: the smaller the company, the larger the abnormal post-earnings announcement return. The importance of firm size to returns will be discussed in Chapter 5.

11. See, for instance, Albrecht, Lookabill, and McKeown [1977] and Watts and Leftwich [1977].

12. Brown and Rozeff hypothesized that the superiority of the *Value Line* analysts' forecast was attributable to new information available in the periods between earnings announcements. Collins and Hopwood [1980] also confirm the *Value Line* analysts' superiority.

13. For an excellent discussion of this test, see Brown and Rozeff [1978, pp. 2-3].

14. The *Earnings Forecaster* provides the EPS forecasts for about 1,500 companies made by Standard and Poor's and other analysts. The forecasts were first published in 1967.

15. Institutional Brokers Estimate System also provides the number of forecasts made and the standard deviation of those forecasts.

16. Conroy and Harris included in their test only those companies for which four or more analysts made earnings predictions.

17. This tendency was noted by Elton, Gruber, and Gultekin [1984].

18. Hassell and Jennings [1986], tested the relative accuracy of management forecasts against those made by analysts. They found a strong relationship between forecast accuracy and the time of the forecasts and found that management forecasts issued before, at the same time, and after analyst forecasts are more accurate than those analysts'. Analyst forecasts were superior beginning nine weeks after the management forecasts were made.

19. Fried and Givoly [1982] also examined analysts' forecasts to see if they could determine the source of their forecast superiority. They found that forecasts late in the year were better than those made using history alone, and they contended that the reason was because analysts appeared at that time "to rely somewhat less on extrapolation of past earnings data and more on autonomous information than early forecasts" (p. 102).

20. Zeikel [1974] and Hitschler [1980] had previously reached the same conclusion.

21. Their risk adjustment was based on efficient-frontier analysis using mean absolute deviation as the measure of risk.

22. In "Consensus Estimate Revisions and Stock Price Performance in Declining Markets," Hawkins [undated] pressed this research one step further. He incorporated investors' appetites for risk in bear markets, on the hypothesis that stocks with the largest upward revisions in analysts' estimates for earnings would not perform as strongly in bear as in bull markets. He found some evidence to support this notion.

23. Nicholson [1960] may have been the first to look at a low-P/E strategy. He found that low-P/E stocks outperformed not only high-P/E stocks, but also the market as a whole. A number of others testing the same thing concurred with Nicholson's findings.

24. See, for instance, McWilliams [1966], Breen [1968], and Nicholson [1960, 1968].

25. These measures are described in Chapter 1.

26. Reinganum [1981] came to much the same conclusion with regard to errors from the model.

27. Their measure of growth was the company's internally sustainable growth for the most recent year for which accounting data were available. Internally sustainable growth was measured by: Earnings retention rate x Return on equity.

28. Goodman and Peavy divided the company's quarterly P/E ratio by the quarterly average for the industry to estimate the PER.

29. See, for example, Banz [1981], Reinganum [1981], and Jaffe, Keim, and Westerfield [1987].

CHAPTER 4

References

Abdel-khalik, A., and Ajinkya, B. "Returns to Informational Advantage: The Case of Analysts' Forecast Revisions." *Accounting Review,* October 1982, pp. 661-80.

Albrecht, W.; Lookabill, L.; and McKeown, J. "The Time-Series Properties of Annual Earnings." *Journal of Accounting Research,* Autumn 1977, pp. 226-44.

Ariel, Robert. "A Monthly Effect in Stock Returns." *Journal of Financial Economics,* 1987, pp. 161-74.

Arnott, Robert. "The Use and Misuse of Consensus Earnings." *Journal of Portfolio Management,* Spring 1985, pp. 18-27.

————, and Copeland, William. "The Business Cycle and Security Selection." *Financial Analysts Journal,* March-April 1985, pp. 26-32.

Ball, R. "Anomolies in Relationships Between Securities' Yields and Yield Surrogates." *Journal of Financial Economics,* June-September 1978, pp. 103-26.

Banz, Rolf. "The Relationship Between Return and Market Value of Common Stocks." *Journal of Financial Economics,* 1981, pp. 3-18.

————, and Breen, William. "Sample-Dependent Results Using Accounting and Market Data: Some Evidence." *Journal of Finance,* September 1986, pp. 779-94.

Basu, S. "Investment Performance of Common Stocks in Relation to Their Price-Earnings Ratios: A Test of the Efficient Market Hypothesis." *Journal of Finance,* June 1977, pp. 663-82.

Beaver, William, and Morse, Dale. "What Determines Price-Earnings Ratios?" *Financial Analysts Journal,* July-August 1978, pp. 65-76.

Benesh, Gary, and Peterson, Pamela. "On the Relation Between Earnings Changes, Analysts' Forecasts, and Stock Price Fluctuations." *Financial Analysts Journal,* November-December 1986, pp. 29-39.

Bidwell, Clinton. "A Test of Market Efficiency SUE/PE." *Journal of Portfolio Management,* Summer 1979, pp. 53-58.

Breen, William. "Low Price-Earnings Ratios and Industry Relatives." *Financial Analysts Journal,* July-August 1968, pp. 124-27.

Brown, Lawrence, and Rozeff, Michael. "The Superiority of Analyst Forecasts as Measures of Expectations: Evidence from Earnings." *Journal of Finance,* March 1978, pp. 1-16.

Brown, P., and Kennelly, J. W. "The Informational Content of Quarterly Earnings: An Extension and Some Further Evidence." *Journal of Business,* July 1972, pp. 403-15.

Brown, S. "Earnings Changes, Stock Prices and Market Efficiency. *Journal of Finance,* March 1978, pp. 17-28.

Chugh, Lal, and Meador, Joseph. "The Stock Valuation Process: The Analysts' View." *Financial Analysts Journal,* November-December 1984, pp. 41-48.

Collins, W., and Hopwood, W. "A Multivariate Analysis of Annual Earnings Forecasts Generated from Quarterly Forecasts of Financial Analysts and Univariate Time Series Models." *Journal of Accounting Research,* Autumn 1980, pp. 340-406.

Conroy, Robert, and Harris, Robert. "Consensus Forecasts of Corporate Earnings: Analysts' Forecasts and Time Series Methods." *Management Science,* June 1987, pp. 724-38.

Curran, John. "Ten Terrible Calls in 1986." *Fortune,* January 19, 1987, pp. 123-26.

Drexel Burnham Lambert. *Anomolies, Inefficiencies and Active Equity Management: Practical Approaches.* New York: Drexel Burnham Lambert, October 20, 1987.

Easton, Peter. "Accounting Earnings and Security Valuation." *Journal of Accounting Research,* Autumn 1985, pp. 54-77.

Elton, Edwin, and Gruber, Martin. "Earnings Estimates and the Accuracy of Expectational Data." *Management Science,* April 1972, pp. B409-23.

―――; and Gultekin, M. "Expectations and Share Prices." *Management Science,* September 1981, p. 982.

―――. "Professional Expectations: Accuracy and Diagnosis of Errors." *Journal of Financial and Quantitative Analysis,* December 1984, pp. 351-63.

Foster, George; Olsen, Chris; and Shevlin, Terry. "Earnings Releases, Anomalies, and the Behavior of Security Returns." *Accounting Review,* October 1984, pp. 574-603.

Fried, Dov, and Givoly, Dan. "Financial Analysts' Forecasts of Earnings: A Better Surrogate for Market Expectations." *Journal of Accounting and Economics,* October 1982, pp. 85-107.

Givoly, Dan, and Lakonishok, Josef. "The Information Content of Financial Analysts' Forecasts of Earnings." *Journal of Accounting and Economics,* December 1979, pp. 164-85

―――. "Properties of Analysts' Forecasts of Earnings: A Review and Analysis of the Research." *Journal of Accounting Literature,* 1984, pp. 117-48.

Goodman, David, and Peavy, John. "Industry Relative Price-Earnings Ratios as Indicators of Investment Returns." *Financial Analysts Journal,* July-August 1983, pp. 60-66.

Graham, Benjamin, and Dodd, D. L. *Security Analysis.* New York: McGraw Hill, 1940.

Hagin, Robert. "Why the Equity Market Has a Low P/E Bias." Paper presented at the Institute for Quantitative Research in Finance, Spring 1985.

Hassell, John, and Jennings, Robert. "Relative Forecast Accuracy and the Timing of Earnings Forecast Announcements." *The Accounting Review,* January 1986, pp. 58-74.

Hawkins, Eugene. "Consensus Estimate Revisions and Stock Price Performance in Declining Markets." (unpublished manuscript).

―――; Chamberlin, Stanley; and Daniel, Wayne. "Earnings Expectations and Security Prices." *Financial Analysts Journal,* September-October 1984, pp. 24-38, 74.

Hitschler, W. A. "The Carribou Weren't in the Estimate." *Financial Analysts Journal,* January-February 1980, pp. 28-32.

Jaffe, Jeffrey; Keim, Donald; and Westerfield, Randolph. "Earnings Yields, Market Values and Stock Returns." Paper prepared for presentation at the Institute for Quantitative Research in Finance, October 1987.

Jahnke, Greg; Klaffke, Stephen; and Oppenheimer, Henry. "Price-Earnings Ratios and Security Performance." *Journal of Portfolio Management,* Fall 1987, pp. 39-46.

Jones, Charles, and Litzenberger, Robert. "Quarterly Earnings Reports and Intermediate Stock Price Trends." *Journal of Finance,* March 1970, pp. 143-48.

————; Rendleman, Richard; and Latane, Henry. "Earnings Announcement: Pre- and Post-Responses." *Journal of Portfolio Management,* Spring 1985, pp. 28-33.

————. "Stock Returns and SUEs during the 1970s." *Journal of Portfolio Management,* Winter 1984, p. 18-22.

Joy, O. M., and Jones, C. P. "Earnings Reports and Market Efficiencies: An Analysis of the Contrary Evidence." *Journal of Financial Research,* Spring 1979, pp. 51-63.

————; Litzenberger, R.; and McEnally, R. "The Adjustment of Stock Prices to Announcements of Unanticipated Changes in Quarterly Earnings." *Journal of Accounting Research,* Autumn 1977, pp. 207-25.

Keim, Donald. "The CAPM and Equity Return Regularities." *Financial Analysts Journal,* May-June 1986, pp. 19-34.

Kerrigan, Thomas. "When Forecasting Earnings, It Pays to Watch Forecasts." *Journal of Portfolio Management,* Summer 1984, pp. 19-26.

Kormendi, Roger, and Lipe, Robert. "Earnings Innovation, Earnings Persistence, and Stock Returns." *Journal of Business,* 1987, pp. 323-45.

Latane, Henry, and Jones, C. "Standardized Unexpected Earnings— A Progress Report." *Journal of Finance,* December 1977, pp. 1457-65.

————. "Standardized Unexpected Earnings—1971-1977." *Journal of Finance,* June 1979, pp. 717-24.

Latane, Henry A.; Joy, O. Maurice; and Jones, Charles P. "Quarterly Data, Sort-Rank Routines, and Security Evaluation." *Journal of Business,* October 1970, pp. 427-38.

McWilliams, James. "Prices, Earnings and P-E Ratios." *Financial Analysts Journal,* May-June 1966, pp. 137-42.

Mendenhall, Richard. "Estimation Risk: A Possible Explanation of Empirical Anomalies." Unpublished paper, Indiana University, Bloomington.

Morse, Dale. "Price and Trading Volume Reaction Surrounding Earnings Announcements: A Closer Examination." *Journal of Accounting Research,* Autumn 1981, pp. 374-83.

Nichols, William, and Brown, Stewart. "Assimilating Earnings and Spilt Information: Is the Capital Market Becoming More Efficient?" *Journal of Financial Economics,* 1981, pp. 309-15.

Nicholson, S. Francis. "Price Earnings Ratios." *Financial Analysts Journal,* July-August 1960, pp. 43-45.

————. "Price Ratios in Relation to Investment Results." *Financial Analysts Journal,* January-February 1968, pp. 104-09.

Niederhoffer, Victor, and Regan, Patrick. "Earnings Changes, and Stock Prices." *Financial Analysts Journal,* May-June 1972, pp. 65-71.

Ozanian, Michael. "Upward Bias." *Forbes,* June 1, 1987, pp. 186-88.

Patell, James, and Wolfson, Mark. "The Intraday Speed of Adjustment of Stock Prices to Earnings and Dividend Announcements." *Journal of Financial Economics*, 1984, pp. 223-52.

Penman, Stephen H. "The Distribution of Earnings News over Time and Seasonalities in Aggregate Stock Returns." *Journal of Financial Economics*, 1987, pp. 199-228.

Pincus, Morton. "Information Characteristics of Earnings Announcements and Stock Market Behavior." *Journal of Accounting Research*, Spring 1983, pp. 154-83.

Reilly, Frank, and Drzycimski, Eugene. "Aggregate Market Earnings Multiples over Stock Market Cycles and Business Cycles." *Mississippi Valley Journal of Business and Economics*, Winter 1974-75, pp. 14-36.

——; Griggs, Frank; and Wong, Wenchi. "Determinants of the Aggregate Stock Market Earnings Multiple." *Journal of Portfolio Management*, Fall 1983, pp. 36-45.

Reinganum, Marc. "The Collapse of the Efficient Market Hypothesis: A Look at the Empirical Anomalies of the 1980s." In Frank Fabozzi, ed. *The Institutional Investor Focus on Investment Management*. Cambridge, MA: Ballinger Publishing, 1989, pp. 9-23.

——. "Misspecification of Capital Asset Pricing: Empirical Anomalies Based on Earnings' Yields and Market Values." *Journal of Financial Economics*, March 1981, pp. 19-46.

——. "Selecting Superior Securities." Unpublished paper, 1987.

Rendleman, Richard; Jones, Charles; and Latane, Henry. "Empirical Anomalies Based on Unexpected Earnings and the Importance of Risk Adjustments." *Journal of Financial Economics*, 1982, pp. 269-87.

Safian, Kenneth. "Corporate Profits and Valuation: A Different Approach." *Financial Analysts Journal*, January-February 1988, pp. 8-13.

Senchack, A. J., and Martin, John. "The Relative Performance of the PSR and PER Investment Strategies." *Financial Analysts Journal*, March-April 1987, pp. 46-56.

Sorenson, E. H., and Kreichman, S. U. B. *Valuation Factors: Introducing the E-MODEL*. New York: Salomon Brothers, Inc. May 12, 1987.

Treynor, Jack. "Are Low P/E Stocks Still Cheap?" Paper presented at the Institute for Quantitative Research in Finance, Fall 1984, summarized in *Institute for Quantitative Research in Finance: Summary Fall 1984 Proceedings*, ed. J. Peter Williamson.

Watts, Ross. "Systematic 'Abnormal' Returns after Quarterly Earnings Announcements." *Journal of Financial Economics*, 1978, pp. 127-50.

——, and Leftwich, R. "The Time Series of Annual Accounting Earnings." *Journal of Accounting Research*, Autumn 1977, pp. 253-71.

Zachs and Company. *Determinants of Performance*. Chicago, Ill.: June 1987.

Zeikel, A. "The Random Walk and Murphy's Law." *Journal of Portfolio Management*, Fall 1974, pp. 20-30.

Fundamental Valuation: Further Issues

In the last chapter, we discussed earnings-based stock-selection strategies. All those methods for selecting profitable stocks relied on earnings, or some ratio that included earnings. What we found was that one might be able to make a profit using earnings forecasts, if the forecasts were good. As for obtaining accurate forecasts, or forecasts of changes in forecasts, there were some encouraging signs.

Earnings are not the only fundamental factor that investors have used in selecting stocks. There are a variety of other ways by which investors and analysts choose what they believe will be profitable equity investments. Some analysts concentrate on particular features of the firm that are revealed on the company's balance sheet or income statement. Other investors follow the company's activities to find reason to buy or sell the stock when specific events are expected to, or do, occur. Such things as merger or divestiture activity are considered by some to signal profit-making investment possibilities.

In this chapter, we will look at both the specific features of a company that make it attractive as an investment, and at the strategies and actions that signal potential profit for the investor. This chapter will certainly not provide an exhaustive survey of all the ways that analysts and investors undertake to make profitable fundamental investment decisions. It will, however, be an extensive survey of what has been tried and what we know about the potential profit of each method.

Dividends

The last chapter discussed earnings and the importance of earnings in stock pricing. In Exhibit 4-1, we showed the fundamental relationship between the price of any asset (its present value) and what the investor would actually receive. In looking at the figure the first time, you would have noticed that, while earnings are the primary source of the investor's returns, the actual returns come in two forms: the dividends that the company pays and the capital that it returns to its shareholders as liquidating payments. Such liquidating payments might be paid as dividends and share repurchases over time, or liquidating payments at the company's dissolution or restructuring. Thus, while earnings are the wellspring of the company's power to pay dividends, dividends are the actual payment.

Although earnings underlie dividends, Hawkins [1977] suggested that earnings have ceased to be reliable forecasts of the cash that a firm would have available to pay dividends, and earnings-based models have thus "lost much of their usefulness" (p. 48). Among other things, inflation and accounting approaches to deal with foreign subsidiaries' income continue to make earnings less than robust indicators of a company's cash flow. Thus Hawkins suggested we return to a model that really takes an investor's returns into account, a dividend discount model (DDM).[1]

Dividend Discount Model

The DDM discounts the expected dividends for any stock by the equity investors' required return. A variety of versions of the basic model have been used, but the most basic is the constant-growth version:[2]

$$Market\ price = \frac{Dividends}{Required\ return - Expected\ growth}$$

This model is a shortened version of one in which the dividends are explicitly forecasted and are expected to increase annually by a constant rate.[3] These dividends are discounted by the investors' required return.

If dividends are not expected to grow at a constant rate, most analysts turn to a two-phase method: the analyst forecasts dividends explicitly for some period of time before assuming future dividends grow at a constant rate. For a high-growth, low- or no-dividend-paying company, the analyst might use a more elaborate model incorporating a period without dividends and a period of high growth, before establishing a final, sustainable, dividend growth rate.[4]

Regardless of which version of the model the analyst or investor uses, the real question is: What value do these dividend discount models have in finding profitable investments? In the last chapter, we saw that there was some profit to be made by the skilled investor who could forecast earnings. Even so, the profits to be made from forecasting dividends could be larger: Sorensen and Williamson [1985] showed that the profit from a price/earnings (P/E) approach was lower than the profit from any of the dividend discount models they tested, and the more sophisticated the version they used, the higher the profit. To reach these conclusions, Sorensen and Williamson used IBES analysts' earnings forecasts to develop their earnings forecasts, and they used two- and three-phase DDMs. As a measure of risk, they used a beta forecasted from information fundamental to the firm.[5] Using these data, they ranked their random sample of 150 of the Standard & Poor's (S&P) 400 into five portfolios. The portfolios contained stocks ranked by their market prices relative to each stock's intrinsic value—the degree of relative undervaluation (DEV). Sorensen and Williamson's results are shown in Exhibit 5-1.

As you can see, the relative risk (systematic risk and standard deviation) of the portfolios was about the same, so the results could not be attributed to differences in risk. What was true was that excess returns were related to the degree of undervaluation, but the returns gained from using the two- and three-period DDMs were larger than those from the P/E method.

DDMs can be improved. Although Sorensen and Williamson showed that multiperiod DDMs outperformed simple one-factor (i.e., P/E) models for their 150-company sample, Jacobs and Levy [1988] documented that DDMs were not nearly as powerful for their larger universe of 1,500 companies. In the larger universe, the simple P/E model dominated their DDMs.

Dividend Announcements

While Sorensen and Williamson showed that profits can be made using dividends, or at least their versions of the dividend discount model, considerable controversy exists about what role dividends actually play in the pricing of shares. Folklore about the price impact of dividend cuts and increases vies with theories about the actual value of dividends to shareholders. In a world where a higher tax rate is assessed on dividends than on capital gains,[6] gains from corporate reinvestments (growth in future dividends) should be preferred by rational investors—at least on purely economic grounds. Many believe, however, that shareholders are either skeptical about the future, and thus prefer a smaller dividend now to a larger dividend later (the bird-in-the-hand theory), or treat dividend payments as an indication of management's intentions about the future prospects for the company (dividends are a signal). In these latter cases, investors prefer dividends to future growth, and the stock price would be higher on higher yielding stocks. One caveat is important. This high-yield conclusion comes only if all else about the company remains the same.

In an intriguing discussion of stock-price movements and shareholders' returns, Shiller [1981] considered whether stock-price volatility came as a result of changes in the expected dividend. He showed that the implied rational S&P Index (the present value of future dividends) was much less volatile than the actual index itself. From data like the graph of his results shown in Exhibit 5-2, Shiller concluded that "the stock market decline beginning in 1929 and ending in 1932 could not be rationalized in terms of subsequent dividends!" (p. 422).

Exhibit 5-1
Performance Measures and Related Statistics, January 1981–January 1983

| | Portfolios | | | | | | |
	1	2	3	4	5	Range	Market
DEV or PE							
3-Period	1.5766	1.1796	0.9513	0.7539	0.5012		0.9980
2-Period	1.4972	1.1733	0.9579	0.7762	0.5292		0.9910
Const. growth	1.5682	1.2424	0.9910	0.7713	0.4853		1.0160
P/E	5.6068	6.9869	8.9353	11.6437	19.9453		10.9453
Annualized Return							
3-Period	0.3046	0.2827	0.1754	0.0622	-0.0517	0.3563	0.1567
2-Period	0.2945	0.2458	0.1412	0.1099	-0.0193	0.3134	
Const. growth	0.2742	0.2277	0.1481	0.0925	0.0346	0.2396	
P/E	0.2705	0.2203	0.1415	0.0975	0.0479	0.2226	
Avg. Annual Excess Return							
3-Period	0.1646	0.1427	0.0354	-0.0778	-0.1917		0.0415
2-Period	0.1545	0.1058	0.0012	-0.0300	-0.1593		
Const. growth	0.1342	0.0877	0.0081	-0.0475	-0.1054		
P/E	0.1305	0.0803	0.0015	-0.0426	-0.0921		
S.D. of Port. Returns							
3-Period	0.1693	0.1751	0.1964	0.1872	0.2168		0.1815
2-Period	0.1651	0.1809	0.1876	0.1903	0.2235		
Const. growth	0.1710	0.1740	0.1844	0.1931	0.2238		
P/E	0.1614	0.1836	0.1745	0.1945	0.2301		
Systematic Risk							
3-Period	0.9279	0.9175	0.9507	1.0037	1.0950		1.0000
2-Period	0.9178	0.9319	0.9463	0.9897	1.1091		
Const. growth	0.9274	0.9071	0.9665	0.9819	1.1074		
P/E	0.9261	0.9064	0.9586	0.9874	1.1154		
Treynor Ratio							
3-Period	0.1774	0.1556	0.0372	-0.0775	-0.1751		0.0170
2-Period	0.1683	0.1135	0.0013	-0.0303	-0.1436		
Const. growth	0.1447	0.0967	0.0084	-0.0484	-0.0952		
P/E	0.1409	0.0886	0.0016	-0.0431	-0.0826		
Sharpe Ratio							
3-Period	0.9722	0.8154	0.1800	-0.4155	-0.8843		0.0917
2-Period	0.9356	0.5845	0.0065	-0.1578	-0.7125		
Const. growth	0.7849	0.5040	0.0439	-0.2460	-0.4711		
P/E	0.7928	0.4375	0.0087	-0.2188	-0.4004		

Source: Adapted from Sorensen and Williamson [1985], p. 65.

Exhibit 5-2
S&P Composite Index Compared with Rational, Implied Price

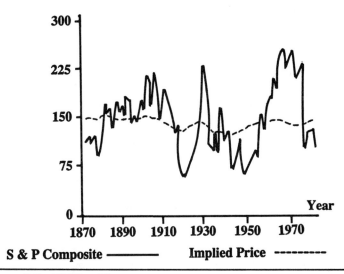

S & P Composite ——————   Implied Price ----------

Source: Shiller [1981], p. 422.

Several things could make the actual index more volatile than theory suggests. First, rather than dividends, earnings might be what the investor expects to receive. Shiller rejected this idea out of hand, saying, "There is no reason why price per share ought to be the present value of expected earnings per share if some earnings are retained " (p. 429). Second, the arrival of new information about real dividends could create the volatility.[7] Shiller rejected this notion also, because the volatility of the stock index has been "five to thirteen times too high . . . to be attributed to new information about future real dividends if uncertainty about future dividends is measured by sample standard deviations of real dividends around their long-run exponential growth path" (p. 434). Third, he tested to determine whether the volatility was caused by changes in expected real interest rates, which he concluded were not the culprit either. From this analysis, he concluded that the excessive volatility was the result of the market being "rightfully fearful of much larger movements than actually materialized" (p. 434). The anticipation was worse than what actually happened.

Shiller looked at the difference between the implied and real impact that dividend changes have on the stock index. Others have investigated the dividend-impact question in other ways. Sakaguchi [1988] used an adaptation of the two-stage DDM that incorporated a factor to account for the Japanese investor's appetite for growth (a combination of the real interest rate and the relationship between the money supply and gross national product plus net imports). He found that the Japanese stock market was appropriately valued in 1986, and 1987, as shown in Exhibit 5-3. You can also see how much importance investors were placing on the first-period returns relative to those in the future.

Exhibit 5-3

DDM Components of Stock Price in the Japanese Stock Market

Year	Returns 1st Period	Future	Price Determined by Model	Actual Price
1972	16.25	186.78	235.32	179.74
1975	.17.29	187.42	190.25	173.88
1980	21.02	233.49	248.75	269.27
1986	27.31	664.12	853.55	851.24
1987	29.13	924.37	1,250.93	1,117.55

Source: Adapted from Sakaguchi [1988], p. 16.

Just how much the dividend portion of expected future payments contributes to an investor's expected return is clear in theory, but the evidence is not so clear. Fama and French [1987] found that forecasted dividend yields are only a small portion of the returns: regressing returns on dividend yield explained 25 percent of the 2-to-4-year return.[8]

We described in the last chapter the results Patell and Wolfson [1984] obtained when they looked at the impact on stock prices of earnings announcements. In the same study, they looked at the impact dividend announcements had on share prices and found that they had a similar, but smaller, effect. You will recall from the last chapter that they found the earnings impact to be measurable, but the information was quickly (within minutes) impounded in share prices. The same was true for dividends.[9]

How do dividend arrangements affect returns? While the early studies produced mixed results, Charest [1978] looked at the profits that could be made from strategies based on announcements of dividend changes. He found, "The evidence . . . is not consistent with the hypothesis that the NYSE [New York Stock Exchange] has been efficient in interpreting selected cash dividend change information in the 1947-67 period. In our estimation, a systematic trader in dividend changing stocks would have earned significant abnormal returns" (p. 326). In contrast to Charest, Divecha and Morse [1983] indicated that most of the effect they found occurred within one day of the announcement and was largest for companies with dividend increases of more than 10 percent. In their study of 735 firms from May 1977 through February 1979, they also found that a simultaneous decrease in the payout ratio also produced higher returns. Their results are shown in Exhibit 5-4.

Exhibit 5-4
Average Return Residuals Surrounding Announcements of Dividend Increases

Positive Dividend Changes
Sample Size = 1,039

Day	Mean	Deviation	t-Test
- 20	0.00046	0.0181	0.82
- 19	-0.00038	0.0183	-0.68
- 18	0.00058	0.0211	0.90
- 17	-0.00007	0.0208	-0.12
- 16	-0.00070	0.0188	-1.21
- 15	-0.00095	0.0328	-0.93
- 14	0.00098	0.0176	1.81
- 13	-0.00106	0.0182	-1.88
- 12	0.00042	0.0174	0.78
- 11	-0.00060	0.0173	-1.13
- 10	-0.00009	0.0181	-0.16
- 9	0.00012	0.0168	0.24
- 8	0.00038	0.0171	0.73
- 7	0.00029	0.0198	0.48
- 6	0.00043	0.0186	0.75
- 5	0.00135	0.0186	2.35[a]
- 4	0.00040	0.0180	0.73
- 3	0.00022	0.0179	0.40
- 2	0.00064	0.0179	1.16
- 1	0.00116	0.0182	2.06[a]
0	0.00843	0.0239	11.37[b]
+ 1	0.00240	0.0207	3.73[b]
+ 2	0.00043	0.0195	0.72
+ 3	0.00144	0.0181	2.57[a]
+ 4	0.00014	0.0180	0.26
+ 5	0.00079	0.0184	1.39
+ 6	0.00022	0.0180	0.40
+ 7	0.00072	0.0182	1.28
+ 8	0.00005	0.0181	0.09
+ 9	0.00009	0.0189	0.16
+ 10	0.00023	0.0193	0.39
+ 11	0.00000	0.0187	0.02
+ 12	0.00053	0.0171	1.00
+ 13	0.00052	0.0179	0.95
+ 14	0.00007	0.0179	0.14
+ 15	0.00071	0.0165	1.39
+ 16	-0.00035	0.0172	-0.67
+ 17	-0.00032	0.0170	-0.61
+ 18	0.00063	0.0161	1.26
+ 19	0.00034	0.0182	0.60
+ 20	0.00061	0.0173	1.51

[a] Significantly different from zero at the 5 percent confidence level.
[b] Significantly different from zero at the 1 percent confidence level.

Source: Divecha and Morse [1983], p. 169.

Most studies, these included, certainly can be questioned as to methodology and data, yet they suggest that information about dividends ought to help us select stocks. Cole [1984] used a different approach to the problem. He wanted to separate the information content of dividends from earnings; he constructed two extreme portfolios—one based on unusual earnings[10] and the other on unusual dividends. Exhibit 5-5 shows the returns from the two portfolios over six different holding periods. As you can see, the high-dividend portfolio (HD) outperformed the portfolio constructed using unexpected earnings (HS) for every holding period.

Exhibit 5-5
Overall Averages of Differences in Holding-Period Returns

Holding Period	HD versus LD	HS versus LS	HD versus HS
1 mo.	.005	.006	.0062
2 mos.	.030	.014	.0106
3 mos.	.043	.024	.0192
4 mos.	.049	.026	.0232
5 mos.	.059	.062	.0176
6 mos.	.073	.069	.0294

Note: HD = High-dividend portfolios.
LD = Low-dividend portfolios.
HS = High-SUE portfolios.
LS = Low-SUE portfolios.

Source: Cole [1984], p. 48.

Perhaps the most complete, and most encouraging, study is by Eades, Hess, and Kim [1985], who tried to determine whether changes in dividends affected returns. They used all NYSE stocks that had made dividend announcements from July 1962 to the end of 1980 and classified the announced dividends as increases, decreases, or no change from the previous dividend. They then calculated the average returns for ten days before and after the announcement. Their results are in contrast to results from earlier studies such as that by Divecha and Morse [1983]. As shown in Exhibit 5-6, they found that the "post announcement day returns for the dividend increase sample are significantly positive for six days after the announcement day" (p. 585). They theorized that part of the first day's returns could be attributed to the fact that some of the announcements were made after trading closed; but this reason did not pertain to the returns on days 2 through 6.[11]

As you can see from Exhibit 5-6, they also found that the same returns were not associated with dividend decreases: the returns all came in the first trading day following the announcement. These results suggest that a profit can

Exhibit 5-6
Test of Timeliness of Market's Reaction to Dividend Announcements

Days Relative to Announcement Day	Average Raw Return (%)	Average Market-Adjusted Excess Return (%)	Average Mean Adjusted Excess Return (%)	Average Standardized Excess Return	Average SER Standard Deviation	t-Statistic for Average SER Relative to Zero	Significance Level
			Panel A: Increases in Regular Dividends				
-10	0.043	-0.047	-0.025	-0.0048	1.122	-0.191	0.8485
-9	0.058	-0.024	-0.009	0.0089	1.142	0.350	0.7264
-8	0.069	-0.014	0.002	-0.0034	1.123	-0.135	0.8924
-7	0.114	0.031	0.046	0.0308	1.250	1.104	0.2697
-6	0.151	0.084	0.083	0.0577	1.173	2.201	0.0278
-5	0.024	-0.038	-0.043	-0.0026	1.200	-0.098	0.9220
-4	0.131	0.059	0.064	0.0641	1.147	2.501	0.0124
-3	0.108	0.042	0.041	0.0488	1.194	1.829	0.0675
-2	0.086	0.040	0.018	0.0185	1.199	0.689	0.4906
-1	0.160	0.125	0.092	0.0862	1.143	3.375	0.0008
AD	0.656	0.619	0.588	0.4484	1.477	13.579	$<10^4$
+1	0.417	0.356	0.349	0.3061	1.549	8.840	$<10^4$
+2	0.158	0.117	0.091	0.0959	1.197	3.584	0.0003
+3	0.077	0.045	0.010	0.0382	1.458	1.173	0.2408
+4	0.053	0.031	-0.014	0.0046	1.148	0.180	0.8570
+5	0.080	0.045	0.013	0.0375	1.077	1.557	0.1196
+6	0.074	0.002	0.006	0.0058	1.087	0.238	0.8116
+7	0.125	0.091	0.058	0.0477	1.173	1.819	0.0691
+8	0.021	-0.010	-0.047	-0.0311	1.141	-1.221	0.2222
+9	-0.009	-0.061	-0.076	-0.0290	1.118	-1.161	0.2456
+10	0.065	-0.012	-0.003	0.0037	1.078	0.155	0.8768

Exhibit 5-6 (continued)

Test of Timeliness of Market's Reaction to Dividend Announcements

Days Relative to Announcement Day	Average Raw Return (%)	Average Market/Adjusted Excess Return (%)	Average Mean Adjusted Excess Return (%)	Average Standardized Excess Return	Average SER Standard Deviation	t-Statistic for Average SER Relative to Zero	Significance Level
		Panel B: Decreases in Regular Dividends					
-10	0.000	-0.064	-0.081	-0.0157	1.222	-0.235	0.8145
-9	0.206	0.075	0.125	0.1027	1.153	1.628	0.1044
-8	0.000	-0.100	-0.081	-0.0339	1.132	-0.547	0.5850
-7	0.033	-0.062	-0.048	0.0230	1.117	0.376	0.7070
-6	-0.012	-0.111	-0.094	-0.0408	1.242	-0.600	0.5488
-5	0.027	-0.058	-0.054	-0.0042	1.304	-0.059	0.9532
-4	0.097	-0.074	0.015	0.0856	1.217	1.285	0.1995
-3	0.125	-0.022	0.044	0.0537	1.340	0.732	0.4647
-2	-0.067	-0.177	-0.149	-0.0324	1.313	-0.451	0.6522
-1	0.011	-0.124	-0.071	-0.0722	1.062	-1.243	0.2149
AD	-0.950	-1.065	-1.032	-0.4903	2.122	-4.224	$<10^4$
+1	-0.684	-0.786	-0.765	-0.3995	2.153	-3.391	0.0008
+2	0.123	-0.004	0.041	0.0746	1.198	1.137	0.2562
+3	0.436	0.325	0.354	0.1548	1.309	2.161	0.0314
+4	-0.100	-0.169	-0.182	-0.0474	1.234	-0.702	0.4834
+5	0.096	0.053	0.015	-0.0226	1.143	-0.362	0.7177
+6	0.085	-0.042	0.003	0.0089	1.190	0.137	0.8913
+7	0.334	0.224	0.252	0.1199	1.122	1.953	0.0516
+8	0.165	-0.087	0.084	0.0550	1.239	0.812	0.4176
+9	0.250	0.190	0.168	0.1234	1.208	-1.867	0.0628
+10	0.087	-0.069	0.005	0.0367	1.173	0.572	0.5677

* Average percentage daily raw returns, market-adjusted excess returns, mean-adjusted excess returns, and standardized excess returns (SER) of equally weighted announcement day (AD) portfolios of all NYSE common stocks in the period July 2, 1962 to December 31, 1980.

be made if the investor buys stocks for which the dividends announced are in excess of the past dividend.[12] Indeed, it appears that profits can be made even if the investor does not react to the information instantly.

Part of the profits that Eades et al. found might be attributable to the impact of the stock going ex dividend: at some point following the announcement, the stock trades and the announced dividend remains with the previous owner. If the ex dividend point were within the first five trading days after the announcement, and a profit was to be made on the ex dividend trading price, the profits that were found could be erroneously attributed to the dividend announcement.

In theory, the ex dividend price plus the dividend should be equal to the price before the stock trades ex dividend. However, when investors are faced with a lower tax rate on capital gains than on dividends, the ex dividend price should be a little more than expected: a higher value is placed on growth. In fact, if the theory holds true, one should be able to deduce the tax rate of the marginal investor from the difference between what the ex dividend price is and what it should be without differential tax rates.

Several researchers have looked at the behavior of stock prices when a stock goes ex dividend. In general, they have found that the ex dividend price drops less than the full value of the dividend.[13] Brealey and Myers [1988] summarized this research in their textbook, the results of which are shown in Exhibit 5-7. As you can see from the exhibit, different researchers have found that quite different tax rates seemed to be in effect.[14] While some of this variability can be attributed to differences in the time periods that each studied, not all the differences can be laid at that door.

Eades et al. [1984] found several other interesting things about the ex dividend behavior of stocks. First, the "ex-day effect occurs overnight and not during the ex-day" (p. 11). Second, the "ex-day excess returns for non-taxable stock dividends and splits are significantly positive, while the ex-day excess returns for non-taxable cash distributions are significantly negative. These results are not consistent with either the simple form of the tax hypothesis or tax-induced dividend clienteles" (p. 32).

Because of these differences, some have questioned whether taxes are the source, or the only source, of the results. To study this question, Poterba and Summers [1984] looked at the impact of dividends on share prices in the United Kingdom. They used data from this market because there had been two major and several minor changes in the way the U.K. tax code dealt with dividend taxation over the previous 30 years. They found that the ex dividend price behaved differently when changes in tax policy affected after-tax dividend values. They also found that their results for some periods were not consistent with the tax rates in existence for those periods.[15]

Eades et al. also found that abnormal returns existed for preferred stocks,

Exhibit 5-7
Some Tests of the Effect of Yield on Returns

Test	Test Period	Interval	Implied Tax Rate (Percent)	Standard Error of Tax Rate
Brennan	1946–1965	Monthly	34	12
Black & Scholes (1974)	1936–1966	Monthly	22	24
Litzenberger & Ramaswamy (1979)	1936–1977	Monthly	24	3
Litzenberger & Ramaswamy (1982)	1940–1980	Monthly	14–23	2–3
Rosenberg & Marathe (1979)	1931–1966	Monthly	40	21
Bradford & Gordon (1980)	1926–1978	Monthly	18	2
Blume (1980)	1936–1976	Quarterly	52	25
Miller & Scholes (1982)	1940–1978	Monthly	4	3
Stone & Bartter (1979)	1947–1970	Monthly	56	28
Morgan (1982)	1946–1977	Monthly	21	2

Sources: See references for this chapter at end of book or below:

M. J. Brennan: "Dividends and Valuation in Imperfect Markets: Some Empirical Tests," unpublished paper, not dated.

F. Black and M. Scholes: "The Effects of Dividend Yield and Dividend Policy on Common Stock Prices and Returns," *Journal of Financial Economics*, 1: 1–22 (May 1974).

B. Rosenberg and V. Marathe: "Tests of Capital Asset Pricing Model Hypotheses," in H. Levy (ed.), *Research in Finance I*, Greenwich, Conn.: JAI Press (1979).

D. F. Bradford and R. H. Gordon: "Taxation and the Stock Market Valuation of Capital Gains and Dividends," *Journal of Public Economics*, 14: 109–136 (1980).

M. E. Blume: "Stock Returns and Dividend Yields: Some More Evidence," *Review of Economics and Statistics*, 567–577 (November 1980).

B. K. Stone and B. J. Bartter: "The Effect of Dividend Yield on Stock Returns: Empirical Evidence on the Relevance of Dividends," W.P.E.-76-78, Atlanta, GA.: Georgia Institute of Technology 1979.

Source: Brealey and Myers [1988], p. 372.

stock dividends, and other noncash distributions, although the results were stronger for cash dividends. These results suggest that something besides tax differentials may be at work.

Kalay [1984] suggested that deducing tax rates from data about ex dividend prices is inappropriate. He came to this conclusion after considering the impact on prices of short-term trading by profit-seeking arbitrageurs: such arbitrageurs have identical tax rates for their dividends and capital gains because of the length of time they hold any stock. Because of the equality of tax rates for these investors, Kalay said, in the absence of transaction costs, opportunities to make a profit should drive the ex dividend value plus the dividend to the dividend value. There are transaction costs, however.

After estimating the transaction costs likely to be paid by a member of the NYSE, Kalay concluded, "These minimum levels of transaction costs are far lower than those paid by the investor community at large, thus it is safe to conclude that the ex-dividend day behavior of stock prices provides no short term profit potential for a typical nonmember [of the NYSE] investor" (p. 1067). In other words, the profits that might be available are not there unless you are able to execute trades at a lower-than-average cost. After adjusting for the problems that he pointed out, Kalay still found that the price drop was less than the value of the dividend: something like taxes is still at work in the pricing of shares ex dividend.

The inspiration for Kalay's first article [1982] about the role of transactions costs in the ex dividend behavior of shares was a much earlier article by Elton and Gruber [1970]. Subsequently, they responded to Kalay's thesis about transaction-cost-induced behavior by looking at the transaction costs that Kalay used to come to his conclusion.[16] Their analysis concluded "that the estimates of the level of transaction costs which Kalay presents . . . are much too low and that true transaction costs make it clear that short-term traders are not setting equilibrium prices on the ex-dividend day" (p. 552). In a further discussion of the issues, Kalay [1984] determined that short-term trading for high-yield stocks may provide those traders a profit.

The behavior of stocks that go ex dividend is unusual. Lakonishok and Vermaelen [1986] hypothesized that, if short-term traders are major players at ex dividend time, the volume of trading in ex dividend stocks should increase dramatically, and it should be related negatively to transaction costs and positively to dividend yield. Using data from Cornell University's Price and Volume file, they examined data about NYSE and American Stock Exchange (ASE) stocks that had declared cash or stock dividends or had had a stock split. They used two time frames to examine the volume data: event and calendar time.[17] For each, they calculated the abnormal volume for five days before and after the dividend was declared. They compared this average abnormal volume for all ex dividend stocks with the normal volume, based on the previous 65 days before the dividend announcement.

Exhibit 5-8 shows that volume increases dramatically at ex dividend time: using the calendar- or event-time methodology, "the cumulative average abnormal percentage change shows a rather spectacular increase in trading volume of 29.8% in the ten days surrounding the ex-day" (p. 299). When they separated their data from 1970 to 1981 into two periods to test for the impact of commission changes in 1975, "the results are even more striking" (p. 299). All "these results are consistent with the hypothesis that short-term traders have significant impact on ex-day behavior" (p. 300)[18] especially since May 1975.

Exhibit 5-8
Cumulative Excess Volume Starting Five Days Before the
Ex Dividend Date (percent)

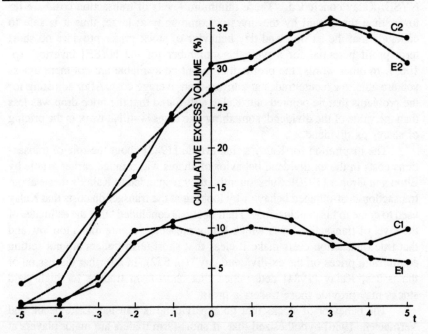

Note: C-2 and E-2 are calendar and event time since May 1975, C-1 and E-1 before 1975.

Source: Lakonishok and Vermaelen [1986], p. 301.

What do we know? Announcements of dividend changes apparently hold information from which the investor may be able to profit. Profits can even be made in the two years subsequent to initial dividend-payment anomalies, as Healy and Palepu [1988] found. Short-term traders may be among those attempting to take advantage of the profits, because volume increases around the ex dividend date, particulary for high-yield stocks and particularly after commissions dropped in 1975. We know that taxes appear to have an impact on the ex dividend price, an impact that will be interesting to measure for the period after the Tax Act of 1986 which made the tax question, at least temporarily, moot. In addition, investors appear to have a preference for dividends that may be somewhat irrational on economic grounds.[19] Such uneconomic preference for dividends may have something to do with risk or information.[20] In short, there are a few things that we know, but many we do not.[21]

Asset Value

Many analysts believe that certain things about a company give special clues to potential profits from its stock. Benjamin Graham [1973], one of the best known and earliest of the fundamental investment proponents, in a book first published in 1930, developed a rule called the net current asset value rule (NCAV): Buy all stocks that sell for less than two-thirds of the value of their current assets minus all liabilities, including preferred stock. In essence, the investor acting on this rule buys a company but pays nothing for the property, plant, and equipment. While Graham suggested other criteria, and those criteria changed over time, he reported that using this rule earned average returns of 20 percent over a 30-year period.

Oppenheimer [1986] retested NCAV using simulation. He created portfolios of undervalued stocks for each year from 1970-82. While survivorship problems certainly existed in his data, Oppenheimer computed the returns adjusted by the mean returns and risk (beta) of these portfolios and compared the returns with those earned on market indexes. He found that the NCAV portfolio's returns were better in every period. His results for 30-month holding periods are shown in Exhibit 5-9.

The abnormal returns were not particularly the result of having an excess of small firms or different levels of risk between the NCAV portfolios and the benchmarks. Vu [1988] confirmed the results using different data and over a more recent period.

Book Value/Market Price

A variation of the NCAV approach is the relationship between the market price of the company's common stock and its book, or adjusted book, value. For example, *Business Week* reported 200 undervalued stocks of the 1,500 largest publicly held U.S. corporations: a low market-book value suggests an undervalued company. However, in reviewing the list, the magazine suggested that a low market price relative to book value might not suggest a valuable company but a company with "uninspiring prospects or . . . stuck in troubled industries" (p. 294) and quoted concerns by one money manager who asked, "'Are you finding value or the dregs of society?' Maybe the stock market is efficiently pricing

Exhibit 5-9

Performance Measures for 30-Month Holding Periods

Purchase Date[a]	Mean Returns		Terminal Wealth of $10,000		Risk-Adjusted Measures				
	R_{pt} (%)	R_{mt} (%)	NAV Issues	Market Index	α (%)	$t(α)$[b]	β	$t(β)$[b]	R_2
Panel A: vs. NYSE-ASE Value-Weighted Index									
1970	0.47	0.56	$19,557	$11,639	-0.21	-0.19	1.64	4.94[d]	0.466
1971	-0.08	-0.47	8,584	8,552	0.62	0.37	1.23	2.69[c]	0.205
1972	1.36	-0.31	11,556	8,599	1.81	0.77	1.14	3.07[d]	0.252
1973	3.60	0.78	24,441	11,930	2.78	1.69	1.19	4.58[d]	0.429
1974	5.37	1.88	42,581	16,993	2.48	1.88[d]	1.70	6.01[d]	0.563
1975	3.70	0.88	28,180	12,726	2.72	3.31[d]	1.23	5.64[d]	0.532
1976	2.75	0.58	21,533	11,624	2.17	3.07[d]	1.05	5.82[d]	0.547
1977	2.64	1.36	19,736	14,473	1.06	1.20	1.37	7.73[d]	0.681
1978	2.86	1.78	22,131	16,446	1.17	1.43	0.90	5.17[d]	0.489
1979	2.16	0.94	18,176	12,767	1.19	1.36	0.73	4.14[d]	0.380
1980	3.88	1.61	30,220	15,635	2.53	3.11[d]	0.61	3.55[d]	0.311
1981[e]	3.53	1.73	21,923	14,798	2.29	1.65	0.48	1.54	0.098
1982[f]	5.85	1.77	18,937	12,297	4.11	1.35	0.97	0.93	0.089
Panel B: vs. Ibbotson and Sinquefield Small-Firm Index[g]									
1970	0.47	-0.27	$19,557	$ 8,778	0.88	1.38	1.22	16.34[d]	0.821
1971	-0.08	-0.98	8,584	6,958	1.03	0.83	1.09	5.99[d]	0.562
1972	1.36	0.14	11,556	9,310	1.32	0.76	1.22	6.21[d]	0.579
1973	3.60	2.17	24,441	17,151	1.11	1.34	1.19	13.08[d]	0.859
1974	5.37	3.74	42,581	27,859	2.22	1.91[d]	1.47	11.28[d]	0.927
1975	3.70	3.34	28,180	25,305	0.57	1.46	0.93	16.89[d]	0.911
1976	2.75	2.70	21,533	19,674	0.58	1.34	0.75	12.26[d]	0.843
1977	2.64	2.42	19,736	18,423	0.17	0.14	0.84	6.73[d]	0.819
1978	2.86	3.32	22,131	24,959	-0.11	-0.11	0.72	5.39[d]	0.744
1979	2.16	1.55	18,176	14,966	0.73	1.12	0.77	7.43[d]	0.664
1980	3.88	1.65	30,220	21,154	1.54	2.49[c]	0.82	7.00[d]	0.636
1981[e]	3.53	2.55	21,923	17,877	1.02	0.91	0.98	4.37[d]	0.465
1982[f]	5.85	2.92	18,937	13,967	1.68	0.76	1.56	3.48[d]	0.548

[a] Purchase on December 31 of designated year.
[b] Significant at 10 percent level.
[c] Significant at 5 percent level.
[d] Significant at 1 percent level.

[e] Holding period of 24 months.
[f] Holding period of 12 months.
[g] Ibbotson Associates.

Source: Oppenheimer [1986], p. 43

these securities. . . . Are these stocks cheap simply because earnings prospects for their companies are comparatively poor?" (p. 294)

To determine whether a strategy based on book/market value would yield profits, Rosenberg, Reid, and Lanstein [1985] estimated the returns that would be earned on a portfolio that bought stocks of high relative book value and sold those with low relative book values. In developing the criteria for their portfolio, they controlled for industry concentration and concentration of a variety of other microeconomic factors such as size, growth, and financial leverage. Using data from 1973 to 1980 to develop the strategy, and from 1980 through 1984 to test the strategy, they found that, about 75 percent of the time, the results were positive, with a mean return of 32 basis points per month. The results were very seasonal; January's returns averaged almost 5 times the average monthly returns. Turnover from the strategy was low, and thus returns from this strategy were still profitable when trading costs were assessed.

Wilcox [1984] went a step further, arguing that the book-value/price ratio (he actually used the price/book value ratio) is not enough.[22] He suggested that incorporating the company's return on equity (ROE) would be superior for selecting stocks. To demonstrate the relationship between the two factors, he plotted them for a large number of stocks. One of his graphs is shown in Exhibit 5-10.

Exhibit 5-10
Price/Book Value and Return on Equity

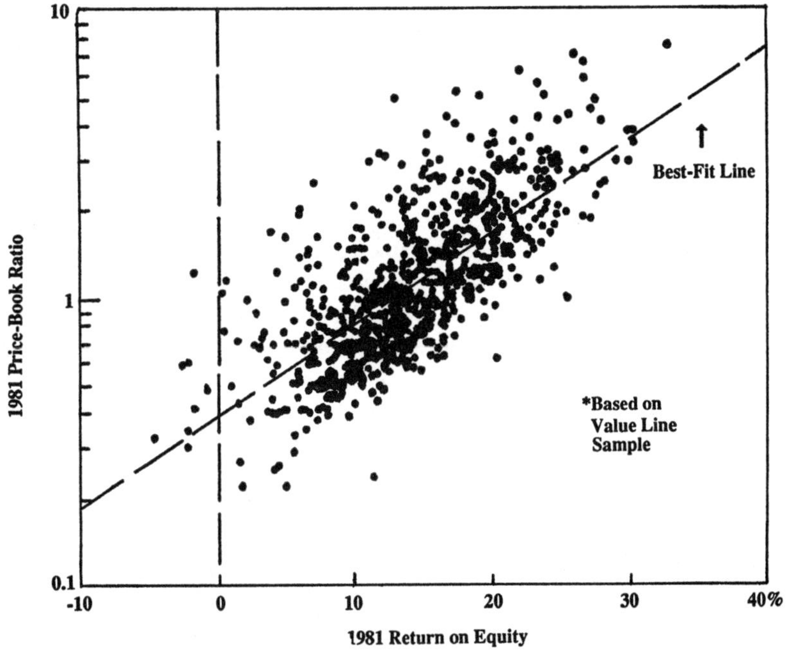

Source: Wilcox [1984], p. 63.

The relationship is quite strong and holds for the years and industries Wilcox examined. Whether the relationship can be used to select securities depends, of course, on whether the variables can be forecasted. From his analysis of these factors and their relationship, he concluded that, contrary to conventional wisdom, (1) stable earnings do not lead to higher prices; (2) dividends matter; (3) leverage does not hurt; (4) stocks with higher betas do not have higher returns. Wilcox [1988] found his strategy worked well for international stocks too.[23]

Another researcher used the price-to-book ratio as part of a scheme to select stocks. Reinganum [1988] examined 222 winners (companies whose prices had doubled in one year) to find commonly held attributes. He considered attributes in four general areas: investment specialists' holdings, measures of valuation, technical indicators, and profitability. He found that, while investment advisors increased their holdings during the period of the price increase, they did not do so in a significant way prior to the price movement. Corporate insiders, another supposedly knowledgeable group, did not buy a stock immediately before or during the price increase: in fact, they sold their shares. As for valuation measures, he tested five: market price/book value, P/E ratio, stock-price level, market capitalization, and beta. He found that, of the 222 price appreciators, 164 sold for less than their book value prior to the price increase, and he concluded that "an investment strategy should isolate firms that sell below book value" (p. 20). He also concluded that "very low P/E ratios are not a necessary ingredient of a successful investment strategy" (p. 21) and neither are small-capitalization stocks or high-beta stocks. He did find that a small number of shares and a price that was within 15 percent of its previous two-year high seemed relevant.

As for the technical indicators, Reinganum found that a positive change in the relative-strength ranking was a common feature among the winners. Finally, positive pretax profits and accelerating earnings with a base of five years of growth were important.

Based on these findings of common features, Reinganum developed several selection strategies. His four-screen strategy used a market/book value ratio of less than 1.0, relative strength greater than that in the previous quarter, fewer than 20 million shares, and accelerating earnings. A stock was bought when it met all four criteria. Using these criteria, the average return after four quarters was 16.7 percent, while the S&P 500 had gained only 7.2 percent. When Reinganum added five more criteria (positive 5-year growth rate, positive pretax profit margins, relative strength of 70 and increasing, and an O'Neil datagraphic ranking[24] of 70), the return after four quarters was 23.71 percent, an improvement over the four-screen strategy.

Reinganum concluded, "What is truly remarkable about the strategies is that they do not exploit characteristics that prior research has revealed to be associated with superior performance" (p. 27). Those characteristics are low

P/Es, substantial price declines, low share prices, and small market capitalization. Still, Reinganum's strategy seemed to provide excess (greater than market average) returns.[25]

Size

Although size was not a critical variable in Reinganum's strategies, it has been important in others' research. At numerous points in this book, we note that researchers have tested to see if their results could be caused by factors other than the primary one or ones they were studying. One of the most frequently examined of these factors is the market-value size of the company. The reason that this factor has been of interest is because research has repeatedly found that firm size has an important bearing on the returns that are earned from a stock. Finding out whether the abnormally high returns of small-company stocks are the result of their being more risky, less frequently traded, harder to research, or more difficult to hold and transfer or because small firms are more flexible and thus better able to take advantage of opportunities or niches that are unsuited to large companies has been the focus of the research of many over the past few years.

Two studies make up the earliest of the work on size: Banz [1981] studied the relationship between risk-adjusted return and the market value of a stock on the NYSE; Reinganum [1981a], studied the same thing for NYSE and ASE stocks. On the basis of his results, Reinganum contended that Basu's [1977] P/E effect[26] was really a proxy for firm size. To see the essence of the argument, look at Exhibit 5-11. From the end-of-the-year market values of the stocks on the NYSE and ASE, the firms were grouped by size. Each portfolio's annual returns were calculated from 1963 to 1980. Reinganum found that the superior performance of the small-firm portfolio was not merely the result of a couple of good years. Using several methods for calculating returns earned on a portfolio held for more than one year, he found that $1 invested at the end of 1963 in the small-capitalization stocks would have increased to $7.50 by the end of 1980, while an investment in the largest stocks would have reached just over $5.40. With annual updating of the portfolio, the value in 1980 would have been $46 and $4, respectively. Small-capitalization investments appear to pay off, especially when they are actively managed.

These abnormal returns seem to exist outside the U.S. capital markets as well. Keim [1986], in his review of anomalies, summarized some international findings as shown in Exhibit 5-12.

Many researchers have been skeptical of the small-firm superior returns. They have sought to ascribe the anomalous returns to some other factor, notably, something that increases the riskiness of buying small-firm stocks. James and Edmister [1983], for example, focused on the infrequent-trading effect.

Exhibit 5-11

Average Annual Returns for the Ten Market-Value Portfolios

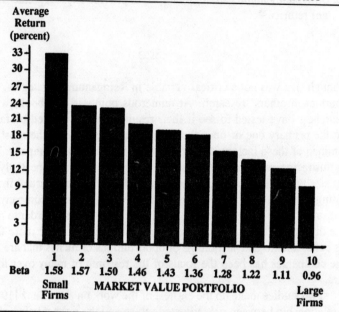

	1	2	3	4	5	6	7	8	9	10
Beta	1.58	1.57	1.50	1.46	1.43	1.36	1.28	1.22	1.11	0.96

Small Firms   MARKET VALUE PORTFOLIO   Large Firms

Source: Adapted from Reinganum [1983], p. 30.

They suggested that investors in the stocks of firms that trade less frequently may require a liquidity premium. They believed that a negative relationship between transactions costs and trading activity would suggest that such a liquidity premium exists, but they found no evidence of such a liquidity premium: the firm-size effect still existed.

Stoll and Whaley [1983] did not agree.[27] They, like Reinganum [1983], found that the average price per share was less for smaller capitalization stocks than for the larger companies. Because of this factor, and infrequent trading, the transaction costs (including bid/ask spread differences) were higher for smaller companies. For instance, the relative spread for the smaller capitalization stocks was 3.23 in 1960 and 3.33 in 1979, while the spreads for the stocks in the largest group were 0.73 and 0.64, respectively. After incorporating transactions costs, Stoll and Whaley found that the "market value effect is reversed when the transaction costs are considered. The largest firms outperform the smallest firms by about seventeen percent a year during the period 1960 through 1979" (p. 74). As Exhibit 5-13 shows, however, the investor's horizon can have an impact on these results.[28] The longer the horizon, the larger the portfolio returns for the small-capitalization stocks.[29]

Stoll and Whaley's work was by no means the end of the argument about the transaction-cost effect on the returns from small firms. Schultz [1983] disagreed with Stoll and Whaley. He looked beyond the Stoll and Whaley universe of the NYSE by including ASE stocks and found "that small firms do

Exhibit 5-12
The Firm-Size Effect: International Evidence

Australia (1958–1981)[a]

Size Portfolio	% Return (std. error)
Smallest	6.75 (0.64)
2	2.23 (0.39)
3	1.74 (0.31)
4	1.32 (0.27)
5	1.48 (0.24)
6	1.27 (0.24)
7	1.15 (0.24)
8	1.22 (0.24)
9	1.18 (0.25)
Largest	1.02 (0.29)

Canada (1951–1980)[b]

Size Portfolio	% Return (std. error) 1951–1972	1973–1980
Smallest	2.02 (0.27)	1.67 (0.58)
2	1.48 (0.22)	1.66 (0.56)
3	1.14 (0.22)	1.41 (0.59)
4	0.99 (0.23)	1.39 (0.56)
Largest	0.90 (0.23)	1.23 (0.58)

Japan (1966–1983)[c]

Size Portfolio	% Return (std. error)
Smallest	2.03 (0.35)
2	1.50 (0.32)
3	1.38 (0.29)
4	1.17 (0.27)
Largest	1.14 (0.27)

United Kingdom (1956–1980)[d]

Size Portfolio	% Return (std. error) 1956–1965	1966–1980
Smallest	1.27	1.00
2	1.18	0.89
Largest	0.98	0.84

[a] Brown, Keim, Kleindon, and Marsh [1983].
[b] Berges, McConnell, and Schlarbaum [1984].
[c] Nakamura and Tereda [1984].
[d] Reinganum and Shapiro [1983].

Source: Keim [1986], p. 26.

Exhibit 5-13

Mean Abnormal Returns on the Lowest Total Market Value Arbitrage Portfolio[a]
for Various Investment Horizons During the Period
January 1960 through December 1979

Investment Horizon (in months)	Number of Time-Series Observations	Before-Transaction-Cost Abnormal Return[b]	After-Transaction-Cost Abnormal Return[c]
1	240	0.0053 (3.49)	−0.0136 (−7.70)
2	120	0.0088 (2.80)	−0.0093 (−2.91)
3	80	0.0129 (2.36)	−0.0058 (−1.09)
4	60	0.0190 (2.61)	0.0004 (0.06)
6	40	0.0266 (2.36)	0.0069 (0.65)
12	20	0.0599 (2.15)	0.0453 (1.75)

[a] To form the arbitrage portfolio return series, the stocks within the lowest market value decile were ranked in ascending order of relative risk and divided into equal-weighted portfolios. One dollar was then allocated between the low-risk and the high-risk portfolios so as to adjust the overall relative risk level to 1. The portfolio return series was then formed and the market return series was subtracted, with the resulting series representing returns on portfolios requiring no net investment and having no relative risk. The values in parentheses are Student t-ratios for the null hypothesis $H_0: a_a = 0$

[b] The before-transaction-cost abnormal return refers to the estimated intercept parameter in the regression $R_{at} = \alpha_a + \beta_a (R_{mt} - R_{ft}) + E_{at}$

[c] The after-transaction-cost abnormal return refers to the estimated intercept parameter in the after-transaction-cost regression $R'_{at} = \alpha_a + \beta_a(R'_{mt} - R_{ft}) + \varepsilon_{at}$

Source: Stoll and Whaley [1983], p. 77.

indeed earn positive excess returns after transaction costs for holding periods of one year or less" (p. 82), although the findings "do not contradict Stoll and Whaley's empirical results. . . . Small firms [do] not earn statistically significant excess returns after transaction costs for a holding period of less than a year—if the holding period does not include a January" (p. 85).

Could all the small-firm excess returns occur in January? Keim [1983] looked at seasonality in relation to the returns on small-capitalization portfolios. What he found is shown in Exhibit 5-14: the January effect is pronounced for small firms but not for others.[30] Thus the small-firm effect appears to be the combination of abnormal returns for small firms and January—in fact, the first five days of January.[31]

Exhibit 5-14

The Relation Between Average Daily Abnormal Returns (in percent) and Decile of Market Value *for Each Month* over the Period 1963-79

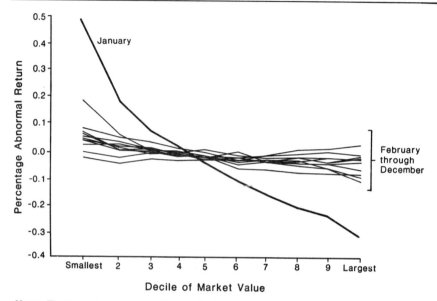

Note: The ten market-value portfolios (deciles) are constructed from firms on the NYSE and ASE. Abnormal returns are provided by CRSP.

Source: Keim [1983], p. 21.

Several researchers have explored the combined impact of other cyclical behavior on the returns from small-capitalization stocks. Keim [1987] looked at the day-of-the-week effect and whether it was related to size (a relationship documented earlier).[32] As you can see in Exhibit 5-15, small firms tended to have large Friday returns. One possible explanation of this effect might be problems in measuring the prices of small firms because of their infrequent trading. There is a bid/ask bias for small firms; that is, the spread is higher than for larger firms.[33]

When Keim looked at the same thing in January, he found that "the weekend-related behavior of returns [high Friday and negative Monday returns] is not different in January versus the other months, once we account for the abnormally high returns at the turn of the year. . . . Friday abnormal returns explain 63% of the average magnitude of the size effect over the period 1963-1985" (p. 46). On the other hand, Jacobs and Levy [1990] report that the January small-size effect is an illusion caused by an improper analytical approach.

Figure 5-15

Average Percentage Returns (standard errors) by Day of the Week for Portfolios
Constructed from Firms in Each Decile of Size on the NYSE and ASE, 1963-85

Size Decile	Market Value of Equity[b] ($ millions)	Average Return[a]						F-Stat[c]	Probability Value
		All Days	Monday	Tuesday	Wednesday	Thursday	Friday		
Smallest	$ 5.02	0.109 (0.011)	-0.064 (0.029)	-0.001 (0.023)	0.148 (0.024)	0.124 (0.025)	0.317 (0.024)	35.42	.0001
2	12.13	0.084 (0.011)	-0.102 (0.029)	-0.016 (0.022)	0.133 (0.023)	0.122 (0.024)	0.276 (0.022)	36.39	.0001
3	22.37	0.078 (0.011)	-0.126 (0.028)	-0.008 (0.022)	0.144 (0.024)	0.116 (0.023)	0.258 (0.022)	37.79	.0001
4	37.06	0.069 (0.011)	-0.136 (0.028)	-0.007 (0.022)	0.129 (0.024)	0.115 (0.024)	0.236 (0.022)	34.36	.0001
5	57.51	0.065 (0.011)	-0.135 (0.028)	-0.012 (0.022)	0.131 (0.024)	0.110 (0.023)	0.223 (0.022)	32.94	.0001
6	93.53	0.060 (0.011)	-0.131 (0.028)	0.004 (0.022)	0.124 (0.024)	0.102 (0.023)	0.195 (0.022)	28.17	.0001
7	154.93	0.056 (0.010)	-0.120 (0.026)	0.001 (0.021)	0.127 (0.023)	0.091 (0.021)	0.177 (0.020)	27.14	.0001
8	276.16	0.053 (0.010)	-0.133 (0.026)	0.020 (0.021)	0.116 (0.023)	0.096 (0.022)	0.161 (0.021)	25.69	.0001
9	551.61	0.048 (0.010)	-0.114 (0.025)	0.022 (0.021)	0.114 (0.023)	0.076 (0.028)	0.139 (0.021)	20.25	.0001
Largest	1394.83	0.041 (0.010)	-0.098 (0.026)	0.036 (0.022)	0.100 (0.023)	0.060 (0.021)	0.104 (0.021)	12.93	.0001
F-Statistic[d]			2.37	3.13	4.96	14.74	99.56		
P-Value			.1238	.0770	.0260	.0001	.0001		

[a] Daily portfolio returns are computed as

$$r_{p,t} = [\sum_{i=1}^{n} (1 + r_{i,t-1})(1 + r_{i,t}) / \sum_{i=1}^{n} (1 + r_{i,t-1})] - 1 \quad \text{for the stocks in each portfolio.}$$

[b] Market value for a portfolio is measured by the average, across all sample years, of the median market values of that size decile in each year.

[c] The F-statistic tests the equality of mean returns across days of the week. Degrees of Freedom: 4,5773.

[d] The F-statistic tests the equality of mean returns across portfolios for a particular day of the week. Degrees of Freedom: 1,5773.

Source: Keim [1987], p.42.

Cyclical behavior is not the only source of the small-firm effect that researchers have investigated. Risk differences have been at the forefront of the theories held by most of those concerned with the reality of the abnormal returns. Looking at the betas in Exhibit 5-11, you will see that the risk (beta) increased as the firm got smaller. Could this riskiness be the source of the differences in returns? If the returns were risk adjusted, would the differences disappear? Reinganum said no. The betas reported in Exhibit 5-11 are unadjusted for infrequent-trading (nonsynchronous) effects: the fact that smaller firms trade less frequently could result in a misstated beta.[34] When Reinganum adjusted the betas,[35] he found that risk differences (at least as measured by beta) were not the source of the superior returns earned by small-capitalization stocks. The total returns were more volatile, however: "Over the 18 years of this study, the odds for a small versus large firm doubling in value were about 10 to 1. On the down side, however, a small firm was almost twice as likely as a large one to experience a one-year return of −25% or less" (p. 35).

Carleton and Lakonishok [1986] looked to industry interrelatedness as a source of undiscovered risk in small-firm portfolios. They extended the notion that there is a seasonality to the abnormal returns, saying,

> Given differences in output markets, cost structures and technologies, some industries were able to benefit from the unforeseen macroeconomic events better than others. If such industries were those made up of smaller firms, then we would be incorrectly attributing industry-related excess returns to a pure size effect. (p. 36)

They grouped NYSE companies with data on the CRSP and COMPUSTAT data tapes into industries; when they further broke down each industry into four equal size-related portfolios, they found a strong relationship between size and abnormal (risk-adjusted) returns (α),[36] and the relationship came from the results for January alone. Their results for 11 basic industries are shown in Exhibit 5-16.

One last potential source of added risk for the stocks of small firms is information or, more precisely, the lack of information. Barry and Brown [1984] offered this explanation of the information problem:

> Securities for which there is relatively little information available may be perceived as riskier. . . . Commensurate with that risk, participants in the market may rationally demand a premium to hold such securities. If so, and if risk is measured empirically without regard to the amount of information available, then there may appear to be "abnormal" returns for low-information securities. (p. 283)

Because relatively little is known about small firms, Barry and Brown used the relative period of listing as a proxy for the amount of available information.[37]

Exhibit 5-16

Returns and Risk Measures by Industries and Size, 1961-80

Industry	SG	GMEAN	AMEAN	SD	Size	β	α	α	α
Transportation	1	15.3	17.6	23.5	63	.83	.31[a]	.21[b]	1.07[a]
	2	10.9	12.6	20.3	170	.73	.03	.05	-.83
	3	8.1	9.6	18.1	396	.66	-.14	-.06	-1.21[a]
	4	5.8	7.0	16.8	1800	.60	-.28[a]	-.17	-1.70[a]
Trade	1	14.2	21.0	41.9	23	1.26	.10	-.11	1.61[a]
	2	12.4	18.0	36.9	62	1.16	-.01	.05	-1.52[a]
	3	10.2	14.9	33.8	157	1.02	-.13	.05	-2.26[a]
	4	7.4	11.1	28.8	1186	.87	-.28[a]	-.03	-3.32[a]
Finance	1	14.4	19.6	34.3	29	1.36	.16	-.11	1.73[a]
	2	14.2	18.9	33.9	88	1.06	.18	.19	-.51
	3	10.3	13.0	23.9	272	.95	-.09	.05	-1.77[a]
	4	10.3	12.0	19.7	1362	.78	-.01	.22[b]	-2.03[a]
Services	1	16.6	22.9	38.9	36	1.33	.31[a]	.15	1.86[a]
	2	12.0	18.1	37.7	74	1.28	-.05	-.15	.09
	3	12.0	17.0	32.9	141	1.21	-.02	.16	-.92
	4	7.9	14.8	40.9	381	1.14	-.30[a]	-.05	-3.52[a]
Mining	1	25.6	34.2	55.1	40	1.06	1.11[a]	.83[a]	6.66[a]
	2	22.2	26.0	32.3	121	.79	.94[a]	.93[a]	3.26[a]
	3	18.7	21.8	29.4	292	.84	.63[a]	.70[a]	2.54[a]
	4	16.6	19.5	26.7	1341	.77	.49[a]	.67[a]	-.47
Food	1	16.6	19.9	29.3	29	.92	.40[a]	.15	2.96[a]
	2	13.9	17.0	27.2	101	.90	.19[a]	.22[a]	-.00
	3	9.4	12.0	25.0	363	.81	-.11	.01	-1.02[a]
	4	8.8	10.3	18.2	1428	.62	-.07	.07	-1.60[a]

Industry	SG	GMEAN	AMEAN	SD	Size	β	α	α	α
Textile	1	13.1	20.8	45.4	18	1.22	.07	-.12	1.33[a]
	2	11.0	16.2	36.1	43	1.13	-.08	-.13	.66
	3	9.1	15.0	36.8	87	1.01	-.18[b]	-.23[a]	-.12
	4	7.9	13.0	33.2	265	.96	-.26[a]	-.15	-1.22[a]
Paper	1	17.4	22.4	38.4	34	1.18	.36[a]	.15	1.82[a]
	2	11.0	14.4	27.5	91	1.02	-.07	.03	-.81
	3	10.6	13.1	24.2	300	.94	-.06	.10	-1.89[a]
	4	6.7	8.6	21.0	1344	.83	-.32[a]	-.08	-3.65[a]
Chemicals	1	16.4	19.8	28.8	50	1.11	.30[a]	.10	3.14[a]
	2	11.7	13.8	21.6	184	.94	.01	.14	-1.03[a]
	3	12.3	13.8	18.6	565	.80	.12	.27[a]	-.65[a]
	4	6.3	7.2	14.2	2537	.61	-.23[a]	.02	-2.08[a]
Petroleum	1	19.6	24.4	34.5	134	.94	.67[a]	.63[a]	2.79[a]
	2	20.4	23.3	26.2	906	.72	.81[a]	.98[a]	.02
	3	15.2	17.7	25.0	2763	.55	.55	.81[a]	-1.13[a]
	4	13.5	15.6	22.9	8369	.50	.43[b]	.63[a]	-1.03[a]
Rubber	1	19.1	24.4	37.1	25	1.12	.54[a]	.43[a]	.90
	2	9.0	12.9	27.9	57	1.06	-.20[b]	-.16	-1.19[a]
	3	10.3	14.5	32.9	212	.93	-.07	-.13	.96
	4	2.5	5.2	23.5	847	.85	-.63[a]	-.54[a]	-1.29[a]

[a] Denotes statistical significance at the 5 percent level for a two-tailed test.
[b] Denotes statistical significance at the 10 percent level for a two-tailed test.
S.G. is the size group.
GMEAN is the geometric mean return (all months) on an annual basis in percent.
AMEAN is the arithmetic mean return (all months) on an annual basis in percent.
SD is the annual standard deviation (all months) in percent.
Size is in millions of dollars.
β is the slope from regression / equation (all months).
α is the intercept from regression / equation (non-January months) in percent.
α is the intercept from regression / equation (January months) in percent.
α is the intercept from regression / equation (all months) in percent.

Source: Carleton and Lakonishok [1986], p. 38.

Using data from 1926 to 1980 on NYSE companies with data on CRSP and COMPUSTAT tapes, they classified each company by size, beta, and number of months since first listed on the exchange. The standardized excess returns (the returns standardized by the 60-month standard deviation) are shown in Exhibit 5-17. As you can see, "The size effect does not dominate the period of listing effect . . . and the small firms listed for the longest periods do not produce statistically excess returns" (p. 291). Barry and Brown concluded that an inter-relationship does exist between size and lack of information.[38]

Exhibit 5-17
Standardized Excess Returns* by Size and Period-
of-Listing Categories for All Months, January 1931 to December 1980

| | | Period of Listing | | | | | | |
		1	2	3	4	5	6	Size Marginal
	1	2.60	2.03	2.19	0.52	0.94	0.68	1.97
	2	1.71	1.99	0.42	-0.64	-0.71	-0.84	0.84
Size	3	-0.26	0.28	1.18	-3.13	-0.56	-0.26	-1.51
	4	-0.82	-1.44	-1.03	-0.45	-1.11	-0.90	-1.51
	5	0.55	-1.42	-0.18	0.53	0.21	-2.36	-0.36
	6	-1.83	-2.25	-2.37	-1.55	-2.81	-2.85	-2.68
Period of listing marginal		2.20	1.21	1.76	-1.24	-1.79	-1.70	

* The standardized excess return category 1 represents a t-value given by $\sum_{t}^{T} = 1 \, S_{lt} / \sqrt{T}$, where $T = 600$. The standard excess return for category 1 in period t, S_{lt}, represents the average excess return for 1 in t standardized by the standard deviation of excess returns estimated on the basis of 60 months of prior data, after correction for the number of securities in 1.

Source: Barry and Brown [1984], p. 291.

Barry and Brown suggested that a more sophisticated measure of information availability might produce different results. Brauer [1986], using a more complex jump-diffusion process (a process designed to represent a situation where information arrives infrequently but has a major price impact), found that portfolios of small stocks have no more frequent informational surprises than do large-stock portfolios. But, the surprises of small-stock portfolios were larger. From his analysis, Brauer concluded there was "convincing support for the proposition that differential information about small versus large firms leads to the well-known firm size anomaly " (p. 455).

Ho and Michaely [1988] also examined the impact of information on share price. They wanted to determine whether risks affected large- and small-capitalization stocks differently. They extracted pessimistic stories from the *Wall Street Journal* and *Barron's* from 1982-84 and determined the stories' impacts on portfolios ranked by size of stocks. Their results are graphically shown in Exhibit 5-18. Information like this led them to conclude that, because the smaller capitalized stocks are riskier than larger stocks and "the prices of small stocks may not incorporate all publicly available information" (p. 53), the small-cap market is not as efficient as the large-cap.

Exhibit 5-18
Cumulative Excess Returns for the Three Groups Around the Event Day,
Where Day Zero Is the Event Day

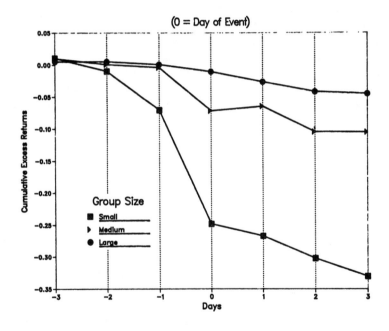

Source: Ho and Michaely [1988], p. 68.

Still the research about size goes on. Chan, Chen, and Hsieh [1985] managed to eliminate the size effect by using arbitrage pricing theory.[39] They too believed that differences in risk underlie the anomalous returns. Using data from the NYSE together with measures for industrial production, expected and unexpected inflation, changes in the term structure of interest rates, the spreads between bonds of different qualities, and new business formations, they found that the difference between the abnormal returns (average residual) for the largest and smallest stock portfolios was 1.5 percent per year (in contrast to 11.5 percent when not risk adjusted), but the difference was insignificant. After further tests, they concluded that the abnormal returns that had been attributed to size were really the result of changes in the risk premium—a premium that changed with changes in business conditions.

In concluding this discussion, we can ask: Can small firms provide abnormal profits for the investor? Many believe that they can and do,[40] and we have seen that raw returns are clearly positive, primarily in January and on Fridays, although the results are diminished when transaction costs are added and risk adjustments are made. Still, the final chapter in this story remains to be written.

There are many other factors besides firm size that analysts use to construct investment strategies; some are based on actions taken, or expected to be taken, by the managers of the company (for example, an offer to repurchase shares or the announcement of a pending merger). Whole investment firms have grown up around advantageous pursuit of these events. We next examine these strategies to discern whether an investor can make money once such events have been announced. If the investor must forecast the announced event, on the other hand, the problem is much more complex, as we saw when forecasting earnings.

Share Repurchases

Share repurchases are an interesting event for shareholders. Most of the research has focused on the managers and their incentives for repurchasing shares. Vermaelen [1984] found an average abnormal return of about 15 percent for firms tendering for their own shares from 1962 to 1977. He went further than had previous researchers, however, by estimating the value of the information conveyed by the tender offer. He, and others, believed that the tender offer was a signal of what management believed about the company and expected to do with it. If this supposition is true, then part of the returns resulting from tender offers would constitute the value of information.[41] Vermaelen estimated the abnormal return from the announcement from 5 days before the offer to 10 days after the offer expired. What he found is shown in Exhibit 5-19.

Using regression, he also found that the "impact of all signals is positive and statistically significant at the 5 percent significance level and the model explains approximately 61 percent of the cross-sectional variance of the perceived value of information" (p. 177). In other words, profit potential exists.

While companies' tenders for their own shares are interesting as potential signals of profit, more interesting to many, including those who manage portfolios where the object is to identify potential merger targets, is the profit potential born of mergers and divestitures.

Exhibit 5-19

Distribution Characteristics of Various Variables in the Signaling Model[a]

Decile	α	Premium	F_p	m_o	f_o	P_σ/E
Min.	−.163	−.188	.01	.001	0	.096
0.1	−.02	.059	.05	.005	0	.344
0.2	+.023	.101	.06	.020	0.002	.447
0.3	.06	.127	.08	.036	0.004	.522
0.4	.095	.159	.10	.058	0.006	.705
0.5	.153	.196	.12	.088	0.009	.759
0.6	.173	.241	.14	.137	0.014	.961
0.7	.220	.273	.18	.215	0.018	1.16
0.8	.280	.333	.22	.330	0.026	1.26
0.9	.350	.429	.29	.481	0.039	1.70
Max.	.694	.846	.60	.87	0.218	13.93
Mean	.157	.227	.147	.175	0.017	1.14
Std Dev.	.155	.175	.108	.199	0.027	1.72

Notes: α is the value of information per share.

Premium is the abnormal return to the tendering shareholders.

F_p is the fraction purchased.

m_o is the fraction of insider holdings.

f_o is the fraction of executive stock options; this distribution is based on 91 available proxy statements.

P_σ/E is the price per share 5 days before the announcement divided by the weighted-average exercise price of the executive stock options; this distribution is based on 76 firms that reported positive amounts of executive stock options.

Source: Vermaelen [1984], p. 176.

Mergers and Divestitures

Research over the past few years shows that, while the shareholders of acquired firms gain as a result of a merger,[42] those of the acquiring firms do not.[43] Dennis and McConnell's [1986] findings, shown in Exhibit 5-20, are typical of what most researchers have found: there is profit to be made by prescient merger watchers.

Dennis and McConnell's sample was firms with assets over $10 million that merged between 1962 and 1980 and were listed on the Federal Trade

Exhibit 5-20

Cumulative Market-Adjusted Returns Surrounding Merger Announcement
Dates for 76 Acquired Companies' Common Stocks over the Period 1962-80

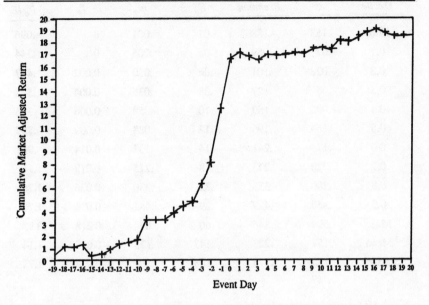

Event Day

Source: Dennis and McConnell [1986], p. 154

Commission's *Statistical Report on Mergers and Acquisitions* and the Conference Board's *Announcements of Mergers and Acquisitions*. Note that all the returns, or at least the majority of the abnormal returns, were earned before the merger was announced. This result suggests either that there was information about the merger circulating before the announcement was made or that the investors were exceptionally canny at forecasting which companies are likely to announce a merger and when.

These abnormal returns have been repeatedly found by various researchers; the size depends on such things as the form of the merger, the method of payment, and the size of the firms. As shown in Exhibit 5-21, Wansley, Lane, and Yang [1983] found that cash-payment mergers yielded higher abnormal returns than did those involving securities. Perhaps the offers involving securities were more often hostile, and the investor had longer to wait to see if the merger would be successful. They also found that, when separated by type of merger, the conglomerates had higher abnormal returns than did nonconglomerate mergers, at least from 1970 to 1978.

Exhibit 5-21
Cumulative Average Residuals by Method of Payment

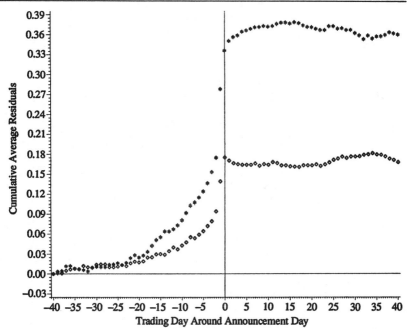

Note: **Day 0 indicates the announcement day. Star indicates cash and diamond indicates merger involving securities**

Source: **Wansley, Lane, and Yang [1983], p. 21.**

Wanting to capitalize on these abnormal returns, several researchers have developed models to forecast those firms likely to merge.[44] Wansley, Roenfeldt, and Cooley [1983] joined the research on abnormal returns with that on firms likely to merge to determine whether profitable investment-screening strategies could be developed. Based on a model with five variables (P/E ratio, long-term debt/assets, size of sales, sales growth, and price/book ratio), they concluded that excess returns are possible from identifying companies as merger candidates.[45] Looking at their results, shown in Exhibit 5-22, the 25 and 50 most attractive candidates clearly outperformed the average of 754 companies for 1973-77. The authors did admit, however, that some of the returns could have come simply because the market identified the companies as merger candidates, not because they actually merged. Of course, if they bought early, investors made profits either way. The top 25 companies earned 17.1 percent for the 21 months that were tested. Although perfect foresight about firms that merged would have earned the investor 29.1 percent for the 7 months before the merger.

Exhibit 5-22
Cumulative Average Residuals (CARs) for Top 25,
Top 50, and 754 Firms

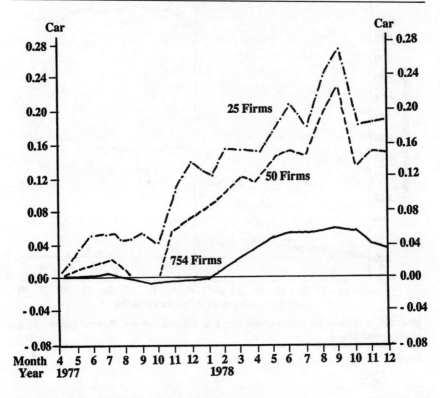

Source: Wansley, Roenfeldt, and Cooley [1983], p. 160.

There is much more research than we can describe here into the reasons for merging and merger returns, the sources of value in mergers, and the market's reaction to merger announcements. What we have discussed summarizes the basic thrust and findings of the research that has been done. What we have not discussed is a closely allied topic: whether the acquired-firm premium also accompanies partial spinoffs—that is, the sale of a portion of the assets of the firm. Hite, Owens, and Rogers [1987] found that sellers and buyers both receive abnormal returns; the sellers reap the largest profits (1.66 versus 0.83 percent). Even ultimately unsuccessful sellers gain at the announcement date (1.41 percent)—a gain that is later lost when the offer expires.[46] Hite, Owens, and Rogers attributed this result not to overenthusiasm in the market place but to an expression of the market's perception that assets will be better utilized after they have been divested.[47]

Other Fundamental Factors

A host of other corporate activities or factors have been used, tested, or considered important in selecting profitable securities. Some investors have attempted to capitalize on popular notions like those contained in such publications as *In Search of Excellence,* by Peters and Waterman [1982] by finding common factors among the excellent firms and using them to select profitable equities.[48] Others have been more concerned with avoiding potential losses in their portfolios by identifying potential bankruptcy candidates.[49] Still others, most notably Jacobs and Levy [1988a, 1988b, 1989, 1990] have and continue to find methods to sort out the real effects and sources of return from those that are illusions created by imperfect technique. There is no doubt that the identification and testing of factors will continue.

Conclusion

This chapter points out areas of profit making from fundamental analysis of firms. We found that small profits may be possible by acting immediately on dividend announcements. We looked at strategies based on events in corporate life, like mergers, and found that profits seem to exist for the investor who can predict them. However, the most important focus of research and speculation about company fundamentals has been market-value size. Some very profitable strategies have been based on book value: Small companies clearly have the potential for above-average returns if low transaction costs can be maintained and if one does not mind taking some additional risk. But are the profits real? Have we measured them correctly, and taken everything into account? Or is the profit an illusion?

    Summers [1986], in an article that is either terribly depressing or very threatening for investors and researchers, contended that we cannot be sure what we know. He suggested that all the tests we have for evaluating market efficiency are relatively powerless. The tests do not discriminate between rational valuations and irrational results.[50] In one description of the problems of testing, Summers said that "even though the market valuations differ from the rational expectation of the present value of future cash flows by more than 30 percent . . . in order to have a 50 percent chance of rejecting the null hypothesis it would be necessary to have data for just over 5000 years" (p. 596). Summers concluded,

> The weakness of the empirical evidence verifying the hypothesis that securities markets are efficient in assessing fundamental values would not be so bothersome if the hypothesis rested on firm theoretical foundations, and if there were no contrary evidence. Unfortunately, neither of these conditions is satisfied in practice. (p. 598)

In other words, profitable opportunities may exist, even if we cannot be confident of our ability to see them in the data. Abandoning fundamental research because of our inability to find profits with certainty is foolish. Instead, exercise intelligence, discrimination, and care.

CHAPTER 5

Notes

1. A number of articles discuss dividend discount models. See, for instance, Farrell [1985] for a primer and Michaud [1985] for a description of a multiphase DDM that adjusts for the simple DDM's biases toward high-yield and low-P/E stocks. In addition, see Sakaguchi [1988] for a discussion of the relevance of the DDM to the Japanese market.

2. This model also is called the Gordon constant-growth model after Myron Gordon [1959] who first described it.

3. The rearranged form of the model may be the more familiar version:

$$Required\ return\ =\ \frac{Dividend}{Market\ price} + Expected\ growth$$

4. See Michaud [1985] and Sorensen and Williamson [1985] for descriptions of these models. In addition, Exhibit 4-1 showed the forecasts needed to use a multiphase DDM.

5. For more information about fundamental betas, see Harrington [1987].

6. The world prior to the 1986 U.S. tax code revision.

7. The impact of information on volatility is discussed by Copeland and Galai [1983], Damodaran [1987], Mahmond and Lobo [1986], and Barry and Brown [1986], among others.

8. See Summers [1986] and Poterba and Summers [1986] for more about this issue.

9. Patell and Wolfson also noted that dividend announcements rarely contain much more information than the facts about the dividend, while earnings announcements were included in long press releases that contained much more information about the company. This difference in information might be the cause of the difference between the earnings and dividend impacts.

10. His earnings portfolio used the SUE (standardized unexpected earnings) technique discussed in Chapter 4.

11. These findings support what others have found: that the information leaks out slowly into the market. See, for instance, Charest [1978].

12. See, for instance, Charest [1978], who found abnormal returns following both positive and negative dividend-change announcements.

13. See, for instance, Durand and May [1960], Elton and Gruber [1970], Kalay [1982], Litzenberger and Ramaswamy [1979 and 1982], and Morgan [1982]. Others have come to different conclusions—for instance, Miller and Scholes [1978].

14. Peterson, Peterson, and Ang [1985] measured the tax rate on dividends for 1979 and estimated it at 40 percent. The average rate in effect was estimated at 30 percent.

15. Lakonishok and Vermaelen [1983] found a larger-than-expected impact (the stock price dropped by only 30 percent of the dividend value) when studying the Canadian market.

16. For a further discussion of transaction costs on the NYSE, see Berkowitz, Logue, and Noser [1988].

17. The purpose of using calendar time is to adjust for intraweek patterns such as Blue Mondays and strong Fridays. When calculating averages such as residual returns on volume, the process is repeated five times beginning on successive days; therefore, the final average is an average of the five daily event averages.

18. Subsequently, Karpoff and Walking [1988] showed that returns during these periods are highly correlated with transaction costs, which further confirms the existence of such short-term trading.

19. See Miller [1986], who provides a review of some of the research relevant to this question.

20. One interesting aside: some of the results we saw in Appendix B to Chapter 1 may have really been attributable to dividend yield. See Cook and Rozeff [1984] for a discussion and test of this thesis.

21. There are a number of potentially transitory things that affect the importance and value of dividends (for instance, Japanese investors' dividend-capture strategies in the mid-1980s).

22. Estep [1985] also argued that book/market value is not enough. He suggested that, to capture companies that are likely to yield a profit for investors, another variable must be added—the company's return spread (return on equity minus growth). He developed what he called the T-model to select stocks:

$$T = Growth + \frac{ROE - Growth}{Market/Book\ value}$$

$$+ \frac{Change\ in\ market\text{-}to\text{-}book\ value}{Market/Book\ value}(1 + Growth)$$

23. He tested the relationship also for U.K. stocks.

24. A proprietary formula based on such things as relative strength and earnings.

25. Others have developed multicriteria models. See, for instance, Estep [1987], who developed a model to turn historical results into returns forecasts, and Zach [1987], who created a proprietary model based on dividend yield, and price/earnings ratios. Gropper [1985] discussed a number of quantitatively based models.

26. As discussed in Chapter 4, Basu [1983] found evidence to dispute Reinganum's findings. When the low-earnings/price-ratio portfolios were controlled for the stock's market capitalization, he found an interactive, and negative, relationship between earnings yield and size. Thus he concluded that the relationship was, at best, complicated. Peavy and Goodman [1983] adjusted for infrequent trading, size, and industry and still found a low-P/E effect. In a later study, Peavy and Goodman [1986] confirmed this finding. Most recently, Jaffe, Keim, and Westerfield [1987] have found that, while an earnings-yield effect exists and is significant only in January, most of the returns came from 1951 to 1968. From 1969 on, the yield effect was marginal.

27. See also Copeland and Galai [1983].

28. Blume and Stambaugh [1983], among others, looked at the impact of using closing prices to estimate returns for small stocks and concluded that half the abnormal returns can be attributed to errors in price estimation. When those errors are eliminated, all the small-firm returns occur in January.

29. None of the returns is statistically significant, which implies no difference in after-transaction-costs returns when risk adjusted.

30. Brown et al. [1983] found that the premium for small firms in Australia is relatively constant across all the months. They concluded that taxes, often supposed to be the main cause of the January effect, are not the culprit behind the abnormal returns of small firms.

31. Keim also tested and found that his results were stable over a number of years. Brown et al. [1983] found that the magnitude of the size effect depended on the period they tested: positive from 1974 to 1979, negative from 1969 to 1973.

32. See, for instance, Keim and Stambaugh [1984].

33. Glosten [1987] looked specifically at what makes up bid/ask spreads.

34. Roll [1981] was one who suggested an infrequent-trading problem might be at the root of the phenomenon.

35. Reinganum adjusted the betas using a method suggested by Dimson [1979].

36. Huberman, Kandel, and Karolyi [1987] supported these results. They further concluded that there are both industry and size effects on returns: controlling for size, industry affected returns; controlling for industry, size affected abnormal returns.

37. Others have used similar proxies for the lack of information. For instance, Klein and Bawa [1977] used the amount of information available: newer, smaller securities have less information available.

38. In addition, Atiase [1985] and Bamber [1986], among others, determined that earnings-report-induced unexpected price changes vary inversely with size.

39. See Appendix A, Chapter 1 for an explanation of arbitrage pricing theory.

40. See, for instance, Breck et al. [1988].

41. Vermaelen explained his process this way:

> In a semi-strong efficient capital market, the price after the expiration of the offer but before the true value of information is revealed, P_E, multiplied by the remaining number of shares outstanding, N_E, must equal the value of the shares before the announcement minus the value of the repurchased shares, $P_T N_P$, plus the market estimate of the dollar change in the value of the shares, I, or $P_E N_E = P_O N_O - P_T N_P + I$.

Using this envelope condition, the abnormal announcement return is estimated as $I/P_O N_O = a P_O$ (p. 172).

42. Torabzadeh and Bertin [1987] found that this statement also holds true for the shareholders of firms acquired through leveraged buyouts.

43. Roll [1983] proposed a different interpretation of the data. Most of the tests of gains to shareholders measure returns on a percentage basis. Roll suggested that percentage gains are not really a good measure of gains because, if the acquired firm were small, "the observed price increase in the target would correspond to such a trivial loss to the bidder that the loss is bound to be hidden in the bid/ask spread and in the noise of daily

return volatility" (p. 21). Bradley, Desai, and Kim [1983] did estimate the dollar returns, with somewhat indeterminant results.

44. See, for instance, Mandelker [1974], who suggested that mergers occurred *after* abnormal returns, and Walking and Edmister [1985], who related the size of tender-offer premiums to the company's leverage, net working capital, market/book value, proportion of bidder-controlled shares, whether the bid was contested, and the proportion of control sought by the suitor.

45. They identified the candidates through an discriminant analysis of 44 companies that merged in 1975-76 and 40 that did not.

46. Linn and Rozeff [1985] found that the vast majority of the returns earned by involuntary spinoffs came before the announcement: of the 20.3 percent return earned in the 90 days before and after the announcement, 13.8 percent came before the event. In addition, about 5 percent came between the 20th and 90th days after the announcment. Just less than 1 percent occurred at the announcement.

47. Davidson and McDonald [1987] looked at the abnormal returns from royalty trust spinoffs and found they were positive also.

48. Clayman [1987] found that the original excellent companies began to decline at the point they were identified as excellent. For those companies, the market/book value declined as well. Clayman also chose an unexcellent group based on the same variables and found that a portfolio of these companies had abnormally superior returns of about 1 percent per month; the excellent companies did not. Using a longer period and more firms, Kolodny, Lawrence, and Ghosh [1988] found that poor performance was more likely from the excellent group than good performance.

49. A number of authors have looked at market and firm-specific factors for forecasting bankruptcy. See, for instance, Altman and Spivack [1983], Altman [1968], Clark and Weinstein [1983], and Altman and Brenner [1981].

50. Others have suggested that irrational-decision-making models of behavior may be more useful in explaining capital market activity (for instance, Arrow [1982]) or have found that stock prices are not rational reflections of changes in dividend expectations (e.g., Shiller [1981]).

CHAPTER 5

References

Aharony, J., and Swary, I. "Quarterly Dividend and Earnings Announcements and Stockholders' Returns: An Empirical Analysis." *Journal of Finance*, March 1980, pp. 1-12.

Altman, Edward. "Financial Ratios, Discriminant Analysis and the Prediction of Corporate Bankruptcy." *Journal of Finance*, September 1968, pp. 589-609.

_____, and Brenner, M. "Information Effects and Stock Market Response to Signs of Firm Deterioration." *Journal of Financial and Quantitative Analysis*, March 1981, pp. 35-51.

_____, and Spivack, Joseph. "Predicting Bankruptcy: The Value Line Relative Financial Strength System vs. the Zeta Bankruptcy Classification Approach." *Financial Analysts Journal*, November-December 1983, pp. 60-67.

Arrow, Kenneth. "Risk Perception in Psychology and Economics." *Economic Inquiry*, January 1982, pp. 1-9.

Asquith, Paul. "Merger Bids, Uncertainty and Stockholder Returns." *Journal of Financial Economics*, April 1983, pp. 51-83.

_____ and Mullins, David. "The Impact of Initiating Dividend Payments on Shareholders' Wealth." *Journal of Business*, January 1983, pp. 77-96.

_____; and Bruner, Robert. "The Gains to Bidding Firms from Merger." *Journal of Financial Economics*, March 1983, pp. 121-39.

Atiase, Rowland. "Predisclosure Information, Firm Capitalization, and Security Price Behavior Around Earnings Announcements." *Journal of Accounting Research*, Spring 1985, pp. 21-36.

Bamber, Linda Smith. "The Information Content of Annual Earnings Releases: A Trading Volume Approach." *Journal of Accounting Research*, Spring 1986, pp. 40-56.

Banz, R. W. "The Relationship Between Return and the Market Value of Common Stocks." *Journal of Financial Economics*, March 1981, pp. 103-26.

Barry, Christopher and Brown, Stephen. "Differential Information and the Small Firm Effect," *Journal of Financial Economics*, May 1984, pp. 283-94.

_____. "Limited Information as a Source of Risk." *Journal of Portfolio Management*, Winter 1986, pp. 66-72.

Basu, Sanjoy. "The Investment Performance of Common Stocks in Relation to Their Price-Earnings Ratios: A Test of the Efficient Market Hypothesis." *Journal of Finance*, June 1977, pp. 663-82.

_____. "The Relationship Between Earnings' Yield, Market Value and Return for NYSE Common Stocks: Further Evidence." *Journal of Financial Economics*, June 1983, pp. 129-56.

Berges, A.; McConnell, John; and Schlarbaum, Gary. "The Turn-of-the-Year in Canada." *Journal of Finance*, March 1984, pp. 105-27.

Berkowitz, Stephen; Logue, Dennis; and Noser, Eugene. "The Total Cost of Transactions on the NYSE." *Journal of Finance*, March 1988, pp. 97-112.

Blume, Marshall, and Stambaugh, Robert. "Biases in Computed Returns." *Journal of Financial Economics*, September 1983, pp. 387-404.

Bradley, Michael; Desai, Anand; and Kim, Han. "The Rationale Behind Interfirm Tender Offers." *Journal of Financial Economics*, April 1983, pp. 183-206.

Brauer, Gregory A. "Using Jump-Diffusion Return Models to Measure Differential Information by Firm Size." *Journal of Financial and Quantitative Analysis*, 1986, pp. 447-58.

Brealey, Richard, and Myers, Stewart. *Principles of Corporate Finance*. Third edition. New York: McGraw Hill, 1988, p. 372.

Breck, William; Posen, David; Collins, Bruce; and Cushing, David. "An Analysis of Small Capitalization Stock Performance." *Index Products Research: Shearson Lehman Hutton, Inc.*, January 28, 1988.

Brennan, Michael. "A Note on Dividend Irrelevance and the Gordon Valuation Model." *Journal of Finance*, December 1971, pp. 1115-22.

Brown, Philip; Kleidon, Allan; and Marsh, Terry. "New Evidence on the Nature of Size-Related Anomalies and Stock Prices." *Journal of Financial Economics*, June 1983, pp. 33-56.

————; and Keim, Donald. "Stock Return Seasonalities and the Tax-Loss Selling Hypothesis." *Journal of Financial Economics*, June 1983, pp. 105-27.

Carleton, Willard, and Lakonishok, Josef. "The Size Anomaly: Does Industry Group Matter?" *Journal of Portfolio Management*, September 1986, pp. 36-41.

Chan, K. C.; Chen, Nai-fu; and Hsieh, David. "An Exploratory Investigation of the Firm Size Effect." *Journal of Financial Economics*, September 1985, pp. 451-71.

Charest, G. "Dividend Information, Stock Returns, and Market Efficiency—II." *Journal of Financial Economics*, June-September 1978, pp. 297-330.

Clapman, Michelle. "In Search of Excellence: The Investor's Viewpoint." *Financial Analysts Journal*, May-June 1986, pp. 54-63.

Clark, T. A., and Weinstein, M. "The Behavior of the Common Stock of Bankrupt Firms." *Journal of Finance*, May 1983, pp. 489-504.

Clayman, Michelle. "In Search of Excellence: The Investor's Viewpoint." *Financial Analysts Journal*, May-June 1987, pp. 54-63.

Cole, John. "Are Dividend Surprises Independently Important?" *Journal of Portfolio Management*, Summer 1984, pp. 45-50.

Cook, Thomas, and Rozeff, Michael. "Coskewness, Dividend Yields and Capital Asset Pricing." *Journal of Financial Research*, Fall 1984, pp. 231-41.

Copeland, Thomas, and Galai, Dan. "Information Effects on the Bid-Ask Spread." *Journal of Finance*, December 1983, pp. 1457-70.

Damodoran, Aswarth. "The Impact of Information on the Structure of Stock Returns." *Journal of Portfolio Management*, September 1987, pp. 53-58.

Davidson, Wallace N., and McDonald, James L. "Evidence of the Effect on Shareholder Wealth of Corporate Spinoffs: The Creation of Royalty Trusts." *Journal of Financial Research*, Winter 1987, pp. 321-27.

Dennis, Debra, and McConnell, John. "Corporate Mergers and Security Returns." *Journal of Financial Economics*, June 1986, pp. 143-87.

Dielman, Terry, and Oppenheimer, Henry. "An Examination of Investor Behavior During Periods of Large Dividend Changes." *Journal of Financial and Quantitative Analysis*, June 1984, pp. 197-216.

Dimson, Elroy. "Risk Measurement When Shares Are Subject to Infrequent Trading." *Journal of Financial Economics*, June 1979, pp. 197-226.

Divecha, Arjun, and Morse, Dale. "Market Responses to Dividend Increases and Changes in Payout Ratios." *Journal of Financial and Quantitative Analysis*, June 1983, pp. 163-67.

Durand, David and May, Alan M. "The Ex-Dividend Behavior of American Telephone and Telegraph Stock." *Journal of Finance*, March 1960, pp. 19-31.

Eades, Kenneth M.; Hess, Patrick J.; and Kim, E. Han. "Market Rationality and Dividend Announcements." *Journal of Financial Economics*, 1985, pp. 581-604.

Elgers, Pieter, and Clark, John. "Merger Types and Shareholder Returns: Additional Evidence." *Financial Management*, Summer 1980, pp. 66-72.

Elton, Edwin, and Gruber, Martin. "Marginal Stockholder Tax Rates and the Clientele Effect." *Review of Economics and Statistics*. February 1970, pp. 68-74.

Estep, Tony. "A New Method for Valuing Common Stocks." *Financial Analysts Journal*, November-December 1985, pp. 26-33.

————. "Security Analysis and Stock Selection: Turning Financial Information into Returns Forecasts." *Financial Analysts Journal*, July-August 1987, pp. 34-43.

Fama, Eugene, and French, Kenneth. "Dividend Yields and Expected Stock Returns." Unpublished Working Paper #215, University of Chicago, July 1987.

Farrell, Christopher. "The Market's Ugly Ducklings." *Business Week*, April 17, 1987, pp. 294, 296, 298.

Farrell, James. "The Dividend Discount Model: A Primer." *Financial Analysts Journal*, November-December 1985, pp. 16-25.

Glosten, Lawrence. "Components of the Bid-Ask Spread and the Statistical Properties of Transaction Prices." *Journal of Finance*, December 1987, pp. 1293-1307.

Goodman, David, and Peavy, John. "The Interaction of Firm Size and Price-Earnings Ration on Portfolio Performance." *Financial Analysts Journal*, January-February 1986, pp. 10-12.

Gordon, D. A.; Gordon, M. J.; and Gould, L. I. "Choice Among Methods for Estimating Share Yield." Unpublished paper, University of Wisconsin, April 1988.

Gordon, Myron. "Dividends, Earnings and Stock Prices." *Review of Economics and Statistics*, May 1959, pp. 99-105.

Graham, Benjamin. *The Intelligent Investor.* Fourth edition. New York: Harper and Row, 1973.

Gropper, Diane. "Mining the Market's Inefficiencies." *Institutional Investor,* July 1985, pp. 81, 84-86, 90, 94.

Harrington, Diana R. *Modern Portfolio Theory, The Capital Asset Pricing Model and Arbitrage Pricing Theory: A User's Guide.* Second edition. Englewood Cliffs, N.J.: Prentice Hall, 1987.

Harris, Robert. "Using Analysts' Growth Forecasts to Estimate Shareholders' Required Rates of Return." *Financial Management,* Winter 1984, pp. 40-47.

Hawkins, David. "Toward an Old Theory of Equity Valuation." *Financial Analysts Journal,* November-December 1977, pp. 48-53.

Healy, Paul, and Palepu, Krishna G. "Earnings Information Conveyed by Dividend Initiations and Omissions." *Journal of Financial Economics,* September 1988, pp. 149-75.

Hite, Gailen, and Owens, James. "Security Price Reactions Around Corporative Spin-off Announcements." *Journal of Financial Economics,* December 1983, pp. 409-36.

———; Owens, James E.; and Rogers, Ronald. "The Market for Interfirm Asset Sales: Partial Sell-offs and Total Liquidations." *Journal of Financial Economics,* June 1987, pp. 229-52.

Ho, Thomas S. Y., and Michaely, Roni. "Information Quality and Market Efficiency." *Journal of Financial and Quantitative Analysis,* March 1988, pp. 53-70.

Huberman, Gur; Kandel, Shmuel; and Kasorlyi, G. Andrew. "Size and Industry Related Covariations of Stock Returns." Paper presented at the Institute for Quantitative Research in Finance, September 1987.

Ibbotson Associates. *Stocks, Bonds, Bills, and Inflation: 1987 Yearbook.* Chicago, Ill.: 1985.

Jacobs, Bruce I., and Levy, Kenneth N. "Disentangling Equity Return Regularities: New Insights and Investment Opportunities." *Financial Analysts Journal,* May-June 1988b, pp. 18-43.

———. "Forecasting the Size Effect." *Financial Analysts Journal,* May-June 1989, pp. 38-54.

———. "On the Value of 'Value'." *Financial Analysts Journal,* July-August 1988, pp. 47-62.

———. "Stock Market Complexity and Investment Opportunity," in *Managing Institutional Assets,* Frank Fabozzi, ed. NY: Ballinger Publishing, 1990.

Jaffe, Jeffrey; Keim, Donald; and Westerfield, Randolph. "Earnings Yields, Market Values and Stock Returns." Paper prepared for presentation at the Institute for Quantitative Research in Finance, October 1987.

James, Christopher, and Edmister, Robert. "The Relation Between Common Stock Returns Trading Activity and Market Value." *Journal of Finance,* September 1983, pp. 1075-86.

Kalay, Avner. "The Ex-Dividend Day Behavior of Stock Prices: A Re-Examination of the Clientele Effect." *Journal of Finance,* September 1982, pp. 1059-70.

———. "The Ex-Dividend Day Behavior of Stock Prices: A Re-Examination of the Clientele Effect: A Reply." *Journal of Finance,* June 1984, pp. 557-61.

Karpoff, Jonathan M., and Walking, Ralph A. "Short-Term Trading Around Ex-Dividend Days." *Journal of Financial Economics,* September 1988, pp. 291-98.

Keim, Donald. "The CAPM and Equity Return Regularities." *Financial Analysts Journal*, May-June 1986, pp. 19-34.

———. "Daily Returns and Size-Related Premiums: One More Time." *Journal of Portfolio Management*, Winter 1987, pp. 41-47.

———. "Size-Related Anomalies and Stock Returns Seasonality: Further Empirical Evidence." *Journal of Financial Economics*, June 1983, pp. 13-32.

———, and Stambaugh, R. "A Further Investigation of the Weekend Effect in Stock Returns." *Journal of Finance*, July 1984, pp. 819-40.

Klein, Roger, and Bawa, Vijay. "The Effect of Limited Information and Estimation Risk on Optimal Portfolio Diversification." *Journal of Financial Economics*, November 1977, pp. 89-111.

Kolodny, Richard; Lawrence, Martin; and Ghosh, Arabinda. "In Search of Excellence . . . For Whom?" *Journal of Portfolio Management*, Spring 1989, pp. 56-60.

Lakonishok, Josef, and Vermaelen, Theo. "Tax-Induced Trading Around Ex-Dividend Days." *Journal of Financial Economics*, July 1986, pp. 287-319.

———. "Tax Reform and Ex-Dividend Day Behavior." *Journal of Finance*, September 1983, pp. 1157-79.

LeRoy, S., and Porter, R. "The Present Value Relation: Tests Based on Implied Variance Bounds." *Econometrica*, forthcoming.

Linn, Scott, and Rozeff, Michael. "The Effects of Voluntary Spinoffs on Stock Prices: The Anergy Hypothesis." *Advances in Financial Planning and Forecasting*, C. F. Lee, ed. Greenwich, Conn.: JAI Press, 1985, pp. 265-92.

Lintner, John. "Dividends, Earnings, Leverage, Stock Prices and the Supply of Capital to Corporations. *Review of Economics and Statistics*, August 1962, pp. 243-69.

Litzenberger, Robert, and Ramaswamy, Krishna. "Dividends, Short Selling Restrictions, Tax-Induced Investor Clienteles, and Market Equilibrium." *Journal of Finance*, May 1980, pp. 469-82.

———. "The Effect of Personal Taxes and Dividends on Capital Asset Prices: Theory and Empirical Evidence." *Journal of Financial Economics*, June 1979, pp. 163-95.

———. "The Effects of Dividends on Common Stock Prices: Tax Effects or Information Effects." *Journal of Finance*, May 1982, pp. 429-43.

Mahmoud, Anal, and Lobo, Gerald. "Relationships Between Differentive Amounts of Interim Information and Security Return Variability." Unpublished paper, University of Wisconsin, January 1986.

Mandelker, Gershon N. "Risk and Return: The Case of Merging Firms." *Journal of Financial Economics*, December 1974, pp. 303-35.

Merton, Robert; Scholes, Myron; and Gladstein, M. "The Returns and Risk of Alternative Call Option Portfolio Investment Strategies." *Journal of Business*, April 1978, pp. 183-242.

Michaud, Richard. "A Scenario-Dependent Dividend Discount Model: Bridging the Gap Between Top-Down and Bottom-Up Forecasts." *Financial Analysts Journal*, November-December 1985, pp. 49-59.

Miller, Merton. "Behavioral Rationality in Finance: The Case of Dividends." *Journal of Business*, October 1986, pp. S451-68.

220   THE NEW STOCK MARKET

————, and Modigliani, Franco. "Dividend Policy, Growth and the Valuation of Shares." *Journal of Business*, October 1961, pp. 411-33.

————, and Scholes, Myron. "Dividends and Taxes." *Journal of Financial Economics*, June 1978, pp. 303-36.

————. "Dividends and Taxes: Some Empirical Evidence." *Journal of Political Economy*, March-April 1982, pp. 1118-41.

Morgan, I. G. "Dividends and Capital Asset Prices." *Journal of Finance*, September 1982, pp. 1071-86.

Nakamura, T., and Terada, N. "The Size Effect and Seasonality in Japanese Stock Returns." Nomura Research Institute, 1984.

Ohlson, James, and Penman, Stephen. "Volatility Increases Subsequent to Stock Splits: An Empirical Abberation." *Journal of Financial Economics*, June 1985, pp. 251-66.

Oppenheimer, Henry. "Ben Graham's Net Current Asset Values: A Performance Update." *Finartcial Analysts Journal*, November-December 1986, pp. 40-47.

————. "A Test of Ben Graham's Stock Selection Criteria." *Financial Analysts Journal*, September-October 1984, pp. 68-74.

Patell, James, and Wolfson, Mark. "The Intraday Speed of Adjustment of Stock Prices to Earnings and Dividend Announcements." *Journal of Financial Economics*, June 1984, pp. 223-52.

Peavy, John, and Goodman, David. "The Significance of P/Es for Portfolios Returns." *Journal of Portfolio Management*, Winter 1983, pp. 43-47.

Peters, Thomas J. and Waterman, Robert H. *In Search of Excellence*. New York: Harper and Row, 1982.

Peterson, Pamela; Peterson, David; and Ang, James. "Direct Evidence on the Marginal Rate of Taxation on Dividend Income." *Journal of Financial Economics*, June 1985, pp. 267-82.

Pettit, Richardson. "Dividend Announcements, Security Performance and Capital Market Efficiency." *Journal of Finance*, December 1972, pp. 993-1007.

————. "The Impact of Dividend and Earnings Announcements: A Reconciliation." *Journal of Business*, January 1976, pp. 86-96.

Poterba, James, and Summers, Larry. "Mean Revision in Stock Returns: Evidence and Implications." Unpublished manuscript, National Bureau of Economic Research, Cambridge, Mass., March 1981.

————. "New Evidence that Taxes Affect the Valuation of Dividends." *Journal of Finance*, December 1984, pp. 1397-1415.

————. "The Persistence of Volatility and Stock Market Fluctuations." *American Economic Review*, December 1986, pp. 1142-51.

Reinganum, Marc. "Abnormal Returns in Small Firm Portfolios." *Financial Analysts Journal*, March-April 1981a, pp. 52-56.

————. "The Anatomy of a Stock Market Winner." *Financial Analysts Journal*, March-April 1988, pp. 16-28.

_____. "The Anomalous Stock Market Behavior of Small Firms in January." *Journal of Financial Economics,* June 1983, pp. 89-104.

_____. "A Direct Test of Roll's Conjecture on the Firm Size Effect." *Journal of Finance,* March 1982, pp. 27-35.

_____. "Misspecification of Capital Asset Pricing: Empirical Anomalies Based on Earnings Yields and Market Values. " *Journal of Financial Economics,* March 1981b, pp. 19-46.

_____ and Shapiro, A. "Taxes and Stock Return Seasonality: Evidence from the London Stock Exchange." University of Southern California Working Paper, 1983.

Rie, Daniel. "How Trustworthy Is Your Valuation Model?" *Financial Analysts Journal,* November-December 1985, pp. 42-48.

Roll, Richard. "On Computing Mean Returns and the Small Firm Premium." *Journal of Financial Economics,* September 1983, pp. 371-86.

_____. "The Hubris Hypothesis of Corporate Takeovers." *Journal of Business,* April 1986, pp. 197-216.

_____. "A Possible Explanation of the Small Firm Effect." *Journal of Finance,* September 1981, pp. 879-88.

Rosenberg, Barr; Reid, Kenneth; and Lanstein, Ronald. "Persuasive Evidence of Market Inefficiency." *Journal of Portfolio Management,* September 1985, pp. 9-16.

Sakaguchi, Yasaku. "A Dividend Discount Model Applied to the Japanese Market." Paper prepared for presentation at the Institute for Quantitative Research in Finance, April 1988.

Schipper, Katherine, and Smith, Abbie. "Effects of Recontracting on Shareholders Wealth: The Case of Voluntary Spin-offs." *Journal of Financial Economics,* December 1983, pp. 437-68.

Schultz, Paul. "Transaction Costs and the Small Firm Effect." *Journal of Financial Economics,* June 1983, pp. 81-88.

Schwert, G. William. "Size and Stock Returns, and Other Empirical Anomalies." *Journal of Financial Economics,* June 1983, pp. 3-12.

Shefrin, H., and Statman, M. "Explaining Investor Preference for Cash Dividends." *Journal of Financial Economics,* May 1984, pp. 253-82.

Shiller, Robert. "Do Stock Prices Move Too Much to Be Justified by Subsequent Changes in Dividends?" *American Economic Review,* June 1981, pp. 421-36.

Sorensen, Eric, and Williamson, David. "Some Evidence on the Value of Dividend Discount Models." *Financial Analysts Journal,* November-December 1985, pp. 60-69.

Stoll, Hans R., and Whaley, Robert E. "Transactions Costs and the Small Firm Effect." *Journal of Financial Economics,* June 1983, pp. 57-80.

Summers, Lawrence. "Does the Stock Market Rationally Reflect Fundamental Values?" *Journal of Finance,* July 1986, pp. 591-601.

Torabzadeh, Khalil, and Bertin, William. "Leveraged Buyouts and Shareholder Returns." *Journal of Financial Research,* Winter 1987, pp. 313-19.

Vermaelen, Theo. "Repurchase Tender Offers, Signaling, and Managerial Incentives." *Journal of Financial and Quantitative Analysis,* June 1984, pp. 163-81.

Vu, Joseph. "An Empirical Analysis of Ben Graham's Net Current Asset Value Rule." *Financial Review,* May 1988, pp. 215-25.

Walking, Ralph, and Edmister, Robert. "Determinists of Tender Offer Premiums." *Financial Analysts Journal,* January-February 1985, pp. 27-37.

Wansley, James; Lane, William; and Yang, Ho. "Abnormal Returns to Acquired Firms by Type of Acquisition and Method of Payment." *Financial Management,* Autumn 1983, pp. 16-22.

————; Roenfeldt, Rodney; and Cooley, Philip. "Abnormal Returns from Merger Profiles." *Journal of Financial and Quantitative Analysis,* June 1983, pp. 149-62.

Watts, Ross. "Comments on 'The Impact of Dividend and Earnings Announcements: A Reconciliation.'" *Journal of Business,* January 1976, pp. 97-106.

————. "Information Content of Dividends." *Journal of Business,* May 1973, pp. 191-211.

Wilcox, Jarrod. "The P/B-ROE Valuation Model." *Financial Analysts Journal,* January-February 1984, pp. 58-66.

Wilcox, Michael. "A Global Search for Value: Expected Return as a Function of Price, Book Value, and Return on Equity." Paper presented at the Institute for Quantitative Research in Finance, April 1988.

Zachs and Company. *Determinants of Performance.* Chicago, Ill.: June 1987.

CHAPTER 6

Common-Stock
Options Strategies

Up to this point, we have discussed what we know and do not know about profiting from buying and selling common stocks. Common stocks are not the only vehicles, however, with which to seek profits from the stock market. Derivative securities—options on stocks, futures, and options on futures—provide alternative ways to capitalize on movements in the price of a stock or the stock market itself, and to tailor the risk of an investor's portfolio. Because these securities are such important and useful instruments, they will be the subject of Chapters 6, 7, and 8.

Options allow investors to mold a portfolio return distribution to fit their particular investment objectives[1] and to do so efficiently. Investors also have used the options market to try to generate abnormal returns. In this chapter, we will review the evidence on common-stock option strategies for return-distribution molding and generating profits. We will focus in this review on two critical empirical questions: Is there, as often suggested in promotional literature, an option strategy that outperforms other option and stock strategies? And is the market for common-stock options efficient? Before we examine these questions, a review of the investment characteristics of options and option strategies will be useful.

Common-Stock Options

A common-stock option is a contract in which the writer of the option grants the buyer of the option the right to purchase from or sell to the writer a specified number of shares of a designated common stock at a predetermined price within a specified period of time. The writer, also referred to as the seller, grants this right to the buyer for a sum of money called the *option price* (or *option premium*). The price at which the designated common stock may be bought or sold is called the *exercise, strike,* or *striking price*. The date after which an option is void is called the *expiration* or *maturity*.

When an option grants the buyer the right to purchase the common stock from the writer (seller) of the option, it is called a *call option*. When the option buyer has the right to sell the designated common stock to the writer (seller), the option is called a *put option*. Notice that it is the writer (seller) of the option who is *obligated* to perform. The buyer of the option can walk away from the contract if no economic value would be realized by exercising the option.

Organized call-option trading began on the Chicago Board Option Exchange (CBOE) in April 1973, and options on common stock are currently traded on several exchanges. All exchange-traded common-stock options sold in the United States may be exercised any time before the expiration date. An option that allows a buyer to exercise it at any time up to and including the expiration date is called an *American option*. When an option permits exercise only on the expiration date, it is called a *European option*. Exchange-traded common-stock options are written for lots of 100 shares of a designated common stock. While the strike price does not take into account cash dividends paid to common stockholders, exchange-traded options are protected against stock dividends and stock splits.

When an investor purchases an option, he or she is said to hold the contract *long* or be in a *long position*. The investor will benefit if the value of the option increases. An option writer (seller) is said to be *short* the contract or to be in a *short position*.

Popular Option Strategies[2]

If the opportunities available with common-stock options are to be understood, the investment characteristics of several option strategies must be understood.

Naked Option Strategies

The simplest strategies are those involving a position in a particular option and no other position in another option or stock. Such strategies are called naked option strategies. There are six naked-option strategies: (1) long call (buying call options), (2) short call (selling call options), (3) long put (buying put options), (4) short put (selling put options), (5) long-call paper buying (buying call options and investing in short-term paper), and (6) cash-secured put writing (writing puts and holding sufficient cash should option be exercised). Each is graphically illustrated in Appendix A to this chapter.

The profit and loss from each strategy depends on the price of the underlying common stock at the expiration date. With each strategy, the most that the option buyer can lose is the amount of the option price. The potential gain, however, is all of the upside potential (reduced by the option price). In contrast, the maximum profit that the option writer can realize is the option price; and the writer is exposed to all the downside risk.

Long-Call Strategy The most straightforward option strategy for profiting from an anticipated increase in the stock price is to buy a call option, to use a *long-call strategy*. For an investor to profit from buying a call option, the stock price at the expiration date must be greater than the exercise price by an amount greater than the option price. If the stock price is less, the investor will lose. The speculative appeal of call options is that, for a given number of investment dollars, an investor can control the appreciation from more shares of common stock than she or he could control by buying stock itself. This characteristic is illustrated in Appendix B to this chapter.

Short-Call Strategy An investor who believes that the price of some common stock will decrease or change little can, if correct, realize income by writing (selling) a call option. This strategy is called a *short-call strategy*. If the price of the underlying common stock is not greater than the exercise price at the expiration date, the writer realizes a profit equal to the option price. If the stock price is above the exercise price by an amount less than the option price, the writer still profits, but by an amount less than the option price. The profit-and-loss pattern for the option writer is the mirror image of that for the option buyer.

Long-Put Strategy The most straightforward option strategy for benefiting from an expected decrease in the price of some common stock is to buy a put option. This strategy is called a *long-put strategy*. The buyer will realize a profit if the stock price at expiration is below the exercise price by an amount equal to the option price. A stock price above the exercise price will result in a loss.

Short-Put Strategy The short-put strategy involves the selling (writing) of put options. This strategy is used if the investor expects that the price of some stock will increase or stay the same. The profit-and-loss profile for a short-put option is the mirror image of the long-put option. The maximum profit from this strategy is the option price. The maximum loss is limited by how much the price of the stock can fall by the expiration date less the option price received for writing the option.

Long-Call Paper-Buying Strategy This naked strategy involves allocating a portion of a portfolio's funds to purchase a call option and investing the balance of the funds in risk-free or low-risk fixed-income securities such as U.S. Treasury bills or commercial paper.[3] This strategy is less risky than allocating all the portfolio's funds to stocks. The long-call option allows the investor to share in any favorable stock-price increase; the funds invested in the fixed-income security provide a cushion against any unfavorable stock-price movements.

Cash-Secured Put-Writing Strategy If an investor makes a decision to purchase a stock at a price less than the prevailing market price, one way of doing so is to place a limit-buy order (an order to buy at a particular price or range of prices). Alternatively, the investor can use the options market to do effectively the same thing. The investor can write a put option with a strike price near the desired price. Sufficient funds to exercise the option are then placed in escrow.

Covered-Option or Hedge Strategies

In contrast to naked-option strategies, *covered-option* or *hedge strategies* involve taking positions in an option and the underlying stock in such a way that one position will help offset any unfavorable price movement in the other. The two popular hedge strategies are: (1) the covered call-writing strategy and (2) the protective put-buying strategy.

Covered Call-Writing Strategy This strategy involves writing a call option on stocks the investor holds in a portfolio—that is, a short position in a call option and a long position in the underlying stock. A decline in the price of the stock will create a loss on the long stock position, but the income generated from the sale of the call option will either (1) fully offset the loss in the long-stock position, (2) partially offset the loss in the long-stock position, or (3) more than offset the loss in the long-stock position so as to generate a profit. This strategy is illustrated in Appendix B.

Protective Put-Buying Strategy If an investor wants to protect the value of a stock held in a portfolio, one way of doing so with options is to buy a put option on that stock. The investor is thus guaranteed the strike price of the put option less the cost of the option. Should the stock price rise rather than decline, the investor is able to participate in the price increase; however, the profit will be reduced by the cost of the option. This strategy is called protective put-writing and involves a long-put position (buying a put option) and a long position in the underlying stock held in the portfolio. This strategy also is illustrated in Appendix B.

A wide variety of other strategies that combine two or more options on the same underlying stock are possible. They include spread strategies (vertical, horizontal, diagonal, and butterfly spreads) and combination strategies (the most popular of which is the straddle). The strategies for specific purposes are discussed in books on option strategies cited at the end of the chapter and will not be presented here.

Is There a Superior Option Strategy?

The development of the option market brought with it a number of myths that particular option strategies consistently generated superior returns relative to the purchase of stocks. For example, popular literature and advertising by the option industry recommended that individual and institutional investors follow a covered-call strategy. This strategy, it was purported, could be expected to generate extra return from the income received by selling (writing) a call option on stocks held in investors' portfolios. The touting of this notion led Black [1975] to write, "For every fact about options, there is a fantasy—a reason given for trading or not trading in options that doesn't make sense when examined carefully" (p. 36).

Still the myths about profits persist. Is there an option strategy that has consistently outperformed a simple strategy of buying common stocks? Let's examine the empirical evidence on this issue—first, a look at call-option strategies.

Call-Option Strategies

Several studies have empirically examined whether there are call-option strategies that might provide superior risk-adjusted results. The first major study was by Merton, Scholes, and Gladstein [1978]. Using simulation analysis, they examined the risk-and-return patterns of the covered call-writing and long-call paper-buying strategies.[4] These strategies were examined not for a single stock-option position but for a portfolio of option positions.

The simulation analysis in Merton et al. was based on two samples of underlying stocks: (1) the 136 stocks on which listed options were available as of December 1975 and (2) the 30 stocks contained in the Dow Jones Industrial Average (DJIA). The time over which the simulations were performed was July 1, 1963, to December 31, 1975, an interval of 12.5 years. This interval encompassed a variety of market environments (bull and bear markets, and periods of high and low volatility). The simulations were performed using 6-month holding periods (25 basic subperiod observations). Transaction costs and taxes were ignored.

For the two call-option strategies investigated, the option prices used in the simulations were calculated using the Black-Scholes model adjusted for dividends.[5] That is, the prices were theoretical, not actual (observed), prices. The simulations were performed for both call-option strategies for four exercise prices: (1) 90 percent of the stock price (in the money), (2) the stock price (at the money), (3) 110 percent of the stock price (out of the money), and (4) 120 percent of the stock price (deep out of the money). All call options purchased had 6-month maturities.

Merton et al. investigated what is called a fully covered call strategy: for each individual stock in the portfolio, a call option for the same number of shares is sold on that individual stock. For the long-call paper-buying strategy, they examined one possible allocation between call options and the risk-free security: 10 percent in call options and 90 percent in a risk-free security; six-month commercial paper was used as the risk-free security.

Exhibit 6-1 provides summary statistics of the semiannual performance results for their fully covered call strategy and for the return of an equally weighted portfolio of the underlying stocks and the return on six-month commercial paper. The results show that investors can reduce their risk exposure significantly by following a fully covered call strategy; they can achieve a lower standard deviation and a lower range of observed returns, regardless of the exercise price. This reduction in risk was not free, however. The cost of the strategy was the reduction in expected return relative to the long-stock portfolio. These findings do not support the claims of those who preach that a covered-call strategy generates "extra income" for investors.

Exhibit 6-1
Summary Statistics for Rate-of-Return
Simulations, Fully Covered Strategies
July 1963-December 1975

| | 136-Stock Sample Exercise Price/Stock Price | | | | | Commercial |
	90%	100%	110%	120%	Stock	Paper
Average rate of return	3.3%	3.7%	4.5%	5.3%	7.9%	3.3%
Standard deviation	4.9	7.1	9.3	11.2	16.6	1.1
Highest return	14.6	19.3	24.7	30.4	54.6	6.2
Lowest return	−9.9	−14.4	−17.4	−19.2	−21.0	6.0
Average compound return	3.0	3.4	4.1	4.7	6.7	3.3
Growth of $1,000	$2,171	$2,328	$2,719	$3,162	$5,043	$2,239
Coefficient of skewness	−0.63	−0.48	−0.26	−0.01	0.73	—

| | DJIA Stock Sample Exercise Price/Stock Price | | | | | Commercial |
	90%	100%	110%	120%	Stock	Paper
Average rate of return	2.9%	2.9%	3.2%	3.5%	4.1%	3.3%
Standard deviation	3.7	6.2	8.6	10.4	13.7	1.1
Highest return	12.3	16.9	22.9	29.5	49.1	6.2
Lowest return	−5.4	−9.2	−11.9	−13.8	−16.4	6.0
Average compound return	2.8	2.7	2.9	3.0	3.3	3.3
Growth of $1,000	$1,992	$1,942	$2,040	$2,103	$2,226	$2,239
Coefficent of skewness	−0.22	−0.21	0.04	0.35	1.25	—

Source: Adapted from Merton, Scholes, and Gladstein [1978], p. 207.

Remember that the option prices used in the study were based on a theoretical option-pricing model, the Black-Scholes model discussed in Appendix A. What would be the impact if the theoretical model provided biased prices? The authors tested for this possibility in two ways. First, they replicated the study for the at-the-money call options, but this time assumed option prices from 70 to 130 percent of the theoretical price. These results, shown in Exhibit 6-2, indicated that, while the option price received by selling call options changed the average return for the study period, the overall volatility of returns remained the same. As a second test, Merton et al. used the actual prices for part of the study period that prices were available—April 1973 (the inception of options trading on the CBOE) to December 1975 (the end of their study period). Using actual prices on 6-month call options and the estimated prices based on the theoretical option-pricing model for this period, they found that, for this short period, the returns on the covered-call strategy were higher using actual prices than when using theoretical prices, but the differences were small.

Exhibit 6-2

Summary Return Statistics for Different Premium Levels, Fully Covered Strategy with Exercise Price Equal to Stock Price, July 1963-December 1975

| | *136-Stock Sample* | | | | | | |
| | *Premium Received/Model Estimate* | | | | | | |
	70%	*80%*	*90%*	*100%*	*110%*	*120%*	*130%*
Average rate of return	0.8%	1.8%	2.7%	3.7%	4.7%	5.7%	6.8%
Standard deviation	6.8	6.8	7.0	7.1	7.2	7.3	7.5
Highest return	13.7	15.5	17.3	19.3	21.3	23.4	25.5
Lowest return	−16.9	−16.1	−15.2	−14.4	−13.5	−12.6	−11.7
Average compound return	0.6	1.5	2.5	3.4	4.5	5.5	5.2
Growth of $1,000	$1,157	$1,457	$1,839	$2,328	$2,957	$3,768	$4,816

| | *DJIA Stock Sample* | | | | | | |
| | *Premium Received/Model Estimate* | | | | | | |
	70%	*80%*	*90%*	*100%*	*110%*	*120%*	*130%*
Average rate of return	0.7%	1.4%	2.1%	2.9%	3.6%	4.4%	5.2%
Standard deviation	6.0	6.1	6.1	6.2	6.3	6.4	6.5
Highest return	12.7	14.0	15.5	16.9	18.4	19.9	21.5
Lowest return	−12.1	−11.1	−10.2	−9.2	−8.2	−7.2	−6.2
Average compound return	0.5	1.2	1.9	2.7	3.4	4.2	5.0
Growth of $1,000	$1,130	$1,351	$1,619	$1,942	$2,334	$2,809	$3,387

Source: Adapted from Merton, et al. [1978], p. 212.

The results of the simulation for the long-call paper-buying strategy are shown in Exhibit 6-3. Unlike the fully covered call writing strategy, risk, as measured by either standard deviation or range of returns, may be higher than for the long-stock strategy. For example, the standard deviation for the 136-stock sample is greater for the deep out-of-the-money option than the long-stock strategy (27.2 percent versus 16.6 percent). The increased risk was accompanied, however, by increased average returns (16.2 percent versus 7.9 percent). Merton et al. found cases in which the long-call paper-buying strategy clearly outperformed the long-stock strategy: the return was higher, and the risk lower. This result is clear for the 136-stock-sample, at-the-money option, and the out-of-the-money option, in which the exercise price is 100 percent of the stock price. Thus for the period investigated, the Merton et al. study suggests that superior returns may have been possible for a long-call paper-buying strategy.

Two explanations are possible for the superior performance of the long-call paper-buying strategy: (1) the price may have been misestimated and/or (2) the results might have been period specific. First, if the theoretical option prices were understated, by using their particular theoretical model to price options, Merton et al. were actually buying cheap or undervalued options. The authors report, however, that the actual prices had to be 20 percent higher than the theoretical prices for the 136-stock sample, and 28 percent higher for the DJIA sample, to have a material impact on some of the results. This misestimation is not likely. Using lower or higher option prices rather than the actual prices did not alter their conclusions.

The other source of error could be the market environment during the study period. For example, if the study period was dominated by many periods of sharply declining stock prices, a long-call paper-buying strategy would outperform a long-stock strategy. When Merton et al. examined the performance over different market environments, however, they did not find that the period studied provided a satisfactory explanation for the superior performance of the long-call paper-buying strategy.

While there have been no other comprehensive studies of the long-call paper-buying strategy, there have been other studies of the covered call-writing strategy, because it is the strategy used by most institutional investors.

Pounds [1978] studied 43 stocks with listed call options for the eight-year period of 1969 through 1976. He used theoretical rather than actual prices and three different exercise prices: out-of-the-money (strike price of 90 percent), at-the-money, and in-the-money (strike price of 110 percent) call options. Commissions were taken into account. The quarterly performance results for his three covered-call strategies are shown in Exhibit 6-4. Also shown is the performance of the stock position.

Unlike the Merton et al. study, Pounds' results showed the at-the-money and in-the-money covered-call option strategies outperforming the long-stock position: the average return was greater, and the standard deviation lower. The

Exhibit 6-3
Summary Statistics for Rate-of-Return Simulations,
Options/Paper-Buying Strategies,
July 1963-December 1975

	136 Stock Sample Exercise Price/Stock Price					
	90%	100%	110%	120%	Stock	Commercial Paper
Average rate or return	6.3%	8.2%	11.1%	16.2%	7.9%	3.3%
Standard deviation	7.8	10.6	15.7	27.2	16.6	1.1
Highest return	25.7	34.7	59.9	121.0	54.6	6.2
Lowest return	–4.7	–5.2	–5.7	–6.1	–21.0	6.0
Average compound return	6.1	7.7	10.1	13.8	6.7	3.3
Growth of $1,000	$4,370	$6,372	$11,178	$25,670	$5,043	$2,239
Coefficient of skewness	0.83	0.87	1.26	2.26	0.73	—

	DJIA Stock Sample Exercise Price/Stock Price					
	90%	100%	110%	120%	Stock	Commerical Paper
Average rate of return	4.2%	5.1%	7.2%	10.6%	4.1%	3.3%
Standard deviation	7.3	10.1	14.6	25.7	13.7	1.1
Highest return	27.1	3.4	42.6	88.1	49.1	6.2
Lowest return	–4.6	–5.7	–7.5	–7.9	–16.4	6.0
Average compound return	3.9	4.7	6.3	8.3	3.3	3.3
Growth of $1,000	$2,627	$3,138	$4,597	$7,287	$2,226	$2,239
Coefficent of skewness	1.26	1.09	1.01	1.64	1.25	—

Source: Adapted from Merton, et al. [1978], p. 219.

out-of-the-money call option had a slightly lower average return (1.14 percent versus 1.20 percent) but a substantially lower standard deviation (4.15 percent versus 10.45 percent). Does this result mean that a covered-call strategy is superior to a long-stock strategy? As Pounds points out, such a conclusion is not possible, because the market did not advance during the period studied: a flat or declining market would favor a covered call-writing strategy. When he investigated rising-market subperiods within the eight years, he found that the long-stock portfolio outperformed all the covered-call option strategies.

Can an investor use Pounds' results to develop a profitable covered-call

Exhibit 6-4

Covered Call Writing—Quarterly Values

	Exercise Price/Stock Price			Stock
	90%	100%	110%	
Arithmetic average return	1.14%	1.75%	1.96%	1.20%
Standard deviation	4.15	6.21	7.91	10.45
Geometric average return	1.05	1.54	1.63	0.65
Maximum return	6.40	10.74	14.60	25.25
Minimum return	−13.42%	−17.60%	−20.54%	−24.44%
Final index value	1.3989	1.6333	1.6792	1.2312

Source: Adapted from Pounds [1978], p. 35.

option strategy? Based on Exhibit 6-4, Pounds argued that an out-of-the-money covered-call strategy gives the best results because of the substantial reduction in risk for a small reduction (0.72 percent) in quarterly average returns. The in-the-money covered-call strategy had the worst results. While these results may be true for the entire period, writing out-of-the-money call options for subperiods resulted in better performance only when stock prices did not rise. Otherwise, the in-the-money covered call-writing strategy was better.

In contrast to the two previous studies, Yates and Kopprasch [1980] investigated the call-writing strategy using actual call option prices for July 1973 to July 1980. They constructed an index, the Institutional Option Writer's Index (IOWI), that institutions could use to measure their option-writing performance. The underlying portfolio for the index was constructed by using all stocks with listed CBOE call options that were in the January, April, July, and October expiration cycles. The quarterly performance of the Standard & Poor's (S&P) 500 Index, the underlying IOWI stocks, and the IOWI is shown in Exhibit 6-5. Commissions were not considered.

The results in Exhibit 6-5 lend support to the position that the covered call-writing strategy would have outperformed both the S&P 500 and the underlying portfolio over the entire time period. While these results might be expected for down markets, Exhibit 6-5 indicates that the IOWI also performed well in up markets. These results, as well as others reported by Yates and Kopprasch, disagree with those of Merton et al.

Put-Option Strategies

In a follow-up study to their earlier study of call-option strategies, Merton, Scholes, and Gladstein [1982] investigated the risk-return patterns of two put-option strategies—uncovered (or naked) put writing and protective put buying.

Exhibit 6-5
Results of Covered Call-Writing Strategy

Date	S&P 500 Index	% Change	Unhedged Underlying Portfolio	% Change	IOWI	% Change
7-27-73	100.00	–0–	100.00	–0–	100.00	–0–
10-29-73	102.16	+2.16	103.14	+3.14	106.30	+6.3
1-30-74	89.98	–11.92	89.37	–63.35	101.11	–4.88
4-26-74	84.40	–6.20	84.77	–5.15	101.97	+.85
7-24-74	76.06	–9.88	75.29	–11.18	97.82	–4.07
10-25-74	65.56	–13.81	63.93	–15.09	89.13	–8.88
1-24-75	69.09	+5.39	66.53	+4.07	96.24	+7.98
4-25-75	82.89	+19.98	84.30	+26.71	105.27	+9.38
7-25-75	86.33	+4.15	86.97	+3.17	112.46	+6.83
10-24-75	87.84	+1.75	85.95	–1.17	118.02	+4.94
1-16-76	95.64	+8.88	92.27	+7.35	125.61	+6.4
4-15-76	100.16	+4.73	97.70	+5.88	130.91	+4.22
7-17-76	105.07	+4.90	104.52	+6.98	138.21	+5.58
10-15-76	102.18	–2.75	99.58	–4.73	138.10	.08
1-21-77	105.62	+3.37	101.43	–1.86	142.74	–3.36
4-15-77	104.37	–1.21	99.43	–1.97	145.27	+1.77
7- -77	104.54	+.16	99.15	.28	147.28	+1.38
10-21-77	97.64	–6.79	90.23	–9.00	141.17	–4.15
1-20-78	96.10	–1.58	90.49	+.29	144.55	+2.40
4-21-78	102.09	+6.23	96.24	+6.35	150.21	+3.92
7-21-78	107.11	+4.92	104.22	+8.29	157.01	+4.53
10-20-78	108.72	+1.50	106.17	+1.87	163.24	+3.97
1-19-79	112.13	+3.14	109.04	+2.70	170.74	+4.59
4-20-79	115.26	+2.79	111.22	+2.00	177.89	+4.19
7-20-79	117.50	+1.94	113.04	+1.64	181.73	+2.16
10-19-79	118.91	+1.20	113.39	+.31	186.35	+2.54
1-18-80	131.69	+10.75	130.89	+15.43	198.26	+6.39
4-18-80	121.00	-8.12	113.98	–12.92	187.24	–5.56
7-18-80	148.72	+22.91	146.96	+28.94	203.79	+8.84

Source: Yates and Kopprasch [1980], p. 76.

They used simulation for the 14 years from July 1, 1963, through June 30, 1977, and the same two stock samples used in their previous study.

For the uncovered-put option-writing strategy, three exercise prices were used, 90 percent of the stock price (in the money), 100 percent (at the money), and 110 percent (out of the money). Exhibit 6-6 summarizes the findings for these strategies and for a fully covered call-writing strategy.[6]

As Exhibit 6-6 demonstrates, the volatility of the uncovered put-writing strategies and the fully covered call-writing strategies is less than that of the two long-stock positions the authors examined. For all three uncovered put-writing strategies, risk (standard deviation) was reduced significantly relative to that of the long-stock positions: 55 percent reduction for the in-the-money, 65 percent for the at-the-money, and 75 percent for the out-of-the-money strategies. However, because the range of observed returns was also reduced, the reduction of volatility came at the expense of a reduction in average return. Once again, Merton et al. found no superior strategy.

As expected, the patterns of returns for the uncovered put-writing strategies were similar to the fully covered call-writing strategy. However, the risk (as measured by either standard deviation or range) of the uncovered put-writing strategies was less than that of the corresponding fully covered call-writing strategy. There are two reasons for this result. First, the uncovered put-writing strategies had less leverage. Second, with the uncovered put-writing strategy, there is the possibility of early exercise of the put option by the buyer. Any position that is exercised early will no longer be a source of variation between the time of exercise and the end of the investment period.

Note that the volatility and average return of the uncovered put-writing strategy and the fully covered call strategy increase substantially when options with higher exercise prices are written.

We can conclude from this study that uncovered put writing is more conservative than fully covered call writing and that both option strategies are more conservative than a long-stock position: the average return for all the option strategies reported in Exhibit 6-6 was less than that of the long-stock position.

The second put-option strategy simulated by Merton et al. was the protective-put strategy. These results and the results of a similar strategy, a long-call paper-buying strategy, are summarized in Exhibit 6-7. For the protective-put strategies, the risk (standard deviation and range of returns) was lower than for the long-stock position: the higher the put-option exercise price, the lower the volatility. The risk reduction comes at the expense of returns.

Summary of Findings

With the exception of the Yates and Kopprasch study, none of the studies examined suggests that a superior option strategy exists. The empirical evidence indicates that option strategies show the expected tradeoff between risk and return: the higher the expected return, the higher the expected risk (volatility). This view is best summarized by Merton et al. in the conclusion to their first [1978] study:

Exhibit 6-6

Summary Statistics for Semiannual Rate-of-Return Simulations, Uncovered Put-Writing Strategies and Fully Covered Call-Writing Strategies, July 1963-June 1977

	Exercise Price = 0.9 Stock Price		Exercise Price = 1.0 Stock Price		Exercise Price = 1.1 Stock Price		Stock Portfolio
	Uncovered Put	Fully Covered Call	Uncovered Put	Fully Covered Call	Uncovered Put	Fully Covered Call	
136-stock sample:							
Average rate of return (%)	3.5	3.4	4.1	3.8	5.0	4.6	7.7
Standard deviation (%)	3.9	4.7	5.6	6.9	7.2	9.1	16.1
Highest return (%)	14.4	14.6	18.8	19.3	23.6	24.7	54.6
Lowest return (%)	-6.0	-9.9	-6.4	-14.4	-5.6	-17.4	-21.0
Average compound return (%)	3.4	3.3	3.8	3.5	4.6	4.1	6.3
Growth of $1,000 ($)	2,571	2,486	2,930	2,691	3,640	3,155	5,901
Coefficient of skewness	.08	-.71	.44	-.50	.58	-.25	.75
DJ stock sample:							
Average rate of return (%)	3.3	3.0	4.0	3.1	5.1	3.6	4.6
Standard deviation (%)	3.1	3.7	4.8	6.1	6.2	8.5	13.7
Highest return (%)	12.1	12.3	16.9	16.9	23.1	22.9	49.1
Lowest return (%)	-2.2	-5.4	-4.0	-9.2	-2.8	-11.9	-16.4
Average compound return (%)	3.2	2.9	3.8	2.9	4.8	3.2	3.7
Growth of $1,000 ($)	2,454	2,233	2,925	2,260	2,819	2,458	2,829
Coefficient of skewness	.35	-.27	.38	-.26	.91	.00	1.16

Source: Merton, Scholes, and Gladstein [1982], p. 26.

Exhibit 6-7
Summary Statistics for Semiannual Rate-of-Return Simulations, Protective Put-Buying Strategies and Call-Option Commercial-Paper-Buying Strategies, July 1963-June 1977

	Exercise Price = 0.9 Stock Price		Exercise Price = 1.0 Stock Price		Exercise Price = 1.1 Stock Price		Stock Portfolio
	Protective Put	Options-Paper	Protective Put	Options-Paper	Protective Put	Options-Paper	
136-stock sample:							
Average rate of return (%)	7.3	6.1	6.7	7.7	5.9	10.4	7.7
Standard deviation (%)	12.0	7.7	9.5	10.5	7.1	15.4	16.1
Highest return (%)	43.6	25.7	37.9	34.7	31.2	60.0	54.6
Lowest return (%)	-8.2	-4.7	-4.0	-5.2	-1.5	-6.3	-21.0
Average compound return (%)	6.5	5.7	6.2	7.0	5.5	9.0	6.3
Growth of $1,000 ($)	6,187	4,882	5,628	7,125	4,654	12,519	5,904
Coefficient of skewness	1.13	.83	1.47	.87	1.93	1.27	.75
DJ stock sample:							
Average rate of return (%)	4.7	4.5	4.5	5.4	4.0	7.3	4.6
Standard deviation (%)	10.4	7.4	7.9	10.4	5.6	14.9	13.7
Highest return (%)	40.8	27.2	35.1	34.4	28.1	42.6	49.1
Lowest return (%)	-7.0	-4.6	-1.8	-5.7	.3	-7.5	-16.4
Average compound return (%)	4.2	4.1	4.2	4.9	3.8	6.2	3.7
Growth of $1,000 ($)	3,218	3,178	3,209	3,895	2,884	5,646	2,829
Coefficient of skewness	1.62	1.18	2.25	1.05	3.02	.97	1.16

The relative risk characteristics of the strategies described by the simulations are representative of the strategies. The specific *levels* of the returns generated, however, are strongly dependent on the actual experience of the underlying stocks during the simulation period. To avoid the creation of new myths about option strategies, the reader is warned not to infer from our findings that any one of the strategies is superior to the others for all investors. *Indeed, if options and their underlying stocks are correctly priced, then there is no single best strategy for all investors.* (p. 184)

Note from the last sentence that in a market that prices options fairly (is efficient), no option strategy should be superior.

The studies we have looked at thus far focused on the profit from simple strategies. Before continuing, a review of the way options are priced will be useful. We will then turn to the question of option-market efficiency.

Option Pricing and Market Efficiency

To implement investment strategies employing options, one must be able to determine the fair value of an option prior to its expiration date. We know that an option must sell for at least its intrinsic value. Based on pure arbitrage arguments, a minimum and/or maximum price for an option can be determined: a boundary can be placed on the option price. If the observed option price violates the boundary (that is, it is less than the minimum price or greater than the maximum price), then a risk-free arbitrage opportunity exists.[7] In addition to being able to establish boundary conditions for option prices, arbitrage arguments can be used to determine the relationship between the price of a put, a call, and the underlying stock. This relationship is referred to as the *put-call parity relationship*. Violations of this relationship lead to arbitrage opportunities.

If one makes some assumptions about the probability distribution of a stock's price, an option-pricing model can be developed. The most popular of these models is the Black-Scholes model [1973].[8] The original Black-Scholes option-pricing model was based on certain restrictive assumptions, but several researchers have modified it by relaxing one or more of the assumptions.

Regardless of which option-pricing model is used, six factors are known to determine an option's price:

1. the current price of the common stock,
2. the exercise (strike) price,
3. the amount of time remaining until the expiration date,

4. the anticipated volatility of the stock price,

5. the riskless interest rate with a maturity equal to the remaining life of the option, and

6. the anticipated cash dividend payments of the stock.

Exhibit 6-8 summarizes how these six factors influence the price of an option.[9]

Exhibit 6-8
Summary of Impact of Six Factors on the Price of an Option

Factor	Effect of an Increase of Factor on Call Price	Put Price
Current stock price	Increase	Decrease
Exercise price	Decrease	Increase
Time to expiration	Increase	Increase
Anticipated stock price volatility	Increase	Increase
Short-term interest rate	Increase	Decrease
Anticipated cash dividends	Decrease	Increase

Efficiency of the Options Market

As we discussed in Chapter 1, a market is considered efficient if investors cannot earn a profit after accounting for risk and transaction costs. In the first five chapters of this book, we discussed the problems associated with testing for the efficiency of the stock market. Many of the same problems exist for testing stock-option efficiency.

A unique problem encountered by stock-option researchers, however, is that their tests require information on the prices of two assets, the stock price and the option price, at the same point in time. When prices are available on both assets at the same time, the data are said to be synchronous. In empirical tests, because of lack of data, prices used may be nonsynchronous; that is, the stock price used in a study may be the closing price for a particular day, while the option price may be the price at the beginning of the same trading day. An empirical study that finds abnormal trading profits using nonsynchronous data does not necessarily confirm that the options market is inefficient.

In addition to the problem of nonsynchronous data, there is a problem in determining the fair price of an option. Recall that, in discussing tests of stock-market efficiency, we found that such tests are joint tests of the efficiency of the market and the model used to estimate the stock returns. Researchers investigating the efficiency of the options market face the same problem. Thus they must rely on an option-pricing model, and empirical tests are then joint tests of market efficiency and the validity of the option-pricing model.

Tests of market efficiency fall into two categories. The first is tests in which no option model is used. Instead, violations of boundary conditions (the range in which the option price must fall) or violations of the relationship between the prices of a stock's put and call options (put-call parity) are examined to determine if abnormal trading profits are possible. The second set of tests uses various option-pricing models to assess whether mispriced options can be identified and exploited using the riskless-hedge strategy.

Tests Not Based on an Option Pricing Model. Both boundary conditions and the put-call parity relationship are derived from a pure arbitrage relationship and all are further explained in Appendix A. We can determine boundary conditions for the price of an option, and violations of these conditions may permit an investor to earn abnormal profits. Violations of the put-call parity relationship create the potential for an investor to earn a return greater than the riskless interest rate. Remember, finding that a boundary condition is violated is not sufficient to conclude that the market is inefficient; it is also necessary that the trading strategies based on any violation produce a profit.

Three studies have examined market efficiency using boundary conditions for call-option prices. Galai [1978] studied the daily closing prices of options traded on the CBOE from April 1973 to October 1973, the first six months of the exchange's operation. His tests found violations of the lower boundary for a call option of a dividend-paying stock. Furthermore, he found that arbitrage trading based on these violations could have generated small profits.

In a later study using data for options traded on the CBOE, Bhattacharya [1983] found that, when transaction costs were accounted for, arbitrage-trading profits from boundary violations disappeared. On the other hand, Halpern and Turnbull [1985], studying the recorded transactions on the Toronto Stock Exchange for the period 1978-79, found that the boundary-violation arbitrage profits more than offset transaction costs. They noted, however, that "observed inefficiencies should not be generalized to current periods where the option market has matured and its growth has leveled off" (p. 500).

If the put-call parity relationship is violated, investors can create a riskless hedge and produce a profit. There have been two studies of market efficiency based on violations of the put-call parity relationship for listed options.[10]

Klemkosky and Resnick [1979] examined 606 hedges for 15 companies having both put and call options listed on the CBOE, the American, and the Philadelphia stock exchanges from July 1977 to June 1978. Of the 606 hedges examined, 540 were riskless: conditions were such that there would be no rational early exercise of the call option. Of these riskless hedges, 306 were unprofitable ex post, while 234 were profitable ex post. After considering transaction costs of $20 (the cost for a member firm to obtain a round-lot position in a hedge), only 147 were still profitable. From this research, Klemkosky and Resnick concluded, "The empirical results of the model tests are consistent with put-call parity theory and thus support this aspect of efficiency for the registered options markets. The small degree of inefficiency detected appears to be the result of overpriced calls" (p. 1154).

In a follow-up study, the authors [1980] further investigated the hedges that produced profits. Specifically, they constructed hedges 5 and 15 minutes after a hedge was initially identified as having an ex post return greater than $20. The purpose was to test the relationship on an ex ante basis by using the ex post results as information from which to construct the hedge. They found the ex ante profitability to be less than the ex post profitability, and prices adjusted rapidly enough to eliminate most, if not all, of the abnormal profit.

Tests Based on Option-Pricing Models. The second category of tests for the efficiency of the options market uses an option-pricing model. These tests involve two steps. First, a model is used to identify under- or overvalued options. There are two approaches to identify a mispriced option. The market price can be compared to the theoretical price. Instead, rather than computing a theoretical option price, an implied volatility can be calculated. How is this done? Recall from the summary of the factors that determine the price of an option (in Exhibit 6-8) that only the expected stock price volatility must be estimated. A volatility consistent with an assumed option-pricing model, the five known factors that determine the price of an option, and the market price of the option, can be estimated. This estimate is called the *implied volatility*. The other approach to identifying a mispriced option is by comparing the implied volatility to the historical volatility. An option is overvalued (undervalued) if the implied volatility is greater (less) than historical volatility. The second step is to create a hedged position to exploit any option that is identified as mispriced and determine if it is sufficiently mispriced to produce a return greater than the risk-free rate.[11]

The first study examining market efficiency using an option-pricing model was reported by Black and Scholes [1972]. Based on the option-pricing model they developed, they could not reject the hypothesis that the market is efficient. Galai [1977], however, did detect evidence of market inefficiency. Stronger evidence of market inefficiency based on implied volatility was found by Trippi [1977] and Chiras and Manaster [1978]. These two studies found trading strategies that could produce abnormally high returns. However, both studies failed to take transaction costs into account.

In the options market, transaction costs include (1) floor trading and clearing costs, (2) New York State transfer taxes, (3) Securities and Exchange Commission transaction fees, (4) margin requirements, (5) net capital charges, and (6) bid/ask spreads. These costs must be considered in any study that investigates market efficiency. Because these costs vary for market makers, arbitrageurs, and individuals in the options markets, the market could be efficient for one type of trader but not for another. When Phillips and Smith [1980] adjusted the Trippi and Chiras-Manaster studies for transaction costs, they eliminated the abnormally high returns.

Finally, Blomeyer and Klemkosky [1983] used transaction-by-transaction option and stock-price data (thereby eliminating the problem of nonsynchronous data) and two option-pricing models to calculate implied volatility. In the absence of transaction costs, they found abnormal returns, but after deducting transaction costs, the abnormal returns were eliminated. Thus the hypothesis that the options market is efficient was supported.

Conclusion

The studies discussed in this chapter suggest two conclusions. First, no option strategy dominates any other. Second, after considering transaction costs, the options market appears to be efficient. Any investor who wishes to use this market should do so for what it was originally intended: to mold return distributions efficiently so that they are consistent with investment objectives.

CHAPTER 6

Notes

1. Options on securities can be used to allow investors to create certain payoffs that otherwise would not be available; that is, they can move an "incomplete" market toward a "complete" one. Economists refer to a complete market as one in which investors can establish any pattern of payoffs. If a market is incomplete, certain payoffs cannot be created. The underlying theory can be found in Ross [1975] and Arditti and John [1980].

2. For basic information about buying and selling put and call options, see the first section of Appendix A to this chapter.

3. While this strategy involves investing in some risk-free or low-risk fixed-income security, it does not involve a long or short position in the stock. For this reason, it is still classified as a naked-option strategy.

4. For a critique of the simulation approach, see Gastineau [1988], Chapter 10.

5. This model is discussed in the latter part of Appendix A to this chapter.

6. As explained in Appendix B, the risk-return profile for a covered call-writing strategy is similar to that of an uncovered put-writing strategy.

7. In general, a risk-free arbitrage means that, without any investment outlay, there is the possibility of realizing a positive payoff.

8. The Black-Scholes model was developed in a general-equilibrium framework. A review of earlier models can be found in Smith [1976].

9. Appendix A reviews boundary conditions, put-call parity relationships, the Black-Scholes option-pricing model, and the factors that influence option prices.

10. For studies investigating put-call parity for over-the-counter options, see Stoll [1969] and Gould and Galai [1974].

11. Remember that the position created is a hedged portfolio, which means its return should be a risk-free rate.

CHAPTER 6

References

Arditti, Fred, and John, Kose. "Spanning the State Space with Options." *Journal of Financial and Quantitative Analysis*, March 1980, pp. 1-9.

Bhattacharya, Mihir. "Transactions Data Tests of Efficiency of the Chicago Board Options Exchange." *Journal of Financial Economics*, August 1983, pp. 161-65.

Black, Fischer. "Fact and Fantasy in the Use of Options." *Financial Analysts Journal*, July-August 1975, pp. 36-41 and 61-72.

————, and Scholes, Myron. "The Pricing of Options and Corporate Liabilities." *Journal of Political Economy*, May 1973, pp. 637-54.

————. "The Valuation of Option Contracts and a Test of Market Efficiency." *Journal of Finance*, May 1972, pp. 399-417.

Blomeyer, Edward C., and Klemkosky, Robert C. "Tests of Market Efficiency for American Call Options." in *Option Pricing*, Menachem Brenner, ed. Lexington, Mass.: D.C. Heath, 1983, pp. 101-21.

Chiras, Donald, and Manaster, Steven. "The Information Content of Option Prices and a Test of Market Efficiency." *Journal of Financial Economics*, June/September 1978, pp. 213-34.

Galai, Dan. "Empirical Tests of Boundary Conditions for CBOE Options." *Journal of Financial Economics*, June/September 1978, pp. 187-211.

————. "Tests of Market Efficiency and the Chicago Board Options Exchange." *Journal of Business*, April 1977, pp. 167-97.

Gastineau, Gary L. *The Stock Options Manual*. Third edition. New York: McGraw-Hill, 1988.

Gould, J.P., and Galai, Dan. "Transactions Costs and the Relationship between Put and Call Prices." *Journal of Financial Economics*, July 1974, pp. 105-30.

Halpern, Paul J., and Turnbull, Stuart M. "Empirical Tests of Boundary Conditions for Toronto Stock Exchange Options." *Journal of Finance*, June 1985, pp. 481-500.

Klemkosky, Robert C., and Resnick, Bruce G. "An Ex Ante Analysis of Put-Call Parity." *Journal of Financial Economics*, December 1980, pp. 363-78.

————. "Put-Call Parity and Market Efficiency." *Journal of Finance*, December 1979, pp. 1141-55.

Merton, Robert; Scholes, M.; and Gladstein, M. "The Returns and Risk of Alternative Call Option Portfolio Investment Strategies." *Journal of Business*, April 1978, pp. 183-242.

————. "The Returns and Risks of Alternative Put-Option Portfolio Investment Strategies." *Journal of Business*, January 1982, pp. 1-55.

Phillips, Susan M., and Smith, Clifford W. "Trading Costs for Listed Options: Implications for Market Efficiency." *Journal of Financial Economics*, June 1980, pp. 179-201.

Pounds, Henry M. "Covered Call Options Writing: Strategies and Results." *The Journal of Portfolio Management*, Winter 1978, pp. 31-42.

Ross, Stephen. "Options and Efficiency." *Quarterly Journal of Economics*, February 1975, pp. 75-89.

Smith, Clifford M. "Option Pricing: A Review." *Journal of Financial Economics*, March 1976, pp. 3-51.

Stoll, Hans. "The Relationship Between Put and Call Option Prices." *Journal of Finance*, December 1969, pp. 801-24.

Trippi, Robert. "A Test of Option Market Efficiency Using a Random-Walk Valuation Model." *Journal of Economics and Business*, Winter 1977, pp. 93-98.

Yates, James W., and Kopprasch, Robert W. "Writing Covered Call Options: Profits and Risks." *Journal of Portfolio Management*, Fall 1980, pp. 74-79.

Appendix A

Arbitrage Relationships and Option-Pricing Models

This appendix briefly reviews option-pricing models and arbitrage relationships, beginning with the factors that affect the price of an option.

Factors Affecting Option Prices

1. Current price of the common stock: The option price will change as the price of the underlying common stock changes. For a call option, as the price of the common stock increases, if all other factors are constant, the option price increases. The opposite holds for a put option.

The responsiveness of an option's price to changes in the stock's price is referred to as the option's *delta.* An at-the-money option will usually have a delta of about 0.5. That is, if the common stock changes by $1, the option-price change will be about $0.50. The further out of the money an option is, the lower its delta will be; a deep out-of-the-money option will have a delta close to zero. An in-the-money option will have a delta greater than 0.5; a deep in-the-money option will have a delta near 1.

2. Exercise (stock) price: The exercise price is fixed for the life of the option, with adjustments arising only when there is a stock split or stock dividend. All other factors being equal, the lower the exercise price, the higher the price for a call option. For put options, the higher the exercise price, the higher the price.

3. Time remaining to the expiration of the option: An option is a wasting asset; that is, after the expiration date, the option has no value. All other factors being equal, the longer the time to expiration of the option, the greater the option price: as the time to expiration decreases, less time remains for the stock price to change to compensate the option buyer for any time value paid. Consequently, for American options, as the time remaining until expiration decreases, the option price approaches its intrinsic value.

4. Anticipated volatility of the underlying instrument: All other factors being equal, the greater the anticipated volatility of the stock price (as measured by standard deviation or variance), the more an investor would be willing to pay for the option and the more an option writer would demand for it: the greater the volatility, the greater the probability that the stock price will move in favor of the option buyer before expiration.

Notice that it is the standard deviation or variance, not the systematic risk as measured by beta, that is relevant in the pricing of options.

5. Level of the riskless short-term interest rate: Buying a call option is an alternative to the direct purchase of common stock. All other factors being constant, the higher the riskless short-term interest rate, the greater the cost of buying the stock and carrying it to the maturity date of the call option. Hence, the higher the riskless short-term interest rate, the more attractive the call option will be relative to the direct purchase of the stock, and the higher the option price.

There is another way to see the impact of the level of the riskless short-term interest rate on the price of a call option. Consider an investor who wants to own the stock at the expiration date. To assure ownership, the investor can (1) buy the call option and (2) place sufficient funds in a riskless short-term investment that matures at the call-option expiration date and has a maturity value equal to the exercise price. The amount that must be invested in the riskless short-term investment will depend on the interest rate offered. The effective exercise price at the expiration date, therefore, can be viewed as the present value of the exercise price, where the discount rate (interest rate) to determine the effective exercise price is the riskless short-term interest rate. Recall that, for a call option, the lower the exercise price, the greater the option price. Because a higher riskless short-term interest rate means a lower effective exercise price, the price of a call option rises as the riskless short-term interest rate rises.[1] For a put option, the opposite holds: the higher the riskless short-term interest rate, the lower the price.

6. Anticipated cash dividend payments of the stock: An investor who purchases stock expects a return from two sources—cash dividends and price appreciation. A call-option investor does not receive any cash dividends paid by the issuer prior to the expiration date. Therefore, the greater the proportion of the stock's expected return that will come from anticipated cash dividends prior to the expiration date, the lower the value of a call option. The opposite is true for a put option: the higher the anticipated cash dividends prior to the expiration date, the higher the option price.

Arbitrage Relationships for Options

Although our ultimate objective is to determine the price of an option, certain relationships can be determined by using pure arbitrage arguments. For example, suppose an investor can establish a portfolio consisting of some stock and short-call positions on that stock in such a way that does not require any initial cash outlay. The purchase price would come from selling call options and borrowing the rest. Assume further that (1) if the price of the stock at the expiration date of the call options is below $50, the value of the portfolio is zero, (2) if its price is higher than $75, the value of the portfolio is zero, and (3) if the stock price is between $50 and $75, the value of the portfolio will be at least $1,000. This condition is a riskless arbitrage opportunity. If markets are efficient, riskless arbitrage opportunities cannot exist for long, because market forces will push the stock price, option price, and/or short-term interest rate in such a way as to eliminate the riskless arbitrage opportunity.

Boundary Price for Options

Based on the riskless arbitrage argument, we can demonstrate that the price of the call option for an American call option in which the underlying stock is not expected to pay cash dividends prior to the expiration date should never fall below the greater of (1) zero and (2) the difference between the current stock price and the present value of the exercise price. Mathematically, we can express this relationship as

$$C \geq Max \; [0, \; S - X \; r^{-t}]$$

where

C = call price,
S = current stock price,
X = exercise price,
r = 1 + riskless interest rate, and
t = time remaining to the expiration date (measured as a fraction of one year).

For a put option on a non-dividend-paying stock, the price of the option should never fall below the greater of zero and the difference between the exercise price and the stock price. Mathematically, this can be expressed as

$$P \geq Max \; [0, \; X - S]$$

Boundary conditions for the price of an option on a dividend-paying stock can also be determined. The boundary conditions can be tightened by making additional assumptions. The extreme case is an option-pricing model that derives a price based on a particular set of assumptions.

Put-Call Parity Relationships for Options

Using arbitrage arguments, the relationship between puts and calls with the same expiration date, exercise price, and underlying stock can be determined. The relationship is known as the put-call parity relationship.

The simplest put-call parity relationship exists for European options: an option where the buyer may not exercise the option prior to the expiration date. For a stock that does not pay dividends, the price of a European put option is equal to the sum of the price of a European call option and the present value of the exercise price minus the current stock price. Using the superscript asterisk (*) to denote a European option, the put-call parity relationship for European options is

$$P* = C* + X \, r^{-t} - S$$

For stock that pays no dividends, the price of an American put option is greater than, or equal to, the sum of the price of an American call option and the present value of the exercise price minus the current stock price.

Option-Pricing Models

Arbitrage conditions provide boundaries for option prices. To identify investment opportunities and construct portfolios to satisfy investment objectives, investors want an exact option price. By imposing certain assumptions (discussed later) and using arbitrage arguments, Black and Scholes [1973] developed the following model to compute the fair price of a call option on a non-dividend-paying stock:

$$C = S \, N(d_1) - X \, e^{-rt} \, N(d_2)$$

where

$$d_1 = [ln \, (S/X) + (r + .5 \, s^2) \, t] \, / \, s \, \sqrt{t},$$

$$d_2 = d_1 - s \, \sqrt{t},$$

C = call price,
S = current stock price,

$X=$ exercise price,

$r=$ riskless interest rate,[2]

$t=$ time remaining to the expiration date (measured as a fraction of one year),

$s=$ standard deviation of the stock price, and

$N(\cdot)=$ the normal-distribution function; its value is obtained from a normal-distribution function that is provided in most statistics textbooks.

Notice that all five factors that influence the price of a call option on a non-dividend-paying stock are included in the Black-Scholes model. Also, the direction of the influence for each of these factors is the same as shown in Exhibit 6-8, and three of the factors—exercise price, stock price, and time to expiration—are easily observed. The riskless interest rate and the standard deviation of the stock price must be estimated; the latter is the most difficult to estimate.

The option price derived from the Black-Scholes option-pricing model is fair, in the sense that, if any other price existed, it would be possible to generate riskless profits by taking an offsetting position in the underlying stock. For example, if the price of the call option in the market is higher than that derived from the Black-Scholes option-pricing model, an investor can sell the call option and buy a certain number of shares in the underlying stock.[3] If the reverse is true (that is, the market price of the call option is less than the fair price derived from the model), the investor can buy the call option and sell short an appropriate number of shares in the underlying stock. This process of hedging by taking a position in the underlying stock allows the investor to lock in a riskless profit. Because the number of shares necessary to hedge the position changes as the factors that affect the option price change, the hedge must be constantly changed.

Assumptions Underlying the Black-Scholes Model and Extensions of the Model

The Black-Scholes model is based on several restrictive assumptions. The assumptions were necessary to develop the hedge that makes possible riskless profits if the market price of the call option deviates from the price obtained from the model.

1. Variance of the stock price: The Black-Scholes model assumes that the variance of the stock price is constant over the life of the option and known with certainty. If it is not constant, an option-pricing model can be developed in which the variance is allowed to change.[4] Violating the known-with-certainty part of the assumption is much more serious. Because the Black-Scholes model depends on the riskless-hedge argument, and, in turn, the variance must be known to construct the proper hedge, if the variance is not known, the hedge will not be riskless. Several researchers (Merton [1976], Johnson and Shannon [1985], Scott [1985], Dothan [1987], and Hull and White [1985]) have extended the Black-Scholes model to allow for a random variance.

2. *Random process generating stock prices:* To derive an option-pricing model, an assumption about the random process generating stock prices is needed. The Black-Scholes model is based on the assumption that the price of the stock can take on any positive value, but that when moving from one price to another, it must take on all values in between: the stock price does not jump from one stock price to another, skipping over interim prices. A pattern of smooth, continuous price movements from one price to the next is called a *diffusion* process. An alternative assumption is that stock prices follow a jump process; that is, prices are not continuous and smooth but jump from one price to the next. Cox and Ross [1976] and Merton [1976] have developed several models based on a jump process.

3. *Riskless interest rate:* In deriving the Black-Scholes model, two assumptions were made about the riskless interest rate: first, the interest rates for borrowing and lending were the same; and second, the interest rate was constant and known over the life of the option. The first assumption is unrealistic, because borrowing rates are higher than lending rates. The effect on the Black-Scholes model of making the assumptions more realistic is that the option price will be between the call prices derived from the model using these two interest rates. The model can handle the second assumption by replacing the riskless rate over the life of the option by the geometric average of the period returns expected over the life of the option.[5]

4. *Dividends:* The form of the Black-Scholes model presented earlier in this appendix is for a non-dividend-paying stock. For a dividend-paying stock, it may be advantageous for an investor to exercise the option early.[6] In addition, if dividends are not known with certainty, a model cannot be developed using the riskless arbitrage argument.

In the case of known dividends, a simple way to adjust the Black-Scholes model is to reduce the stock price by the present value of the dividends. Black [1975] suggested an approximation technique to value a call option for dividend-paying stock;[7] more accurate models for pricing calls in the case of known dividends were developed by Roll [1977], Geske [1979 and 1981], and Whaley [1981].

5. *Taxes and transaction costs:* The Black-Scholes model ignores taxes and

transaction costs. The model can be modified to account for taxes, but the problem is a lack of one unique tax rate. The transaction costs include both commissions and the bid/ask spreads for the stock and the option that an investor must pay the market maker, as well as other costs associated with option trading.

Summary

There are six factors that determine the price of an option: (1) current price of the common stock, (2) exercise price, (3) time remaining to expiration, (4) anticipated volatility of the underlying stock, (5) short-term riskless interest rate, and (6) anticipated cash dividends. Based purely on arbitrage arguments, the relationship between the prices of a put option, a call option, and the underlying stock can be determined for European options and, under more restrictive conditions, for American options.

By making additional assumptions about the factors that affect the option price, an option-pricing model can be developed. The most popular one is the Black-Scholes model. Several researchers have extended the basic Black-Scholes model. A model that has become popular in the investment community because of its simplicity and flexibility is the binomial option-pricing model developed by Sharpe [1978], Cox, Ross, and Rubinstein [1979], and Rendleman and Bartter [1979]. A detailed explanation of the binomial pricing model is provided by Bookstaber [1988, Chapter 3].

CHAPTER 6   APPENDIX A

Notes

1. This analysis has been simplified, in that it assumes that changes in interest rates do not affect any of the other factors. In particular, it does not consider the impact of changing interest rates on the anticipated stock-price volatility.

2. Note that r here is the riskless interest rate, while in the other relationships presented earlier, the interest rate is 1 plus the riskless interest rate.

3. The number of shares is not necessarily equal to the number of shares underlying the call option. The reason is that the change in the value of the call price will generally be less than the change in the stock price. In the Black-Scholes model, the number of shares is given by $N(d_1)$.

4. A closed-form solution is not available for the generalized formula. Instead, numerical solution techniques must be used.

5. The effects of variable interest rates are considered by Merton [1973].

6. For a discussion of optimal early exercise of an option, see Chapter 5 of Jarrow and Rudd [1983].

7. The approach requires that the investor specify, at the time of purchase of the call option and for every subsequent period, the exact date the option will be exercised.

CHAPTER 6   APPENDIX A

References

Bookstaber, Richard. *Option Pricing and Investment Strategies*. Chicago, Ill.: Probus Publishing, 1987.

Cox, John; Ross, Stephen; and Rubinstein, Mark. "Option Pricing: A Simplified Approach." *Journal of Financial Economics*, September 1979, pp. 229-63.

————, and ————. "The Valuation of Options for Alternative Stochastic Processes." *Journal of Financial Economics*, March 1976, pp. 145-66.

Dothan, Michael U. "A Random Volatility Correction for the Black-Scholes Option-Pricing Formula." *Advances in Futures and Options Research*, Vol. 3, 1987, pp. 97-115.

Geske, Robert. "Comment on Whaley's Note." *Journal of Financial Economics*, June 1981, pp. 213-15.

————. "A Note on an Analytical Formula for Unprotected American Call Options on Stocks with Known Dividends." *Journal of Financial Economics*, December 1979, pp. 375-80.

Hull, John, and White, Alan. "An Analysis of the Bias in Option Pricing Caused by a Stochastic Volatility." *Advances in Futures and Options Research*, Vol. 3, 1988, pp. 29-62.

Jarrow, Robert A., and Rudd, Andrew. *Option Pricing*. Homewood, Ill.: Dow Jones-Irwin, 1983.

Johnson, Herbert, and Shannon, Donald. "Option Pricing When the Variance is Changing." Unpublished manuscript, 1985.

Merton, Robert. "Option Pricing When Underlying Stock Returns Are Discontinuous." *Journal of Financial Economics*, March 1976, pp. 125-44.

————. "The Theory of Rational Option Pricing." *Bell Journal of Economics and Management Science*, Spring 1973, pp. 141-83.

Rendleman, Richard, and Bartter, Brit. "Two-State Option Pricing." *Journal of Finance*, December 1979, pp. 1093-1110.

Roll, Richard. "An Analytic Formula for Unprotected American Call Options on Stocks with Known Dividends." *Journal of Financial Economics*, November 1977, pp. 251-58.

Scott, Louis. "Option Pricing When the Variance Changes Randomly: Theory, Estimation, and an Application." Unpublished manuscript, 1985.

Sharpe, William. *Investments*. Englewood Cliffs, N.J.: Prentice Hall, 1978.

Whaley, Robert. "On the Valuation of American Call Options on Stocks with Known Dividends." *Journal of Financial Economics*, June 1981, pp. 207-11.

CHAPTER 6

Appendix B

Details of Common-Stock Option Strategies

This appendix describes the various option strategies in greater detail than was practical in the chapter.

Long-Call Strategy

To illustrate this strategy, assume there is a call option on 100 shares of a common stock with a strike price of $100, an option price of $500, and a current stock price of $100. Because the strike price is equal to the current price of the common stock, this option is at the money. The profit and loss of the strategy will depend on the price of the stock at the expiration date. The following outcomes are possible:

1. If the price of the stock at the expiration date is less than $100 per share, then the investor would not exercise the option: why bother exercising the option and paying the option writer $100 per share when the same stock can be purchased in the market at a lower price? Notice, however, that $500 is the maximum loss that the option buyer will realize regardless of how low the price of the stock declines.

2. If the price of the stock is equal to $100 per share, no economic value will result from exercising the option. The buyer of this call will lose the entire option price.

3. If the price of the stock is greater than $100 but less than $105, the option buyer would exercise the option. By exercising, the option buyer purchases 100 shares of stock for $100 per share (the strike price) and sells it in the market for a higher price. Suppose, for example, that the price of the stock is $103 at the expiration date. The buyer of this call

option will realize a $3 gain per share by exercising the option, a $300 gain for 100 shares. Because the cost of purchasing the call option was $500, $200 is lost on this strategy, but failing to exercise the option would have lost the investor $500 instead of just $200.

4. If the price of the stock at the expiration date is equal to $105 per share, the investor would exercise the option: the investor breaks even, realizing a gain of $5 per share on the stock, or $500 for 100 shares. This gain offsets the $500 cost of the option.

5. If the price of the common stock at the expiration date is greater than $105 per share, the investor will exercise the option and realize a profit. For example, if the price of the stock is $120 per share, exercising the option will generate a profit per share of $20, or $2,000 for 100 shares. The investor will realize a profit from this strategy of $1,500 after deducting the option cost of $500.

Exhibit 6B-1 graphically portrays the profit-and-loss profile for the call-option buyer. The breakeven point and the loss will depend on the option price. You can see that the maximum loss is the option price and that there is substantial upside potential.

Compare the profit-and-loss profile for a long call-option position with a long-stock position. The payoff from the option strategy depends on the price of the underlying stock at the expiration date. Consider again the five previous price outcomes. If the price of the stock is

1. less than $100 per share at the expiration date, the investor will lose the entire option price of $500. However, the long-stock position has three possible outcomes. If the price of the stock is
   a. less than $100 per share but greater than $95, the loss on the long-stock position will be less than $500;
   b. $95, the loss on the long-stock position will be $500;
   c. less than $95, the loss on the long-stock position will be greater than $500. For example, if the price at the expiration date is $70, the long-stock position will result in a loss of $3,000 ($30 per share for 100 shares);

2. exactly $100 per share, the buyer of the call option will realize a loss equal to the cost of the option—$500. There will be no gain or loss on the long-stock position;

3. greater then $100 but less than $105 per share, there will be no loss or gain from buying the call option. The long-stock position will produce a gain of $500 ($5 per share for 100 shares);

4. greater than $105 per share at the expiration date, both the call-option buyer and the long-stock position will result in a profit. The profit for the

THE NEW STOCK MARKET

Exhibit 6B-1
Profit/Loss Profile for a Long-Call Position*

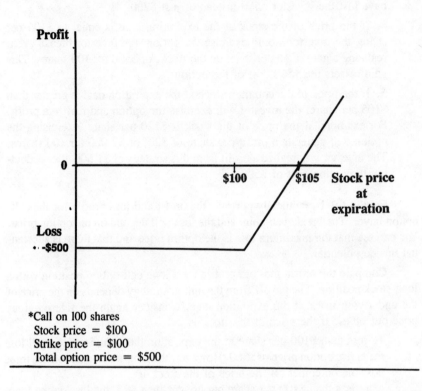

*Call on 100 shares
Stock price = $100
Strike price = $100
Total option price = $500

buyer of the call option will be $500 less, however, than on the long-stock position. For example, if the price of the stock is $120 per share, the profit from the long-call position is $1,500, while the profit from the long-stock position is $2,000 ($20 per share for 100 shares).

Exhibit 6B-2 graphically compares the long-call strategy and the long-stock strategy and clearly demonstrates the way in which an option can change the risk-return profile available to investors. This long-stock strategy allows an investor who takes a position in 100 shares of the common stock we have used in our example to realize a profit of $1 for every $1 increase in the price of the stock. However, some or all of the $10,000 investment ($100 per share for 100 shares) can be lost. If the price decreases by more than $5 per share, this strategy will result in a loss of more than $500. The long-call option strategy limits the loss to the option price of $500. In addition, it retains most of the upside potential of the long-stock position.

Exhibit 6B-2
Comparison of Long-Call and Long-Stock Positions*

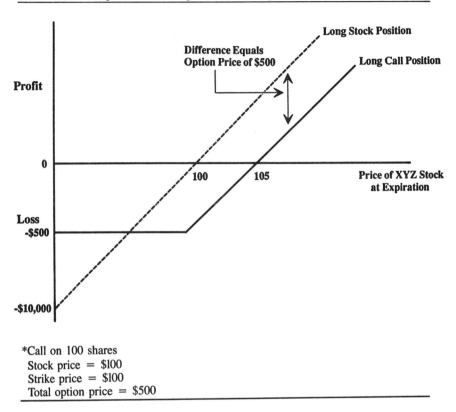

*Call on 100 shares
  Stock price = $100
  Strike price = $100
  Total option price = $500

We can also use this hypothetical option to understand the speculative appeal of options. Suppose an investor with only $500 is confident that the price of the stock will increase substantially from its current price of $100. With an option price of $500, a long-call position will allow the investor to control 100 shares of the stock. If the stock price increases to $120, the long-call strategy will result in a profit of $1,500, a return of 300 percent on the $500 investment in the call option. With $500, the investor can purchase only 5 shares of stock. This long-stock strategy results in a profit of only $100 ($20 per share for 5 shares), a 20 percent return. It is this greater leverage that an option buyer can achieve that attracts investors to options when they want to speculate on price movements. But notice that if the price of the stock at the expiration date is unchanged at $100, the long-call strategy would result in a loss of the entire investment of $500. The long-stock strategy would produce neither a gain nor a loss.

Short-Call Strategy (Selling or Writing Call Options)

The profit-and-loss profile of the short-call strategy (the position of the call-option writer) is the mirror image of the profit-and-loss profile of the long-call strategy (the position of the call-option buyer). That is, the profit (loss) of the short-call position for any given price of the stock at the expiration date is the same as the loss (profit) of the long-call position. Consequently, the maximum profit that the short-call strategy can produce is the option price; the maximum loss is limited only by how high the price of the common stock increases by the expiration date, less the option price. This relationship can be seen in Exhibit 6B-3, which shows the profit/loss profile for a short-call strategy.

Exhibit 6B-3
Profit/Loss Profile for a Short-Call Position

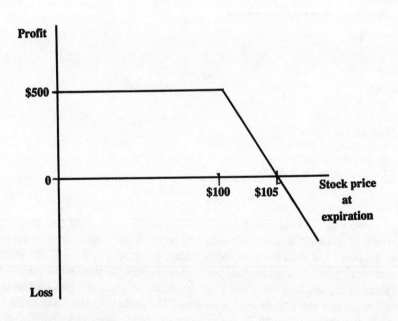

*Call on 100 shares
Stock price = $100
Strike price = $100
Total option price = $500

Buying a Put Option

To illustrate this strategy, consider a put option for 100 shares of common stock with a strike price of $100 selling for $700. The current price of the common stock is $100; hence, the put option is at the money. The profit or loss for this strategy at the expiration date depends on the price of the stock. Five outcomes are possible. If the price of the stock at the expiration date is:

1. greater than $100, the buyer of the put option will not exercise it. Exercising it would mean selling the stock to the writer for a price that is less than the market price. A loss of the option price ($700) would result from the long-put position. Once again, the option price represents the maximum loss to which the buyer of the put option is exposed;

2. equal to $100 per share, the put will not be exercised, leaving the long-put position with a loss equal to the option price of $700;

3. less than $100 but greater than $93, a loss will result, but the loss by exercising the put option will be less than the option price ($700). For example, a price of $95 for the stock at the expiration date results in a gain of $500; because the buyer of the put option can sell each share purchased for $95 in the market to the writer for $100, realizing a gain of $5 per share or $500 for 100 shares. Deducting the $700 cost of the option results in a loss of $200.

4. $93 per share, the long-put strategy will break even: the investor realizes a gain of $7 per share by selling the stock to the writer of the option for $700 for 100 shares, offsetting the cost of the option ($700);

5. below $93, the long-put position will generate a profit. For example, if the price of the stock is $88 at expiration, the long-put position will produce a profit of $500—a gain of $12 per share, or $1,200 for 100 shares less the option price of $700.

The profit-and-loss profile for the long-put position is shown in Exhibit 6B-4. As with all long-option positions, the loss is limited to the option price. However, the profit potential is substantial (the theoretical maximum profit being generated if the stock price falls to zero).

Again we can see how an option alters the risk-return profile for an investor by comparing the option with a position in the stock. A long-put position would be compared with a short-stock position, and the option strategy would realize a profit if the stock price declined. Suppose an investor sells 100 shares of ABCD stock short for $100. The short-stock position produces the following profit and losses (ignoring the cost of carrying the short position) if the price of the stock at the expiration date is:

1. above $100, the long-put option will result in a loss of $700, but the short-stock position will realize a loss that is
   a. less than $700 if the price of the stock is less than $107;
   b. the same as the long-put position ($700) if the price of the stock is equal to $107;
   c. greater than $700 if the price of the stock is greater than $107. For example, if the price is $110, the short-stock position will result in a loss of $10 per share, or $1,000 for 100 shares;

2. equal to $100 per share, the long-put strategy will realize $700. There will be no profit or loss on the short-stock position;

3. less than $100 but greater than $93, a loss of less than $700 will result for the long-put position but a profit will result for the short-stock position. For example, a price of $95 for the stock at the expiration date will result in a loss for the long-put position but a profit of $500 for the short-stock position;

Exhibit 6B-4
Profit/Loss Profile for a Long-Put Position*

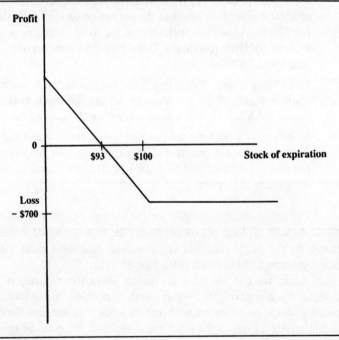

*Call on 100 shares
Stock price = $100
Strike price = $100
Total option price = $500

4. $93 per share for the stock at the expiration date, the long-put position will break even, but the short-stock position will generate a profit;

5. below $93 per share for the stock, both positions will generate a profit, but the profit will always be $700 less for the long-put position.

A comparison of the profit-and-loss profile for the long-put and short-stock strategies is shown in Exhibit 6B-5. While the investor in a short-stock strategy faces all upside potential and downside risk, the long-put strategy allows the investor to limit the downside risk to the option price but maintain upside potential. However, the upside potential is less than for a short-stock position by an amount equal to the option price.

Exhibit 6B-5
Comparison of Long-Put Position and Short-Stock Position*

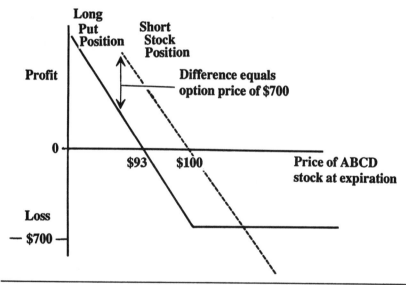

*Put on 100 shares
Stock price = $100
Strike price = $100
Total option price = $500

Short-Put Strategy

To illustrate this strategy, we will use the same put option we used to illustrate the long-put strategy. The profit/loss profile for the writer of a put option is the mirror image of the long-put strategy. Exhibit 6B-6 graphically depicts the profit-and-loss profile.

Exhibit 6B-6
Profit/Loss Profile of a Short-Put Position

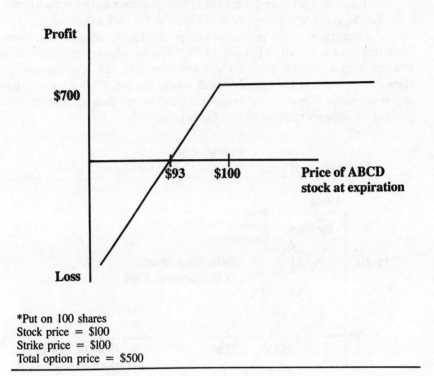

*Put on 100 shares
Stock price = $100
Strike price = $100
Total option price = $500

Covered Call-Writing Strategy

If an investor owns stock and writes a call option on the stock, the strategy is referred to as covered call-writing. The profit or loss for this strategy will depend on the price of the stock at the expiration date. Suppose an investor owns 100 shares at a current price of $100. The total value of the portfolio (assuming that it has only 100 shares) is $10,000. Also suppose that a call option on the 100 shares with a $100 strike price that matures in 3 months can be sold for $700. One of five outcomes will occur. If the price of the stock at the expiration date is:

    1. greater then $100, the call-option buyer will exercise the option and pay the option writer $100 per share. Because 100 shares are in the portfolio, they are exchanged for $10,000. The value of the portfolio at

the expiration date is then $10,700 ($10,000 received from the stock plus $700 received from writing the call option). In fact, more than $10,700 will be in the portfolio if the $700 was invested when it was received. At a minimum, the profit from this strategy, if the price of the stock is greater than $100, is $700, the option price;

2. $100, the call-option buyer will not exercise the option. The value of the portfolio will still be at least $10,700: 100 shares with a market value of $100 per share and the $700 received from writing the call option;

3. less than $100 but greater than $93, there will be a profit, but it will be less than $700. For example, suppose the price of the stock is $96. The portfolio value will be equal to $10,300 ($9,600 for the stock plus $700 from the sale of the call option), resulting in a $300 profit;

4. $93, the portfolio value will be equal to $10,000 ($9,300 for the stock plus $700 from the sale of the call option); therefore, no profit or loss results;

5. less than $93, the investor will realize a loss. For example, if the price of the stock at expiration is $88, the portfolio value will be $9,500 (the long-stock position will be worth $8,800, and the short-call position will have produced $700), for a loss of $500.

The profit-and-loss profile for this covered call-writing strategy is graphically portrayed in Exhibit 6B-7. You should recognize two important points from this illustration. First, this strategy has allowed the investor to reduce the downside risk for the portfolio. In this example, for the at-the-money option, the risk is reduced by an amount equal to the option price. In exchange for this reduction of downside risk, the investor has agreed to limit potential profit. For the at-the-money option used in our illustration, the maximum profit is the option price.

The second point can be seen by comparing Exhibits 6B-6 and 6B-7. Notice that the shape of the two profit-and-loss profiles is the same; that is, the covered call-writing strategy has the same profit-and-loss profile as a short-put strategy. In fact, in our example, the covered call-writing strategy has the same profit-and-loss outcomes as writing a 3-month put on 100 shares of the stock with a strike price of $100. This effect is not an accident; it is a result of the put-call parity relationship explained in the chapter and discussed further in Appendix A.

Protective Put-Buying Strategy

A protective put-buying strategy is employed to protect the value of a portfolio. To illustrate, suppose that an investor has 100 shares of stock in a portfolio and

Exhibit 6B-7
Profit/Loss Profile of Covered-Call Position*

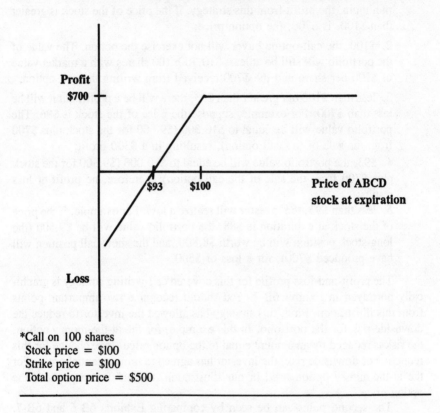

*Call on 100 shares
Stock price = $100
Strike price = $100
Total option price = $500

the current market value of the stock is $100 per share (a portfolio value of
$10,000). Assume further that a 2-month put option can be purchased for $500
on 100 shares of the stock with a strike price of $100. At expiration, 2 months
from now, there are four possible outcomes. If the price of the stock is

1. greater than $105, the investor will realize a profit. For example, if the
   price is $112, the long-stock position will have a value of $11,200.
   Because the cost of purchasing the put option was $500; however, the
   value of the portfolio is $10,700, for a net profit of $700;

2. less than $105 but at least $100, a loss will result. For example, a price
   of $102 will result in a loss of $300—a gain in the long-stock position of
   $200, but a loss of the $500 to acquire the put option;

3. equal to $105, no profit or loss will be realized from a protective put;

4. below $100 per share, the option will be exercised: at any price below $100 per share, the investor is assured of receiving $100 per share for the 100 shares of stock. Thus the value of the portfolio will be $10,000 minus the cost of the option ($500), resulting in a loss from this strategy of $500.

The graphical presentation of the profit-and-loss profile for this protective put-buying strategy is shown in Exhibit 6B-8. The investor, by implementing this strategy, has effectively assured a price of $95 per share while maintaining the upside potential. That potential is reduced, however, by the cost of the put option.

Exhibit 6B-8
Protective-Put Buying Option Strategy*

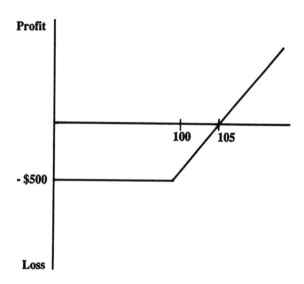

*Put on 100 shares
Stock price = $100
Strike price = $100
Total option price = $500

Conclusion

The basic options strategies are the (1) long-call strategy, (2) short-call strategy, (3) long-put strategy, and (4) short-put strategy. In the chapter, we referred to these strategies as naked option strategies. The long-call and long-put strategies have limited downside risk and substantial upside potential. The reverse is true for the short-call and short-put strategies: the profit is limited to the option price and there is substantial downside risk. The covered call-writing strategy and protective put-buying strategy are called covered-option or hedge strategies. The risk and reward characteristics of option positions allow investors to mold portfolio returns.

Stock-Index Futures[1]
and Stock-Index Options

Since the inception of stock-index futures contracts in 1982, and stock-index options in 1983, trading volume in these contracts has grown rapidly. The great popularity of stock-index futures and options may have several explanations. First, investors who believe they can predict the direction of the overall market better than they can predict which stocks to buy or sell use stock-index futures and options to capitalize on their forecasts. Second, investors holding large stock portfolios can use equity-index products as a timing device to protect cash values, accelerate market entry, or enhance portfolio returns. Third, professional arbitrageurs use stock-index futures and options to profit from the market inefficiencies they discover. Finally, the leverage possible when using the futures and options markets means that while they are risky investments, their potential payoff can be substantial.[2]

In this chapter, we review the evidence about profitability in the stock-index futures and stock-index options markets. We first review what we know about the pricing efficiency in the stock-index futures market. Next we examine whether some of the market anomalies observed in the stock market also exist (i.e., the weekend, January and small firm effects) in the stock-index futures market. In the last section of the chapter, we review the scant evidence on pricing efficiency of the stock-index options markets.

Empirical Evidence from the Stock-Index Futures Market

A futures contract is a legal agreement between a buyer (seller) and an established exchange, or its clearinghouse, in which the buyer (seller) agrees to take (make) delivery of a designated item at a specified price at a particular time, called the *settlement date*. When the parties agree to take or make delivery of a financial benchmark representing a common-stock index, the futures contract is referred to as a stock-index futures contract. Settlement for stock-index futures contracts is done on a cash basis rather than delivery of the stocks in the index.

In 1982 three futures contracts based on broadly based common-stock indexes made their debut: the Standard & Poor's 500 futures contract traded on the International Monetary Market of the Chicago Mercantile Exchange, the New York Stock Exchange Composite futures contract traded on the New York Futures Exchange, and the Value Line Average traded on the Kansas City Board of Trade. Since then, other broad-based and specialized stock-index futures contracts have been introduced. A summary of the currently traded contracts is presented in Exhibit 7-1.

Exhibit 7-1
Currently Traded Stock-Index Futures Contracts

Contract	Exchange
S&P 500	Chicago Mercantile Exchange
Major Market Index	American Stock Exchange
NYSE Composite Index	New York Futures Exchange
Value Line Index	Kansas City Board of Trade

Note: The contract size for all but the Major Market Index is equal to 500 times the index. For the MMI it is 250 times the index.

Pricing Efficiency of the Stock-Index Futures Market

The appendix to this chapter explains how the theoretical price of a futures contract can be determined. When looking at stock-index futures markets, one of the first questions the potential investor should ask is: Do actual futures prices differ sufficiently from their theoretical prices such that abnormal profits can be earned? If the stock-index futures market is efficient, abnormal profits will be very hard to earn.

The first study to examine the pricing of stock-index futures empirically was by Cornell and French [1983]. Exhibit 7-2 shows their results of comparing actual and theoretical futures prices for the S&P 500 and New York Stock Exchange (NYSE) futures contracts on the first days of trading of June, July, August, and September 1982. In all but two of the cases shown, the theoretical (predicted) futures price was higher than the actual futures price.

To determine the reasons for the discrepancy between the theoretical and actual prices, Cornell and French relaxed the assumptions of the pricing model (described in the appendix) and found that the most important problem was that taxes were not considered. There are two ways in which taxes must be considered. First, there are taxes on the capital gain or loss on the sale of stocks and the futures contract as well as taxes on dividends and interest income. Exhibit 7-3 shows the actual prices and Cornell and French's theoretical, tax-adjusted futures prices. While the actual prices were closer to the tax-adjusted theoretical prices, they were still less.

Exhibit 7-2

Actual versus Theoretical Stock-Index Futures Prices,
June-September 1982

Contract Month	Days to Maturity	Actual Prices	Perfect Markets Prices
		June 1, 1982: S&P 500	
Spot		111.68	
June	18	110.05	112.13
September	108	110.10	113.99
December	199	110.55	116.19
March 83	290	111.00	118.49
		June 1, 1982: NYSE	
Spot		64.37	
June	28	63.35	64.75
September	120	63.45	65.91
December	211	64.05	67.26
March 83	304	64.55	68.69
		July 1, 1982: S&P 500	
Spot		108.71	
September	77	109.85	110.61
December	168	110.25	113.05
March 83	259	110.65	115.77
June	350	111.20	118.48
		July 1, 1982: NYSE	
Spot		62.51	
September	90	63.20	63.80
December	181	63.45	65.20
March 83	272	63.75	66.79
June	363	64.05	68.35
		August 2, 1982: S&P 500	
Spot		108.98	
September	45	110.00	109.40
December	136	110.75	110.99
March 83	234	111.35	113.22
June	318	111.90	115.33
		August 2, 1982: NYSE	
Spot		62.49	
September	58	63.20	62.88
December	149	63.65	63.84
March 83	240	64.10	65.02
June	331	64.55	66.39
		September 1, 1982: S&P 500	
Spot		118.25	
September	15	117.00	118.42
December	106	117.30	119.32
March 83	197	118.10	121.33
June	288	118.80	123.29

Exhibit 7-2 continued

Contract Month	Days to Maturity	Actual Prices	Perfect Markets Prices
	September 1, 1982: NYSE		
Spot		67.90	
September	28	67.25	68.07
December	119	67.45	68.62
March 83	210	67.85	69.77
June	301	68.25	71.13

The prices predicted by the perfect-markets model are based on the assumption that there are no taxes and that both the interest rate and the dividend yield are constant;

$$F(t,T) = P(t)\{e^{r(T-t)}[1-d/r]+d/r\}$$

The dividend yield is assumed to be 6 percent per year. The interest rate is measured by the rate on the Treasury bill that matures closes to the maturity of the futures contract.

Source: Cornell and French [1983], pp. 679-80.

Taxes can influence theoretical and actual prices in another way: investors can postpone taxes when trading in the cash market, but not in futures. In the cash market, the investor can choose when to realize a capital gain or loss: if a stock rises in price, taxes can be postponed by not selling the stock; if the stock falls, the investor can recognize the tax loss by selling the stock.[3] Stock-index futures traders, however, do not have this option, since futures contracts have a finite life: when there is a gain or loss, taxes must be paid. The gain or loss is taxed either at the investor's tax-year end or at the time the futures contract settles, whichever is first. Thus the lack of a tax-timing option for futures-market participants has a cost, and that cost causes a discrepancy between the actual and theoretical futures prices. While there is a real reason for a discrepancy between the cash and futures markets, we still must determine whether it is large enough to exploit.

Modest and Sundaresan [1983] studied whether actual futures prices were outside their theoretical bounds. To develop their test, the authors made three assumptions about how short sellers used the proceeds from selling the cash-index short: short sellers used none, half, or all of the proceeds of the short sale. In addition, Modest and Sundaresan constructed theoretical price limits with and without adjusting for dividends, because the theoretical futures price also depends on the expected dividend yield. In total, six theoretical price limits were developed for two S&P 500 futures contracts: the June 1982 S&P futures contract from April 21, 1982, to June 16, 1982, and the December 1982 S&P 500 futures contract from April 21, 1982, to September 15, 1982.

Exhibit 7-3

Actual versus Theoretical Stock-Index Futures Prices
Considering Taxes
June-September 1982

Contract Month	Days to Maturity	Actual Prices	Theoretical Prices without Taxes	Theoretical Prices with Taxes
		Actual Versus Theoretical Prices*		
		June 1, 1982: S&P 500		
Spot		111.68		
June	18	110.05	112.10	111.94
September	108	110.10	114.22	113.24
December	199	110.55	116.42	114.58
March 83	290	111.00	118.95	116.11
		June 1, 1982: NYSE		
Spot		64.37		
June	28	63.35	64.74	64.61
September	120	63.45	66.01	65.39
December	211	64.05	67.29	66.17
March 83	304	64.55	68.79	67.05
		July 1, 1982: S&P 500		
Spot		108.71		
September	77	109.85	110.51	109.86
December	168	110.25	112.93	111.31
March 83	259	110.65	115.65	112.94
June	350	111.20	118.36	114.56
		July 1, 1982: NYSE		
Spot		62.51		
September	90	63.20	63.75	63.28
December	181	63.45	65.17	64.14
March 83	272	63.75	66.72	65.09
June	363	64.05	68.29	66.01
		August 2, 1982: S&P 500		
Spot		108.98		
September	45	110.00	109.18	109.10
December	136	110.75	110.88	110.16
March 83	234	111.35	113.08	111.51
June	318	111.90	115.19	112.78
		August 2, 1982: NYSE		
Spot		62.49		
September	58	63.20	62.71	62.63
December	149	63.65	63.73	63.26
March 83	240	64.10	64.91	63.98
June	331	64.55	66.22	64.78
		September 1, 1982: S&P 500		
Spot		118.25		
September	15	117.00	118.37	118.32
December	106	117.30	119.42	118.98
March 83	197	118.10	121.44	120.22
June	288	118.80	123.77	121.64
		September 1, 1982: NYSE		
Spot		67.90		
September	28	67.25	68.03	67.98
December	119	67.45	68.69	68.40
March 83	210	67.85	69.88	69.13
June	301	68.25	71.23	69.94

* The theoretical prices estimated by authors.

Source: Cornell and French [1983], p. 686.

Modest and Sundaresan found that no arbitrage profits were possible (that the actual futures prices were within the theoretical bounds) when the contract was adjusted for dividends and the investor could not use the proceeds from short selling. While there were occasional instances when the theoretical bounds were violated,[4] generally no arbitrage profits were possible. In fact, the actual futures prices were different from what theory suggested only when the investor had full use of the proceeds from short selling the cash-market index. In general, and using realistic assumptions, violations of the theoretical price limits provided few opportunities for arbitrage profits.

While Cornell and French [1983] and Modest and Sundaresan [1983] examined pricing efficiency when the contracts first began trading, Peters [1985] investigated whether the futures market had become more efficient over time. He examined market efficiency for the S&P 500 and the NYSE futures contracts from the September 1982 contracts to the December 1983 contracts and found the actual prices moved closer to the theoretical prices. He attributed this to better estimation of the dividend stream for each index contract.

Collins [1987] also tested for increasing futures-market efficiency by examining the profits that could have been earned from buying the cash-market index and selling the futures contract: selected S&P 500 futures contracts from the December 1982 contracts to the September 1985 contracts were studied. Transaction costs were included. While in an efficient market the return on this strategy should be equal to the return on a Treasury security with a maturity equal to the maturity of the futures contract, Collins found that there were few instances of pricing inefficiency and that the market became more efficient over time.

Market Anomalies in the Futures Market

There appear to be no consistently exploitable pricing inefficiencies in the stock-index futures market today. But does this market have the same anomalies we found in the stock market: day-of-the-week, weekend, and January effects? Furthermore, if they exist in this market, is it possible to exploit them for profit? Transaction costs in the stock-index futures market are only a fraction of the cost for stocks; thus anomalies in futures should be easier to exploit than they are in the stock market.[5]

Day-of-the-Week and Weekend Effects

Chapter 2 found that stock returns tend to be, on average, negative on Mondays and positive on Fridays. Does this hold true in the futures markets? The evidence is mixed. Rogalski [1984] partitioned price movements into those in nontrading periods (overnight and weekends) and trading periods (hours when stocks are traded). He found that the negative Monday returns appear to be confined to the nontrading periods—before the market opened.

Smirlock and Starks [1986] and Harris [1986] disagreed. Looking at an earlier time period than Rogalski, Smirlock and Starks found that the negative returns occurred during the trading day; Harris [1986], using NYSE transaction-by-transaction data for the 14 months ending January 1983, found negative returns for both the nontrading period and during the first 45 minutes of Monday's trading.

Cornell [1985] found the effect to be a weekend effect. His data consisted of daily opening and closing prices for the S&P 500 futures contract for the period May 3, 1982, to July 24, 1984, and prices for the next futures contract to settle.[6] Excluded from the sample were all holidays and days following holidays. Note, during the period he tested, the market rose approximately 25 percent.

Exhibit 7-4 shows Cornell's average returns for (1) close-to-open (nontrading periods), (2) open-to-close (price changes during the trading day), and (3) close-to-close (the sum of the first two) prices for each day of the week, as well as returns for the spot (cash) index. The net mean return is the difference between the mean return for the day and the overall mean. Statistically significant negative returns from the close on Friday to the open on Monday suggest that the Monday effect really is a weekend effect.

More recent work by Dyl and Maberly [1986a, 1986b], who replicated the Cornell study, did not come to the same conclusion. They found negative returns and negative price changes on Monday; however, the return and price changes were not statistically different from those found for the other four days of the week. Note that there are minor differences between their and Cornell's study: Dyl and Maberly covered a slightly different time period (May 3, 1982, to December 31, 1985) and used a different method for switching from contracts as the settlement date approached.

Panel A of Exhibit 7-5 shows Cornell's mean returns. Panel B shows the results when Dyl and Maberly replicated the Cornell study. As you can see, even when they adjusted to use the same switching approach and time period, their results did not support Cornell. Exhibit 7-5 reports both mean rate of return (R_t) and mean price change (P_t).[7] Dyl and Maberly measured the return on futures as the natural logarithm of the price on day t divided by the price on day $t-1$. They argued, and it is an important point, that futures' performance cannot be measured by rate of return on investment because the investment essentially is a performance bond equal to the initial margin, and it is only a fraction of the actual futures contract's value. They suggested that a more appropriate measure of return is the mean dollar price change.[8]

The last panel of Exhibit 7-5 shows the results for Dyl and Maberly's larger sample (the period May 3, 1982, through December 31, 1985). In

Exhibit 7-4
Day-of-the-Week Statistics: Spot and Futures Returns, May 3, 1982—July 24, 1984

Contract	Mon.	Tue.	Wed.	Thur.	Fri.	F-Statistic[a]
Spot S&P 500: close to close						
Mean	-0.0300	0.945	0.1577	-0.0229	0.0411	0.74
t-statistic	(-0.31)	(1.01)	(1.73)	(-0.25)	(0.44)	
Net mean	-0.0798	0.0447	0.1079	-0.0727	-0.0087	
Spot S&P 500: close to open						
Mean	-0.1285	0.0715	0.0915	0.0176	0.0971	3.13[b]
t-statistic	(-2.38)[b]	(1.38)	(1.82)	(0.35)	(1.90)	
Net mean	-0.1618	0.0382	0.0582	-0.0157	0.0638	11.01[c]
Spot S&P 500: open to close						
Mean	0.0986	0.0230	0.0662	-0.0405	-0.0560	0.60
t-statistic	(1.10)	(0.27)	(0.79)	(0.48)	(-0.66)	
Net mean	0.0821	0.0065	0.0497	-0.0570	-0.0725	1.03
S&P 500 futures: close to close						
Mean	0.1090	-0.0302	0.0627	0.0806	-0.0584	0.39
t-statistic	(0.90)	(-0.26)	(0.55)	(0.71)	(-0.51)	
Net mean	0.0772	-0.0620	0.0309	0.0487	-0.0902	0.50
S&P 500 futures: close to open						
Mean	0.0139	0.0137	0.0608	0.0664	0.0387	0.26
t-statistic	(0.27)	(0.28)	(1.27)	(1.38)	(0.81)	
Net mean	-0.0258	-0.0260	0.0221	0.0267	-0.0010	0.31
S&P 500 futures: open to close						
Mean	0.0951	-0.0440	0.0019	0.0140	-0.0971	0.38
t-statistic	(0.80)	(-0.38)	(0.17)	(0.13)	(-0.86)	
Net mean	0.1030	-0.0361	0.0098	0.0219	-0.0892	0.92
Observations	99	107	104	103	111	

[a] The first F-statistic is for the hypothesis that all the coefficients are equal in the regression $R_t = a_1 D1 + a_2 D2 + a_3 D3 + a_4 D4 + a_5 D5 + u_t$, where R_t is the return on the market index and $D1$ through $D5$ are day-of-the-week dummies. The second F-statistic is for the hypothesis that Monday's return is equal to the average of the other four days.

[b] Denotes significance at the 5 percent level.

[c] Denotes significance at the 1 percent level.

Exhibit 7-5
Day-of-the-Week Close-to-Open Statistics of
Stock-Index Futures

Statistic	Mon.	Tues.	Wed.	Thurs.	Fri.	F-Statistic[a]
		A. Cornell's results, May 3, 1982–July 24, 1984				
Mean R_t	.0139	.0137	.0608	.0664	.0387	0.26
t-statistic	(0.27)	(0.28)	(1.27)	(1.38)	(0.81)	
Observations	99	107	104	103	111	
		B. Replication, May 3, 1982–July 24, 1984				
Mean R_t	−.0618	.0278	.0423	.0717	.0317	1.38
t-statistic	(−1.56)	(0.11)	(0.52)	(0.70)	(0.19)	
Mean ΔP_t	−.0817	.0434	.0604	.1039	.0353	1.36
t-statistic	(−1.47)	(0.17)	(0.52)	(1.38)	(0.01)	
Observations	101	106	115	113	111	
		C. New results, May 3, 1982–December 31, 1985				
Mean R_t	−.0413[b]	.0613	.0406	.0627	.0388	2.25[c]
t-statistic	(−2.10)	(1.20)	(0.32)	(1.03)	(0.20)	
Mean ΔP_t	−.0547[b]	.1060	.0628	.0951	.0563	2.33[c]
t-statistic	(−2.05)	(1.46)	(0.26)	(1.02)	(0.05)	
Observations	171	175	187	184	182	

[a] The F-statistic is for the hypothesis that all the coefficients are equal in the regressions R_t (or ΔP_t) = $\alpha_1 D1 + \alpha_2 D2 + \alpha_3 D3 + \alpha_4 D4 + \alpha_5 D5$, where $D1$ through $D5$ are day-of-the-week dummies.
[b] Denotes significance at the 5 percent level.
[c] Denotes significance at the 10 percent level.

Source: Dyl and Maberly [1986b], p. 1150.

contrast to the findings in the second section of the table, the mean return and price change for Mondays were negative, statistically significant, and statistically different from the other four days of the week. These results support the existence of the weekend effect, at least for this larger sample.

Junkus [1986] studied the Monday effect for three stock-index futures contracts (S&P 500 futures, NYSE futures, and Value Line futures). She used daily returns based on closing prices for approximately two years after trading began in 1982. She partitioned the time period into two subperiods corresponding to the first and second year of futures contracts trading, and used only the nearest contract.[9] For the full two-year period and the two subperiods, the returns for the three cash-market indexes were not significantly negative on Mondays, as shown in Exhibit 7-6, and the distribution of returns in the cash market did not differ by the day of the week.

Keim and Smirlock [1987] used a different approach to find exploitable, cyclical profits and found opportunity existed on Thursday. They examined the S&P 500 and the Value Line futures contracts over a longer time period than did the previous studies.[10] Their conclusions, as shown in Exhibit 7-7, were the same whether they used returns or price changes,[11] and were similar to those of Dyl and Maberly for the S&P 500 futures contract: negative Monday price changes accrued during nontrading hours. However, the Value Line contract did not act in the same way as the S&P 500 futures contract: price changes were negative over the nontrading period but positive during the trading day. For the S&P 500 futures, only the negative price change in the nontrading period was statistically significant.

Different contracts have different patterns, and depending upon how and when we study the data, there are different results. Keim and Smirlock [1987] confirmed higher price changes over the last three days of the week in the cash market, but the higher price change was on Thursday alone in the futures market.

Does the high positive average price change Keim and Smirlock found on Thursday mean that there is a profit opportunity?[12] The answer depends on price variability. For example, if an investor had purchased an S&P 500 futures contract on the close of Wednesday and sold it on the close of Thursday, based on the results reported in Exhibit 7-7, the average price change would have been 17.46 in basis points or $87.30. However, this position would have been exposed to substantial losses. For example, while profits would have been realized about 58 percent of the time, Keim and Smirlock report losses of over $600 would have been realized in several instances. Moreover, their $87.30 does not include transaction costs.

Strategies involving holding a futures contract for several days and then selling on Thursday also must take price variability into account. For example, if an investor had purchased an S&P 500 futures contract on Monday morning and sold it at the end of the trading day on Thursday, the average profit would

Exhibit 7-6
Mean Returns[a,d] and T-Statistics[b,d] for Stock Indexes
and Futures Contracts

Contract or Index	Mon.	Tue.	Wed.	Thur.	Fri.
Value Line Index	-.093	.084	.165	.102	.097
February 28, 1982–March 30, 1984	(-1.057)	(1.120)	(2.012)[e]	(1.478)	(1.406)
Futures[c]	.147	-.097	.117	.169	-.002
February 28, 1982–March 30, 1984	(1.081)	(-.719)	(.959)	(1.496)	(-.018)
VL Index	-.055	.229	.166	.155	.158
February 28, 1982–February 25, 1983	(-.355)	(1.908)	(1.239)	(1.435)	(1.463)
Futures	.294	.024	.022	.370	-.067
February 28, 1982–February 25, 1983	(1.205)	(.104)	(.154)	(1.958)	(-.362)
VL Index	-.132	-.067	.165	.049	.036
February 28, 1983–March 30, 1984	(-1.553)	(-.761)	(1.719)[d]	(.557)	(.419)
Futures	.000	-.223	.211	-.033	.062
February 28, 1983–March 30, 1984	(0.000)	(-1.582)	(1.530)	(-.277)	(.521)
NYSE Index	.002	.079	.270	.013	.047
April 28, 1982–March 30, 1984	(.018)	(.745)	(2.070)	(.160)	(.522)
Futures	-.005	-.033	.063	.109	-.072
April 28, 1982–March 30, 1984	(-.041)	(-.202)	(.529)	(.746)	(-.605)
NYSE Index	-.028	.247	.215	.064	.090
April 28, 1982–March 18, 1983	(-.144)	(1.380)	(1.272)	(.496)	(.584)
Futures	-.159	.161	-.140	.395	-.121
April 28, 1982–March 18, 1983	(-.664)	(.463)	(-.683)	(1.312)	(-.511)
NYSE Index	.033	-.097	.198	-.037	.007
March 21, 1983–March 30, 1984	(.340)	(-.882)	(1.752)[d]	(-.373)	(.071)
Futures	.114	-.188	.222	-.114	-.034
March 21, 1983–March 30, 1984	(1.046)	(-1.504)	(1.552)	(-.974)	(-.293)
S&P 500 Index	.037	.081	.236	-.016	.033
May 6, 1982–March 30, 1984	(.327)	(.704)	(2.206)[e]	(-.175)	(.359)
Futures	.155	-.019	.159	.068	-.047
May 6, 1982–March 30, 1984	(1.107)	(-.131)	(1.169)	(.571)	(-.385)
S&P 500 Index	.030	.259	.246	.051	.046
May 6, 1982–March 18, 1983	(.150)	(1.328)	(.382)	(.336)	(.293)
Futures	.207	.089	.105	.214	-.115
May 6, 1982–March 18, 1983	(.812)	(.344)	(.438)	(1.034)	(-.530)
S&P 500 Index	.045	-.105	.225	-.082	.022
March 21, 1983–March 30, 1984	(.413)	(-.873)	(1.829)[d]	(-.781)	(.216)
Futures	.100	-.132	.213	-.079	.017
March 21, 1983–March 30, 1984	(.901)	(-1.031)	(1.664)[d]	(-.699)	(.152)

[a] Returns expressed in percentage form.
[b] t-statistics for null hypothesis mean equals 0.
[c] Futures series represents nearest to maturity contract.
[d] Indicates significance at 5% level.
[e] Indicates significance at 2.5% level.

Source: Junkus [1986], p. 400.

Exhibit 7-7

Daily Price Changes in Basis Points for Stock-Index Futures
by Day of the Week, April 1982–December 1986[a]

	All Days	Mon.	Tues.	Wed.	Thurs.	Fri.	F-Statistic[b] (p-value)
S&P 500							
Close-to-open	1.95	-10.38	7.88	3.17	2.95	5.40	2.99
	(1.08)	(-2.05)	(2.23)	(.93)	(.68)	(1.42)	(.0181)
Open-to-close	5.57	22.79	-2.42	3.58	14.50	-9.56	1.30
	(1.10)	(1.94)	(-.20)	(.32)	(1.31)	(-.97)	(.2691)
Close-to-close	7.43	12.41	5.47	6.29	17.46	-4.15	.47
	(1.41)	(.99)	(.44)	(.55)	(1.41)	(-.40)	(.7559)
Spot close-to-close	10.63	-4.97	11.12	18.17	12.41	15.57	.79
	(2.36)	(-.46)	(1.04)	(1.92)	(1.19)	(1.77)	(.5336)
Value Line							
Close-to-open	8.00	-2.69	11.49	10.18	10.23	10.19	1.22
	(3.38)	(-.47)	(1.94)	(1.97)	(2.06)	(2.25)	(.3019)
Open-to-close	-3.28	5.97	-19.86	-10.07	17.82	-9.33	1.60
	(-.62)	(.46)	(-1.63)	(-.87)	(1.50)	(-.81)	(.1716)
Close-to-close	4.71	3.28	-8.37	.04	28.05	-4.15	1.17
	(.83)	(.24)	(-.63)	(.00)	(2.12)	(-.08)	(.3234)
Spot close-to-close	8.06	-28.00	4.72	17.28	17.33	27.13	6.15
	(2.09)	(-3.04)	(.52)	(2.09)	(2.00)	(3.68)	(.0001)
Number of observations	1,190	227	243	242	238	239	

[a] The T-statistics are shown in parenthesis.

[b] The F-statistic is for the hypothesis that all the coefficients a_i are equal in the regression $\Delta P_t = \sum_{i=1}^{5} a_i D_i$, where D_1 through D_5 are day-of-the-week dummies.

Source: Keim and Smirlock [1987], p. 148.

have been $208.15. There were times, however, when this strategy would have lost more than $1,500. Even without considering transaction costs, this strategy was profitable just over half the time.

Instead of looking for futures contracts' daily returns patterns, Keim and Smirlock later [1989] looked for patterns in the difference (spread) in prices between futures contracts. In particular, they examined a strategy that took a long position in the Value Line contract and a short position in the S&P 500 contract. They argued that these two contracts were not the same things, because the S&P 500 futures contract is a market-value-weighted proxy for the performance of large-capitalization firms, while the Value Line futures contract is a geometric-equally-weighted proxy for the performance of small-capitalization firms.[13] Earlier Keim and Smirlock [1987] had examined the average daily returns of stocks listed on the NYSE and American Stock Exchange (ASE) for

10 portfolios ranked by size for the period 1963-81. They compared these returns with the average daily returns on two composite indexes consisting of the same stocks,[14] and, as shown in Exhibit 7-8, found that moving from small- to large-capitalization firms, the average daily returns decreased. In addition, the value-weighted composite index had an average return that was the same as the portfolio consisting of large-capitalization stocks. The equal-weighted composite index (Value Line) performed much like that of the small-capitalization stocks. Because of these differences, an intermarket-spread position created by buying the Value Line futures contract and shorting the S&P 500 contract should capture the performance of small-capitalization firms more than a long position in the Value Line contract alone.

Exhibit 7-9 summarizes the average daily price change by day of the week for each of the two futures contracts (a long position in each) and the intermarket-spread position. The price changes are based on close-to-close prices. The results reported in the first two panels are the same as reported in Exhibit 7-7 for the two futures contracts based on close-to-close prices.

Exhibit 7-8
Average Daily Returns for 10 Portfolios of Common Stocks
Listed on the NYSE and ASE and for Two Indexes
Composed of All the Stocks on the NYSE
and ASE, 1961-81

Portfolio / Index	Average Market Capitalization ($ millions)	Average Return (%)
Smallest	4.5	.107
2	10.8	.082
3	19.6	.076
4	31.9	.066
5	49.4	.060
6	79.0	.056
7	128.3	.051
8	226.9	.048
9	463.5	.043
Largest	1114.5	.034
Value-weighted composite		.034
Equal-weighted composite		.072

Source: Adapted from Keim and Smirlock [1987], p. 145.

Unlike the pricing pattern for the individual futures contracts, the results in Exhibit 7-9 suggest a consistent, time-related, pricing pattern for the intermarket-spread position.[15] In particular, an average price change for the spread is

Exhibit 7-9
Daily Price Changes in Basis Points for Stock-Index Futures
by Day of the Week, April 1982–December 1986

	All Days	Mon.	Tue.	Wed.	Thurs.	Fri.
S&P 500						
Average	7.42	12.41	5.46	6.28	17.46	–4.15
Standard error	(5.28)	(12.49)	(12.56)	(11.34)	(12.34)	(10.26)
Percentage increase/decrease	51.6/48.4	56.3/43.7	48.9/51.1	47.7/52.3	58.8/41.2	46.8/53.2
K.C. Value Line						
Average	4.70	3.28	–8.37	0.04	28.04	.85
Standard error'	(5.70)	(13.84)	(13.35)	(12.21)	(13.24)	(10.96)
Percentage increase/decrease	49.8/50.2	52.4/47.6	46.9/53.1	48.1/51.9	57.9/42.1	43.9/56.1
Spread Position						
Average	–2.71	–9.12	–13.84	–6.24	10.58	5.01
Standard error	(1.89)	(4.44)	(4.25)	(4.00)	(4.24)	(4.11)
Percentage increase/decrease	46.3/53.7	43.1/56.9	38.2/61.8	45.6/54.4	55.8/44.2	48.5/51.5
Number of Observations	1189	227	243	242	238	239

Source: Keim and Smirlock [1989], p. 148.

negative in the first three days of the week and positive in the last two days, and it is inconsistent with what has been observed in the cash market: a positive Friday and negative Monday price change. Thus, for small-capitalization firms, there may be a weekend effect.

It is interesting to note that the price-change variability of the intermarket-spread position is less than that of the individual futures contracts. Lower variability may allow one to capitalize using the intermarket-spread position: instead of buying the Value Line futures contract and shorting the S&P 500 futures contract, the reverse can be done. The resulting price change would be the opposite of that shown in Exhibit 7-9. If this strategy were initiated on the close of Friday and liquidated on the close of Tuesday (a day with stable negative price changes), the average profit would have been 23 basis points, or $115, and 60 percent of the trades would have been profitable. When there were losses, they would have been considerably less than those from the earlier strategy designed to take advantage of the higher Thursday price change.

Even without a weekend effect or day-of-the-week effect, Keim and Smirlock [1989] suggest that an intermarket-spread position based on the weekend effect that highlights the performance of small-capitalization firms may produce stable trading profits.[16] They tested a strategy that went long the S&P 500 futures contract and short the Value Line futures contract on the close of Friday and liquidated at the close of Tuesday. With the exception of 1982, this two-day trading strategy would have earned an average of about $125 per trade. Without considering transaction costs, a profit would have been realized on 60 percent of the trades.

The intraday performance for the Toronto Stock Exchange (TSE) 300 cash index and futures index has been investigated by Chamberlain, Cheung, and Kwan [1988]. They observed a Monday effect in both the cash and futures markets. For the cash-market index, the data consisted of time-ordered records of the closing levels of the TSE 300 index between March 1978 and December 1984. For the futures contract, the daily closing levels from January 1984 to December 1986 were included. Performance was measured in terms of dollar price changes based on close-to-close prices. Exhibit 7-10 summarizes the daily means for each day of the week.

Panels A and B show the results for the cash-market index. Panel A includes the entire period, while Panel B covers the time for which the futures were observed. Regardless of the time period, the cash-market results were similar: Monday's price change was negative, statistically significant, and in absolute value, larger than the other trading days. Panel C reports that the futures results were similar to those for the cash market.

Intraday Trading Patterns

Finnerty and Park [1988] analyzed cash and futures price data over 15-minute intervals. Exhibits 7-11 and 7-12 show the results for their futures and cash markets, respectively. For the Major Market Index (MMI) futures contract, average prices trended continually lower on Wednesdays; Fridays had the most intraday volatility with little change during the day. Returns on the other three days had an upward trend. Exhibit 7-11 also shows that, on average, the futures price tended to open down on Mondays for the first 30 minutes and then move upward for the remainder of the trading day. The other four days exhibited a positive return for the first 15 minutes of trading. A closer examination of these results indicates that, with the exception of Mondays and Fridays price changes tended to diminish between noon and 1 p.m. Finnerty and Park referred to this phenomenon as the "lunch-hour effect."

Focusing on the cash-market results in Exhibit 7-12 shows that the negative weekend effect in the cash market seemed to start about 1:30 p.m. on Friday (not Friday's close) and end at 9 a.m. on Monday.

The January Effect and The Turn of the Year Effect

The information about a weekend effect is mixed. What about the curious, but seemingly persistent, January effect? Do we also see it in the futures market? The empirical evidence reported in Chapter 2 suggested that stock returns in

Exhibit 7-10

Summary Statistics for the Daily Close-to-Close Price Changes of the TSE 300 Index and TSE 300 Index Futures

Statistic	Monday	Tuesday	Wednesday	Thursday	Friday	F_{4, n_2}
	Panel A: Cash; March 7, 1978, to January 15, 1984					
Mean	-3.4408	1.3317	3.2051	2.0276	2.3440	6.328[a]
Standard deviation	18.3955	15.5447	16.5151	19.0571	15.6785	$(n_2 - 1410)$
t-statistic	-3.022[a]	1.400	3.345[a]	1.840	2.550[b]	
Observations	261	267	297	299	291	
	Panel B: Cash; January 16, 1984, to December 31, 1986					
Mean	-3.1842	0.3990	1.6267	1.5165	3.1684	3.471[a]
Standard deviation	14.5691	16.0154	15.1797	16.6314	13.2342	$(n_2 - 718)$
t-statistic	-2.549[b]	0.293	1.313	1.117	2.922[a]	
Observations	136	138	150	150	149	
	Panel C: Futures; January 16, 1984, to December 31, 1986					
Mean	-2.8976	0.2090	0.5685	1.2414	2.0915	1.828
Standard deviation	16.6928	17.5816	15.5980	17.7460	12.3856	$(n_2 - 689)$
t-statistic	-1.956	0.138	0.440	0.842	2.012[b]	
Observations	127	134	146	145	142	

[a] Significant at 1%.
[b] Significant at 5%.

Source: Chamberlain, Cheung, and Kwan [1988], p. 332.

Exhibit 7-11

Cumulative 15-Minute Intraday Percentage Returns, MMI Futures

	Mon.	Tues.	Wed.	Thurs.	Fri.
OPEN - 9:00 a.m.	-.018	.020	.008	.009	.018
9:00 - 9:15	-.017	-.005	-.002	.039	.049
9:15 - 9:30	-.014	.038	.002	.017	.059
9:30 - 9:45	.012	.029	-.0003	.031	.032
9:45 - 10:00	-.0001	-.002	-.034	.037	.054
10:00 - 10:15	.004	-.014	-.064	.059	.052
10:15 - 10:30	-.0003	-.008	-.023	.037	.023
10:30 - 10:45	.006	.013	-.040	.064	.045
10:45 - 11:00	.007	.040	-.027	.068	.077
11:00 - 11:15	.017	.037	-.002	.071	.058
11:15 - 11:30	.057	.049	-.032	.088	.077
11:30 - 11:45	.035	.041	-.022	.128	.080
11:45 - 12:00	.083	.036	-.035	.115 ⎤	.089
12:00 - 12:15	.071	.064 ⎤	-.069	.115 ⎥ *	.129 ⎤
12:15 - 12:30	.051 ⎤	.061 ⎥ *	-.043 ⎤	.115 ⎦	.128 ⎦ *
12:30 - 12:45	.052 ⎥ *	.065 ⎦	-.042 ⎦ *	.142	.063
12:45 - 1:00	.051 ⎦	.003	-.048	.139	.057
1:00 - 1:15	.067	.024	-.050	.102	.029
1:15 - 1:30	.056	.046	-.077	.135	.069
1:30 - 1:45	.034	.048	-.059	.170	.080
1:45 - 2:00	.080	.063	-.108	.149	.034
2:00 - 2:15	.088	.050	-.143	.152	.056
2:15 - 2:30	.113	.070	-.114	.108	-.002
2:30 - 2:45	.124	.073	-.102	.137	-.026
2:45 - 3:00	.135	.082	-.111	.174	-.033
3:00 - CLOSE	.127	.094	-.100	.174	.005

* Changes are not significantly different from zero at the 10 percent level of significance.

Source: Finnerty and Park [1988], p. 306.

January are significantly higher than in other months. This January effect is much more pronounced for small- than for large-market-capitalization firms. Keim and Smirlock [1987 and 1989] investigated the January effect using the S&P 500 and the Value Line futures contracts. As we saw earlier, the spread between the Value Line futures contract and the S&P 500 futures contract represented an intermarket-spread position that heightens the performance of small-capitalization firms. Exhibit 7-13 shows the average daily price change for both stock-index futures contracts and the spread for each month based on close-to-open and open-to-close prices; the average price change for both con- tracts in January was positive overnight and during trading hours, but not

THE NEW STOCK MARKET

Exhibit 7-12

Cumulative 15-Minute Intraday Percentage Returns, MMI Spot

	Mon.	Tues.	Wed.	Thurs.	Fri.
OPEN - 9:00 a.m.	-.015	-.011	.026	.005	.001
9:00 - 9:15	-.055	.045	.027	.032	.060
9:15 - 9:30	-.046	.068	.028	.016	.110
9:30 - 9:45	-.026	.050	.028	.011	.088
9:45 - 10:00	-.024	.056	.008	.032	.018
10:00 - 10:15	-.023	.050	-.014	.048	.082
10:15 - 10:30	-.021	.039	-.014	.049	.063
10:30 - 10:45	-.016	.057	-.006	.054	.087
10:45 - 11:00	-.021	.053	-.017	.056	.086
11:00 - 11:15	-.011	.076	-.005	.062	.084
11:15 - 11:30	-.001	.077	.008	.077	.090
11:30 - 11:45	.013	.083	.004	.094	.087
11:45 - 12:00	.025⎤	.089	-.021⎤*	.115	.104⎤*
12:00 - 12:15	.028	.100⎤	-.022⎦	.131⎤	.103⎦
12:15 - 12:30	.028 *	.099 *	-.028	.127	.114
12:30 - 12:45	.027⎦	.103	-.031	.127	.113
12:45 - 1:00	.007	.096⎦	-.049	.129 *	.090
1:00 - 1:15	.008	.074	-.026	.125	.089
1:15 - 1:30	.007	.083	-.038	.131⎦	.098
1:30 - 1:45	-.007	.092	-.036	.141	.099
1:45 - 2:00	.021	.110	-.052	.139	.070
2:00 - 2:15	.040	.103	-.054	.161	.065
2:15 - 2:30	.071	.146	-.070	.131	.045
2:30 - 2:45	.064	.128	-.069	.117	.033
2:45 - CLOSE	.096	.134	-.041	.167	.031

*Changes are not significantly different from zero at the 10 percent level of significance.

Source: Finnerty and Park [1988], p. 307.

statistically significant. In fact, few months contained statistically significant average price changes. In other words, they found no January effect.

Exhibit 7-14 shows that the daily price change was higher in January than for the other months, but the spread was not statistically significant for any month. Moreover, when Keim and Smirlock tested the hypothesis that the average price change of the spread was the same for all months, the hypothesis could not be rejected.

However, Keim and Smirlock [1987 and 1989] did find a difference between the results for the S&P and Value Line contracts. They tested a strategy that bought the futures contract on the penultimate trading day of the year at the closing price and sold it after the first four trading days of the new year. In the

Exhibit 7-13

Daily Price Changes (T-Statistics) for Stock-Index Futures by Month of the Year, April 1982–December 1986

Month	Value Line		S&P 500		Value Line–S&P 500		
	Close-to-Open	Open-to-Close	Close-to-Open	Open-to-Close	Close-to-Open	Open-to-Close	
January	7.43	17.63	1.33	15.48	6.10	2.15	86
	(1.06)	(.81)	(.18)	(.78)	(1.50)	(.22)	
February	6.91	−4.90	−.71	11.04	7.62	−15.94	77
	(.79)	(−.22)	(−.12)	(.54)	(1.23)	(−1.63)	
March	21.05	−6.92	5.81	8.84	15.23	−15.76	86
	(2.02)	(−.43)	(.95)	(.54)	(1.63)	(−1.31)	
April	−2.56	−.93	2.17	3.57	−4.72	−4.51	91
	(−.16)	(−.92)	(.38)	(.18)	(−.32)	(−2.75)	
May	3.36	−1.00	−2.47	4.74	5.83	−5.74	106
	(.47)	(−.07)	(−.52)	(3.57)	(.93)	(−.71)	
June	11.75	−6.19	.68	4.89	11.08	−16.08	106
	(1.98)	(−.36)	(.11)	(.64)	(3.18)	(−2.63)	
July	−.24	−39.91	−4.24	−25.76	4.00	−14.14	106
	(−.04)	(−2.25)	(−.77)	(−1.68)	(1.06)	(−2.09)	
August	12.39	20.32	4.38	32.69	8.01	−12.38	111
	(1.87)	(1.10)	(.72)	(2.02)	(1.70)	(−1.46)	
September	7.75	−34.81	.51	−28.70	7.25	−6.12	102
	(.92)	(−1.52)	(.06)	(−1.34)	(1.72)	(−.90)	
October	3.44	15.21	1.41	26.93	2.04	−11.72	111
	(.50)	(.87)	(.21)	(1.59)	(.72)	(−2.14)	
November	6.20	16.79	2.65	15.78	3.55	1.01	102
	(.84)	(.88)	(.47)	(.84)	(.96)	(.16)	
December	18.91	−13.95	11.73	−7.20	7.18	−6.75	106
	(2.98)	(−.80)	(1.92)	(−.44)	(1.84)	(−.87)	
F-Statistic*	.72	1.20	.44	1.19	.60	.52	
(p-value)	(.7176)	(.2812)	(.9360)	(.2857)	(.8347)	(.8939)	

* The F-statistic is for the hypothesis that all the coefficients are equal in the regression $\Delta P_i = \Sigma^{12}_{i=1} a_i D_i$, where D_1 through D_{12} are month-of-the-year dummy variables.
Source: Keim and Smirlock [1987], p. 153.

Exhibit 7-14

Daily Price Changes for Stock-Index Futures by Month of the Year,
April 1982–December 1986 (based on close-to-close prices)

Month	S&P 500	Value Line	Spread Position
January	16.80	25.05	8.25
	(20.33)	(22.36)	(8.17)
February	10.32	2.01	-8.31
	(20.05)	(23.04)	(7.26)
March	14.65	14.12	-0.05
	(17.07)	(19.18)	(7.33)
April	4.50	-3.55	-8.05
	(20.30)	(20.54)	(5.30)
May	2.26	2.35	0.09
	(13.57)	(15.09)	(6.02)
June	10.56	5.56	-5.00
	(16.64)	(18.01)	(6.02)
July	-30.00	-40.14	-10.14
	(17.22)	(19.85)	(6.91)
August	37.07	32.70	-4.36
	(16.95)	(19.35)	(7.17)
September	-28.18	-27.05	1.12
	(22.18)	(23.80)	(6.54)
October	28.33	18.64	-9.68
	(17.74)	(18.53)	(5.18)
November	18.43	22.99	4.55
	(19.70)	(19.96)	(6.06)
December	4.52	4.95	0.42
	(16.43)	(17.32)	(6.40)

Source: Keim and Smirlock [1989], p. 152.

case of the intermarket-spread position, they initiated it on the penultimate trading day of the year at the closing price and liquidated it at the close of the fourth trading day of the new year. Their results, using close-to-close prices for the S&P 500 futures contract, the Value Line futures contract, and the spread, are summarized in Exhibit 7-15.

While it is difficult to draw conclusions from such a small sample (only four years), the results are interesting. The Value Line futures contract outperformed the S&P 500 futures contract in all four years, even when the market declined in 1985. The average daily profit from a long position in the Value Line futures contract was $425, and a profit would have been realized in 16 of the 20 trading days. The spread would have produced a profit of $1,050 and realized losses in only 4 of the 20 trading days. Keim and Smirlock [1989] reported that, had this strategy been used at the beginning of 1987, a profit of $7,825 and

$1,425 would have been realized from the Value Line futures contract and the intermarket-spread position, respectively. In other words, they did find a January effect in one contract and using a strategy that capitalized on intermarket spreads. No doubt, more research on this will be coming.

Exhibit 7-15
Turn-of-the-Year Effect, by Year, 1983-86 (based on close-to-close prices)

		Trading Day, Current Year				
	Last Trading Day, Previous Year	*First*	*Second*	*Third*	*Fourth*	*Total Basis-Point Change*
S&P 500						
1983	.65	−2.80	3.50	.40	4.05	5.80
1984	.15	−1.50	3.10	1.20	.60	3.55
1985	−.20	−1.80	−1.35	−.65	.65	−3.35
1986	−1.00	−.90	1.40	.30	2.80	2.60
K.C. Value Line						
1983	1.40	−2.40	3.20	.50	4.65	7.35
1984	.90	−.55	3.80	2.30	1.15	7.60
1985	.00	−1.85	−1.15	.05	1.25	−1.70
1986	−.25	.05	1.80	.10	2.05	3.75
Spread Position						
1983	.75	.40	−.30	.10	.60	1.55
1984	.75	.95	.70	1.10	.55	4.05
1985	.20	−.05	.20	.70	.60	1.65
1986	.75	.95	.40	−.20	−.75	1.15

Source: Keim and Smirlock [1989], p. 154.

Stock-Index Options

In the previous chapter, we discussed options on individual issues of common stock. In March 1983, options on a stock index, the S&P 100 (originally called the CBOE 100), began trading on the Chicago Board Options Exchange. This was followed by ASE trading of options on the MMI.[17] As with stock-index futures, options on stock indexes (simply, index options) are settled in cash. Within one year, trading volume in options on stock indexes reached about 20 percent of all options' daily volume. Exhibit 7-16 lists the currently traded index options. The total put-and-call volume for all cash-settled broad- and narrow-based index options routinely accounts for more than 50 percent of the total volume of options traded on all exchanges.

Exhibit 7-16
Currently Traded Stock-Index Options

Contract	Exchange
S&P 500	Chicago Board Options Exchange
S&P 100	Chicago Board Options Exchange
Major Market Index	American Stock Exchange
Institutional Index	American Stock Exchange
NYSE Composite Index	New York Futures Exchange
Value Line Index	Kansas City Board of Trade

Note: The contract size for each index option is equal to 100 times index.

Despite the huge volume of trading and the use of index options by institutional investors, little empirical research has been published on the efficiency of this market. Empirical tests of the pricing of index options suffer from some of the same problems as the tests on stock options we discussed in Chapter 6. In addition, there is another problem: the amount and timing of dividends for the stocks contained in the index must be estimated. In spite of these problems, two types of studies are important to our understanding of the profit potential in this market. The first looks for violations of the price boundary for an option, and the second, for violations of put-call parity.

Evnine and Rudd [1985] tested for violations of the lower boundary of the price of a call option[18]—that is, instances in which the ask price of the call option was below the difference between the value of the cash index and the strike price. They used real-time prices for S&P 100 and MMI index options from June 26, 1984, to August 30, 1984. For each trading day, prices for every hour were included, a total of 1,798 observations. The information was essentially the same information that would have been displayed on electronic monitors on the exchange floor.[19] Exhibit 7-17 shows the number of times that a violation was observed and its mean dollar value.

There were 30 times when the lower boundary for the call-option price on the S&P 100 was violated and 11 times for the MMI. Evnine and Rudd reported that the sizes of the discrepancies became so large at times, even upstairs traders[20] would have been capable of taking advantage of them. Evnine and Rudd noted that one possible explanation for this phenomenon was that, during the week these violations were observed (August 1 to August 6), there was a dramatic increase in the level of market prices. Thus, it was possible that violations occurred because the value of the cash index was updated faster than the bid/ask prices.

Exhibit 7-17
Call Price Lower-Boundary Violations for Index Options

	Violation		
Contract	Number Observed	$ Mean	$ Standard Deviation
S&P100			
Aug. 145	16	0.22	0.14
Aug. 150	9	0.29	0.13
Aug. 155	5	0.07	0.03
MMI			
Aug. 110	11	0.48	0.36
Aug. 115	0		

Source: Evnine and Rudd [1985], p. 751.

Evnine and Rudd [1985] also tested for violations of the put-call parity relationship.[21] Exhibits 7-18 and 7-19 present the results of their tests of European and American put-call parity relationships, respectively, and suggest that, when the index options were treated as European options, significant profit opportunities were possible. The violations suggest that the S&P 100 index call options were underpriced. The reverse was true for the MMI options. Even if the options were treated as American options, the results in Exhibit 7-19 suggest that there were opportunities to profit.

Exhibit 7-18
European Put-Call Parity Violations

	Call Underpriced			Call Overpriced		
Contract	Number Observed	$ Mean	$ Standard Deviation	Number Observed	$ Mean	$ Standard Deviation
S&P100						
Aug. 145	241	0.45	0.31	39	0.11	0.08
Aug. 150	264	0.54	0.34	35	0.12	0.08
Aug. 155	293	0.66	0.36	42	0.15	0.10
MMI						
Aug. 110	40	0.26	0.25	208	0.27	0.24
Aug. 115	97	0.33	0.35	79	0.28	0.21

Source: Evnine and Rudd [1985], p. 751

Exhibit 7-19
American Put-Call Parity Violations

	Call Underpriced			Call Overpriced		
Contract	Number Observed	$ Mean	$Standard Deviation	Number Observed	$Mean	$Standard Deviation
S&P 100						
Aug. 145	10	0.11	0.08	39	0.11	0.08
Aug. 150	21	0.17	0.10	35	0.12	0.08
Aug. 155	30	0.29	0.18	42	0.15	0.10
MMI						
Aug. 110	1	–	–	133	0.22	0.18
Aug. 115	1	–	–	65	0.29	0.20

Source: Evnine and Rudd [1985], p. 752.

Chance [1987] tested put-call parity in investigating the S&P 100 index options for the period January 3, 1984, to April 27, 1984, using a data base supplied by a regional brokerage and investment banking firm. The prices were market-makers' bid/ask quotes as the market closed and the final index level. Because the prices were quotes rather than closing transaction prices, the problem of nonsynchronicity of the option and index prices was not present.[22]

Chance created two portfolios. Portfolio A consisted of a long position in the call option and risk-free bonds and short positions in the put option and the cash-market index, and Portfolio B consisted of long positions in the put option and the cash-market index and short positions in the call option and risk-free bonds. Chance showed that, for Portfolio A, there should not be a negative payoff, while for Portfolio B, the payoff should not be positive: put-call parity would be violated if Portfolio A had a negative payoff and Portfolio B had a positive payoff.

Chance found that, of the 1,690 portfolios he examined, Portfolio A violated put-call parity 735 times and Portfolio B, 645 times: there were only 310 times that there were no violations. The average violations for Portfolio A and Portfolio B were $69.84 and $65.98, respectively. Both values are statistically significant. Profitable opportunities appeared to exist.

Why? The cause is probably the result of the difficulty of arbitraging between the index-options market and the cash market: the expense of creating a portfolio to replicate the performance of the cash-market index and estimating dividends for the stocks in the index. Either problem could be the source of Chance's abnormal returns.

The put-call parity relationship involves a put, a call, and the cash-market index. Chance [1987] devised a test to determine whether there was parity between only the put and call options for an index.[23] Based on the expected payoffs from this parity relationship, Chance found that, while there were violations, the frequency and size of the violations were not sufficient to reject the hypothesis that the puts and calls were priced correctly in relation to each other.

Summary

Individual and institutional investors who use stock-index futures and/or stock-index options to accomplish investment objectives must be aware of the pricing efficiency in these markets. Because of the difficulty of arbitraging a derivative market in which the underlying instrument is an index, there will be a zone around the theoretical futures price that will be free of arbitragable returns. Empirical studies of the stock-index futures market indicate that, after considering taxes and the use of proceeds for the short seller of the cash market index, there was little mispricing in the early stages. As the market grew, mispricing became even less frequent. The little evidence we have for the stock-index options markets suggests that there is some mispricing between puts, calls, and the cash index. However, puts and calls appear to be priced in line with each other.

The market anomalies observed in the cash market are not necessarily observed in the futures market. Evidence on the presence of the weekend effect in the futures market is mixed. The most comprehensive studies did not find a weekend effect in the futures market. There is evidence, however, that an intermarket-spread position that appears to heighten the performance of small-capitalization firms may exhibit a weekend effect and that, even after the introduction of stock-index futures trading, there is a weekend effect in the cash market. As for the January effect there is no evidence of it in the stock-index futures market, but a turn-of-the-year effect offers potential trading profits if the Value Line futures contract and the intermarket spread are used. Scanty research and the newness of the market open opportunity, but opportunity that should be tempered with caution. Future research in these areas will be worth watching.

CHAPTER 7

Notes

1. Readers who are unfamiliar with stock-index futures and how they are priced should review the appendix to this chapter before proceeding.

2. Trading and portfolio strategies using stock-index futures and options are described in Fabozzi and Kipnis [1988].

3. Constantinides [1983] discussed the importance of this tax-timing option for capital-market equilibrium.

4. This occurred when the short seller of the cash-market index had use of 50 percent of the proceeds and futures contracts were dividend adjusted.

5. Round-trip commissions, for example, on stock-index futures are between $50 and $100 for individual investors and less than $15 for institutional investors. Assuming a round-trip commission of $50 per contract, the cost of transacting is typically less than 0.1 percent of the contract value. In contrast, a round-trip commission for a portfolio consisting of the S&P 500 stocks would be roughly 1 percent of the value of the stocks.

6. Except during the delivery month, when the next most distant contract was used.

7. The price changes reported represent the change in the futures price. To obtain the price change in dollars, the values reported in the table should be multiplied by $500.

8. Referring to futures contracts, Black [1976] noted, "Since his investment is zero, it is not possible to talk about the percentage or fractional return on the investor's position in the futures market. Both his risk and his expected return must be defined in dollar terms " (p. 171).

9. She did not switch to the next-to-nearest contract as did Cornell and Dyl and Maberly.

10. Their study period was from April 21, 1982 (the day trading began on the S&P 500 futures contract), to December 31, 1986, a bull market.

11. The price change reported in Exhibit 7-7 is in terms of basis-point price changes. Because the futures contracts are designed so that a basis-point price change is equal to $5, the dollar value for the numbers reported in the table can be obtained by multiplying by $5. The results reported by Dyl and Maberly in Exhibit 7-5 are in terms of the change in the futures price and can be translated into a dollar value by multiplying by $500.

12. To capitalize on it, one would buy the futures contract at the close on Wednesday and sell on Thursday.

13. The S&P 500 Index is composed of 500 firms traded primarily on the NYSE. The Value Line average includes stocks traded on the NYSE, on the American and Canadian exchanges, and in the over-the-counter market.

14. The composite indexes were constructed in different ways. They first weighted each stock in the portfolio by its market value (value-weighted composite). The other composite index assigned an equal weight to each stock.

15. Finnerty and Park [1988] studied intraday returns from the Major Market Index (MMI) and the related futures contract using transactions reported for the futures contract and the value of the spot index one to four times every minute of the trading day

(which meant that a return could be calculated every minute). They also found no weekend effect.

16. Other studies have attempted to investigate the day-of-the-week effect. Pieptea and Prisman [1988] found no weekend effect in the futures market for either the nearby futures or the next-nearby futures contracts.

17. The index was constructed to be similar to the Dow Jones Industrial Average and included 20 stocks.

18. In Chapter 6, we explained that, by using arbitrage arguments, a lower boundary can be placed on the price of a call option.

19. Even so, the last option trade recorded for the hour was not synchronized with the last value recorded for the index. However, the index option prices included bid/ask prices; thus part of the cost of transacting was considered in the study's analysis.

20. Block trades (that is, trades of 10,000 shares or more) are typically negotiated between traders and institutional investors using a network that links them together. This market is referred to as the upstairs market.

21. In Appendix A of Chapter 6, we showed that there is a relationship between the price of a call option, the price of a put option, and the value of the underlying instrument: the put-call parity relationship.

22. While there are problems in updating both the option quotes and the index, Chance argued that all quotes reflect transactions that could have been executed.

23. He tested the payoff for a box spread. See Gastineau [1988], p. 90-92, for a detailed description of this strategy.

CHAPTER 7

References

Black, Fischer. "The Pricing of Commodity Contracts." *Journal of Financial Economics*, June 1976, pp. 167-79.

Chamberlain, Trevor W.; Cheung, C. Sherman; and Kwan, Clarence C. Y. "Cash versus Futures Prices and the Weekend Effect: The Canadian Evidence." *Advances in Futures and Options Research*, 1988, pp. 329-39.

Chance, Don M. "Parity Tests of Index Options." *Advances in Futures and Options Research*, 1987, pp. 47-64.

Collins, Bruce M. *An Empirical Analysis of Stock Index Futures Prices.* Unpublished doctoral dissertation, Fordham University, 1987.

Constantinides, George M. "Capital Market Equilibrium with Personal Taxes." *Econometrica*, May 1983, pp. 611-36.

Cornell, Bradford. "The Weekly Pattern in Stock Returns: Cash versus Futures: A Note." *Journal of Finance*, June 1985, pp. 583-88.

————, and French, Kenneth R. "Taxes and the Pricing of Stock Index Futures." *Journal of Finance*, June 1983, pp. 675-94.

Dyl, Edward A., and Maberly, Edwin D. "The Daily Distribution of Changes in the Price of Stock Index Futures." *Journal of Futures Markets*, Winter 1986a, pp. 513-21.

————. "The Weekly Pattern in Stock Index Futures: A Further Note." *Journal of Finance*, December 1986b, pp. 1149-52.

Evnine, Jeremy, and Rudd, Andrew. "Index Options: The Early Evidence." *Journal of Finance*, July 1985, pp. 743-56.

Fabozzi, Frank J., and Kipnis, Gregory M. *The Handbook of Stock Index Futures and Options.* Homewood, IL: Dow Jones-Irwin, 1989.

Finnerty, Joseph, and Park, Hun. "Intraday Return and Volatility Patterns in the Stock Market: Futures versus Spot." *Advances in Futures and Options Research*, 1988, pp. 301-17.

Gastineau, Gary L. *The Options Manual,* Third edition. New York: McGraw-Hill, 1988.

Harris, Lawrence. "A Transaction Data Study of Weekly and Intradaily Patterns in Stock Returns." *Journal of Financial Economics*, May 1986, pp. 99-118.

Hill, Joanne M.; Fabozzi, Frank J.; and Jankus, Jonathan C. "Stock Market Indicators." Chapter 7 in Frank J. Fabozzi and Gregory M. Kipnis, eds. *The Handbook of Stock Index Futures and Options.* Homewood, IL: Dow Jones-Irwin, 1989.

Junkus, Joan C. "Weekend and Day of the Week Effects in Returns on Stock Index Futures." *Journal of Futures Markets*, Autumn 1986, pp. 397-407.

Keim, Donald B., and Smirlock, Michael. "The Behavior of Intraday Stock Index Futures Prices." *Advances in Futures and Options Research*, 1987, pp. 143-66.

———. "Pricing Patterns in Stock Index Futures." Chapter 10 in Frank J. Fabozzi and Gregory M. Kipnis, eds. *The Handbook of Stock Index Futures and Options*. Homewood, IL: Dow Jones-Irwin, 1989.

Modest, David M., and Sundaresan, Mahadevan. "The Relationship between Spot and Futures Prices in Stock Index Futures: Some Preliminary Evidence." *Journal of Futures Markets*, Spring 1983, pp. 15-42.

Peters, Ed. "The Growing Efficiency of Index-Futures Markets." *Journal of Portfolio Management*, Summer 1985, pp. 52-56.

Pieptea, Dan, and Prisman, Eliezer. "Intraday Return and Volatility Patterns in the Stock Market: Futures versus Spot." *Advances in Futures and Options Research*, 1988.

Rogalski, Richard J. "New Findings Regarding Day-of-the-Week Returns over Trading and Non-Trading Periods: A Note." *Journal of Finance*, December 1984, pp. 1603-14.

Smirlock, Michael, and Starks, Laura., "Day-of-the-Week and Intraday Effects in Stock Returns." *Journal of Financial Economics*, September 1986, pp. 197-210.

Appendix

Introduction to Stock-Index Futures Contracts

Stock-Index Futures Characteristics

When an investor takes a position in the market by buying a futures contract, the investor is said to be in a *long position* or *long the futures*. If, instead, the investor's opening position is the sale of a futures contract, the investor is said to be in a *short position* or *short the futures*.

A distinctive feature of stock-index futures contracts is that they are cash-settlement contracts; that is, the parties must settle in cash on the settlement date. The contract value at any time is equal to $500 times the futures price. For example, if the futures price for the S&P 500 futures contract is $245.10, then the total contract value is $122,550.

Most financial futures contracts expire in March, June, September, or December, which means that, at that time, the contract stops trading and a settlement price is determined by the exchange. The contract with the closest settlement date is called the *nearby* futures contract. The *next* futures contract is the one that settles just after the nearby contract. The contract furthest away from settlement is called the *most distant* futures contract.

Mechanics of Futures Trading[1]

When a position is first taken in a futures contract, the investor must deposit a specified amount per contract. This amount is called the *initial margin* and is put up as a *good faith deposit* for the contract.[2] The initial margin may be in the form of an interest-bearing security such as a Treasury bill. As the price of the futures contract fluctuates, the value of the investor's equity in the position changes. At the close of each trading day, an investor's position is *marked to market,* so that any gain or loss from the position is reflected in the investor's equity account. The price used to mark the position to market is the settlement price for the day.

Maintenance Margin is the minimum level specified by the exchange to which an investor's equity position may fall, as a result of an unfavorable price movement, before the investor is required to make an additional margin deposit. The additional margin that must be deposited is called *variation margin.* If it is required, the amount of variation margin the investor must deposit is an amount necessary to bring the equity in her or his account back to its initial margin level. If there is excess margin in the account, that amount may be withdrawn by the investor.

The investor can liquidate a stock-index futures position in two ways. Prior to the settlement date, the investor must take an offsetting position in the same contract, which means, for a long position, selling an identical number of contracts; for a short position, it means buying an identical number of contracts. Otherwise, the investor must wait until the settlement date and settle in cash.

When an investor takes a position in the futures market, there is another investor taking the opposite position and agreeing to satisfy the terms set forth in the contract. After an order is executed, the relationship between the two parties is severed. The *clearing corporation* interposes itself as the intermediary.[3] Thus the investor is free to liquidate his or her position without involving the other party in the original contract, and without worry that the other party may default.

Futures versus Forward Contracts

A forward contract, just like a futures contract, is an agreement for the future delivery of a designated item at a specified price and a designated time. Futures contracts are standardized agreements as to the delivery date and the quality and quantity to be delivered. They are traded on organized exchanges. A forward contract is usually nonstandardized, and secondary markets for them are often nonexistent or extremely limited.

Futures contracts are marked to market at the end of each trading day; forward contracts are not. Thus interim cash flows are associated with futures contracts, as margin may be required or freed up as prices change. Because no variation margin is required with forward contracts, they involve no interim cash flows. However, because either party may default on his or her obligations, forward contracts have one risk that futures do not—credit risk.

Pricing of Stock-Index Futures

Based on arbitrage arguments, an equilibrium (theoretical) price can be determined based on the following information:

1. The price of the index in the cash market, the *spot* price.

2. The dividend yield on the stocks in the index that would be earned between the purchase date and the settlement date.

3. The interest rate for borrowing and lending from the purchase date to the settlement date, the financing cost.

The theoretical futures price that will prevent arbitrage profits is

> *Futures price = Cash market price*
> *+ Cash market price (Financing cost − Dividend yield)*

This price indicates that the futures contract may sell at a premium or discount to the cash-market price, depending on the financing cost and the dividend yield. The difference between the financing cost and the dividend yield is called the net financing cost, because it adjusts the financing cost for the *cost of carry* (or simply, carry): it adjusts the financing cost for the yield earned. *Positive carry* means that the yield earned is greater than the financing cost; *negative carry,* that the financing cost exceeds the yield earned.

To derive the theoretical futures price using the arbitrage argument (also called the *cost-of-carry model*), several assumptions must be made. When these assumptions are not reasonable, there will be a difference between the theoretical and actual futures prices.

The first assumption is that there are no interim cash flows as a result of variation margin or dividend payments, even though we know that interim cash flows can and do occur for both these reasons. Note that, because a forward contract is not marked to market at the end of each trading day, and there is no variation margin, the theoretical futures price is technically the theoretical forward contract price.[4] Incorporating interim dividend payments into the pricing model is not difficult, but the value of the dividend payments at the settlement date depends on the interest rate at which the dividend payments can be reinvested in the interim. The shorter the maturity of the futures contract and the lower the dividend yield, the less important the reinvestment income is in determining the futures price.

Second, to determine the cost of carry, we need to know both the financing cost and the dividend yield. While the financing cost may be known, the dividend rate is not known with certainty. It must be projected. In addition, we assume that the borrowing rate and lending rates are equal, even though they are not: the borrowing rate typically is greater than the lending rate.

Third, the model assumes there are no transaction costs or taxes. We know, however, that transaction costs of entering into and closing the cash position, as well as the round-trip transaction costs for the futures contract, are important.

Fourth, when the futures price is below its theoretical value, for arbitrage to be profitable, the investor must be able to use the proceeds from selling the cash-index short. In practice, individual investors do not receive the proceeds; they are required to put up margin (securities margin not futures margin) to sell short. For institutional investors, the securities may be borrowed, but at a cost. The model also assumes that, in the case of a short sale of the stocks in the index, all stocks are sold simultaneously. The up-tick rule for short sales of stock[5] may prevent the arbitrage strategy from bringing the actual futures price in line with the theoretical futures price.

Yet another difficulty in arbitraging the cash and futures market is that buying or selling every stock included in the index is expensive. Instead, a portfolio containing a smaller number of stocks may be constructed to reflect the index. This portfolio will not track the index exactly, which introduces another source of risk, known as *tracking-error risk*.

The violation of the assumptions made in developing the cost-of-carry model results in discrepancies between the actual and theoretical futures prices: there will be a band within which the futures price will trade that will not permit arbitrage profits.[6]

CHAPTER 7   APPENDIX

Notes

1. For a more detailed discussion of the trading mechanics of stock-index futures, see Collins and Fabozzi [1989].

2. Although there are also initial and maintenance margin requirements for buying securities on margin, the concept of margins differs for securities and futures. When securities are acquired on margin, the difference between the price of the security and initial margin is borrowed from the broker. The purchased security serves as collateral for the loan, and interest is paid by the investor. For futures contracts, the initial margin serves as good faith money, indicating that the investor will satisfy the obligation of the contract. No money is borrowed by the investor.

3. Because the exchange operates as a clearing corporation, the investor need not worry about the financial strength and integrity of the other investor.

4. For a technical discussion of the difference between futures and forward prices, see Cox, Ingersoll, and Ross [1981], Jarrow and Oldfield [1981], and Richard and Sundaresan [1981]. Hanson and Kopprasch [1989] suggest a procedure for adjusting the forward price to account for variation margin.

5. The short-selling rule for stocks specifies that a short sale can only be made at a price that is higher than the previous trade (referred to as an up-tick) or at a price that is equal to the previous trade but higher than the last trade at a different price (referred to as a zero-tick).

6. Modest and Sundaresan [1983] derived upper and lower bounds for the theoretical futures price that take into consideration several of the factors discussed here.

CHAPTER 7   APPENDIX

References

Collins, Bruce M. and Fabozzi, Frank J. "Mechanics of Trading Stock Index Futures," Chapter 5 in Frank J. Fabozzi and Gregory M. Kipnis, eds., *The Handbook of Stock Index Futures*. Homewood, IL: Dow Jones-Irwin, 1989.

Cox, John C.; Ingersoll, John E.; and Ross, Stephen A. "The Relationship between Forward and Futures Prices." *Journal of Financial Economics*, December 1981, pp. 321-46.

Hanson, Nicholas, and Kopprasch, Robert. "Pricing of Stock Index Futures." Chaper 8 in Frank J. Fabozzi and Gregory M. Kipnis, eds. *The Handbook of Stock Index Futures and Options*. Homewood, IL: Down Jones-Irwin, 1989.

Jarrow, Robert A., and Oldfield, George S. "Forward and Futures Contracts." *Journal of Financial Economics*, December 1981, pp. 373-82.

Modest, David M., and Sundaresan, Mahadevan. "The Relationship between Spot and Futures Prices in Stock Index Futures: Some Preliminary Evidence." *Journal of Futures Markets*, Spring 1983, pp. 15-42.

Richard, Scott F., and Sundaresan, M. "A Continuous Time Equilibrium Model of Forward Prices and Futures Prices in a Multigood Economy." *Journal of Financial Economics*, December 1981, pp. 347-72.

Stock-Index Futures and Options, Stock-Price Volatility, and Black Monday

In the previous chapter, we discussed the empirical evidence on the efficiency of stock-index futures and option markets. In this chapter, we will concentrate on two related questions: First, has the introduction of stock-index futures and options trading, and strategies using these contracts, increased the volatility of the stock market as the press and critics have often claimed? Second, to what extent did the presence of these contracts contribute to the October 1987 market crash, popularly known as Black Monday? Before we present the empirical evidence, the next two sections will provide background information. The next section briefly describes the role of stock index futures in financial markets. Then, we will describe index-related trading innovations and strategies that have been alleged to contribute to greater stock price volatility—program trading, index arbitrage and portfolio insurance.

Stock-Index Futures and Their Role in Financial Markets

In the absence of stock-index futures and options markets, investors had only one way to alter their portfolios when new information was received—to buy or sell in the cash market. If there was economic news that they believed would adversely affect the expected cash flow from all stocks, investors could reduce their equity exposure by selling stocks. There were and are, of course, transaction costs when doing this—commissions and hidden, or execution costs (bid/ask spreads and market-impact costs).

Stock-index futures provide an alternative way for equity investors to alter their exposure to risk. Should investors use the cash or futures market to alter their positions? The answer is simple: Investors should use the one that is the more efficient in achieving their objective. By efficient, we mean the one that offers the lowest commissions, smallest bid/ask spreads, lowest market-impact costs, and most leverage. The market that investors feel is the one that is more efficient to use to achieve their investment objective will be the one in which price discovery takes place. Price information will then be transmitted to the other market. So, for example, if the futures market is the market of choice, it will serve as the price discovery market. That is, it will be the market where investors send their collective message about how any new information is expected to impact the cash market. Then, there must be a mechanism for transmitting that message to the cash market. We'll discuss that mechanism later.

Transaction costs are substantially lower in the futures market. Typically, transaction costs in this market are between 5 to 10 percent of those in the cash market. For example, the transaction costs associated with trading a $120 million portfolio of stocks would be about $161,000; using the Standard & Poor's (S&P) 500 stock-index futures it would be only $10,000.[1]

The speed at which orders can be executed gives a further advantage to the futures market. Byrne [1986], for example, estimated that selling a block of stocks at a reasonable price takes 2 to 3 minutes. A futures transaction can be made in 30 seconds or less. The advantage is also on the side of the futures market when it comes to leverage, the amount of money that must be put up in a transaction. In the cash market, margin requirements are set by the Federal Reserve as a proportion of the stock price. Thus, the dollar value of the margin required changes as the stock price changes. As of early 1989, the initial margin was 50 percent, with a 25 percent maintenance margin. In contrast, the margin or good-faith deposit for stock-index futures is a fixed dollar amount established by the exchange on which they are traded. On October 19, 1987, the initial and maintenance margins were $10,000 and $50,000, respectively, for speculators in the S&P 500 contract. By June 1988 the requirements had doubled. Even with these higher margins, however, the leverage was 600 percent greater than when purchasing equities on margin.

A study by the Division of Market Regulation of the Securities and Exchange Commission (SEC) [1987] concluded:

> [institutions can] sell portions of their equity positions in a faster, less expensive manner by using index futures than by selling direct-ly on stock exchanges. . . .

> Futures are used instead of stocks because of the increased speed and reduced transaction costs entailed in trading a single product in the futures market. . . .

> As a result of the futures market's liquidity, investors can execute large transactions with much smaller market effects than is possible in the separate stocks.

In the face of these transaction-cost advantages, which market has been selected by investors for altering risk exposure? Merrick [1987b] found that, prior to 1985, the cash market dominated the price-discovery process.[2] Since 1985, however, the S&P 500 futures market has played the dominant price-discovery role. This reversal of which was the dominant market was not an accident; it followed the pattern of trading volume. When trading volume in the futures market surpassed that of the cash market, the futures market dominated in the price-discovery process. In her testimony before Congress on July 23, 1987, Susan Phillips, then the chairperson of the Commodity Futures Trading Commission, stated, "The depth and liquidity of the futures markets facilitate the absorption of new fundamental information quickly, thus improving the efficiency of the stock markets."[3]

Could the futures market take on a life of its own—a life where the futures price did not reflect the economic value of the underlying instrument? Could the values in the cash market be different from those reflected in the futures market? Yes, if there were no mechanism to synchronize futures prices and cash-market prices. There is a mechanism, however, and that mechanism is index arbitrage.

Trading Innovations and Futures Strategies

Index Arbitrage

For markets to be integrated, and prices efficient, there must be a way to transmit investors' expectations from one market to another. We know from our discussion in the appendix to the previous chapter that only if the cost of carry is zero will the futures price and cash price be the same. Otherwise, the futures price will differ from the cash price by the cost of carry. Because of such things as transaction costs,[4] there is a range around the theoretical futures price in which it is not possible to generate arbitrage profits. But what happens if the futures price is outside that band? An investor can generate arbitrage profits by selling the more expensive and buying the cheaper instrument.

To do this if the cash market is cheap relative to the futures market, an investor would buy the stock and sell the futures contract. At the expiration of the contract, the stock would be sold to provide cash to cover the futures position (which must be settled in cash). To obtain the necessary funds, the investor would liquidate the stock position by submitting market-on-close[5] sell orders at the expiration of the futures contract. If, however, buying the futures contract is cheaper than buying the stock, the investor would buy the futures and sell the stock (sell short). At the expiration date, the investor must cover the short sale of the stock by buying the stock: the investor covers the short position by submitting market-on-close orders to buy the stock. Either of these strategies will drive the price of the expensive instrument down and the price of the cheaper one up until the futures price is back within the theoretical range.

A strategy for taking advantage of mispriced futures is called *index arbitrage*. It is index arbitrage that keeps the futures and the cash markets in line with each other. This link prevents futures contracts from taking on lives of their own and allows hedgers to use stock-index futures for carrying out strategies to protect portfolio values at a fair price.

Critics of index arbitrage argue that arbitrageurs only consider the relationship among cash, futures, and transactions costs, rather than making decisions based on the economic value of the underlying stock. The response to these critics is that there must be a movement in at least one of the markets for arbitrage trading to be profitable. As long as nonarbitrageurs are pricing in that market based on economic information, all price changes will capture the price impact of the information.

Information about the volume of index-arbitrage activity is not readily available. Merrick [1987c] deduced the level of arbitrage activity by looking at the growth in the number of contracts settled in cash on expiration day. His rationale for using this measure was that market participants other than arbitrageurs (namely, hedgers and speculators), typically close out their positions prior to expiration dates. Hedgers roll over their positions in order to maintain hedged positions; speculators close out their positions in the nearest contract and establish a new position in a more distant contact. Thus it is generally arbitrageurs who settle in cash on expiration days.

Using this information, Merrick found that, between 1983 and 1986, the volume of contracts settled in cash on the expiration day increased from 6,000 to about 33,000, as shown in Exhibit 8-1. Not only had the growth of arbitrage been substantial, but a comparison of the number of contracts settled in cash relative to the growth of the average month-end open interest suggested that the relative importance of arbitrageurs had increased. This effect can also be seen in Exhibit 8-1, which shows the growth of the average month-end open interest. Between 1983 and 1986, the proportion of cash-settled futures contracts increased from about 28 percent to 38 percent of the average month-end open interest.

In the last chapter, we explained how futures prices were getting much closer to their theoretical prices over time. Merrick argued that it is arbitrageurs that have pushed actual prices close to their theoretical counterparts. This situation is illustrated in Exhibit 8-2, which shows the amount of near-futures contract mispricing from May 17, 1982, to May 30, 1986. The shaded area shows the band for the theoretical futures price resulting from the transaction costs. In the earlier years, there was frequent violation of the theoretical band. With the growth of arbitrage activity in 1985 and 1986, fewer violations in excess of transaction costs occurred.

The relationship between prices in the cash and futures markets is critical. If they are unrelated, or outside theoretical bonds, arbitrage is possible. Two

Exhibit 8-1
Deduced Growth of Arbitrage Activity

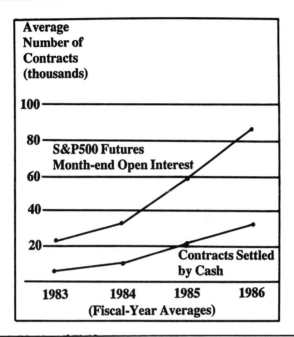

Source: Merrick [1987c], p. 19.

studies have investigated the relationship between intraday price movements of stock indexes and stock-index futures. Both investigated the time-series relationship between the S&P 500 stock index and the S&P 500 futures contract.

One of the critical questions that both studies asked is whether the futures market serves as a price-discovery market for stock prices. Kawaller, Koch, and Koch [1987], examining the period from the second quarter of 1984 to the last quarter of 1985, found that futures prices consistently led index movements by 20 to 40 minutes, while movements in the cash-market index rarely affected futures prices for longer than a minute. Stoll and Whaley [1987a] using data from April 21, 1982, to December 31, 1986, also found that futures prices led cash prices, but the lead time was usually no more than 5 minutes on average, with occasional leads of as long as 15 minutes.

Some investors believe that a lead/lag relationship provides opportunities to profit from changes in the difference between the futures and cash prices, called the *basis*. They believe that changes in the basis can be used as an

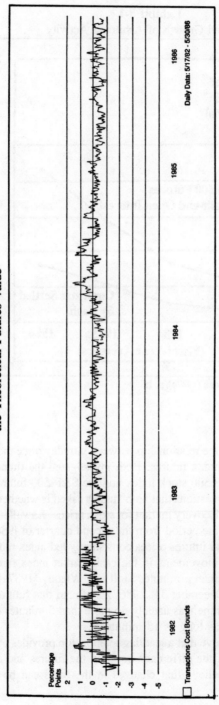

Exhibit 8-2
Near-Contract S&P 500 Futures Mispricing as a Percentage of the Theoretical Futures Value

Percentage Points

2
1
0
-1
-2
-3
-4
-5

1982   1983   1984   1985   1986

☐ Transactions Cost Bounds

Daily Data: 5/17/82 - 5/30/86

Source: Merrick [1987c], pp. 20-21.

indicator of forthcoming movements in the cash-market index. For example, an extraordinarily large basis is believed to be an indicator of rising stock prices, and a fall would be signaled by an extraordinarily small or negative basis. Kawaller et al. concluded it was unlikely that the lag structure they observed could be exploited in this way.

Stoll and Whaley [1987b] also investigated whether the futures market overshot its true value as a result of market congestion or speculative activity. They found no evidence to support this hypothesis.

Program Trading

How do investors index arbitrage? Program trading is an important activity for index arbitrage and other equity strategies. *Program trading* is a technique for trading groups of stocks as simultaneously as possible, not, as it is often characterized in the popular press, a profit-seeking trading strategy. Program trades are typically implemented electronically using the automated order-execution facilities of the exchanges (e.g., the Super DOT [Designated Order System] of the New York Stock Exchange), in which the orders are transmitted simultaneously to the appropriate specialists' posts. While program trading can also be implemented manually by someone quickly carrying preprinted order tickets to the specialists' posts, the automated order-execution facilities are more efficient and less costly.

Several investment strategies depend on executing a list of orders as simultaneously as possible. One of those strategies is indexing. Indexing rests squarely on efficient-market theory. An efficient portfolio is one that has the highest expected return for a given level of risk, and the market portfolio is the efficient portfolio: it offers the highest return per unit of risk.[6] The theoretical market portfolio consists of a market-value weighted portfolio of all risky assets. In an efficient stock market investors should construct their portfolios to mirror the market portfolio. The strategy of matching the performance of an equity portfolio to the performance of the market is known as *indexing*. About 30 percent of the total assets of the 200 largest defined-benefit pension funds was indexed as of September 1986.[7]

Three related problems arise in implementing an indexing strategy. First, since there is no way to construct the theoretical market portfolio, a proxy market portfolio must be chosen.[8] Once the index is chosen, the investor faces a second problem: how to construct a portfolio to replicate the index. Here the decision is whether to purchase all the stocks in the index or a sample that has characteristics similar to those of the index. Third, and most importantly for our discussion, when new money is invested in or withdrawn from the equity portfolio, the investor must determine how simultaneous orders for all stocks in the market-proxy portfolio can be executed at the closing prices so that the portfolio's performance will mirror the index. This third problem creates the advantage program trading has in index-fund management.

Portfolio Insurance (Dynamic Hedging)

Program trading is also used in dynamic hedging, also called portfolio insurance. *Dynamic hedging* is a strategy that seeks to insure the value of a portfolio using a synthetic put option.[9] In Chapter 6, we explained how a put option can protect the value of an asset. At the expiration date of the put option, the minimum value of the asset will be the strike price minus the cost of the put option. Put options or synthetic put options on stock indexes can do the same for a diversified portfolio of stocks. An institutional investor can synthetically create a put option by using either (1) stock-index futures or (2) stocks and a riskless asset. The allocation of the portfolio's funds to either stock-index futures or to stocks and a riskless asset is adjusted as market conditions change.

If portfolio managers can use put options on stock indexes, why should they bother with synthetic puts and dynamic hedging? There are two reasons. First, the market for options on stock indexes is not as large as the market for stock-index futures and therefore may not easily accommodate large portfolio-insurance programs without moving the price of the option substantially. Second, the transaction costs of a put option may be higher than those associated with dynamic hedging. Note, however, that while the cost of a put option is known (determined by its expected price volatility), the cost of creating portfolio insurance by using stock-index futures or stocks is not known and is a function of the actual price volatility in the market.[10] One thing is certain: the greater the actual price volatility in the market, the more the portfolio must be rebalanced and the higher the costs of portfolio insurance.

How does dynamic hedging work using stocks and a riskless asset? When stock prices decline, stocks are sold, and the proceeds invested in the riskless asset. When stock prices rise, stocks are purchased with proceeds obtained from selling a portion of the riskless asset.[11] Program trading is used to execute the orders to buy or sell stocks.

Instead of implementing dynamic hedging by changing the allocation of the portfolio between stocks and a riskless asset, stock index futures can be used. When stock prices decline, stock index futures are sold. This is equivalent to selling stocks and investing the funds in a riskless asset. When stock prices rise, stock index futures are purchased, which is equivalent to buying stocks and reducing the portfolio's allocation to a riskless asset.

The Impact of Futures on Stock-Price Volatility

The view held by some investors and the popular press is that stock index futures and options, program trading and index-related strategies (index arbitrage and dynamic hedging) have resulted in an increase in the volatility of stock prices. This criticism of futures contracts is not confined to stock index futures. It has been a criticism leveled against all futures contracts and can be referred to as the *destabilization hypothesis.*

Harris [1987] noted two variants of the destabilization hypothesis: the liquidity variant and the populist variant. According to the liquidity variant, large transactions that are too difficult to accommodate in the cash market will be executed in the derivative-contract markets because of the latters' better liquidity. The increased volatility that may occur in the derivative-contracts markets is only temporary, because prices tend to revert when liquidity arrives. Thus there should be no long-term impact on the value of the underlying cash-market security. The impact of the liquidity variant would be that the variance of stock prices for short time intervals, such as one day, would be greater than otherwise expected. However, over long intervals, the variance of stock prices should be largely unaffected by the introduction of derivative contracts.

In contrast, the populist variant asserts that, as a result of speculative trading in derivative contracts, the cash-market instrument does not reflect fundamental economic value. The result would be a larger-than-expected variance of stock prices over all time periods.[12]

Several studies have investigated the effect of the introduction of futures trading, trading innovations, and index-related strategies on the volatility of the underlying cash-market price. There are several problems each such study faces. First, what the volatility of the cash-market price would be in the absence of futures trading must be determined. A simple comparison of price volatility before and after the introduction of futures trading, while informative, is not sufficient, because other factors influence volatility. For example, an increase in price volatility may be the result of an increase in the variability of economic information that affects the price of the cash-market instrument, rather than any interaction between trading in the cash and futures markets. An alternative to comparing price volatility before and after futures trading is to attempt to control for the other factors that affect price volatility.

A second, and even more fundamental problem is that there is no universal definition of stock-market volatility. By volatility we could mean the overall distribution of stock prices, a sharp price fluctuation, or the frequency of turning points (reversals) that reflect changes in market sentiment. In spite of these problems, we have gained some insight.

Interday Price Volatility

Davis and White [1987] examined several time periods to test whether a change in stock-price volatility had occurred. They compared volatility in 1986-87, when index-related trading was believed to be substantial, with volatility in the 1970s and early 1980s, when it was not. Comparisons were also made with the decades after World War II, a period in which index-related trading was insignificant and economic conditions were viewed as more stable.

Davis and White used three measures of price volatility in investigating the volatility of aggregate indexes and individual stocks: (1) percentage changes in prices, (2) absolute percentage changes in prices, and (3) frequency of turning points in prices. Closing prices for six indexes were examined: the NYSE Composite Index, the Dow Jones Industrial Average (DJIA), the S&P 500 Index, the NASDAQ Composite, the American Stock Exchange (ASE) Composite Index, and the Wilshire 5000 Index.

Davis and White pointed out that their tests were not direct tests of any index-related trading strategies, but that inferences could be drawn about the impact on prices of these strategies. They argued that, if the price effects were not quickly reversed, an increase in the proportion of days with relatively large price swings would be expected if stock-index futures and options and index-related strategies increased stock-price volatility. They also argued that a comparison of returns over longer holding periods with daily returns could provide evidence about the persistence of price influences from the use of derivative techniques: the effect of any overshooting should be reversed in a week or month.

Exhibit 8-3 shows the average values of daily percentage changes in the NYSE Composite Index for each year from 1970 through 1987. The volatility (standard deviation) varies substantially from year to year. The results were similar regardless of the index investigated.

Exhibit 8-4 is a plot of the frequency distribution of day-to-day price changes for two periods: 1970 to 1985 and 1986 to May 1987. The shapes of the two distributions are similar, but losses of more than 1.5 percent occurred more often during 1986-87.

Standard deviation is only one measure of volatility or risk.[13] Investors may also be concerned about the frequency of extreme price changes—that is, the outliers of the distribution. Thus risk can be viewed in terms of unusually large price changes. The skewness and kurtosis statistics reported in Exhibit 8-3 can be used to examine whether there were large price changes in a period.

Of the 18 years examined, 11 years exhibited positive skewness,[14] 8 of which were statistically significant. Of the 7 years that exhibited negative skewness, only 3 were statistically significant. The frequency distributions for 1986 and 1987 were negatively skewed, but only 1986 was statistically significant. This suggests that 1986 had more days with unusually large price declines than did most of the earlier years in the study. In addition, the kurtosis[15] values reported in Exhibit 8-3 indicate that, for most years, a large number of the observations were clustered at the mean and far from the mean in the tails. This suggests that relatively few of the price changes observed for each year represented medium-sized deviations from the mean.

Exhibit 8-5 provides the same summary statistics for the S&P 500 Index

Exhibit 8-3

Daily Changes in the NYSE Index, 1970-87

Year	Mean (percent)	Standard Deviation		Skewness		Kurtosis[a]	
		Measure	Test of Equality with 1986–87[b]	Measure	Significance Test[c]	Measure	Significance Test
1970	−.010	.98	n.s.	.62	.01	3.42	.01
1971	.048	.64	.01(−)	.53	.01	2.86	.01
1972	.054	.50	.01(−)	−.08	n.s.	.00	n.s.
1973	−.082	1.00	n.s.	.13	n.s.	.41	n.s.
1974	−.133	1.36	.01(+)	.52	.01	.67	.05
1975	.114	.96	n.s.	.15	n.s.	.02	n.s.
1976	.072	.79	.02(−)	.31	.05	6.01	.01
1977	−.027	.56	.01(−)	.11	n.s.	.95	.01
1978	.012	.87	n.s.	−.01	n.s.	6.87	.01
1979	.064	.68	.01(−)	−.52	.01	2.49	.01
1980	.089	1.03	.02(+)	−.26	.05	.47	n.s.
1981	−.032	.83	n.s.	−.16	n.s.	.70	.05
1982	.057	1.08	.01(+)	.62	.01	1.75	.01
1983	.067	.83	n.s.	.47	.01	2.98	.01
1984	.008	.74	.01(−)	.85	.01	1.43	.01
1985	.094	.59	.01(−)	.39	.01	.33	n.s.
1986	.055	.85	—	−.95	.01	3.51	.01
1987[d]	.166	1.01	—	.32	n.s.	.36	.01

[a] The measure is standardized so that the value for a normal distribution equals zero. Negative values imply flatter distributions with shorter tails, such as the uniform distribution. Positive values imply a distribution with thicker tails. Significance test indicates whether a value is significantly different from the normal distribution and, if so, at what level.

[b] The equality of the standard deviation of the indicated year and that of 1986–87 was tested. If the difference was statistically significant, the level of significance is indicated; (+) indicates that the given year's standard deviation was significantly larger than that in 1986–87; indicates that the 1985-87 standard deviation was larger than the year's. An dash signifies that the test is not meaningful.

[c] The level of significance is indicated if the skewness measure was statistically significantly positive or negative in a one-tailed test.

[d] Data through May

n.s. No statistically significant difference.

Source: Davis and White [1987], p. 62.

Exhibit 8-4
Frequency Distribution of Day-to-Day Price Changes in
the NYSE Index

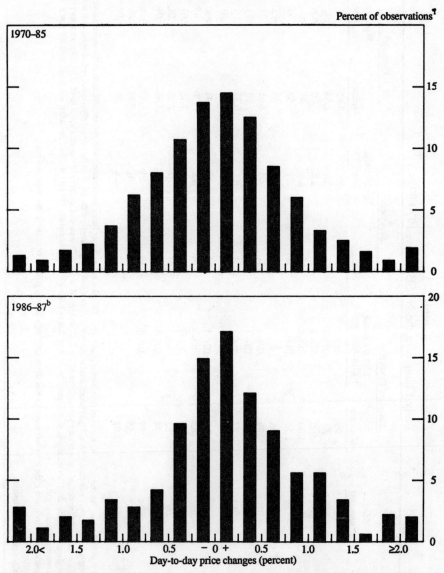

Percent of observations[1]

1970–85

15

10

5

0

20

1986–87[b]

15

10

5

0

2.0<   1.5   1.0   0.5   − 0 +   0.5   1.0   1.5   ≥2.0
Day-to-day price changes (percent)

[1] Each observation is the percentage change in the index from the close of trading on one day to the
close of trading on the next.

[2] Data through May 1987.

Source: Davis and White [1987], p. 2.

Exhibit 8-5
Daily Changes in the S&P 500 Index, by Decade

Decade	Mean (percent)	Standard Deviation		Skewness		Kurtosis[a]	
		Measure	Test of Equality with 1970s and 1980s[b]	Measure	Significance Test[c]	Measure	Significance Test
1950s	.052	.71	.01(−)	−.65	.01	9.35	.01
1960s	.019	.64	.01(−)	−.41	.01	10.16	.01
1970s	.011	.88	*	.26	.01	4.09	.01
1980s[d]	.056	.93	*	.16	n.s.	1.90	.01

[a] The measure is standardized so that the value for a normal distribution equals zero. Negative values imply flatter distributions with shorter tails, such as the uniform distribution. Positive values imply a distribution with thicker tails. Significance test indicates whether a value is significantly different from the normal distribution and, if so, at what level.

[b] The equality of the standard deviation of the indicated decades and that of the 1970s and 1980s was tested. If the difference was statistically significant, the level of significance is indicated; (+) indicates that the given decade's standard deviation is significantly larger than that in the 1970s and 1980s; (−) indicates that the standard deviation in the 1970s and 1980s was larger than the decade's. An asterisk signifies that the test is not meaningful.

[c] The level of significance is indicated if the skewness measure was statistically significantly positive or negative in a one-tailed test.

[d] Data through May 1987.

n.s. No statistically significant difference.

Source: Davis and White [1987], p. 10.

by decade rather than by year, and Exhibit 8-6 is a graph of the day-to-day percentage price changes. The last two decades have been characterized by greater relative frequency of large positive and negative price changes. This can be seen from the thicker tails of the two distributions and the smaller number of observations clustered at the mean. Thus, the increase in day-to-day percentage price changes apparently began back in the 1970s and should not be attributed to index-related trading. Davis and White believed this increased volatility was the result of "unexpected changes in fundamental macroeconomic conditions, such as business activity and interest rates" (p. 10). This is the same conclusion that was reached in the SEC study of the rapid market decline in September 1986 we will discuss later in this chapter.

Exhibit 8-6
Daily Percentage Changes in the S&P 500 Index, by Decade

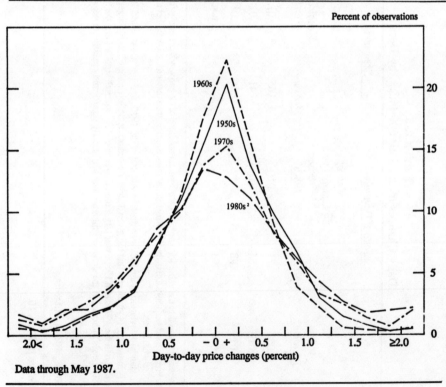

Percent of observations

Data through May 1987.

Source: Davis and White [1987], p. 9.

Davis and White also examined absolute percentage price changes for the NYSE Index for 1970-87. Exhibit 8-7 shows that the mean absolute percentage price change in 1986 was not out of line with historical experience, even though it was higher than in the two previous years. In 1987 it increased, slightly. Using daily data, Davis and White concluded that volatility increased in the 1970s and 1980s, but the increased volatility in the 1980s could not be attributed to index-related trading.

Exhibit 8-7
Daily Absolute Changes in the NYSE Index, 1970-87

Year	Mean (percent)	Standard Deviation
1970	.699	.68
1971	.470	.44
1972	.395	.30
1973	.785	.62
1974	1.050	.87
1975	.771	.57
1976	.590	.53
1977	.427	.36
1978	.614	.62
1979	.500	.47
1980	.817	.63
1981	.639	.52
1982	.800	.73
1983	.630	.55
1984	.562	.49
1985	.465	.38
1986	.616	.59
1987[*]	.770	.67

[*] Data through May.

Source: Davis and White [1987], p. 8

Davis and White tested the notion that, if index-related trading results in mispriced stocks, then daily percentage price changes should be more volatile than monthly percentage price changes. They found that changes in daily and monthly returns were similar, concluding that their tests did not find index-related trading increases volatility.

Stock-price volatility can also be examined by looking at the pattern of market turning points, price-change reversals. If index-related futures trading has increased volatility, one would expect the frequency of market turning points to increase: new information would be captured in stock prices with greater speed. More frequent price reversals could also be attributed, however, to more variable economic conditions. The average number of days between market turning points from 1973 to May 1987 is shown in Exhibit 8-8. The average number of days between market turning points in 1986 and 1987 does not appear much different from prior years.

Exhibit 8-8
Average Number of Days Between Market Turning Points, 1973-87[a]

Year	Days
1973	2.60
1974	2.29
1975	2.26
1976	1.96
1977	2.19
1978	2.17
1979	1.89
1980	2.00
1981	2.07
1982	2.04
1983	1.98
1984	2.12
1985	1.95
1986	1.92
1987[b]	2.39

[a] Based on turning points in the DJIA.
[b] Data through May.

Source: Davis and White [1987], p. 9.

Merrick [1987c] looked at daily data for nonexpiration months from 1982-86 to determine whether index arbitrage had increased stock-price volatility. He found a direct link between futures/cash mispricings and trading volume in the NYSE cash market, and during 1985-86, increased trading volume accompanied increased arbitrage activities. However, for the NYSE and the S&P 500 indexes, he failed to find evidence that arbitrage mispricing was related to any significant percentage of the variation in daily return volatility.

Harris [1987] tried to isolate the effects of index-related trading on stock-price volatility. He took advantage of two things: (1) not all stocks are included in an index, and (2) there is a predictable cross-sectional relationship that can be used to partially account for volatility by using regression analysis. The independent variables that can partially explain volatility (stock-price variance) include firm size, price level, beta, and frequency of trade. Because of these two things, one can test whether the stocks in an index have higher volatilities than would be predicted from a similar control sample of stocks not included in an index. Assuming that no other factors explain the results, the test is a test of the hypothesis that derivative instruments destabilize stock prices. The limitation of this approach, as Harris noted, is that it will not detect destablization if stock-index futures and options affect the volatility of stocks not included in the index.

Harris's study covered 1978 to 1986. He found that, beginning in 1985, the volatility of those stocks listed in the S&P 500 increased relative to that observed for a comparable list of stocks not included in the S&P 500. By 1986 the daily standard deviation of stock returns for stocks in the S&P 500 Index was, on average, 14 basis points higher than for stocks not included in the index. For longer time intervals (10 to 20 days), the average difference was about half that amount. The average difference was statistically significant; Harris noted, however, that if this excess volatility was evenly distributed over all days of the year, it was too small to be of much economic significance.

Finally, Edwards [1988a], using several measures of volatility, examined periods before and after the introduction of S&P 500 and Value Line futures. Two pre-futures periods were investigated. One included the entire pre-futures time period; the other excluded the period October 10, 1979, to September 30, 1982, because of the change in monetary policy established by the Federal Reserve in October 1979.[16] Exhibit 8-9 shows his results based on close-to-close daily prices. As can be seen, if the October 1, 1979–December 31, 1982, period is excluded, volatility for the S&P 500 was greater before the introduction of futures than after. No statistically significant difference between the two periods was found if the 1979-82 period was included. Nor was there any statistically significant difference in volatility before and after the introduction of the Value Line Index futures.

Edwards also reported the results for individual years, as shown in Exhibit 8-9. These findings indicate that, prior to late 1986, volatility was lower each year when compared with the pre-futures periods. From late 1986 through 1987 there was an increase in volatility. While Edwards noted that there is no clear explanation for the recent increased volatility observed in the stock market, he argued that it probably is not attributable to the introduction of stock-index futures trading:

> The most likely causes are the exceptional rise in stock prices during recent months, the sharp fall of the dollar against leading currencies and the persistence of significant economic problems, such as the federal deficit and trade imbalance. Higher volatility has also occurred in the bond market and in other markets not associated with stock index futures trading.
>
> The upswing in volatility should be interpreted in the context of the nearly five years of stock index futures trading that we have

experienced. During most of that time, volatility was lower than it was before futures trading began (p. 68).

Exhibit 8-9
Variances of Rates of Return: Close-to-Close Daily Prices
(number of observations in parentheses)

	S&P 500 (A)	Value Line (B)
Pre-Futures		
Entire Period	0.8559	0.5979
(A) 6/1/73–4/20/82	(2245)	
(B) 1/1/75–2/23/82		(1800)
Excluding 79–82	0.8311	0.5187
(A) 6/1/73–9/30/79	(1610)	
(B) 1/1/75–9/30/79		(1193)
Post-Futures		
Entire Period	0.7783	0.5212
(A) 4/21/82–12/31/86	(1189)	
(B) 2/24/82–12/31/86		(1229)
Excluding 79–82	0.7417[a]	0.5095
(A) 10/1/82–12/31/86	(1075)	
(B) 10/1/82–12/31/86		(1075)
1983	0.8394	0.6745
1984	0.8003	0.6618
1985	0.6376	0.5129
1986	0.9291	0.8361
1986[b]	0.8635	0.7165
1/1/87 to		
5/18/87	1.0664	0.8224

[a] Variance for the pre-futures period (excluding the time period 10/1/79 to 9/30/82) is greater than variance for the post-futures period at the 5 percent level of significance.
[b] Observations on expiration days of S&P 500 futures and September 11 and 12, 1986, are excluded.

Source: Adapted from Edwards [1988], p. 66.

Could these results be caused by other factors—in particular, unanticipated changes in economic factors that affect investor expectations for returns from their investments?

Officer [1973] found that the variability of stock returns on the NYSE from 1897 to 1969 was influenced by business fluctuations. More recently,

Chen, Roll, and Ross [1986] found that stock prices and nonequity prices are affected by macroeconomic variables such as unexpected changes in industrial production growth, inflation, risk premiums, the term structure of interest rates, and real per capita consumption. Davis and White [1987] adjusted the volatility of stock returns for the influences of the macroeconomic factors found by Chen et al. The results for the adjusted NYSE Index, shown in Exhibit 8-10, support the position that, after adjusting for the variability of macroeconomic factors, stock-price volatility was not significantly different in the 1980s than in the previous three decades.

Exhibit 8-10
Changes in the NYSE Index Adjusted for Macroeconomic Factors, by Decade[a]

Decade	Mean[b] (%)	Standard Deviation	
		Measure	Test of Equality with 1980s
1950s	.86	2.80	n.s.
1960s	.60	3.01	n.s.
1970s	.22	3.84	n.s.
1980s[c]	.72	3.28	—

[a] Percentage changes in the NYSE index are equal to the function of term structure, risk premium, real interest rate, change in inflation, change in industrial production, and change in oil prices. Monthly data.

[b] Regression residuals for each decade have been used to adjust the overall mean value for the dependent variable, and the mean can be interpreted as monthly percentage changes for each subperiod.

[c] Data through December 1986.

n.s. means no statistically significant difference. A dash signifies that the test is not meaningful.

Source: Davis and White [1987], p. 13.

Intraday Price Volatility

All this research has addressed interday volatility. What happens to volatility during a trading day? Birinyi and Hanson [1986] examined the absolute percentage price changes for an index over 15-minute intervals and the absolute percentage price changes for the spreads between high and low values for individual days from 1982 to mid-1986. They concluded that intraday volatility had not increased in the early 1980s.

Stoll and Whaley [1987b] examined intraday price volatility in an extreme case, the "triple witching day." Until late 1987, the third Friday in every quarter was called the triple witching day because the derivative contracts (stock-index futures, stock-index options, and options on individual stocks) all expired on that day. For the time period Stoll and Whaley studied, stock-index contracts (both futures and options) expired at the close of trading on the third Friday of the contract-expiration month. The last hour of trading on which all these contracts expired simultaneously was called the triple witching hour. Since June 1987, futures and futures-related contracts have expired at the opening rather than the close of the market on that Friday, and options on individual stocks and options on stock indexes have expired at the market close. [17]

Exhibit 8-11 shows Stoll and Whaley's results for the last hour of the expiration day for the period July 1, 1983, through December 27, 1985 (26 expiration days and 97 nonexpiration Fridays). They show the percentage rate of return by expiration date and index type, as well as the return for non-S&P 500 and 100 stocks. Stoll and Whaley found that, when both futures and options expired on the same day, the prices on the S&P 500 and S&P 100 were more volatile than on nonexpiration days. Price volatility was not statistically different from nonexpiration days for the S&P 500 Index when only the options on the stock index expired. It was significantly higher for the S&P 100. [18]

Any change in volatility would be expected for stocks in the S&P 500 Index as arbitrageurs unwind their positions. There should be no impact, however, on the volatility of stocks not listed in the S&P 500. This conclusion is supported by the results in Exhibit 8-11 showing that the volatility for the non-S&P 100 stocks did increase. One possible explanation is that many of the stocks not included in the S&P 100 are included in the S&P 500.

While these results suggest that an order imbalance existed during the triple witching hour, one could not know in advance whether this imbalance would produce a rise or fall in the market. In all the cases in Exhibit 8-11 where there was a significant change in volatility, there was a decline in the market, but the decline was statistically significant only when futures and options expired together.

If the observed price changes were abnormal, and caused by the unwinding of positions by arbitrageurs, then a reversion of the price to its normal level would be expected on the next day. When Stoll and Whaley calculated the average percentage price reversal over the first half hour on the day following expiration, they found large reversals for both the S&P 500 and S&P 100 when all futures and options expired together.

Using minute-by-minute data for the S&P 500, Stoll and Whaley analyzed each expiration day separately. They divided each trading day by type of expiration based on (1) S&P 500 Index futures and options expiring on Thursday, (2) S&P 500 futures and options expiring on Friday, and (3) S&P 100 Index options expiring on Friday. A daily standard deviation was calculated based on

Exhibit 8-11
Mean and Standard Deviation of the Percentage Rates of Return in the Last Hour of Expiration Day by Index Type and Expiration Type (July 1, 1983, through December 27, 1985)

	Expiration Type		
Index Type	*Futures and Options Expiration*	*Options–Only Expiration*	*Nonexpiration*
S&P 500 Index			
Mean	-0.352[b]	0.026	0.061
Std. deviation	0.641[b]	0.26	0.211
No. of obs.	10	16	97
S&P 100 Index			
Mean	-0.452[b]	-0.007	0.033
Std. deviation	0.699[b]	0.401[b]	0.252
No. of obs.	10	16	97
Non-S&P 500 Stocks[c]			
Mean	0.064	0.079	0.077
Std. deviation	0.230	0.211	0.264
No. of obs.	10	16	97
Non-S&P 100 Stocks[c]			
Mean	-0.168	0.059	0.079
Std. deviation	0.423[b]	0.202	0.160
No. of obs.	10	16	97

[a] The data base contains hourly price observations from closing the day before expiration to 10:30 a.m. on the first day after expiration.
[b] The null hypothesis of equal means (t-test) or equal standard deviation (F-test) is rejected at the 5 percent probability level.
[c] The rate of return for the value-weighted index of non-S&P 500 stocks, R_x, is computed from the following equation: $R_{NYSE} = kR_1 + (1 - k)R_x$, where R_{NYSE} is the rate of return on the NYSE composite index, R_x, is the rate of return on the S&P 500 or S&P 100 index, and k is the fraction of the NYSE index in the S&P 500 or S&P 100. For the S&P 500, k is 0.79; for the S&P 100, k is 0.34.

Source: Stoll and Whaley [1987b], p. 23.

the standard deviation for each 15-minute period over the last 3 hours of trading. These standard deviations were averaged for the type of expiration day. Only on Fridays when both the S&P 500 futures and options expired was price volatility higher than other days.

For each index-futures expiration day, Exhibit 8-12 shows the value of the S&P 500 for the following four intervals: (1) 30 minutes before the 4 p.m. close, (2) the 4 p.m. close, (3) the next day's open, and (4) 30 minutes after the next day's open. The same data are presented in Exhibit 8-13 for the S&P 100 Index option. The results indicate substantial percentage price changes in the last half hour of some of the more recent S&P 500 futures expirations.

Stoll and Whaley also investigated the magnitude of price effects by measuring the degree of reversal in prices on the morning after the expiration day. They found that the average magnitude of the price effect for the futures contract was about 0.4 percent of the closing index value at expiration. Considering that a price impact resulting from bid/ask spreads of roughly 0.25 percent would be expected, the average expiration-day price effect of 0.4 percent was not large: the additional cost of liquidity was 0.15 percent (0.40 percent minus 0.25 percent).

Price effects are frequently observed in large block transactions. For example, Kraus and Stoll [1972] found a price effect of 0.7 percent, which is much higher than that found by Stoll and Whaley for futures.[19]

So what does all this evidence show? A fair conclusion is that the introduction of stock-index options and futures and index-related strategies has not increased stock-price volatility except around expiration dates. Even then, the price effects are not as great as in block trading.

One Way Volatility—The Cascade Effect

The SEC Division of Market Regulation and other critics of dynamic-hedging strategies are concerned that this activity may have a cascading effect when stock prices decline. To understand their concern, consider what would happen if stock prices declined and dynamic hedging were used with stocks and a riskless asset. This strategy requires that stocks be sold, but if the amount of stocks sold is substantial, the result will be a further decline in stock prices. In turn, more stocks must be sold, leading to a further decline in stock prices. The same thing could happen, however, if stock-index futures were used to implement the portfolio-insurance program; in a market decline, portfolio insurers would sell stocks index futures (which is equivalent to selling stocks and investing the funds in a riskless asset).[20] This action, it is argued, would further lower prices, causing portfolio insurers to sell futures, and so on—a so-called cascading or spiraling effect.

Proponents of dynamic hedging argue that the cascade effect is unlikely: value-oriented investors would step in when stocks were priced below their value based on economic fundamentals.

Exhibit 8-I2

Rates of Return on the S&P 500 During the Last Minutes of S&P 500 Index Futures Contract-Expiration Day and the Opening Minutes of the Day after Expiration (April 21, 1982, through December 31,1985)

Exp. Date (t)	Day After (t+1)	Index Level				Rates of Return			
		Close −30 Minutes	Close	Open	Open +30 Minutes	Last 30 t	First 30 t+1	Last 15 t	First 15 t+1
820617	820618	107.77	107.60	107.60	107.37	-0.158	-0.214	-0.009	-0.139
820916	820917	123.85	123.77	123.76	123.27	-0.065	-0.396	0.081	-0.242
821215	821216	135.43	135.24	135.22	135.69	-0.140	0.348	0.044	0.259
830317	830318	149.54	149.59	149.59	149.86	0.033	0.180	0.027	0.074
830616	830617	169.31	169.14	169.11	168.94	-0.100	-0.101	-0.100	-0.089
830915	830916	164.92	164.38	164.39	164.50	-0.327	0.067	-0.231	0.024
831215	831216	162.25	161.66	161.66	161.96	-0.364	0.186	-0.210	0.136
840315	840316	157.84	157.41	157.46	160.10	-0.272	1.677	-0.241	0.845
840615	840618	149.57	149.03	149.02	148.81	-0.361	-0.141	-0.268	-0.268
840921	840924	166.40	165.67	165.67	165.99	-0.439	0.193	-0.072	0.109
841221	841224	164.65	165.53	165.50	165.98	0.534	0.290	0.133	0.290
850315	850318	177.97	176.53	176.53	177.03	-0.809	0.283	-0.563	0.317
850621	850624	188.02	189.61	189.50	187.93	0.846	-0.828	0.021	-0.649
850920	850923	182.96	182.05	182.12	184.60	-0.497	1.362	-0.328	1.065
851220	851223	210.60	210.94	210.94	210.00	0.161	-0.446	0.200	-0.465

Source: Stoll and Whaley [1987b], p. 25.

Exhibit 8-13

Rates of Return on the S&P 100 During the Last Minutes of S&P 100 Index Option Contract-Expiration Day and the Opening Minutes of the Day after Expiration (March 18, 1984, through December 31, 1985)

Exp. Date (t)	Day After (t + 1)	Index Level				Rates of Return			
		Close −30 Minutes	Close	Open	Open +30 Minutes	Last 30 t	First 30 t + 1	Last 15 t	First 15 t + 1
840419	840423	157.83	158.02	158.02	158.02	0.120	0.000	0.184	−0.057
840518	840521	155.30	155.77	155.80	155.99	0.303	0.122	0.225	0.019
840720	840723	149.15	149.55	149.55	147.91	0.268	−1.097	0.268	−0.822
840817	840820	164.11	164.14	164.14	163.90	0.018	−0.146	0.091	−0.085
841019	841022	167.60	167.96	167.96	167.46	0.215	−0.298	0.305	−0.363
841116	841119	164.51	164.10	164.17	164.23	−0.249	0.037	−0.110	0.085
850118	850121	171.00	171.32	171.31	171.74	0.187	0.251	0.216	0.152
850215	850219	181.63	181.60	181.61	181.10	−0.017	−0.281	0.177	−0.270
850419	850422	180.83	181.11	181.11	180.98	0.155	−0.072	0.094	0.050
850517	850520	187.90	187.42	187.50	189.33	−0.255	0.976	−0.181	0.779
850719	850722	194.65	195.13	195.13	194.48	0.247	−0.333	0.221	−0.323
850816	850819	186.76	186.12	186.14	186.46	−0.343	0.172	−0.118	0.134
851018	851021	187.19	187.04	186.98	187.08	−0.080	0.053	0.016	0.021
851115	851118	198.01	198.11	198.11	198.16	0.051	0.025	0.056	−0.056

Source: Stoll and Whaley [1987b], p. 25.

Evidence from Recent Market Breaks

September 11-12, 1986

The DJIA dropped 86.61 points (a 4.61 percent decline) on September 11, 1986. The next day it dropped by another 34.17 points (1.91 percent). The Division of Market Regulation of the SEC [1987] investigated this two-day decline in stock prices to determine the role index-related strategies may have played. On these two days, index arbitrage required the sale of the underlying index; futures were cheap relative to cash. These sales took the form of program trades. There were 244 program trades on these two days, carried out by 7 brokerage firms, of which 208 (84 percent) were index-arbitrage trades. The index-arbitrage trades accounted for about 18 percent of trading volume for the two days and represented about 40 percent of the trading volume of the 7 firms involved. Thus a substantial amount of the trading volume in the market was not index related.

However, the 244 program trades may have been so large that they had a significant impact on the market; that is, they were not easily accommodated within the prevailing market mechanisms. The SEC study found that, of the 244 program trades, 131 involved the S&P 500 Index and tended to be the larger program trades. While one program trade exceeded $100 million, the average size was $24 million. The SEC study concluded that the size of the program trades was such that they should have been easily handled by the computerized order-transmission system of the NYSE:

> The magnitude of the September decline was a result of changes in investors' perception of fundamental economic conditions, rather than artificial forces arising from index-related strategies.
>
> . . . index-related futures trading was instrumental in the rapid transmission of these changed investor perceptions to individual stock prices, and may have condensed the time period in which the decline occurred.

Support for the view that the market decline was a result of changes in fundamental factors rather than program trading was thus provided by the SEC. They investigated the price movements on the two days for both the stocks that were not included in the index underlying a futures contract and in the index itself. They found that non-index stocks decreased in price by an amount equivalent to those stocks in the index, thus confirming the fundamental-factors view of the market decline.

The SEC study also examined the cascade effect resulting from the implementation of portfolio-insurance strategies and potential manipulation using stock-index futures. The SEC found neither present on September 11 and 12. Moreover, with respect to the cascade effect, the SEC study concluded that economic forces were sufficient to counteract it. As for potential manipulation, the SEC conclusion was that manipulation was more costly and risky here than in other potential manipulation targets.

> The SEC study exonerated index-related strategies, saying, analysis of this particular market decline does not provide an independent basis to conclude that radical regulatory or structural changes are necessary at this time. . . . However, close monitoring should be maintained.

Black Monday: October 19, 1987

On Monday, October 19, 1987, known as Black Monday, the DJIA declined by 508 points, the largest single-day change in history. This was, however, only the climax to changes that had occurred in previous weeks. The DJIA had fallen more than 90 points on each of three days prior to Black Monday: Tuesday, October 6, Wednesday, October 14, and Friday, October 16. The decline was also not unique to the United States stock market. Every major stock market in the world suffered a decline in value based in local currency.

In response to the crash, six studies were commissioned in the United States to assess its causes and make recommendations as to how to reduce the likelihood of another crash. Studies were commissioned by (1) President Reagan (the Presidential Task Force on Market Mechanisms), (2) the General Accounting Office, (3) the SEC, (4) the NYSE, (5) the Chicago Mercantile Exchange, and (6) the Commodity Futures Exchange.

According to the popular press and many market observers, no study was needed. The culprits were well known—market participants who used index-related strategies. For example, the *Wall Street Journal* the day following the crash reported, "In a nightmarish fulfillment of some traders' and academicians' worst fears, the five year old index futures for the first time plunged into a panicky, unlimited free-fall, fostering a sense of crisis throughout U.S. capital markets" (McMurray and Rose [1987], p. 28). The evidence that has accumulated since then, however, does not confirm that index-related trading was the culprit.

Index-Related Trading and the Crash Program trading was severely limited on October 19 and the morning of October 20 because the NYSE DOT system was suspended and executing trades was made very difficult.[22] DOT-system suspension gave the impression that program trading had caused the chaotic market, but the actual motivation for DOT suspension was the fear that the specialist system could not execute program trades. The fact is that index-arbitrage traders could not operate in the chaotic market environment even before the suspension of the DOT system.

Index arbitrageurs could not execute cash-market transactions at the outset on October 19 because most of the major issues in the S&P 500 did not open for trading until 11 a.m. at the earliest. Executing the program trades necessary to implement an index-arbitrage strategy in the futures market was difficult because prices were too volatile. Later in the day, the execution of an index-arbitrage strategy became even more difficult. Delays in reporting trades in the cash market meant that identifying profitable arbitrage opportunities between the cash and futures market was impossible. Delays in executing orders in the cash market, particularly after the suspension of the DOT system, meant that, even if a profitable arbitrage opportunity could have been identified, there was no assurance that it could have been executed at the quoted price. Index arbitrage was not the culprit behind the October 19 decline. Did the stock-index futures market play a major role in the crash?

By looking at trading-volume statistics, Hill [1988] provided evidence on the minor role that the stock-index futures market played on October 19 and 20. On Monday, S&P 500 futures trading volume was 162,022 contracts, approximately 1.5 times the average daily number of contracts traded in the previous week. However, trading volume on the NYSE was 2.7 times greater than the average daily number of shares traded in the previous week (604 million versus 224 million shares). Based on normal levels of S&P 500 futures trading in relation to NYSE stock trading, approximately 250,000 to 300,000 contracts should have been traded, rather than the below normal 162,022 that were. This low level of futures trading continued on Tuesday, with NYSE trading remaining at 600 million shares, and futures trading volume down to 126,462 contracts.

Hill suggested other reasons, in addition to futures trading volume, why portfolio insurers should not be singled out as the major culprits of the stock market fall:

> Some further evidence that the insurers do not deserve the major part of the blame comes from other equity markets worldwide in which this strategy [portfolio insurance] is not a major factor. Comparable declines in Australia, Japan, and London cannot be explained by portfolio insurance or futures-related arbitrage. Futures markets in these countries are small compared to the U.S. and program trading and portfolio insurance are not widely used. Interestingly, in these markets the story was very similar to the U.S. in terms of strains on the market mechanisms. . . .

> Finally, if the selling was the result of a snowball effect from portfolio insurance and stock index arbitrage, why did the U.S. market not recover a large part of the decline as portfolio managers motivated by value analysis saw a terrific opportunity created by "informationless" traders? (p. 35)

Roll [1989] provided additional evidence that computer-directed trading may have mitigated the the crash. To do this, he looked at the decline for the stock market in 23 countries. For five of the countries (Canada, France, Japan, the United Kingdom, and the United States), computer-directed trading was prevalent; for the other 18 countries, it was not. In terms of local currency, the average decline for the 18 countries where computer-directed trading was not widespread was 27.89 percent; for the five countries where it was prevalent, the decline was less (21.25 percent).

It is fair to conclude on the basis of the evidence that the major reason for the rapid decline in stock prices was not institutional trading based on "mechanical, price-insensitive selling," as the Report of the Presidential Task Force on Market Mechanisms (commonly referred to as the Brady Report) contended.

Explanations for Black Monday other than that attributed to stock-index futures and options include: (1) presence or absence of institutional arrangements, (2) overvaluation of stock prices prior to the crash, and (3) overreaction to economic news. A study by several well-respected university-affiliated researchers sponsored by the Mid-America Institute (MAI) for Public Policy Research[23] helps eliminate some misconceptions about the causes. The MAI task force study also critically evaluated some of the recommendations made by the six Black Monday-commissioned studies. Such an evaluation is needed because, as noted by Meltzer [1989], one of the contributors to the MAI-sponsored study,

> A striking but generally disregarded feature of the recommendations made is that, often, no claim is made and no evidence offered that the events of October would have been different if the recommended changes had been in effect. Indeed, in some reports, there is little relation between the problems described and some of the solutions proposed. (p. 16)

Institutional Arrangements The six commissioned studies focused on institutional characteristics of the market such as (1) the presence of a specialist, (2) the presence of computer-directed trading, (3) the nature of price limits, (4) continuous versus single auctions, (5) the existence of derivative instruments (futures and options), and (6) the level of margin requirements.

Roll [1989] looked at the institutional arrangements in 23 countries with major stock markets. He estimated a regression relating the change in the decline in a country's stock market to the presence or absence of 10 institutional arrangements. His regression results do not provide support for the position that institutional arrangements can be used to explain the decline in stock prices in the 23 stock markets studied.

Overvaluation of Stock Prices prior to Black Monday Others suggested that the decline in stock prices in the United States was a result of a permanent adjustment to changes in fundamental values. Fama [1989] cited two pieces of evidence to support this position: the level of the S&P 500 dividend/price ratio and the default spread (as measured by the difference between yields on A/Baa bonds and Aaa bonds).

There is additional support for this explanation for the cause of the crash. As the Brady Report and Bernstein and Bernstein [1988] documented, evidence is strong that the market was overvalued and that the bull market was coming to an end. As Bernstein and Bernstein stated,

> . . . careful studies of stock selection techniques published by Goldman Sachs & Company and Zachs Investment Research during the summer of 1987 demonstrated that, for at least a year, sheer price momentum had been the only functioning model for selected stocks: The stocks that moved were the stocks that were moving. Valuation parameters of all kinds had been left far behind in the dust, a common complaint among managers all during 1987. (p. 175)

Overreaction to Economic News Some market observers suggested that the price decline resulted from an overreaction to some economic news. Candidates for such economic news include concern about the negative impact of the merchandise trade news, additional increases in interest rates, proposed tax legislation, and news over the October 16 weekend about the further decline in the value of the dollar expressed by Treasury Secretary Baker. However, because the decline was not temporary, this conclusion does not seem reasonable.

Mechanical Breakdown Finally, an analysis by Bernstein and Bernstein [1988] leads us to the culprit. Bernstein and Bernstein attributed the dramatic drop in stock prices to the inability of the existing market structure to handle the widespread selling of shares by great numbers of small investors. That is, it was not the dollar amount of the transactions that the system could not handle, but the large number of transactions. It appears that a major problem was that the computers were simply overloaded.

Conclusion

Even though almost half a century has passed since the October 29, 1929, market crash, no consensus has been reached as to the reason for that decline. Not surprisingly, therefore, no real consensus has been reached about the causes for Black Monday, October 19, 1987.

Were stock index futures a cause? If one accepts the hypothesis that the price decline was caused by overvaluation of stock prices, would financial markets have been better served if the process had taken longer to move to the new equilibrium price? According to Fama [1989], "If there are bubbles, economic efficiency is best served by letting them burst rather than leak" (p. 77). Were stock-index futures the pin that burst the bubble? Evidence about the efficiency and the speed with which prices are transmitted between the cash and futures markets suggests they were the mechanism, not the culprit.

CHAPTER 8

Notes

1. *Program Trading* (New York: Morgan Stanley, October 8, 1987).

2. If the futures market is the investors' market of choice, it will serve as the market in which prices are set or discovered; that is, it will be the market from which investors send their collective message about how any new information is expected to affect the cash market.

3. Testimony before the Subcommittee on Telecommunications and Finance, Committee on Energy and Commerce, U.S. House of Representatives, July 23, 1987, p. 1.

4. These other factors include (1) interim cash flows resulting from variation margin or dividend payments, (2) uncertainty about the timing and amount of dividends, (3) inability to use the proceeds from short selling, (4) the up-tick rule, and (5) risk associated with tracking the index with a sample of stocks.

5. A market-on-close order is a market order executed on the day it is entered at the official closing of the market.

6. See the works by Sharpe [1964] and Lintner [1965].

7. *Pension and Investment Age,* January 26, 1987, p. 16.

8. Institutional investors often have used the S&P 500 Index as a proxy.

9. For a more detailed explanation of this strategy, see Rubinstein and Leland [1981] and Leland [1989].

10. Hill, Jain, and Wood [1988] and Zhu and Kavee [1988] reported simulation results for dynamic-hedging strategies.

11. The allocation of the portfolio's funds between stocks and the riskless asset depends on (1) the difference between the current market value of the portfolio and the minimum value, or floor, established for the strategy and (2) the length of the portfolio-insurance program.

12. Stein [1984] concluded that a substantial number of irrational investors would be required to destabilize the cash markets.

13. Rothschild and Stigliz [1970] showed that the standard deviation does not capture all the information about the relative risk of investing in securities.

14. Skewness measures how symmetric the distribution is around the mean. For example, a negatively skewed distribution for the daily price change indicates that there were more large losses than large gains. A positively skewed distribution suggests that there were more large gains than large losses. If the distribution was not skewed, then the relative frequency of large positive and negative payoffs was equal.

15. Kurtosis measures how extreme values (i.e., large gains and large losses) affect the peakedness of the distribution. The measure of kurtosis used by Davis and White was standardized to the normal distribution. Positive kurtosis in this case means that the distribution had a sharper peak than the normal curve and more observations in the tails

(i.e., extreme values). Negative kurtosis means that the distribution was flatter than the normal distribution.

16. Prior to October 1979, the operating target of the Federal Reserve was to smooth short-term interest rates. After October 1979, control of the money supply was paramount.

17. Prior to June 1987, index arbitrageurs typically unwound their positions in the stock market during the triple witching hour. The impact on prices and volatility depended on whether there was an imbalance of orders between arbitrageurs who were long and those who were short the stock. Consider what might happen on the expiration date when the stock portfolio in an index arbitrage must be liquidated (in the case of a long-stock position) and stocks purchased (in the case of a short position). There will certainly be an increase in orders, but the effect on prices will depend on the composition of the orders: if they are balanced between arbitrageurs who have created long and short positions, there should be no significant price movement; if not, there should be a significant change in prices. Therefore, stock-price volatility could increase on futures' contracts expiration dates.

18. These findings provide evidence of a change in June 1987 of triple witching conditions: futures contracts and options on the futures contracts expired at the opening of the market on Friday, while the stock index options expired at the close.

19. Similar findings for large block transactions were reported by Holthausen, Leftwich, and Mayers [1985].

20. Conversely, when stock prices rise, stocks or stock-index futures would be purchased (which is equivalent to buying stocks and reducing the portfolio's allocation to a riskless asset).

21. The system was reinstated three weeks later.

22. The MAI is an organization created to generate and disseminate original academic research on matters related to economic policy issues. The organization was created in 1984.

CHAPTER 8

References

Bernstein, Peter L., and Bernstein, Barbara S. "Where the Postcrash Studies Went Wrong." *Institutional Investor,* April 1988.

Birinyi, Laszlo, Jr., and Hanson, H. Nicholas. *Market Volatility: Perceptions and Reality.* Salomon Brothers, December 1985.

_____. *Market Volatility: An Updated Study.* Salomon Brothers, July 1986.

Byrne, Thomas. "Program Trading—A Trader's Perspective." *Commodities Law Letter,* 1986.

Chen, Nai-Fu; Roll, Richard; and Ross, Stephen. "Economic Forces and the Stock Market." *Journal of Business,* July 1986, pp. 383-403.

Dann, Larry Y.; Mayers, David, and Raab, Robert J., Jr. "Trading Rules, Large Blocks and the Speed of Price Adjustment." *Journal of Financial Economics,* January 1977, pp. 3-22.

Davis, Carolyn D., and White, Alice P. *Stock Market Volatility.* Staff Study, Board of Governors of the Federal Reserve System, August 1987.

Edwards, Franklin R. "Does Futures Trading Increase Stock Price Volatility?" *Financial Analysts Journal,* January-February 1988a, pp. 63-69.

_____. "Futures Trading and Cash Market Volatility: Stock Index and Interest Rate Futures." *The Journal of Futures Markets,* August 1988b, pp. 421-39.

Fama, Eugene F. "Perspectives on October 1987 or What Did We Learn from the Crash?" *Black Monday and the Future of Financial Markets.* Homewood, IL: Dow Jones-Irwin, 1989.

Harris, Lawrence. "S&P 500 Futures and Cash Stock Price Volatility." Unpublished paper, October 1987.

Hill, Joanne M. *Program Trading, Portfolio Insurance, and the Stock Market Crash: Concepts, Applications and an Assessment.* Kidder, Peabody, January 1988.

_____; Jain, Anschuman; and Wood, Robert A., Jr. "Insurance: Volatility Risk and Futures Mispricing." *Journal of Portfolio Management,* Winter 1988, pp. 23-29.

Holthausen, Robert W.; Leftwich, Richard W.; and Mayers, David. "Block Trades of Securities and the Price Pressure Hypothesis." Working paper, Graduate School of Business, University of Chicago, October 1985.

Kawaller, Ira G.; Koch, Paul D.; and Koch, Timothy W. "The Temporal Price Relationship between S&P 500 Futures and the S&P 500 Index." *Journal of Finance,* December 1987, pp. 1309-29.

Kraus, Alan, and Stoll, Hans. "Price Impacts of Block Trading on the New York Stock Exchange." *Journal of Finance,* June 1972, pp. 569-88.

Leland, Hayne. "Portfolio Insurance." Chapter 12 in Frank J. Fabozzi and Gregory M. Kipnis (eds.). *The Handbook of Stock Index Futures and Options.* Homewood, IL: Dow Jones-Irwin, 1989.

Lintner, John. "Security Prices, Risk and Maximal Gains from Diversification." *Journal of Finance*, December 1965, pp. 587-616.

Markowitz, Harry M. "Portfolio Selection." *Journal of Finance*, March 1952, pp. 77-91.

McMurray, Scott, and Rose, Robert L. "Chicago's 'Shadow Markets' Led Free Fall in a Plunge that Began Right at Opening." *Wall Street Journal*, October 20, 1987.

Meltzer, Alan H. "Overview." *Black Monday and the Future of Financial Markets*. Homewood, IL: Dow Jones-Irwin, 1989.

Merrick, John J., Jr. "Fact and Fantasy about Stock Index Futures Program Trading." *Business Review: Federal Reserve Bank of Philadelphia*, September/October 1987a, pp. 13-25.

———. "Price Discovery in the Stock Market." Federal Reserve Bank of Philadelphia Working Paper No. 87-4, March 1987b.

———. "Volume Determination in Stock and Stock Index Futures Markets: An Analysis of Volume and Volatility Effects." *Journal of Futures Markets*, October 1987c, pp. 483-96.

Officer, R. "The Variability of the Market Factor of the New York Stock Exchange." *Journal of Business*, July 1973, pp. 434-53.

Roll, Richard W. "The International Crash of October 1987." *Black Monday and the Future of Financial Markets*. Homewood, IL: Dow Jones-Irwin, 1989.

Rothschild, Michael, and Stigliz, Joseph E. "Increasing Risk: I.A. Definition." *Journal of Economic Theory*, September 1970, pp. 225-43.

Rubinstein, Mark, and Leland, Hayne. "Replicating Options with Positions in Stock and Cash." *Financial Analysts Journal*, July-August 1981, pp. 63-79.

Securities and Exchange Commission, Division of Market Regulation. "The Role of Index-Related Trading in the Market Decline on September 11 and 12, 1986." March 1987.

Sharpe, William F. "Capital Asset Prices: A Theory of Market Equilibrium under Conditions of Risk." *Journal of Finance*, September 1964, pp. 425-42.

Stein, Jerome. "Real Effects of Futures Speculation: Rational Expectations and Diverse Predictions." Unpublished working paper No. 88, Center for the Study of Futures Markets, Columbia University, 1984.

Stoll, Hans R., and Whaley, Robert E. "The Dynamics of Stock Index and Stock Index Futures Prices." Unpublished paper, October 16, 1987a.

———. "Expiration Day Effects of Index Options and Futures." *Financial Analysts Journal*, March-April 1987b, pp. 16-28.

———. "Volatility and Futures: Message versus Messenger." *Journal of Portfolio Management*, Winter 1988, pp. 20-22.

Zhu, Yu, and Kavee, Robert C. "Performances of Portfolio Insurance Strategies." *Journal of Portfolio Management*, Spring 1988, pp. 48-54.

CHAPTER 9

Future Strategies for Profit

You *can* profit in the stock market. A prescient investor would have made over 15 percent per year if that investor had bought five now recognizable companies' shares at the time they were initially issued and held them until January 31, 1989 (see Exhibit 9-1). These returns do not even take into account any dividends these companies paid. These are much better returns than could have been made on average stock investments. So despite our worst fears, profits are possible from equity investing. However, as we have seen, to profit is not easy, and there are more strategies that promise profits than there are profitable strategies.

Since our lucky-5 strategy clearly is one of stock selection, let's look at a strategy that relied less on value-based prescience and more on technical analysis or cycle-spotting skill. What would have been the return if an investor had bought a randomly chosen group of 35 stocks at the low on October 20, 1987 (the day following Black Monday) and held them until the close on January 31, 1989? The portfolio's average return would have been 38.3 percent, as shown in Exhibit 9-2. If the investor was not lucky or skilled enough to hit the October 20, 1987 low, and bought at the close, the return for the lucky 35 would still have been 23 percent.

Two economists, Grossman and Stiglitz [1980] describe why they believe positive returns like these (returns above all costs including risks) can be earned in the highly competitive stock market:

> If competitive equilibrium is defined as a situation in which prices are such that all arbitrage profits are eliminated, is it possible that a competitive economy will always be in equilibrium? Clearly not, for then those who arbitrage make no (private) return from their (privately) costly activity. Hence the assumptions that all markets, including that for information, are always in equilibrium and always perfectly arbitraged are inconsistent when arbitrage is costly. (p. 393)

Disequilibrium, inefficiencies, or anomolies create pockets of profitable

Exhibit 9-1
Value on January 31, 1989, of Six
Limited Public Offerings

	Year of Issue	Price at Issue	1/31/89 Close	Portfolio Holdings[a]	Value of One Share Today	Compound Annual Return[b]
IBM[c]	1917	$46.00	$128.75	2,967	$382,001.25	13.35%
American Express[d]	1965	60.00	30.25	36	1,089.00	12.83
Apple Computer	1981	22.00	37.38	2	74.75	16.52
Morgan Stanley	1986	56.50	89.00	1	89.00	16.35
J.P. Industries	1983	10.00	13.25	2	26.50	17.64

[a]Recognizes stock splits and stock dividends.
[b]Not including dividend payments.
[c]From Moody's Manuals, 1988, and the companies.
[d]American Express was incorporated in 1965; prior to that, it was organized in the form of a joint stock association, a hybrid between a corporation and a partnership.

opportunity. The result of academic research into market inefficiencies has often been the basis on which new and potentially profitable strategies have been developed. However, as we have seen throughout this book, research must be treated with care, and the costs of implementing a strategy based on the research, must be considered fully:

> Once an investor becomes aware of a study, he must decide whether the reported historical relations will apply in the future. On the expected duration of this decision, I need only mention that six years have passed since publication of the first study on the "small-firm effect," and we in academic finance have yet to agree on whether it even exists. Resolving this issue is presumably no easier a task for investors. Beyond this decision, the investor must also determine whether the potential gains to him are sufficient to warrant the cost of implementing the strategy. Included in the cost are the time and expense required to build the model and create the data base necessary to support the strategy. Moreover, professional money managers may have to expend further time and resources to market the strategy to clients and to satisfy prudence requirements before implementation. If profitable implementation requires regulatory and business practices changes or the creation of either new markets or new channels of intermediation, then the delay between announcement of an anomaly and its elimination by corrective action in the market place can, indeed, be a long one. (Merton [1987], p. 486.)

Exhibit 9-2

Gains in 35 Randomly Chosen Stocks

October 20, 1987–January 31, 1980

	Buy at Low on 10/20/87		Buy at Close on 10/20/87	
	Price Changes	Total Returns	Price Changes	Total Returns
Abbott Labs	17.5%	20.2%	5.0%	7.3%
Air Products	25.9	28.7	23.8	26.6
American Brands	45.2	47.0	34.6	36.3
American Express	32.8	36.1	18.8	21.7
AT&T	25.0	29.6	12.7	16.8
Anheuser Busch	23.4	25.7	4.9	6.8
Atlantic Richfield	34.2	40.3	12.7	17.8
Bowater	6.5	9.9	0.7	3.9
Bristol Myers	46.8	51.8	19.0	23.0
Castle & Cooke	89.3	89.3	55.1	55.1
Compaq Computer	57.2	57.2	29.6	29.6
Cray Research	23.9	23.9	–4.3	–4.3
Delta Airlines	39.1	42.0	28.1	30.8
Dow Chemical	38.3	42.4	27.4	31.1
Dupont	25.6	23.0	15.5	19.6
General Electric	15.5	19.5	4.7	8.3
General Motors	58.7	67.0	39.8	47.1
Genuine Parts Co.	29.2	32.6	13.3	16.3
Helene Curtis	43.7	44.5	42.7	43.5
Hewlett Packard	32.4	33.1	13.1	13.6
IBM	13.3	17.0	9.5	12.1
International Paper	64.4	68.3	41.4	44.8
JWP Inc.	70.2	70.2	49.6	49.6
K Mart Inc.	54.7	59.6	30.6	34.8
Eli Lilly	43.7	47.1	28.4	31.4
McDonald's Corp.	46.8	48.3	23.0	24.2
Pepsico	40.6	43.3	20.8	23.1
Pitney Bowes	42.9	45.5	35.4	37.9
Procter & Gamble	32.5	36.4	17.1	20.5
Quaker Oats	53.9	56.8	33.8	36.3
Rubbermaid	32.9	34.6	18.5	20.1
Stanley Works	27.5	31.3	18.0	21.5
Toys R Us	55.4	55.4	38.4	38.4
Walgreen	32.4	34.5	27.1	29.1
Xerox	20.4	25.9	11.0	16.1
S&P 400 Industrials	28.8		19.9	
S&P 500 Composite	27.2		18.6	
Dow Jones Industrial Average	32.7		19.9	
Average for 35 companies	38.3		22.9	

As we have seen throughout this book, careful consideration of research results has led to some opportunities for profit. But the research we have discussed is already available for the diligent reader of academic journals. The aggressive profit-seeker will want to know what is on the horizon. What are the new ideas, and are there profits to be made?

Risk and Risk Premia Have Cycles

One thing researchers have recently begun to look at is the very nature of risk.[1] For example, French, Schwert, and Stambaugh [1987] have hypothesized that investors' perceptions of risk change over time. When perceived risk increases, required rates of return must rise to compensate investors. Using a statistical technique that simultaneously estimated risk and return,[2] these researchers found that risk premia did indeed vary (Exhibit 9-3) and that investors could expect high returns following periods of high risk. The important word is *following*.

Exhibit 9-3
Predicted Percentage Monthly Risk Premium to the S&P's
Composite Portfolio from the Daily GARCH-in-Mean
Model for the Standard Deviation,* 1928-84

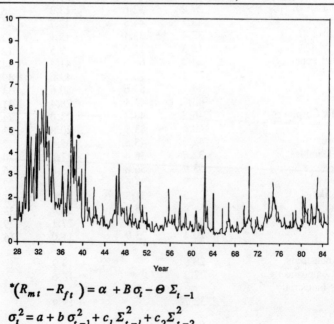

$$^*(R_{mt} - R_{ft}) = \alpha + B\sigma_t - \Theta \Sigma_{t-1}$$

$$\sigma_t^2 = a + b\,\sigma_{t-1}^2 + c_1 \Sigma_{t-1}^2 + c_2 \Sigma_{t-2}^2$$

Source: French, Schwert, and Stambaugh [1987], p. 6.

Others have found further interesting results when examining risk over time. For instance, Arnott [1987] found that both stocks and bonds showed significant correlation between subsequent returns and the preceding month's volatility. Ferson, Kandel, and Stambaugh [1987] concluded that both expected premiums for risk and market betas shift.[3] In looking at small-stock returns, Conrad and Kaul [1988] discovered that up to 26 percent of these stocks' weekly variation in realized returns was predictable from the previous week's realized risk premium.[4] There appears to be a relationship between risk, return, and time, which some have characterized by saying returns are sticky.

Looking specifically at small stocks and risk cycles from 1926 to 1985 and for two subperiods, 1926-53 and 1954-85, Brock by himself [1988] and with Dechert and Scheinkman [1986, 1987] found that randomness existed among the returns of large firms during the latter time period but that small firms' returns exhibited more nonrandomness (pattern), particularly in the later period. This decline in nonrandomness throughout the period was confirmed for somewhat different periods by LeBaron [1987]. Whatever the exact relationships are, we do know that recent research is finding increasing evidence of a relationship between short-term changes in risk and subsequent levels of return.[5]

The implications of this research are important for long-term investors; however, some caution is appropriate. As seen in Exhibit 9-4, returns have a tendency to be mean reverting (a variance ratio less than 1.0); that is, risk over the longer term is less than short-run risk, and this tendency seems to be more pronounced for smaller stocks, as indicated by the lower coefficients for the equal-weighted portfolios. On the other hand, the magnitude of the effect has diminished since 1940.[6]

Why is there a tendency for risk to diminish as the horizon gets longer? Fama and French [1987b] and Poterba and Summers [1988] found a predictable component to the three-to-five-year stock-return variance. Fama and French [1987a] found that dividends may be one culprit; that is, simple regressions that included dividend yield explained more than 25 percent of the variances of two-to-four year returns.

Researchers have just begun to delve into the mysteries of risk and time. There appears to be a relationship, but we are not sure why and whether the relationship is changing over time and is different for different stocks. What has been even less investigated, and is ripe for research, is the relationship between risk, time, and economic cycles.[7]

Nonlinear Patterns and Chaos[8]

After October 19, 1987, articles began to appear in the finance literature on chaos theory of stock-price behavior. Such articles often have appeared after major market changes. We can find immediate use of such an abstract and

Exhibit 9-4
Variance Ratios for U.S. Monthly Data, 1926-85

Data Series	Annual-Return Standard Deviation	1 Month	24 Months	36 Months	48 Months	60 Months	72 Months	84 Months	96 Months
Value-weighted real returns	20.6%	0.797 (0.150)	0.973 (0.108)	0.873 (0.177)	0.747 (0.232)	0.667 (0.278)	0.610 (0.320)	0.565 (0.358)	0.575 (0.394)
Value-weighted excess returns	20.7	0.764 (0.150)	1.036 (0.108)	0.989 (0.177)	0.917 (0.232)	0.855 (0.278)	0.781 (0.320)	0.689 (0.358)	0.677 (0.394)
Equal-weighted real returns	29.6	0.809 (0.150)	0.963 (0.108)	0.835 (0.177)	0.745 (0.232)	0.642 (0.278)	0.522 (0.320)	0.400 (0.358)	0.353 (0.394)
Equal-weighted excess returns	29.6	0.785 (0.150)	1.010 (0.108)	0.925 (0.177)	0.878 (0.232)	0.786 (0.278)	0.649 (0.320)	0.487 (0.358)	0.425 (0.394)

Notes: Calculations are based on the monthly returns for the value-weighted and equal-weighted New York Stock Exchange portfolios, as reported in the CRSP monthly returns file. Values in parentheses are Monte Carlo estimates of the standard deviations of the variance ratio, based on 25,000 replications under the null hypothesis of serially independent returns. Each variance ratio is corrected for small-sample bias and has a mean of 1.0 under the null hypothesis of no serial correlation.

Source: Poterba and Summers [1988], p. 37.

embryonic topic as chaos theory in finance by looking no further than the Elliott wave theory described in Chapter 2. Elliott wave theory is based on fractal structure analysis: the analysis of irregular patterns that can be superimposed within smaller and smaller areas. The up-5/down-3 Elliott structure is exactly this—a fractal structure—and fractal structures have been known for some time to abound in chaotic systems.

What is new is finance academics' interest in nonlinear systems and the realization that complex patterns can exist. This complexity creates the possibility that several different and simultaneous patterns (correlations) can exist and also increases the complexity of the problem of identifying and exploiting patterns in stock-price behavior.[9]

Recent evidence suggests that nonlinear patterns do exist in stock market returns. Scheinkman and LeBaron [1986] used a method that points toward the maximum number of patterns (correlation dimensions) and concluded that there is "no doubt that past weekly returns help predict future ones even though they are uncorrelated." (p. 10) This conclusion casts serious doubt on the randomness of stock prices, one of the basic ideas long held as true by academics.[10] It also points to a direction for research into the nature of risk over time.

This research is exciting but extremely new. Not only are techniques for analyzing nonlinearities in their infancy, but researchers are drawing conclusions by using very few data; data for stock returns are much fewer than the tens of thousands of observations on the natural science problems where these sorts of research techniques have been used more extensively.[11]

One practical way to capture some of the complex patterns and nonlinear effects is to add additional variables to a model. The Jacobs and Levy [1988] study described in Chapter 5 is an example of such a multiple-variable analysis. They used 25 variables, including many we have discussed in other parts of this book: price/earnings ratios, size, earnings surprises, and time of the year. Their results are repeated here in Exhibit 9-5 so that you may recall the relationships across time (autocorrelations) they found for low-P/E and high-relative-strength strategies.[12]

Will strategies like those found by Jacobs and Levy produce profits in the future? To answer this question, Speidell [1988] constructed a series of high- and low-value portfolios for 12 strategies and graphed their relative performance over time. Exhibit 9-6 shows his results: the portfolio returns of the low-price/book strategy seem to have declined, while high-quality and high-market-capitalization portfolios or strategies seemed to be coming back into favor.

Obviously, betting on factor strategies entails risk. Yet, because some of these factor strategies represent particular types of risk that will persist in the future, they can be profitable. The problem with adding variables in this way is that they may cease to be effective. Since we do not really understand the underlying process or factor for which these variables proxy, we cannot predict

Exhibit 9-5
Each Strategy's Monthly Profit
(1978–86)

Anomaly	Overall Return		January/Non-January Return				
	Monthly Average	t-Statistic	Average January	t-Statistic	Average Non-Jan.	t-Statistic	t-Statistic of Difference
Low P/E	0.46%	4.7[b]	0.09%	0.5	0.49%	4.7[b]	-1.1
Small size	0.12	2.7[b]	0.14	1.3	0.12	2.5[a]	0.2
Yield	0.03	0.5	0.67	3.4[b]	-0.03	-0.4	2.9[b]
Zero yield	0.15	1.3	1.00	1.9[a]	0.08	0.6	2.1[a]
Neglect	0.10	1.7[a]	0.36	1.8[a]	0.08	1.3	1.3
Low price	0.01	0.2	0.38	2.0	-0.02	0.4	2.1[a]
Book/price	0.09	1.2	0.51	2.4[a]	0.05	0.7	1.9[a]
Sales/price	0.17	3.7[b]	0.05	0.2	0.18	4.1[b]	-0.8
Cash/price	0.04	0.6	-0.15	-2.0[a]	0.05	0.8	-1.0
Sigma	0.07	0.6	0.62	2.1[a]	0.02	0.2	1.4
Beta	0.04	0.3	-0.05	-0.1	0.05	0.4	-0.2
Coskewness	0.04	0.7	0.10	0.5	0.04	0.6	0.3
Controversy	-0.05	-0.8	-0.01	-0.1	-0.06	-0.8	0.2
Trend in estimates:							
1 month	0.51	8.1[b]	0.60	3.8[b]	0.50	7.5[a]	0.5
2 months	0.28	4.9[b]	0.25	1.6	0.29	4.7[b]	-0.2
3 months	0.19	3.8[b]	0.13	0.6	0.19	3.8[b]	-0.4

Earnings surprise:							
1 month	0.48	3.7[b]	1.36	1.6	0.42	3.4[b]	1.8[a]
2 months	0.18	0.8	0.14	2.0	0.18	0.7	-0.1
3 months	-0.21	-1.1	-0.01	0.0	-0.22	-1.1	0.3
Earnings torpedo	-0.10	-1.7[a]	0.08	0.3	-0.12	-1.5[a]	0.9
Relative strength	0.34	3.5[b]	-0.13	-0.2	0.39	4.0[b]	-1.4
Residual reversal:							
1 month	-1.08	-17.8[b]	-1.38	-6.0[b]	-1.06	-16.8[b]	-1.5
2 months	-0.37	-8.1[b]	-0.56	-2.5[a]	-0.35	-7.7[b]	-1.3
Short-term tax	0.04	-0.4	0.38	1.8[a]	-0.08	-0.7	1.2
Long-term tax	-0.00	-0.1	0.78	3.2[b]	-0.07	-1.2	3.6[b]

[a] Significant at 10 percent level.
[b] Significant at 1 percent level.

Source: Adapted from Jacobs and Levy [1988], pp. 25 and 33.

Exhibit 9-6
Relative Performance of High Versus Low Portfolios

Portfolio Strategies

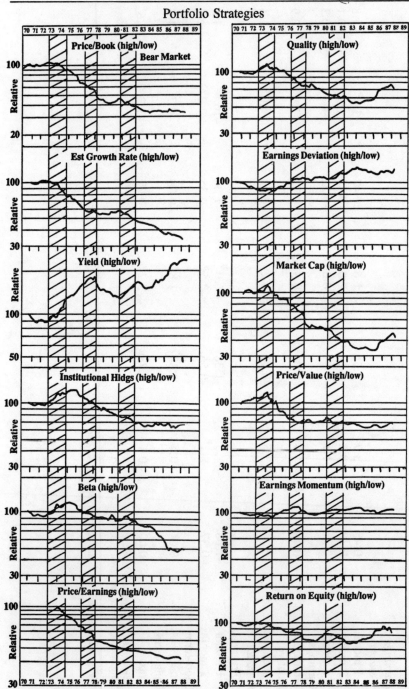

Source: Speidell [1987], p. 10.

their usefulness. Clearly, understanding and measuring risk must be carefully done.

Adapting the Basic Theory

The basic premise in all current valuation is the rational or efficient-market, hypothesis: the market price of a security is the expected present value of future cash flows from the security. Another way to think of the rational market hypothesis is that "the quality of the information embedded in that expectation is high relative to the information available to the individual participants in the market." (Merton in Dornbusch, Fischer, and Bossons [1987], p. 93.) If, however, prices depend in "an important way on factors other than fundamentals underlying future cash flows and discount rates, or the quality of information reflected in stock prices is sufficiently poor that investors can systematically identify significant differences between stock prices and fundamental value" (Merton in Dornbusch, Fischer, and Bossons [1987], p. 93), then a new theory must be developed. Because we have found reasons to believe that profits can be made, there is reason to look for new theories. What new theories about basic stock-pricing behavior wait in the wings?

A number of researchers have begun to think about adapting the theory[13] and applicability of behavioral theories to stock market behavior. Rational bubbles,[14] cognitive misperception,[15] overreaction,[16] and fads[17] are descriptions of how people do behave. These ideas are being applied to investors to counter the usual finance-theory approach of defining prices in terms of how investors should behave. The should, or normative, theory is rational market behavior. The positive, or how investors do behave, theories are behavioral. Whether one of these or some yet-to-be-tried or undiscovered theory will replace the widely used, but somewhat suspect, theory of market rationality and efficiency remains to be seen—and profited from.

Conclusion

In this book, we have tried to bring to you what is and is not known about profiting from equity investing. As is apparent by now, there is much we know, but a great deal more we do not. Some investors seem especially skilled in their ability to make profits on their equity investments. Whether it is because they have unique information, interpret commonly known data differently, or act in a way that is different from the rest of us, we do not know. Our best approach is to try to learn what the most successful investors may know and use, and develop theories and strategies that capitalize on the opportunities they perceive.

We continue to examine the market itself, while developing and testing new theories—drawn from such disciplines as physics and the study of human

348 The New Stock Market

behavior. In the meantime, there are five worthwhile conclusions that you can draw from this book:

1. Whatever you do should be supported by a logical economic explanation.
2. When looking at empirical research, be wary of the possible errors in methodology.
3. Profits must take into account explicit and implicit transaction costs.
4. Investing is a zero-sum game.
5. Do not underestimate the collective intelligence of your competition.

Good skill and good luck.

CHAPTER 9

Notes

1. Indeed, probability and risk may have characteristics we still understand only in the most rudimentary way. Quantum physics is leading the way in reexamining this area. See, for instance, Zukav [1979] for a basic introduction to the subject.

2. French, Schwert, and Stambaugh demonstrated and used a technique that relied on GARCH—generalized auto regressive conditional heteroskadicity model. This model, and its forerunner, ARCH (not generalized) attempts to measure variance and return jointly, thus capturing changes in volatility. Separate equations for return and variance avoid biased estimates. See Engle [1983] for more on this subject.

3. In addition, changes in risk have been related to the term structure of interest rates by Campbell [1987] and to business cycles by Ferson and Merrick [1987], and Burmeister and McElroy [1988] have worked on a multi-beta theory.

4. This high weekly autocorrelation decayed over a four-week period and was significantly greater than could be explained by the nonsynchronous trading effects discussed in Chapter 2.

5. See Lo and MacKinlay [1988], who found that, for shorter intervals like a week, autocorrelations of returns were common.

6. See Fama and French [1987a].

7. Among others, Kandel and Stambaugh [1988] are currently looking into these relationships.

8. See Gleick [1987] for a layman's introduction to chaos theory.

9. Priestly [1981, p. 868] described the problem as follows: Suppose excess stock returns in period t, r_t, were related to previous and current unanticipated earnings, E_t, and that unanticipated earnings were random. Also, assume the actual relationship was

$$r_t = E_t + \beta\epsilon_{t-1\ t-2}$$

In this nonlinear relationship, stock returns would not be independent over time, but there would be no correlation between successive returns. This lack of correlation stems from successive unanticipated earnings being uncorrelated. Dependence exists, however, because of the scaling effect of β [i.e., the expected value of a third-order term in r_t is not zero]. Thus, there is white noise, but it has dependence.

Such third-order dependence is detected by calculating the expected value from groups of three successive terms; i.e.,

$$c_{rrr\ j,k} = E\ [r_{t+j} r_{t+k} r_t]$$

When $c_{rrr} = 0$ and there is no correlation between the terms, the series is independent for lags of j and k.

10. See Fama [1970].

11. The impact of this lack of data was vividly shown by Ramsey, Sayers, and Rothman [1988] when, replicating Scheinkman and LeBaron's 1962-85 study without the 25 weeks from July 1974 through January 1975, they found significantly different results.

12. In addition, they found that both beta and relative-strength-based strategies depended on market direction.

13. See, among others, Miller [1987]; Ibbotson, Diermeier, and Siegel [1984]; and Keane [1986].

14. See, for instance, Tirole [1982].

15. See, for instance, Kahneman and Tversky [1979, 1982] and Arrow [1982].

16. See, for instance, De Bondt and Thaler [1985].

17. See, for instance, Schiller [1984].

CHAPTER 9

References

Arnott, Robert D. "Risk and Reward—An Intriguing Timing Tool." Salomon Brothers, Inc., April 6, 1987.

Arrow, Kenneth J. "Risk Perception in Psychology and Economics." *Economic Inquiry,* January 1982, pp. 1-9.

Brock, W. A. "Applications of Nonlinear Science Statistical Inference Theory to Finance and Economics." Innisbrook, FL: Institute for Quantitative Research in Finance, March 1988.

————; Dechert, W.D.; and Scheinkman, J. "A Test for Independence Based on the Correlation Dimension." Department of Economics, University of Wisconsin, Madison, University of Houston, and University of Chicago, 1986, 1987.

Burmeister, Edwin, and McElroy, Marjorie B. "Joint Estimation of Factor Sensitivities and Risk Premia for the Arbitrage Pricing Theory." *Journal of Finance,* July 1988, pp. 721-33.

Campbell, John Y. "Stock Returns and the Term Structure." *Journal of Financial Economics,* June 1987, pp. 373-99.

Chan, K. C. "On the Contrarian Investment Strategy." *Journal of Business,* April 1988, pp. 147-63.

Conrad, Jennifer, and Kaul, Gautam. "Time-Variation in Expected Returns." *Journal of Business,* October 1988, pp. 409-25.

DeBondt, Werner F. M., and Thaler, Richard. "Does the Stock Market Overreact?" *Journal of Finance,* July 1985, pp. 793-805.

Dornbusch, Rudiger; Fischer, Stanley; and Bossoms, John (eds.). *Macroeconomics and Finance: Essays in Honor of Franco Modigliani.* Boston: M.I.T. Press, 1987.

Engle, Robert F. "Estimates on the Variance of U.S. Inflation Based Upon the ARCH Model." *Journal of Money, Credit and Banking,* August 1983, pp. 286-301.

Fama, Eugene F. "Efficient Capital Markets: A Review of Theory and Empirical Work." *Journal of Finance,* May 1970, pp. 383-417.

————, and French, Kenneth R. "Dividend Yields and Expected Stock Returns." *Journal of Financial Economics,* October 1988, pp. 3-25.

————. "Forecasting Returns on Corporate Bonds and Common Stocks." Working paper, Center for Research in Security Prices, Graduate School of Business, University of Chicago, April 1987a.

————. "Permanent and Temporary Components of Stock Prices." *Journal of Political Economy,* April 1987b, pp. 246-73.

Ferson, Wayne E., and Merrick, John J., Jr. "Non-Stationarity and Stage-of-the-Business-Cycle Effects in Consumption-Based Asset Pricing Relations." *Journal of Financial Economics,* March 1987, pp. 127-46.

Fogler, H. Russell. "Normal Style Indexes—An Alternative to Manager Universes." Delivered at Institute for Chartered Financial Analysts Conference on Performance Measurement, January 24, 1989.

French, Kenneth R.; Schwert, G. William; and Stambaugh, Robert F. "Expected Stock Returns and Volatility." *Journal of Financial Economics*, September 1987, pp. 3-29.

Gleick, James, *Chaos: Making a New Science*, New York: Viking Penquin, 1987.

Grossman, Sanford J., and Stiglitz, Joseph E. "On the Impossibility of Informationally Efficient Markets." *American Economic Review*, June 1980, pp. 393-408.

Hinich, Melvin J., and Patterson, Douglas M. "Evidence of Nonlinearity in Daily Stock Returns." *Journal of Business & Economic Statistics*, January 1985, pp. 69-77.

Ibbotson, Roger; Diermeier, Jeffrey; and Siegel, Laurence. "The Demand for Capital Market Returns: A New Equilibrium Theory." *Financial Analysts Journal*, January-February 1984, pp. 22-23.

Jacobs, Bruce I., and Levy, Kenneth N. "Disentangling Equity Return Regularities: New Insights and Investment Opportunities." *Financial Analysts Journal*, May-June 1988, pp. 18-45.

Jones, Robert C. "Portfolio Strategy: Stock Selection." Goldman Sachs, August 31, 1988.

Kahneman, D., and Tversky, A. "Intuitive Prediction: Biases and Corrective Procedures." In *Judgment Under Certainty: Heuristics and Biases*, D. Kahneman, P. Slovic, and A. Tversky (eds.), Cambridge University Press, 1982.

―――. "Prospect Theory: An Analysis of Decision Under Risk." *Econometrica*, March 1979, pp. 263-91.

Kandel, Shamuel, and Stambaugh, Robert F. "Modeling Expected Stock Returns for Long and Short Horizons." The Wharton School, University of Pennsylvania, 1988.

Keane, Simon. "The Efficient Market Hypothesis on Trial." *Financial Analysts Journal*, March 1986, pp. 58-63.

Keim, Donald B., and Stambaugh, Robert F. "Predicting Returns in the Stock and Bond Markets." *Journal of Financial Economics*, December 1986, pp. 357-90.

LeBaron, B. "Nonlinear Puzzles in Stock Returns." Department of Economics, University of Chicago, 1987.

Lo, Andrew W., and MacKinlay, A. Craig. "Stock Market Prices Do Not Follow Random Walks: Evidence from a Simple Specification Test." *Review of Financial Studies*, Spring 1988, pp. 41-66.

Loeb, Thomas F. "Trading Cost: The Critical Link Between Investment Information and Results." *Financial Analysts Journal*, May-June 1983, pp. 39-44.

Maravall, Agustin. "An Application of Nonlinear Time Series Forecasting." *Journal of Business & Economics Statistics*, vol. 1, January 1983, pp. 66-74.

Merton, Robert C. "A Simple Model of Capital Market Equilibrium with Incomplete Information." *Journal of Finance*, July 1987, pp. 483-510.

Miller, Edward M. "Bounded Efficient Markets: A New Wrinkle in the EMH." *Journal of Portfolio Management*, September 1987, pp. 4-13.

Poterba, James M., and Summers, Lawrence H. "Mean Reversion in Stock Prices: Evidence and Implications." *Journal of Financial Economics*, October 1988, pp. 27-59.

Priestley, M. *Spectral Analysis and Time Series*, Vol. 2. New York: Academic Press, 1981.

Ramsey, James B.; Sayers, Chera L.; and Rothman, Philip. "The Statistical Properties of Dimension Calculations Using Small Data Sets: Some Economic Applications." Working paper, Department of Economics, University of Houston, August 16, 1988.

Reinganum, Marc R. "The Anatomy of a Stock Market Winner." *Financial Analysts Journal*, March-April 1988, pp. 16-28.

Rosenberg, Barr; Reid, Kenneth; and Lamstein, Ronald. "Persuasive Evidence of Market Inefficiency." *Journal of Portfolio Management*, Spring 1985, pp. 9-16.

Scheinkman, Jose A., and LeBaron, Blake. "Nonlinear Dynamics and Stock Returns." Department of Economics, University of Chicago, Working Paper #181, 1986.

Schiller, Robert J. "Theories of Aggregate Stock Price Movements." *The Journal of Portfolio Management*, Winter 1984, pp. 28-37.

Speidell, Lawrence S. "Guest Speaker." *Financial Analysts Journal*, July-August 1988, pp. 9-12.

Tirole, J. "On the Possibility of Speculation Under Rational Expectations." *Econometrica*, September 1982, pp. 1163-81.

Zukav, Gary. *The Dancing Wu Li Masters*. New York: William Marrow, 1979.

Index